LEVELLER MANIFESTOES
OF THE
PURITAN REVOLUTION

LEVELLER
MANIFESTOES

of the

PURITAN REVOLUTION

Edited, with introduction and commentaries
by

DON M. WOLFE
New York University

Foreword by
CHARLES A. BEARD

THOMAS NELSON AND SONS

NEW YORK · LONDON · EDINBURGH

TORONTO · MELBOURNE

1944

PRINTED IN THE UNITED STATES OF AMERICA
BY J. J. LITTLE & IVES COMPANY, NEW YORK

TO
WILLIS H. WILCOX
in grateful memory of
an intellectual
awakening

FOREWORD

This volume deserves a permanent place as a fundamental exhibit in the history of constitutional government and liberty in England, the United States, indeed the whole English-speaking world. It is a collection of primary manifestoes issued by the popular group or party, generally known as Levellers, who played an active and influential role in the English revolution of 1642-49 that marked the end of royal tyranny. Within the covers of a single book Mr. Wolfe has brought together rare pamphlets and tracts that are seldom available even in many of the largest libraries in England and America. By orderly arrangement and informed comment he has smoothed the way for a study of the relations among them and of the evolution in the ideas and interests they expressed. Thus his work constitutes a well-rounded unity of thought and plan which forms an indispensable part of the whole record representing the struggle for constitutional government from Magna Carta to our own age.

As a contribution to critical scholarship, Mr. Wolfe's book serves many useful purposes. It makes easily available to inquirers everywhere numerous documents requisite to the study of a stormy and creative period in English history. No library that pretends to provide essential materials for English history can fail to have the volume on its shelves. No course of instruction in English history that rises above the most elementary level can fail to require an examination of the remonstrances, declarations, and appeals contained in this collection. For these reasons alone students will be grateful to Mr. Wolfe for sparing them laborious days prosecuting searches which they would otherwise have to make and for furnishing them guidance in interpretations.

Now that the history of ideas is beginning to receive in the United States some of the thoughtful attention it deserves, Mr.

Wolfe's work possesses what may be called "current interest" in the strict sense of the words. In the materials he reprints and in the supplementary comments from his own pen are to be found early origins and formulations of ideas that have bulked large in the history of the Western world for more than two centuries. No person seriously concerned with the rise and development of these ideas can afford to neglect a line by line scrutiny of the pages Mr. Wolfe has prepared.

For the history of the United States, Mr. Wolfe's work has a special significance. Important colonies were rising to power on the shores of America when the Puritan revolt broke into full storm in 1642-49. To these colonies fled many participants in that struggle, before, during, and after it exploded in revolution. In all parts of the colonies reverberations of the conflict were heard. It was to the traditions of this contest that leaders in the American Revolution, such as John Adams, James Otis, Alexander Hamilton, and Thomas Jefferson appealed in justification of their cause.

In the Declaration of Independence and in the Constitution of the United States were incorporated ideas, maxims, and principles which are cherished as distinguishing features of American life and institutions. But these doctrines were not all newly designed and formulated by the founders of our Republic and proclaimed to the world as original discoveries. No one knew better than Thomas Jefferson that the axioms of the Declaration were already well known and tenaciously held among masses of the American people. Even boys and girls in American high schools are now aware that Jefferson drew heavily on John Locke for many essentials deemed "self-evident" in the immortal document of 1776. What is not generally known is that nearly all the fundamentals of government and liberty had been set forth or foreshadowed in the declarations of English Levellers long before John Locke published his celebrated treatises on government.

In support of this contention a few citations from Mr. Wolfe's pages may be made:

"Originally men and women 'were by nature all equall and alike in power, digny [sic], authority, and majesty,' no one possessing any right of dominance except by mutual consent." (p. 8)

"So ought the whole nation to be free therein even to alter and change the publique forme, as may best stand with the safety and freedome of the people." (p. 7)

"By naturall birth, all men are equally and alike borne to like propriety, liberty, and freedom." (p. 11)

"We are resolu'ed upon our Natural Rights and Freedoms." (p. 11)

"The only and sole legislative Law-making power is originally inherent in the people, and derivatively in their Commissions chosen by themselves by common consent and no other." (p. 14)

On such statements no comment is needed. By comparing them with the opening passages of the Declaration of Independence anyone can see that levelling ideas of 1646-49 were in fact self-evident truths of 1776.

In "Foundations of Freedom or an Agreement of the People Proposed as a Rule for Future Government" (pp. 293 ff.) are laid down many essentials of constitutional government long recognized in the United States as basic to liberty under law, if often violated in practice. These include apportionment of representatives on the basis of population, a broad though not universal suffrage, a safeguarded system of popular elections, exclusion of salaried officials from legislatures, limited government, and a bill of rights. In other words here are the doctrines that government must rest upon a popular basis, that it is limited and not sovereign in powers, and that, in the interest of human liberty, certain rights of persons and property must be protected against governmental encroachments.

Nor were the Levellers indifferent to the condition of the people. They opposed monopolies and special privileges. They called for reforms in the laws which anticipated achievements commonly ascribed to the enlightenment of the nineteenth century. That a civilized government must resort to social legislation and safeguard the people against the hazards of misfortune, Levellers were firmly convinced, despite the fact that they stood to the right of their more radical contemporaries, "the Diggers." To this conviction "The humble Petition of many thousands," among other documents, bore eloquent witness (pp. 135 ff.).

It is, therefore, to the history of civilization, as well as government and liberty, that Mr. Wolfe makes an enduring contribution.

CHARLES A. BEARD.

New Milford, Conn.,

Spring, 1944.

PREFACE

Like most searchers in seventeenth-century intellectual history, I have long felt a need for a volume of documents containing the three great constitutional sallies of the Levellers,[1] the *Agreements* of 1647, 1648, and 1649. Once engaged in the project, however, I found that to trace the genesis and maturation of *Agreement* ideas required a more elaborate plan, one that would incorporate the chief petitions and pamphlet proclamations of the three-year period. Hence the final scope of the project: to exemplify the basic ideological patterns of the Leveller movement.

Of the nineteen complete documents reprinted here, sixteen are undeniably Leveller tracts and proclamations, and the remaining three were written under Leveller influence. One, the officers' *Agreement* of 1649, is of Independent authorship; one, *No Papist nor Presbyterian,* is of doubtful origin, though asserting its loyalty to *Agreement* tenets; the third, *Several Proposals,* was written by Lieut. Col. John Jubbes as a compromise *Agreement.* Two of the documents have appeared in a recent collection;[2] several others have been reprinted in the past three centuries. Except in the words and phrases noted (see *Appendix 3*), the text of each document has been reprinted in its original spelling, punctuation, upper and lower case, variation of roman with italic type. The marginal notes of the original manuscripts have been arranged in footnote form. The title pages are imitations, not exact reproductions, of the original typography.

Without the diligent assistance of libraries in supplying photostat copies of rare pamphlets, this project could not have gone forward. I am indebted to the National Library of Wales, Aberystwyth, present custodians of the Thomason Collection, for

[1] Though I have used the word *Leveller* throughout to designate the party of Lilburne and Overton, the term did not actually appear until November, 1647. It came into use as a nickname. Gardiner, *Civil War,* III, 380.

[2] *A Remonstrance Of Many Thousands* and the Petition of March, 1647, appeared in Professor W. H. Haller's *Tracts on Liberty in the Puritan Revolution,* 1934.

photostats of dozens of tracts not elsewhere available; to the Henry E. Huntington Library, the New York Public Library, and the Princeton Theological Seminary Library, for similar service. To the Union Theological Seminary Library I am especially indebted, and to the workers there who have given me unwearied assistance for the past four years; to Mrs. Charlotte Knight, Mrs. Hugh M. Foster, Mrs. Marcia Feibush, Dr. Lucia W. Markley, Mr. Robert Schroeder, and Mrs. H. N. Bigelow. Dr. Theodore Jones of New York University Library, University Heights, gave important aid in securing microfilm reproductions. In the difficult work of reading proof and preparing the index, I have had the generous aid of Dr. Florence Maly, Miss Nellie Schlatter, and Dr. Ruth A. Firor of Hunter College.

To Dr. S. Marion Tucker, of Brooklyn Polytechnic Institute, I am indebted for suggestive counselling and unfailing encouragement, drawn from the rich lore of his profound culture; to Professors Leo E. A. Saidla and Thomas L. Donahue for scholarly comradeship and many zestful hours of discussions; to Dr. Albert S. Borgman, of New York University, for valuable suggestions on notes and textual arrangement; to Professor Paul Haines, New York University, for much provocative, timely analysis of ideas; to Dr. Putnam F. Jones, University of Pittsburgh, for his steady interest and exact, rich criticism; to Dr. Charles Beard, for the warmth of his encouragement and the inspiration of his intellectual zeal.

D. M. W.

New York,
March 31, 1944

CONTENTS

DOCUMENTS AND COMMENTARIES

LEVELLER MANIFESTOES
OF THE
PURITAN REVOLUTION

INTRODUCTION

1. Sectaries: Brood of Presbyterian Hatching

AMONG the reformers of the Puritan Revolution none were such active and skillful propagandists as the Levellers, whose manifestoes presaged with amazing fullness political and constitutional patterns that were to stir England and America for twenty decades. Like their rebellious contemporaries, even Gerrard Winstanley and his Digger communists, the Levellers began their agitation as theological radicals; they agitated first against the bishops and then against the rigid Calvinism and state-church doctrines of the Presbyterians. Throwing their energies at last into secular Reformation, the Levellers in 1646 and 1647 sowed the ideological seed from which were to spring the revolutionary changes of 1649.

In the early years of the Civil War the Presbyterians achieved such ascendancy in Parliament as to impose upon all England the Solemn League and Covenant, binding the citizens to support Calvinistic tenets. The Presbyterians sought to replace the Anglican state church with the Presbyterian; politically, as members of the rising commercial classes, they sought the annihilation of absolutism and the supremacy of the Commons. Of the four or five million people in England, the Presbyterians could count on the largest mass support of any Puritan group; moreover, their leadership among the barristers, financiers, and clergymen was able and energetic. Of nine thousand ministers, Hobbes estimated the Presbyterians to number no more than a thousand, but these were fanatical and fearless. Upon these ministers Hobbes placed the blame for the rupture between king and Parliament. Not only had they urged the efficacy of Bible-reading, an explosive and divisive force, but they had "publicly taught rebellion in the pulpits." [1] "Had it not been much better," asked Hobbes, "that

---

[1] *Behemoth,* in *The English Works of Thomas Hobbes,* edited by Molesworth (11 vols., London, 1839), VI, 343.

those seditious ministers, which were not perhaps 1000, had been all killed before they had preached? It had been, I confess, a great massacre; but the killing of 100,000 [in the Civil War] is a greater." [2]

From the Bible-reading ranks of the Presbyterians sprang a multitude of sectaries, introducing, says Hobbes, "many strange and many pernicious doctrines, out-doing the Reformation, as they pretended, both of Luther and Calvin." [3] Of these sects the most powerful was the Independents, probably no more than one-tenth as numerous as the Presbyterians, but gifted in leadership: Sir Henry Vane, Oliver Cromwell, John Goodwin, John Milton. The Independents, wrote Milton, were "for the most part, men of the better conditions of life, of families not disgraced if not ennobled, of fortunes either ample or moderate . . . prepared, not only to debate, but to fight; not only to argue in the senate, but to engage the enemy in the field." [4] In contrast to the Presbyterians, the Independents stood for toleration of strange sects, Papists excepted; many of them were opposed to any state church. In their political and economic demands the Independents were at first no more drastic than the Presbyterians; only in the heat of the second Civil War did they emerge as king-haters and republicans, influenced in part by the intense Leveller propaganda in the New Model army. In their military dictatorship the Independents remained an unpopular minority, neither placating the Presbyterians nor fulfilling the demands of the Levellers for the abolition of economic and legal oppressions.

2. Baptists and Levellers: Puritans of the Left

On the title page of *A Remonstrance Of Many Thousand Citizens* (July 7, 1646), a contemporary observer wrote the following words: "For the Baptists." The phrase is significant of the sharp deviation into drastic secular demands that characterized many leaders of the hated sect, men far more rational in their outlook and revolutionary in their aims than the Independents. Rebels against the Separatists of Amsterdam, the Baptists of Lon-

---

[2] *English Works*, VI, 282. Hobbes says that the sectaries were the worst enemies of the Presbyterians, though the very "brood of their own hatching."

[3] *Ibid.*, VI, 333.

[4] *The Second Defence*, in *Prose Works* (Bohn edition), I, 291.

don as early as 1614 had anticipated, in Leonard Busher's *Religions Peace*,[1] the extreme tenets of Roger Williams' *Bloudy Tenent* and the seething tolerationist ferment of the New Model army. To the ranks of the Baptists belonged few university graduates, but many tradesmen, apprentices, small merchants, printers. Apprenticed to a merchant in his early years in London, John Lilburne had been a member of a Baptist congregation, as had Richard Overton, printer. From the ranks of the Baptists, often of humble and obscure origins, men in Cromwell's army had risen to high place, among them Robert Overton, William Allen, Henry Danvers, John Wigan, Robert Bennet, Charles Howard, Richard Deane, Edmund Chillenden, John Desborough, Richard Lawrence, Henry Jones, Henry Denne, Daniel Axtell, William Packer, Thomas Harrison. Ludlow alone at one time commanded twenty-five Baptist officers.[2] Henry Hills, the army printer, was a Baptist, as was John Canne, clergyman, who preached often to the army and later denounced the Levellers in *The Discoverer*. The march of the New Model soldiery was often followed by the establishment of Baptist churches. Most men of Cromwell's army carried Bibles. It was not thought strange, therefore, that officers and men should ascend pulpits and harangue congregations, bearing with them the prestige of conquest on the battlefield.

Though many Baptists veered into mysticism and Fifth-Monarchy expectations of Christ's second coming, Lilburne and Overton, after experience with economic and judicial injustices, threw their energies into secular reforms, gradually assuming a rational rather than a theological validity for their premises. In this agitation they often found the Baptist congregations their staunch supporters. But the army was the spearhead of Leveller radicalism; there men read Lilburne's pamphlets "as statute law," elected agitators to represent each regiment, braved the wrath of the officers to petition for their civil rights. In 1645-46, when Lilburne and Overton waged a constant warfare against Presbyterian intolerance, the army was a hotbed of toleration, with Cromwell himself lending high approval. Meanwhile, however, the Leveller leaders were evolving revolutionary constitutional concepts that

---

[1] *Tracts on Liberty of Conscience* (Hanserd Knollys Society, 1846).
[2] I am here following W. T. Whitley, *A History of British Baptists* (London, 1923), pp. 74-76.

the New Model army was to absorb and adopt with equal enthusiasm. These revolutionary principles culminated in the *Agreement Of The People* presented to the officers November 3, 1647. No constitutional documents of the Puritan Revolution deserve more prolonged examination than the first *Agreement* and its successors of December, 1648, and May, 1649 (all incorporated in the present volume). Anticipating the chief principle of the American constitution, the *Agreement* defined and limited the powers of Parliament itself, setting down rights and privileges perennially inviolate.

3. Forerunners: Prynne and Parker

Before Lilburne and Overton projected themselves into secular controversy, the premises of their initial assumptions had appeared in the works of William Prynne and Henry Parker. In the heavy pages of *The Soveraigne Power of Parliaments & Kingdomes* Prynne anticipated most the Leveller heresies that he was later to reject. "The High Court of Parliament," he had written, "and the whole Kingdome which it represents, may in divers respects be truly and properly said, *to be the Highest Soveraigne power of all others, and above the King himselfe.*" [1] Kings are created for the benefit of the people; they cannot change the laws without the people's consent; they have no absolute veto of Parliament's actions; they acknowledge the superiority of the law when they take their oaths; they may be deposed or set up by the people.[2] But Henry Parker was a much more skilful advocate than Prynne of the rising democratic surge. Master of lucid, stinging prose, Parker unhesitatingly tested all institutions by "the Charter of nature," a visualization of perfection through the unaided reason of man. By this law of nature states are formed for the safety and benefit of the people, in whose hands resides the sovereign

[1] *The Treachery and Disloyalty of Papists* (contains *The Soveraigne Power,* First Part), second edition, May 2, 1643, p. 33. Three other parts of *The Soveraigne Power* appeared May 28, 1643, June 23, and August 28. These heavy volumes of Prynne (an incredibly industrious man) contain many of the source documents that Lilburne later studied and quoted with much more skill than Prynne. He was undoubtedly indebted to some extent to Prynne for his habitual reliance on docu ments and citations. Lilburne quotes from the Appendix to *The Soveraigne Power* (Fourth Part) in *Innocency and Truth Justified.*

[2] *The Treachery and Disloyalty,* pp. 35, 37, 45, 74, 75, 79, 86, 92.

power to delegate or no, as they choose. "The Major part of Kings are so farre from being the best Judges, the profoundest States-men, the most expert souldiers, that when they so value themselves they prove commonly most wilfull, and fatall to themselves and others." [3] Any agreement a people may have made to obey a king absolutely is against reason and the law of nature.[4] In the begin-ning God created no such inequality between man and man as between man and beast. A king therefore should deport himself as a brother, not as a lord. Yet the royalists seldom speak of the people "but under the notion of the rude multitude . . . with termes of derision." [5] Parker set forth the interpretation of Eng-lish history later used so effectively by both Levellers and In-dependents: William the Conqueror had deprived the native English of their property and privileges, inscribing new laws in a foreign tongue to perpetuate their robberies. Like Prynne, how-ever, Parker was enunciating theories he could not extend illimit-ably; a few years later he denounced Lilburne and Levelling ideas, even as Lilburne and his fellows were to denounce the Diggers of St. George Hill.[6]

4. The Democratic Seed Time: 1645-46

On October 10 and 11, 1645, two pamphlets appeared that foreshadowed the ringing accents of *A Remonstrance Of Many Thousand Citizens* and the principles of the first *Agreement.* They were *Englands Birth-Right Justified* and *Englands Lamen-table Slaverie.* In *Englands Birth-Right* Lilburne and Overton [1]

[3] *Jus Populi,* October 16, 1644, p. 10. This pamphlet contains a more complete exposition of Parker's position than the provocative *Observations upon some of his Majesties late Answers and Expresses.*

[4] *Ibid.,* pp. 8, 18.   [5] *Ibid.,* p. 19.

[6] *A Letter of Due Censure, and Redargution To . . . Lilburne,* June 21, 1650. Parker attacks effectively the legal quibbling of Lilburne's defense, which he calls (p. 17) "a great weight hang'd upon a small threed." Parker summarizes Lilburne's Levelling position thus (p. 21): "The Judges because they understand Law, are to be degraded, and made servants to the Jurors: but the Jurors, because they under-stand no Law, are to be mounted aloft . . . The Judges because they are com-monly Gentlemen by birth, and have had honorable education, are to be exposed to scorn: but the Jurors, because they be commonly Mechanicks, bred up illiterately to handy crafts, are to be placed at the helme."

[1] Much of the first half of *Birth-Right* may have been written by Overton, who was more adept at theorizing than Lilburne, less persistent in the use of docu-ments, page references, quotations. The reasoning about equity and justice has traces of Overton's later phrasing, and the short, compact paragraphs are typical of

protest against Parliament's violations of the common law, Magna Charta, and Petition of Right. The Petition says no man may be imprisoned "without cause shewed or expressed." It is absurd, says Lilburne, for the Parliament to disobey this injunction: *"It cannot be imagined that ever the People would be so sottish, as to give such a power to those whom they choose for their Servants."* [2] Throughout *Birth-Right* runs a tone of hostility to Parliament's arbitrary proceedings that anticipates *A Remonstrance.* Parliament is accountable to the people in its interpretation and observance of the common law. Lilburne's special skill lay in tracing "equity and reason" and the people's privileges in charters and legal precedents; but he and his fellow-pamphleteer were aware that the common law needed codification: "Ought there not to be a plaine platforme," he asks, "agreed on, and laid down by the Parliament concerning things of so high consequence to all the Commons of *England?"* [3] This is the germinative idea of the *Agreement:* a plain statement of constitutional rights unalterable by Parliament itself.

In *Englands Lamentable Slaverie* (October 11, 1645), written evidently after discussions with his friend Lilburne, William Walwyn struck out, with significant deviations, for the same constitutional reforms. He protests against the theory that once the people have trusted Parliament it is "bound to no rules, nor bounded by any limits . . . they are above *MAGNA CHARTA."* [4] He asserts that "most Parliament men are to learn what is the just power of a Parliament, what the Parliament may doe, and what the Parliament . . . may not doe." [5] But neither Magna Charta nor the Petition of Right, nor any known charter at all, can assure the reformation the people need. Has not Magna Charta been used to justify oppressions as well as freedoms? Have not the kings endeavored to weaken what few guarantees it possessed, often with Parliament's help? Parliament itself has been very erratic, now enlarging the prerogatives of both king and bishops, now occupying itself with trivial or burdensome law-making such as pun-

---

his style. Lilburne undoubtedly collaborated in the writing of *Birth-Right*, probably after discussions with Overton and Walwyn, but he nowhere claims it as his own. It is significant that *Innocency And Truth Justified,* acknowledged by Lilburne as his own, is less mature in its constitutional reasoning than *Birth-Right,* though *Innocency* appeared several months later.

[2] P. 4. [3] P. 8. [4] P. 3. [5] *Ibid.*

ishment for pigeon-killing, regulation of trades, the keeping of greyhounds, the wages of poor laborers.[6] No, says Walwyn, the old charters, even if mended, are not enough. What England needs is a new charter, founded not on precedents, but on reason and equity, man's sense of universal justice. As a man may change his code of life, "so ought the whole Nation to be free therein even to alter and change the publique forme, as may best stand with the safety and freedome of the people." [7] In such language did Walwyn justify a sharp break from England's traditional constitution. Older, more daringly theoretical than Lilburne, though much less familiar with English charters and their interpreters, Walwyn anticipated even more clearly than his friend the revolutionary principle of the *Agreement*.

Though not so pointed as *Birth-Right* and *Slaverie* in their foreshadowing of the *Agreement,* Lilburne's pamphlets of early 1646 show a continued fertilization of the democratic theories to be so boldly set forth in the *Remonstrance*. In *Innocency And Truth Justified* (January 6) Lilburne emphasizes Prynne's declaration that the people and Parliament are the "highest power." If kings are subject to the law adds Lilburne, Parliament must obey it also. When Parker says, in *Observations,* "Power is but secondary and derivitive in Princes," Lilburne adds, "And say *I* in counsells likewise." [8] Long passages from Parker on the origin of power Lilburne sets down with high approval.[9] In *The Ivst Mans Ivstification* (June 6) Lilburne breaks into a long denunciation of the common law under which the courts operate, quoting Speed, Daniel, Coke, and Martin to prove that the legal protections and judicial machinery of Edward the Confessor had been destroyed by William the Conqueror and his successors. He cannot find the common law written, nor do any two lawyers agree on its substance; he concludes that it "flowed out of *Normandy . . . from the* Will *of a* Tyrant." [10] Though some written laws, among them Magna Charta and the Petition of Right, are "gallant Lawes," yet

[6] Parliament, says Walwyn (pp. 4-5), has been "so unskilfull in the nature of common and just freedom, as to call bondage libertie, and the grants of Conquerours their Birth-rights . . . and when they might have made a newer and better Charter, have falne to patching the old."

[7] P. 6.   [8] P. 57.

[9] Parker denied that conquest had abolished the people's power (p. 58): "For meere force cannot alter the course of nature, or frustrate the tenour of the law."

[10] P. 13.

even they are inferior to the laws of Edward the Confessor; Lilburne petitions Parliament *"to annihilate this Norman innovation, and reduce us back to . . . the ancient frame of government in this Kingdome,"* [11] particularly the hundred courts and their monthly meetings. Only thirteen days after *The Ivst Mans Ivstification* (June 19) [12] appeared *The Free-Mans Freedome Vindicated,* notable for its first full statement of Lilburne's conception of the origin of society and the social compact, afterward restated in *Vox Plebis* and *Regall Tyrannie.*[13] Whether or not Overton or Walwyn provided the ideas for this statement, the language is undeniably Lilburne's. He contends that originally men and women "were by nature all equall and alike in power, digny [sic], authority, and majesty," no one later possessing any right of dominance except by mutual agreement.[14] In his prison cell Lilburne had sought justice in the ancient laws and charters; this knowledge he was now gradually synthesizing with philosophical justifications common to the liberal pamphleteers of the Puritan Revolution. Lacking Overton's biting satire and skill in abstractions, as well as Walwyn's mature historical sense, Lilburne, now only thirty, was a more dramatic and appealing leader than his fellows: victim of the bishops' tyranny, soldier hero, fearless pleader at the bar, resourceful amateur lawyer, quoter of Coke and Magna Charta, jailed spokesman for English freedoms.

Meanwhile Marten, Overton, and Walwyn were also setting forth the revolutionary implications of the democratic surge. Replying to the Presbyterian *Remonstrance* of May 26 with *The Interest Of England Maintained* (June 8), Marten weighed the sacrifices of the sectaries, and their right to Parliament's protection,[15] against those of the Presbyterians. Parliament was bound, insisted

---

[11] P. 15.

[12] Thomason records this pamphlet as appearing June 16, and I have used this date in *Milton in the Puritan Revolution.* Lilburne's postscript is dated, however, June 19.

[13] Overton paraphrases parts of it in the opening paragraphs of *An Arrow Against All Tyrants* (October 12, 1646). A similar statement by Lilburne appears again in *Londons Liberties In Chains Discovered* (October, 1646).

[14] P. 11.

[15] "That which some judge *Heresie* and *Schisme*," wrote Marten, "others judge sound Doctrine, and warrantable Separation . . . find a proper Judge in these Cases, and you doe something; but that cannot be found without the indowment of Infallibility." Even if such an unerring judge were to appear, added Marten, his judgment could be executed only by persuasion, not by force.

Marten, *"to Free the People not onely from the present burden; but the future danger of him* [the king] *or his Adherents . . . That so the People may be in some measure recompenc'd for the hazards they have runne, and the blood they have lost: and that so the worke of this Kingdome may be once thoroughly done."* [16] The reigns of all the kings, Marten declared, beginning with William the Conqueror, had been filled with attempts at tyranny. Had Parliament and the people not blocked their efforts, the population would long since have passed into slavery. On June 23 appeared *A Pearle In A Dovnghill,*[17] a fiery pamphlet anticipating in both tone and phrasing many of the ideas of the *Remonstrance* of July 7. Picturing Lilburne as a chief agent in the overthrow of the bishops, as a military hero, and now as the imprisoned champion of common liberties, especially the constitutional supremacy of the House of Commons, the author castigates the Lords for imprisoning Lilburne and trampling down the rights of the commoners. The Lords are "a meer Clog" to the Commons in all their actions. "And why presume ye thus Oh ye Lords," exclaims the author. "Set forth your merit before the People, and say, *for this good it is, that we will raign over yee.* Remember your selves, or shall wee remember yee? Which of ye before this Parliament, minded anything so much as your pleasures?" [18] The Leveller writer taunts the Lords for their failures as military leaders, and reminds them that in all the New Model there is not one Lord. Another appeal for Lilburne, and a similar attack on the Lords, appeared in *The Ivst Man In Bonds,* written and distributed in late June. "The power of the *House of Lords,"* wrote the author, "is like a shallow, un-even water, more in noise then substance." They have usurped the rights of the commoners, having issued not from the people, or gained power by their consent, but rather attached themselves like wens to the body politic, "the extuberances [sic] and mushromes of Prerogative." [19]

---

[16] P. 11.

[17] E. 342 (5). The fiery language and satirical sallies of this pamphlet indicate that its author was Overton, not Walwyn.

[18] P. 3.

[19] E. 342 (2). The Thomason catalog dates this pamphlet June 23. The date in Thomason's handwriting, however, is June 29. The style, which is more persuasive, less provocative, than that of *A Perle,* appears to be that of Walwyn. A comparison of only the opening sentences of the two pamphlets makes it difficult to believe they were written by the same man.

5. Ideas at Harvest: The *Remonstrance*

The constitutional ideas of the Levellers, hitherto tentative and fragmentary, now realized full integration in a remarkable pamphlet pleading Lilburne's cause, *A Remonstrance Of Many Thousand Citizens*,[1] July 7, 1646. Written in the main by Overton, filled with trenchant, pregnant phrasing, the *Remonstrance* calls peremptorily for a democratic revolution as the fruition of the war against Charles. More completely than any other document of 1646 it anticipates the Leveller program of three years to follow: overthrow of kingship and Lords, supremacy of the Commons, responsibility of the Commons to the people, annual Parliaments, unlimited religious toleration, constitutional guarantees against Commons' tyranny, redress of economic grievances. For the first time extreme Puritan opposition not only to Charles but to all kings is bitter and unqualified. As the Levellers had led the opposition to Presbyterian intolerance, so now they were the first to attack the Presbyterians as political conservatives, plotting to defeat the king but not destroy his power, to redress no grievances, to use the state clergy to repress the people's aspirations. In short, say the writers, *"a change of our bondage is the uttermost is intended us, and that too for a worse, and longer."* [2] Asserting that "wee are your Principals, and you our Agents," the *Remonstrance* accuses the Commons itself, now predominantly Presbyterian, not only of blocking the way to true liberation, but also of subverting the very principles of law they should be most jealous of defending.[3] The Commons must create guarantees against all arbitrary proceedings, including its own. Thus did the Levellers anticipate again the conception of irrevocable rights inherent in the *Agreement* of sixteen months later. Thus also did they foreshadow the strategy of 1647: appeal from the Commons to the army as spokesmen for England's democratic demands.

In the months that followed the Leveller leaders carried on their agitation with heightened intensity, expanding and underlining the demands of the *Remonstrance*. On July 31 Overton sent forth his *Alarum To the House of Lords,* bitterly upbraiding the peers for their imprisonment of Lilburne, and renouncing

---

[1] Document 1, and commentary, pp. 109-130 of this volume.
[2] P. 124 of this volume.   [3] P. 113 of this volume.

again their right to any law-making power. The Lords were merely heirs to the usurped power of their ancestors, who had gained it "by adhering to Kings, in subduing and oppressing the *Commons.*" [4] The power of the Lords must be curbed: "Wee are resolu'd upon our Natural R*ights* and *Freedoms,* and to be enslaved to none, how Magnificent soever, with Rotten Titles of Honour." [5] On August 21 appeared Lilburne's *Liberty Vindicated against Slavery,* a protest pregnant with his long study of documents, particularly Coke's *Institutes,* and bristling with attacks on jailors' extortions of poor prisoners. Some men have suffered imprisonment for debt, he complains, for ten, twenty, thirty, forty years together, with no provision made for food or raiment, neglected by the agencies of justice. *"What is the reason of this their great neglect?"* demands Lilburne. "Because we are *Poore, Poore* I say, and not able to see Lawyers, Atturneys, Sollicitors and Gaolers; for if we had moneys to satiate these Horse-leeches, then (though our causes were never so unjust, and debts never so great) we should no wayes doubt the gaining of our Liberties." [6] Imprisoned by the Lords on August 11, Overton sent forth less than a month later (September 9) his *Defiance Against All Arbitrary Usurpations,* assailing the "new upstart Presbyters" for truckling to the Lords and "accounting it their honour to rob themselves and their posterities, of their just Birth-rights and Freedoms." [7] The Presbyterians, claims Overton, have made it their business to be propaganda agents for arbitrary power, keeping the people in "a state of ignorance and vassalage." [8] On October 12 appeared *An Arrow Against All Tyrants,* a pamphlet also loaded with barbs against the Presbyterians and their new ordinance against heresies (September 10), but richly expressive of Overton's secular philosophy as it had emerged in the *Remonstrance.* "By naturall birth," he insisted, "all men are equally and alike borne to like propriety, liberty and freedom . . . every man by nature being a King, Priest and Prophet in his owne naturall circuite and compasse." [9] In a postscript letter to Marten, Overton urges the implications of Leveller democracy upon him thus: "Let not the *greatest Peers* in the Land, be more respected with you, then so

---

[4] P. 4. [5] P. 6. [6] P. 25. [7] P. 2.
[8] P. 2. "I was not born for myself alone," writes Overton (p. 5), "but for my neighbor as well as for myself; and I am resolv'd to discharge the trust which God hath repos'd in me for the good of others." [9] Pp. 3-4.

many *old Bellowes-menders, Broom men, Coblers, Tinkers or Chimney-sweepers,* who are all equally *Free borne,* with the *hudgest men,* and *loftiest Anachims* in the Land." [10] Such sentiments reflect the explosive implications of the democratic surge, implications of one piece with Overton's and Lilburne's wearing their hats before the Lords, Walwyn's satire of the "silken Independents" in their fine clothes and coaches, a Digger leader standing covered before Fairfax, saying "he was but their fellow creature."

His mind still immersed in documents and charters, Lilburne in October sent forth from his cell *Londons Liberties In Chains discovered,* asserting the right of all London freeholders to vote for mayor and aldermen, denouncing again the heavy taxes laid upon the poor, while those in high places receive a thousand, fifteen hundred, or two thousand pounds a year. Less flexible and imaginative than Overton, Lilburne nevertheless was documenting and clarifying his political credo. "The Fundamental Law of the Land," he wrote, "is the PERFECTION *of reason, consisting of Lawfull and Reasonable Customes, received and approved of by the people. . . But such only as are agreeable to the law Eternall and Naturall.*[11] On November 6 appeared *An Anatomy of the Lords Tyranny,* Lilburne's speech before the Commons' committee appointed, with Henry Marten chairman, to investigate his case. In the *Anatomy* Lilburne describes the prison hardships and indignities inflicted upon him by the sentence of the Lords, his refusal to kneel, remove his hat, or listen to his sentence; quoting Magna Charta, he repeatedly denies the right of the Lords to try him, a commoner. As always with Lilburne, these bitter personal struggles agitated and crystallized his constitutional reflections. Like Milton, Lilburne unfailingly identified his personal with the just rights of all his countrymen, projecting individual tyrannies into pervasive social oppressions.

In November and December Leveller tracts continued their insistent democratic demands, justifying the war against Charles

[10] Pp. 19-20.

[11] P. 41. In this tract Lilburne reprinted the petition which his wife Elizabeth had presented to the Commons on September 23, pleading for her husband's right to plead his case before the bar of the Commons, for prohibition of the Lords' arbitrary actions, and for a Commons' investigation of the Earl of Manchester and Lilburne's charges against him. In this petition Lilburne speaks of Englishmen as "born equally free, and to whom the law of the land is an equall inheritance."

as the means to a revolutionary end, denouncing the Presbyterians
for their repressive tactics against the sectarians. On November
19 *Vox Plebis* appeared, buttressing Lilburnian arguments with
Latin quotations and classic references. The Levellers made it
plain that they regarded ownership of property as a basic right:
"Liberty of conscience in matters of Faith, and Divine worship;
Liberty of the Person, and liberty of Estate: which consists properly in the propriety of their goods, and a disposing power of
their possessions." [12] The imprisonment of Lilburne, claims the
author, is a violation of the ancient rights of English freemen,
rights of which the Conquest defrauded them, and Magna Charta
has restored but not perfected.[13] Again the radicals complain of
arbitrary proceedings unjustifiable by any statute: *"We know
that it is better to live under an hard and harsh known written
law . . . then under the mildest arbitrary government, where the
Subject is condemned at the will of their Judges."* [14] On November 30 Overton sent forth his *Vnhappy Game At Scotch And
English,* a biting attack on the Scotch papers of October 20. In *An
Vnhappy Game* Overton seeks to channel nationalist enthusiasm
into an attack on Scottish and Presbyterian royalism. "Our Lawes
. . . and Liberties," he exclaims, "are more pretious, then to be
prostitute to the exhorbitant boundlesse *will* of any mortall
Steuart under the Sun." [15] The question to be resolved is
"whether his will, or the two Kingdomes consent . . . must stand
irrevocable." [16] Though the Commons replied with asperity to
Scotch claims of a share in the disposal of the king's person, Overton's bold words were for them gallingly provocative. On the day
of its publication, *An Vnhappy Game* was ordered burned by the
common hangman and a committee set on the trail of the
printer.[17] In the evolution of Leveller attacks on monarchy, to

---

[12] Pp. 3-4.

[13] "It is a most sure Rule in State policy," adds the author, "That all the Lawes
that are made in favour of liberty, spring first from the disagreement of the people
with their Governours."   [14] P. 67.

[15] P. 10. On October 26 *A Corrector Of the Answerer* (attributed to Henry
Marten) condemned the king even more rashly than Overton, asking if Parliament
were not bound by the Covenant, if it found the sovereign guilty of tyranny, "to
bring him to condign punishment, as the chiefe of all delinquents." Having set
Strafford and Canterbury to work, has not the king "infinitly transcended them in
Treasons against the Commonwealth?"

[16] P. 14.   [17] *Commons' Journals,* IV, 731-32.

culminate in *Regall Tyrannie* and *Putney Projects, An Vnhappy Game* provided a decisive impetus.[18]

On December 18 Lilburne published *The Charters Of London,* a tract resounding not only with threats to kingship, but also, significantly enough, a justification of manhood suffrage. Continuing his argument of *Londons Liberty In Chains,* Lilburne denied the right of the Lord Mayor and the Court of Aldermen to share the legislative power of the Common Council. Since the king himself has no legislative power, claimed Lilburne, he cannot invest his appointees, the Mayor and Aldermen, with any authority whatever. They are executives, not legislators, and have no right to sit in the Common Council. "The only and sole legislative Law-making power," writes Lilburne, *"is originally inherent in the people, and derivatively in their Commissions chosen by themselves by common consent, and no other.* In which the poorest that lives, hath as true a right to give a vote, as well as the richest and greatest." [19] The four great evils of the world Lilburne summarizes as follows:

First, the Popes unwritten verities. Secondly, Kings unlimited Prerogatives. Thirdly, Parliaments unknown Priviledges. Fourthly, the Lord Major, Court of Aldermen, and the rest of the Prerogative men of Londons implicit faith, who in the second desire of their most pernitious Atheisticall, Papisticall Remonstrance, pag. 7. would have all those fully declared against, and some effectuall course setled, for proceeding against all such persons as will not be conformable to the publick Discipline established, or to be established.[20]

In these statements Lilburne anticipates two cardinal principles of the first *Agreement:* manhood suffrage and a written guarantee and clarification of constitutional privileges. Ten months later the clash between Leveller and Independent on the issue of the suffrage was to illuminate as did no other debate the cleavage in outlook between apprentices and masters, workers and property-

[18] In *Putney Projects* Wildman elucidates repetitiously but effectively the implications of the king's will as the source of power.   [19] P. 4.

[20] P. 5. Lilburne's harsh words against the *Remonstrance* of May 26 reflect his conviction that Presbyterian insistence on a state church would mean persecution of all other sects. The Leveller war for toleration and against a compulsory state church I have traced in detail in *Milton in the Puritan Revolution.* Leveller insistence on toleration was to be also a cardinal principle of the *Agreement.*

owners, small business men and gentlemen. In the phrase, "Parliaments unknown Priviledges," Lilburne symbolized his mounting discontent with the Commons' violations (as he thought) of the elementary rights of all Englishmen. Underlying these principles Lilburne assumed, of course, the broader one inherent in previous Leveller tracts: the social compact, implicit in the words, "by common consent."

6. Thomas Edwards: Mirror of Puritan Piety

No tracts reflect more suggestively the attitude of conservative Puritans toward the Levellers than Thomas Edwards' *Gangraena*, the third part of which appeared December 28. The first two *Gangraena* sallies had pictured Overton and Lilburne as theological heretics. But London agitation in the last six months of 1646, together with the rising ferment in the army, had revealed to Edwards the still more dangerous secular demands of the democratic surge. "I Desire to know of these Sectaries," asked Edwards, ". . . whether all the men, women, and children born in *England*, men-servants, maid-servants, poore people and beggars, together with those of the better sort . . . be the state universall, have they the like Soveraigne power over the King and Parliament." [1] Lilburne is "head of the Sectaries in these Anti-Parliamentary principles," "the great darling of the Sectaries," leaning not only to democracy but to "Anarchicall Principles," a man who wants to overthrow king and Lords, to change totally the laws and customs of the country.[2] Overton, "a desperate Sectary, one of *Lilburne's* Breed and followers," is equally rash and heinous, desiring nothing less than the "overthrow of the fundamentall constitution of this Kingdome." [3] These audacious leaders, laments Edwards, are determined to "set up an Utopian Anarchie of the promiscuous multitude." Upon the heads of such men, and those who allow them to escape without punishment, Edwards as a minister pronounces "the plague of God." [4]

Though Edwards did not yet realize its secular implications,

---

[1] Thomason E 368 (5), eighth unnumbered page following p. 16.
[2] *Ibid.*, pp. 153, 159.   [3] *Ibid.*, pp. 148, 149.
[4] *Ibid.*, p. 218. Edwards of course levels the usual charges against the sectaries (pp. 187-92) that they are guilty of adultery, incest, fornication, drunkenness, Sabbath-breaking, card-playing, cheating, lying.

he was particularly fearful of the rising tide of sectarianism in the
New Model army. Independents and Anabaptists held high favor,
but "because a man is a Presbyterian, he shall be turned out of
his command." [5] Poisoned by army sectarianism, Hugh Peters was
now its arch-sectary, boasting of his converts among the Presbyterians themselves. Many soldiers, complained Edwards, want no
ministers at all; they "cal the Citizens Preist-riden slaves." [6] One
of them "laid his hand on his sword, and said, this sword should
never be laid down, nor many thousands more, whilst there was a
Priest left in *England*." [7] Another soldier had shown his contempt
of churches by leading a bald-headed horse into a church, filling
the font with urine, baptizing the horse *Ball Esau,* even naming
for him a godfather and godmother! [8] Liberty of conscience is
their cry, liberty even to Papists! A universal toleration! "Our
Armies," concludes Edwards, "are the Nurseries of all errours and
all our evills . . . it will never be well with the Kingdome, till the
Armies be disbanded." [9]

With what accuracy Edwards had gauged the spirit of the New
Model soldiery may be judged in the pages of the moderate and
patient Richard Baxter. Had Edwards accompanied Baxter in the
latter's conversations around the campfires, his exclamations of
horror would have resounded with understandable panic. The
endless passionate disputes, the vehement preaching of the soldiers,
the rise of Anabaptist officers, Cromwell's encouragement of toleration, the founding of Baptist churches in the wake of victorious
marches, the recognition, for the first time in English military
history, of soldiery merit alone as the basis of promotion—these
were the revolutionary seedground soon to be planted thick again
with the pamphlets of Lilburne and Overton. "A few proud, self-
conceited, hot-headed Sectaries had got into the highest places,"
wrote Baxter sadly, "and were *Cromwell's* chief Favourites." [10]
The soldiers "took the King for a Tyrant and an Enemy, and . . .
intended absolutely to master him, or to ruine him." [11] Moreover,
"What were the Lords of *England* but *William* the Conqueror's
Colonels? or the Barons but his Majors? or the Knights but his
Captains?" [12] Baxter estimated that no more than one-half the

5 Thomason E 368 (5), p. 70.   6 *Ibid.*, p. 228.
7 *Ibid.*, p. 173.   8 *Ibid.*, p. 18.   9 *Ibid.*, p. 266.
10 *Reliquae Baxterianae* (London, 1696), p. 52.
11 *Ibid.*, p. 53.   12 *Ibid.*, p. 53.

soldiers were tainted with these notions; but they yielded through
ignorance and indifference to the arguments of the hot-headed
few, "sometimes for State Democracy, and sometime for Church
Democracy." [13] The godly, orthodox ministers, had they remained
with the army, might have prevented the accumulated ferment of
errors and heresies opened to the men in Lilburne's pamphlets;
but their discouragement and retreat had let fall the barriers to all
abominable heresies of immature, impulsive minds. As the dire
events of 1649 were to demonstrate, Baxter's fears held the substance of truth. Nowhere in England did the intellectual restlessness of Protestantism, and the fluid shiftings of social forces, assert
themselves more freely or destructively than in Cromwell's strange
army. Unchecked by the community's authority, each man his
own confident, unseasoned interpreter of truth, revolving cease-
lessly the Biblical ideal with the face of ancient inequalities,
listening, arguing, searching, making England's history by day,
prophesying her future by night, the soldiers passed from a vague
realization of their strategic power into an explosive revolutionary
resolution. To the intensification and direction of the army's
radicalism, which they had helped to create, the Leveller leaders
were now determined to address themselves, after futile pleas to
the Commons.

7. Of Tyrants and Oppressors

On January 6 the Leveller leaders distributed *Regall Tyrannie
discovered,* a remarkable tract synthesizing their theoretical justifications of a democratic program, expanding and clarifying their
conception of the social compact. "In *nature and reason,*" they
wrote, "there is none above, or over another, against mutuall consent and agreement." [1] Equal by birth, born in the image of God,
*"the people in generall are the originall sole legislaters, and the
true fountain, and earthly well-spring of all just power."* [2] Only
by mutual agreement did people nominate magistrates to be their
executives, these to be subject to the law the people had created.
When they have taken the oath of office,[3] the kings of England
have admitted their responsibility to the law and their compact

---

13 *Ibid.*   1 P. 11.   2 P. 99.
3 On pp. 31 and 32 the authors quote the actual oath taken by Charles and his
predecessors.

with the people. More fully than in any other pamphlet the authors elaborate their conception of the history of England since the Conquest as a theft of property and violation of ancient privileges. William gave away the lands to his Normans, levied heavy taxes and set up courts to collect them, had the laws written in French so that "the poor miserable people might be gulled, and cheated, undone and destroyed," [4] created *"Dukes, Earles* and *Barons* for helping him to subdue, and enslave the *free Nation of England."* [5] From time to time, admit the Levellers, as at the signing of Magna Charta, kings have been forced to bow to the supremacy of the law and the wishes of the people. But Charles I relentlessly opposes the will of his subjects; he has repeatedly broken his contract. He deserves no respect or consideration; the origins of English kings have been *"wicked, triviall, base, and tyrannical."* As for the Lords, they have no right to sit in Parliament; in the earliest Parliaments prelates had no place, temporal Lords little or none. Like the kings who created them, the Lords have usurped their power by abridging the rights of the people. In such terms did the Levellers recapitulate their demands, planting the seed for explosive army radicalism, anticipating the theory by which, two years later, Milton and his fellow-Independents were to justify the annihilation of both kingship and Lords.

8. Appeal to all England

Disillusioned by the failure of the Commons to free him from prison and redress his grievances, finding that even Henry Marten, *"the glory of his Age amongst Parliament men,"* delayed to press his cause, Lilburne now resolved to appeal to the common people and the rank and file of the army. He hoped to rouse them to an espousal of the rights and privileges that the Commons had often justified as the grounds of their war against Charles. By January 30, 1647, when he published *The Oppressed Mans Oppressions declared,* he was convinced that Parliament had betrayed the principles of its own declarations, declarations that "may very well serve against themselves." [1] By its tyrannical actions Parliament

---

[4] P. 15.   [5] P. 45.

[1] *The Oppressed Mans Oppressions,* p. 34. *The Commoners Complaint,* which is dated by Overton February 1, contains a graphic account of his prison adventures and clashes with Parliament's officers. Overton's theme is that of Lilburne, the tyranny of Parliament.

has nullified Magna Charta and the ancient liberties of free-born Englishmen. *"Tyrannie, is tyrannie,"* Lilburne wrote, "exercised by whom soever; yea, though it be by members of Parliament, as well as by the King, and they themselves have taught us by their Declarations and practises, that tyrannie is resistable . . . what is tyrannie, but to admit no rule to govern by, but their own wils?" [2] Lilburne apparently saw no incongruity in making his personal wrongs the basis of his appeal to the populace: "I am now determined . . . if I speedily have not that Justice, which the Law of *England* affords me . . . to make a formall Appeale to all the Commons of the Kingdome of *England,* and Dominion of *Wales."* [3] Issuing a joint manifesto from prison on February 28 (*The out-cryes of oppressed Commons*), Lilburne and Overton excoriated the failure of the Commons to redress grievances and receive petitions, to protect prisoners from rapacious jailers, to preserve their position against the encroachments of the Lords. The writers have indeed been loyal to the Commons, acknowledging it as the supreme authority; but for their own preservation, when the Commons fails to act for liberty, they must appeal to the people as the ultimate source of all power. "By suffering will and lust, but not law to rule and govern us," the Commons is disqualifying itself to represent the nation. Moreover, it is dissolving the kingdom *"into the originall Law of nature,"* in which every man is bound to "preserve and defend himselfe the best he can." Thus did Lilburne and Overton justify, when precedents failed them, their impending appeal to the soldiers and citizens. "We for our preservation shall tread in the Parliament steps by *appealing to the People* against them, as they did against the King." [4] How such a denunciation could secure wide acceptance of their revolutionary proposals the radicals did not pause to reflect. From this point onward, finding the army sharply responsive to their propaganda, they had no hesitation in urging the dangerous device of military intimidation of the House of Commons. However unrepresentative the House, however unrespon-

---

[2] *Oppressed Mans Oppressions.* Of Parliament's economic policy Lilburne writes: (pp. 33-34): "Was a Parliament in *England* ever called for that end, as to rob and poll the poore common people, and to force those that have scarce bread to put in their mouthes, to pay excise, and other taxations . . . and then share it amongst the members of both houses; as 10000. 1. to one man, 6000. 1. to another, 5000. 1. &c."   [3] *Ibid.,* pp. 37-38.   [4] P. 14.

sive to democratic pressures, the alternative of military expediency, as the Levellers were to learn to their sorrow, would bring in its wake an unstable dictatorship more autocratic than Charles himself.

From the dire threats of *The out-cryes* one would suppose that the radicals' formal appeal to the people was imminent, forthcoming within a few days or weeks. While intensifying their agitation among the soldiers, however, Lilburne and Overton were constrained to delay by the work of their colleagues on the great March petition. Possibly Walwyn, undoubtedly the main author of the petition, had less confidence than his fellow-leaders in the efficacy of military intervention for democratic gains. Whether or not this was true, the strategy adopted by the Levellers in this emergency was typical of their later program. Unable consistently to appeal to Parliament as the "supreme authority" and simultaneously urge the people to renounce its power, the radicals withheld their renunciation but lighted the fuse in the army for a timed explosion in London. While their adherents circulated petitions in the army for indemnity and arrears, the Levellers of London impetuously plied their followers for support of the great petition. The hostility of the Commons' Presbyterian majority they knew well enough; no doubt they expected a blunt rebuff to their far-reaching proposals. But the petition would crystallize the issues and unite their forces while army discontent was mounting to the point of explosion and coercion. From this time forward army and London Levellers planned their common strategy with the closest integration.[5]

[5] According to Lilburne, Cromwell opposed the first soldiers' petition of March, 1647, which they had evidently planned to co-ordinate with the great March petition of the London Levellers. On March 25 two men, an officer and a special messenger, told Lilburne that Cromwell and his agents "are likely to dash in peeces the hopes of our outward preservation, *Their petition to the House,* and will not suffer them to petition till they have laid down their Armes." Simultaneously the Levellers were directing the agitation in London and the army. Of Cromwell's motives Lilburne was already suspicious. He warns him against the "snares . . . laid for thee in that vote of the House of Commons of two thousand five hundred pounds per annum." If Cromwell persists in opposing the army's petition, then will "deliverance arise to us poore afflicted ones . . . from another place then from you silken Independents, the broken reeds of Egypt." Lilburne also admonishes Cromwell against disbanding until the army has petitioned for reforms. This is the earliest hint of the line of agitation followed in April by the army radicals. *Ionahs Cry out of the Whales belly,* pp. 2, 3, letter to Cromwell dated March 25, 1647.

9. Compound of Heresies: The March Petition

The worst fears of Edwards and his fellow-Presbyterians were realized in the famous document of March.[1] It was a compound of the army's extreme heresies, both religious and secular. Not only did it demand toleration of all religious opinions, both spoken and written (and Papist ideas not excepted), but it called unequivocally for the abolition of tithes, hence the elimination of the state-supported clergy, the bulwark of Presbyterian strength. Moreover the economic planks of the petition ran counter to the interests of many wealthier Presbyterians: the abolition of the Company of Merchant Adventurers, the relief of imprisoned debtors, assistance to the poor. "Thousands of men and women," avowed the petitioners, "are still (as formerly) permitted to live in beggery and wickednesse . . . to breed up their children in the same idle and vitious course . . . and no effectual meanes used to reclaim either." [2] Such a demand not only threatened pockets; it also repudiated a settled conviction of the wealthier Puritans that only the lazy and sinful suffered the distresses of poverty. The petitioners' insistence, furthermore, that the fees of all judges, magistrates, lawyers, and government officials be limited and published struck directly at the livelihood of influential Presbyterians and their underofficers. Beneath these disturbing innovations, however, loomed a revolutionary proposal still more menacing: the abolition of the negative voices of king and Lords. A stiff-backed emphasis on the rights of the Commons, voiced in many declarations since 1642, had now brought in its train an unexpected danger not only to Presbyterian vested interests but also to their control of the Commons itself. Vigorously as they had opposed the king, his power was no such ogre as the rising tide of revolutionary fervor, born of ferment among the poorer sectaries and the strange, heretical propaganda of the New Model army. In effect, then, the petition of March crystallized the issue of the Civil War's purpose and direction: an extension of the democratic principle into resolute popular control of the House of Commons, opening the way to still more dangerous innovations; or a stabilization of the fundamental constitution with a Presbyterian Com-

[1] Document 2 and commentary, pp. 131-43 of this volume.   [2] P. 137.

mons effectively checking the monarch's will. Against this stabilization ran the fierce tide of the Independents' military might and the Levellers' resourceful propaganda.

10. Ferment in the New Model

The strategy of the Presbyterians, as Edwards had anticipated in December, was to disband the army, thus destroying the main collective strength of the rebellious sectaries. It was a strategy fraught with unforeseen disaster. Nevertheless, to accomplish this end, they pressed for the organization of an army to invade Ireland, the men of the New Model to volunteer. On March 11 a Presbyterian petition urged haste in this procedure upon the House.[1] Cromwell himself assured the House about this time that the army would disband upon their command. On March 22 fourteen officers sympathetic to Presbyterianism submitted a petition to both Houses, urging the expedition to Ireland, but calling for payment of arrears and indemnity and the removal of county committees.[2]

Only the day before a deputation from the Commons had conferred with Fairfax and his officers at Saffron Walden, urging volunteers for Ireland. It was an opportunity for the unburdening of army grievances. Yes, said the officers, they would urge their men to volunteer; but as for themselves, they could not agree to do so until answers to pertinent questions were forthcoming. The questions show the officers' suspicions: What regiments and companies were to remain in England? Who was to command in Ireland? What assurance of pay would be forthcoming for the volunteers? What assurance of arrears and indemnity for those who had already served?[3] Meeting again on March 22, the officers resolved

[1] Commons' *Journals*, V, 115; John Rushworth, *Historical Collections* (8 v., London, 1721), VI, 451.

[2] *The Parliamentary or Constitutional History of England* (23 v., London, 1761-63), XV, 338. Hereafter referred to as *Old Parliamentary History*.

[3] *A Declaration of the Engagements, Remonstrances, Representations . . . from . . . Fairfax, and the Generall Councel of the Army,* 1647, p. 4. Hereafter referred to as *Book of Army Declarations.* The questions underlying these queries may be summarized as follows: Were predominantly Presbyterian or sectarian regiments to be sent to Ireland? Was the Commons trying to get rid of the army sectaries by sending them on a foreign expedition? Would Cromwell and Fairfax be left behind? Would the men be commanded by Presbyterian officers in Ireland, that is, by men unsympathetic with their religious and political demands? Would the army be paid for past and future services? On the last point the men of the army, what-

to formulate their resolutions in a petition to Parliament. At news of a petition the deputation took offense, and after private appeals by Fairfax twenty-nine of the forty-three officers agreed to volunteer. But the rumbling voices would not cease. Blowing the smouldering protest into a feeble flame, the common soldiers phrased with the officers a comparatively mild petition to be submitted to Fairfax. Affirming their loyalty to the Parliament, the soldiers pointed out that they have never "disputed their Commands, disobeyed their Orders, nor disturbed them with Petitions." Ever cheerful in the line of duty, they have "done Summer Service in Winter Seasons." [4] But now they "humbly desire," before disbanding, the assurance of payment for their services, freedom from impressment (for those who have volunteered in England), provision for the wounded, the widows and orphans, recompense for their losses, and funds to pay for their present quarters. This petition, circulated in the days following March 22, provoked an inflammatory response from the Presbyterian majorities of Lords and Commons. Should the petitioners persist in their appeal, said the Parliament's declaration, they "shall be look'd upon, and proceeded against, as Enemies to the State, and Disturbers of the Public Peace." [5] In such language did the Presbyterians throw down the gauntlet to the whole army, providing the radicals with unanswerable propaganda among the unpaid rank and file. Thus, too, did the Presbyterians reveal their utter failure to evaluate the power of sectarian explosiveness soon to be turned against them.

In April the tension between army and Commons continued to mount, each protest and declaration provoking a still sharper reply, and Leveller leadership rousing the soldiers to decisive action. On March 30 Fairfax had written to the Earl of Manchester saying that he would stop the circulation of the objectionable petition as described in the Lords' letter of March 27. The soldiers' intentions, however, said Fairfax, were "no other than by way of Petition to represent unto me those inconveniences, which would necessarily befal most of the army after disband-

ever their rank or persuasion, were unanimous. The foot soldiers had not been paid for eighteen weeks, the horsemen for forty-three. Gardiner, *Civil War,* III, 225. In one of their letters the soldiers name the arrears as over two years for the foot soldiers and thirteen months for the horse, but this evidently is an exaggeration. *Book of Army Declarations,* p. 10.

[4] *Old Parliamentary History,* XV, 343-44. [5] *Ibid.,* XV, 345.

ing." [6] Writing from Saffron Walden on April 3, an army spokesman expressed alarm at Parliament's condemnation: "Have the
Souldiers only, who have been Instruments to recover the lost
Liberties of the Nation, fought themselves into Slavery? Sure
there is Right of petitioning for us, as well as there was a Petition of Right for the Parliament." [7] In a second letter of the
same date, the spokesman deplores again Parliament's denial of
the right of petition to the army, while its enemies are heard with
respect. On April 6 the House received a sharp Essex petition for
disbanding, but asked its members from Essex to persuade the
petitioners to desist from their appeal.[8] On April 20 sixteen common soldiers of Colonel Lilburne's regiment appealed to Fairfax
against going to Ireland without their old commanders, and upon
threat of not being paid, saying that they represented the minds
of the whole company. This happening appears to be the first
hint of an organization among the private soldiers; the word
agitator appeared for the first time, significantly enough, on the
same day.[9] On April 27 the House received *The Vindication of
the Officers,* a document reviewing the history of the soldiers' first
petition, deploring the misrepresentations spread abroad about
the army, and stoutly defending the right of the soldiers and officers to petition Parliament. "We hope, by being Soldiers," wrote
the officers, "we have not lost the capacity of Subjects . . . that in
purchasing the Freedoms of our Brethren, we have not lost our
own." The officers quote the Parliament's own declaration of 1642
on the right of petitioning, and add: "We know not any thing
more essential to Freedom, without Grievances are remediless, and
our Condition most miserable." [10] This demand for freedom of
petitioning, like many another plank in army manifestoes, was a
portent of events to come: As Parliament had asserted it against
the king, so the army upheld it against Parliament's condemnations; and in turn the Levellers were to plague the army leaders
with their own declarations for the same basic privilege.

In the midst of army agitation over disbanding appeared the
fiery and provocative *A New Found Stratagem*,[11] evidently in good

---

[6] *Book of Army Declarations*, p. 5.   [7] Rushworth, VI, 446.
[8] *Ibid.,* VI, 450, 451. This is the petition attacked in *A New Found Stratagem.*
[9] S. R. Gardiner, *History of the Great Civil War* (4 v., London, 1886), III, 237.
[10] Rushworth, VI, 469-70.
[11] Thomason records that the *Stratagem* "was scattered abroad in yᵉ Armie

part the work of Overton. After quoting the Essex petition in favor of disbanding, Overton breaks forth in peremptory appeal: "O Foolish men of *Essex!* who hath bewitched you? yee did run well, who hath hindred you? for indeed ye were with the first, and most forward, in assisting the Parliament, for the recovering and regaining our then lost Lawes and liberties." [12] Overton insists that if the New Model is disbanded, Parliament will merely raise another for the invasion of Ireland. Hence the mounting expense of a standing army so bitterly complained of by the petitioners is certain to continue. The army has now become the people's refuge, the means "to keep you and yours from sudden vasalage and slavery." To put their trust in the present Commons is "to offer your selves slaves." [13] Would the men of Essex have the army disband without payment of their arrears? "Aske your daily Thresher, your plow-man, and dayes labourer, if they will be contented with the like dealing?" [14] Overton asserts that the petition, like the scheme for disbanding the army, is the work of "a company of false, traiterous, and deceitfull men; in both Houses of Parliament, and of proud, coveteous Priests . . . suddenly to inthrall & inslave us." [15] Nothing stands in the way but the incorruptible army, an army that has neither stolen nor pillaged nor stood at ease, but fought *"in the face of death, in frost, snow, rain, cold, heat, wet, and dirt, by day, by night, in hunger and thirst . . . to suppresse the fury of your bloodthirsty enemies."* [16] But the present enemies, being pretended friends, are more dangerous than the king and his armies. Thus Overton urges in passage after passage the urgency of the crisis, and concludes, "Alasse we are at the *pit brinke, and see not."* [17]

11. The Soldiers Force an Issue

By April 28, when the soldiers presented to Fairfax *The Apologie,* Leveller agitation [1] was plainly at work. The first soldiers'

when ye Commissioners were sent from ye Parliament to disband ym." This was about April 15, when the soldiers appeared at Saffron Walden. Thomason's date on the pamphlet (E 384, 11) is April 18, but it appears in the catalog under the date of April 4.

12 P. 4.   13 P. 7.   14 P. 8.
15 P. 9.   16 P. 12.   17 P. 15.

1 Lilburne later claimed he had contributed both funds and leadership to effect the organization of the common soldiers: "I had been instrumentall with the expence of a great deale of money, and withall the interest and industry I had in

petition of a month before, filtered through the phrasing of minds
more cautious and tactful than their own, had emphasized economic grievances. But the aim of *The Apologie* and *A Second
Apologie* was to strike, in a tone deliberately provocative, for political freedoms as well. If the army's present enemies, wrote the
soldiers, stood face to face with them, they would have no fear
of the outcome. But "a farre worse enemy we have to deale with,
who like Foxes lurke in their Dennes . . . this plot is but a meere
cloake for some who have lately tasted of Sovereignty . . . seek
to become Masters, and degenerate into Tyrants . . . we must
. . . shew ourselves averse to that service [Ireland] until our desires be granted, the just Rights and liberties of the Subjects vindicated and maintained.[2] In *A Second Apologie* the soldiers all
but name Lilburne and Overton when they complain of "cordiall
friends to the Parliament and us, and to the just Rights and Liberties of this Nation, that with us are slighted, abused, beaten,
and dragged to Jayles." [3] The soldiers demand that the army's
honor be vindicated (in putting forth their first petition); that indemnity be provided; that assistance be given wives and children
of slain soldiers; that volunteers for England may not be con-
scripted for service in Ireland; finally, that *"Iustice and Iudgement
may be dealt to the meanest Subject of this Land, according to
old Law."* *The Apologie* was signed by Edward Sexby, William
Allen, and Thomas Sheppard, with fourteen other representatives of the soldiers, called "commissioners," evidently in ironic
contradistinction to the commissioners of Parliament.[4] On April
30 *The Apologie* was presented to the House by Major General
Skippon, with whom the troopers had intrusted it the day before.
So shocking was this letter, in contrast to the *Vindication,* that the
House ordered an immediate examination of Sexby, Allen, and

the world; acted both night and day to settle the Souldiers in a compleat and just
posture, by their faithfull agitators chosen out by common consent from amongst
themselves, as resolute, fit, and just instruments to effect my Liberty, to give a
checke to tyranny, and settle the peace and justice of the Kingdome, not looking
for any good at all from your selfe, and the rest of your fellow great ones." *Ionahs
Cry,* p. 9, letter to Cromwell dated July 7, 1647.

On May 4 a letter was circulated in the army advising the men on details of
organization of "Councells of the Army." This letter, which may have been written,
in Firth's opinion, by Edward Sexby, describes the propaganda strategy followed
by the agitators. *Clarke Papers,* I, 24.

2 *Book of Army Declarations,* p. 8.   3 *Ibid.,* p. 9.
4 *Ibid.,* pp. 9, 11.

Sheppard. The answers of the three men to the House's questions showed how effectively the common soldiers of eight regiments of horse were now organized to give expression to their grievances. The three agitators evaded questions about the times and places of meetings and signatures. When Allen was asked his opinion of the phrases "tasted of Sovereignty" and "degenerated into Tyrants," he refused to interpret them, saying that the letter was a joint declaration and that only the men of the regiments could answer the question.[5] The House's response to the perilous conflict represented in *The Vindication* and *The Apologie* was a pause and a retreat. It voted assurance of "a considerable Sum" before disbanding, of an auditing of soldiers' accounts, of an ordinance for indemnity. Cromwell, Skippon, Ireton, and Fleetwood were to bear the news to the army. But the retreat was too late, and the promises too vague, to avoid the explosions to follow. Most portentous of all, the agitators had had their first taste of the integrated political power of the common soldiers.

12. Lilburne on the Tyranny of the Commons

Sent forth April 30, Lilburne's *The resolved mans Resolution* resounded with bold accusations against the Parliament and fierce cries for its dissolution. The Commons is so corrupt, claims Lilburne rashly, that three-quarters of the country's revenue go into the pockets of its members. Even the new members, some of them fresh from the battlefield and eager for liberty, lose their zeal with the payment of their arrears. Lord of the people's lives and property, the Parliament is more menacing and tyrannical than any king since Magna Charta; it "destroyes us with unknown, unlimitted and arbitrary priviledges." [1] Lilburne repeatedly cries out for a new Parliament, a Parliament chosen annually according to the ancient laws of Edward III. No newly chosen Parliament, however base its members, could work one-thousandth the injustices of the Long Parliament. "O *England*, England!" he bursts forth, "woe unto thee! when thy chosen preservers turne to be thy grand destroyers, and in stead of easing thee of thy grievances, with a high hand of violence protect from violence those that commit them . . . that body . . . not able to *evacuate its ex-*

5 *Clarke Papers* (4 v., Camden Soc. Pub., London, 1891-1901), I, 430-31.
1 P. 20.

crements is nigh unto the giving up the Ghost." [2] Daily the members of the Commons destroy those very laws they have sworn to
uphold. Lilburne's fiery castigations he was directing in the main,
of course, at the Presbyterian majority, now attempting to disband
the Independent army. But he has no good word either for the
Independents, or for *"sluggish Mr. Henry Martin, whose prisoner
principally I now am."* [3] On February 13 he had written to John
Goodwin, accusing his congregation of having conspired to keep
him and his fellows in prison; [4] on March 25 he had addressed himself impetuously to Cromwell, holding him to blame should the
army disband before its demands were met.[5] Already he has used
the term "silken Independents" and mentioned Cromwell's salary
as a bribe to betray the liberties of his country.[6] Lilburne was
quick to recognize, therefore, the cooperation between Presbyterian and Independent for the suppression of the Leveller fire-
brands.

Infuriated by the belligerent reception of their petitions, the
Levellers in May attacked the House of Commons with a sharp
and bitter virulence. Since March the House had postponed
promised consideration of the stolen petition. On April 23 the
petitioners, expecting an answer, waited at the House until five
in the afternoon, but again met the rebuff of postponement and
delay. Finally, on May 4, the House declared its disapproval of
the petition. The Levellers, however, would not desist; from
March to May they had appealed to the Commons upon five occasions. On May 20, in considering the fourth petition, the House
ordered it and the March petition to be burned by the common
hangman.[7] Convinced that all appeals to the House were useless,
that his only hope for liberty, either his own or his countrymen's,
lay now in the army, Lilburne launched his most violent condem-

---

[2] P. 16.   [3] P. 26.   [4] *Jonahs Cry,* p. 5.   [5] *Ibid.,* p. 3.

[6] At the convention of officers at Saffron Walden on May 15, Cromwell urged
upon them a sober consideration of Parliament's efforts to meet their demands. He
advised the officers to encourage in the men "a good opinion of that authority that
is over both us and them," adding, "If that authority falls to nothing, nothing can
followe but confusion." *Clarke Papers,* I, 73. Perhaps because he visualized more
clearly than they this confusion, Cromwell was much more reluctant than the
Levellers and his radical officers to use military coercion to effect redress of grievances. Once embarked on this course, however, Cromwell held it unflinchingly,
making little pretense of constitutional sanction for the intimidation of armed
might.

[7] See p. 133.

nations of the Commons in *Rash Oaths unwarrantable* (May 31). They have now degenerated, he exclaims, into "a conspiracy . . . of lawlesse, unlimited, and unbounded men . . . that will have no rule to walke by but their owne corrupted and bloody wills." [8] Instead of shepherds they have become "a company of devouring Lions and ravening Wolves," betrayers of their trusts, breakers of their oaths, ten times more tyrannical than the king himself.[9] "You have forfeited your essence and being," cries Lilburne, "& absolutely nullified the end of your sitting." [10] The people have now no other alternative than to wage war against the Commons as they have against the king, "to root up and destroy these tyrants" by force of arms.[11] Anticipating again elements of the *Agreement,* Lilburn points to the unrepresentative elections, the rotten boroughs, the House's arbitrary disregard of commoners' rights. He calls again for annual Parliaments, according to "the ancient and just unrepealed Law of the Land." [12]

13. June 5, 1647: Compact of Citizen-Soldiers

Meanwhile, toward the end of May, the temper of the army was rising feverishly, with the new organization of agitators more and more dominant in the shaping of army policy. On May 17, after the meeting at Saffron Walden, where a few officers disagreed about the soldiers' willingness to accept Parliament's terms, sixteen agitators made a declaration of soldier unanimity on the grievances presented.[1] On May 28 the Commons, still adamant, dispatched an order to Fairfax for the disbanding of the foot soldiers. Fairfax' response was to call a council of war at Bury, where two hundred officers resolved that the orders to disband were unsatisfactory to the soldiers; the soldiers expressed their amazement at Parliament's order for such an early disbanding (June 1), this to take effect without redress of grievances.[2] In support of their position, the officers then presented a petition from

8 Pp. 6-7.　　9 P. 38.　　10 *Ibid.*　　11 P. 47.　　12 Pp. 27, 49.

1 *Clarke Papers,* I, 78. The growth of the soldiers' organization is indicated in part by the enlarged number of agitators. On April 28, sixteen agitators had signed; on May 17, sixteen; on May 29, thirty-one. Letters in May from London to the agitators, several from Sexby, indicate close correspondence with Lilburne and his fellow-leaders. *Clarke Papers,* I, 84, 85, 92, 100, 105. In the code letter on p. 101, the numerals 59 and 89 probably refer to Lilburne and Overton.

2 Rushworth, VI, 497; *Two Letters of His Excellencie,* E. 391(2), May 29. The soldiers' petition was signed by thirty-one agitators.

the soldiers signed by the agitators. Beseeching an immediate rendezvous of the whole army, the soldiers urged Fairfax to use his "utmost Endeavours that it [the army] be not disbanded before our sad and pressing Grievances be heard, and fully redressed." [3] The soldiers protested also against the unprecedented Parliamentary action of disbanding the army piecemeal. The next May 30, in justifying his course to the Earl of Manchester, Fairfax wrote: *"I am forc'd to yeeld something out of order, to keep the Army from disorder, or worse inconveniences."* [4] Nothing then written more clearly reveals the conviction of the leaders that the army was in a desperate mood. Fairfax at once yielded to the demand of the soldiers and officers for a general rendezvous.

The rendezvous near New Market on June 4 and 5 crystallized army sentiment on a level proposed and sustained by the common soldiers and their radical leaders. In *An Humble Representation of the Dissatisfactions of the Army,* the officers and soldiers [5] boldly and unanimously voiced grievances that only the more daring would have dared to utter two months before; citing twelve particulars of the Commons' failure to satisfy their demands; expanding and reaffirming not only their right to arrears, but also their privilege of petitioning; evaluating Parliament's concessions in terms of their effect on the common soldier and his family. Not content with these criticisms, the army grasped the opportunity of the rendezvous to weld themselves into a cohesive political entity. In issuing *A Solemn Engagement of the Army* (June 5),[6] the soldiers and officers not only bound themselves not to disband until their grievances had been redressed, thus applying the principle of the social compact later to be incorporated in the *Agreement;* they also set up machinery by which they would proceed to voice democratically the political decisions of the whole army. For the first time in English history a body of soldiers had organized itself on a democratic basis to exert its collective will on crucial national events. The ideas of the *Solemn Engagement,* whatever pen phrased them, had sprung from the agitation among

---

[3] Rushworth, VI, 498.   [4] *Book of Army Declarations,* p. 12.

[5] Letters in *Clarke Papers* from and to the agitators reveal that their early strategy was to keep at all costs the good will and active cooperation of the officers in their designs.

[6] See Document 3 and commentary, pp. 142-53 of this volume. *A Solemn Engagement* begins on p. 146.

the common soldiers, who now had secured not only the cooperation of their officers, but also the tacit approval of Fairfax, Ireton,
and Cromwell. The willingness of the leaders to yield to the will
of the radical spirits doubtless arose in part from the tactless opposition of the Presbyterian majority, and in part from the mutinous
spirit of the troops. Thus far the army was united in its demands
for arrears, indemnity, sustenance for the families of the slain and
wounded; united, too, in their resentment of Presbyterian insults
and denial of the right of petition. The cleavage between officers
and men on the reshaping of England's social structure was still
months in the offing.

"Itt is incredible the Unitie of Officers and Soldiers," an army
spokesman had written on May 29.[7] In the face of such resolute
unity, the Commons were beginning to yield, and in June the
march of events kept pace with army manifestoes and the strategy
of the agitators. Apparently at the instigation of the agitators,
Cornet Joyce seized the king at Holdenby on June 4. On June 5
Parliament ordered expunged its declaration of March 30 against
the soldiers' first petition; it also ordered foot soldiers to be paid
in full upon their disbanding.[8] On June 10 Fairfax and his officers
wrote a stern letter to London's lord mayor, denying any revolutionary intentions, but asserting again the army's intention not
to disband until the country was assured *a full and perfect Settlement.*[9] On June 14 the army issued its *Declaration,* a more
comprehensive program of reform than it had yet voiced, reading
here and there as if it had been written by Lilburne himself, denouncing corrupt elections, demanding the purging of the Commons, regular elections at fixed intervals, the unqualified right of
petition, release or trial of imprisoned patriots.[10] Only two days
later, on June 16, the army presented the names of the eleven
members it demanded the House expel, charging them with false
and malicious attacks on the army, raising forces against the army,
infringing oppressively the rights and liberties of the citizens, especially petitioners.[11] The impact of these actions on Presbyterian
sentiment was reflected in William Prynne's *VIII Queres* on

[7] *Clarke Papers,* I, 112.   [8] Rushworth, VI, 518.
[9] *Ibid.,* VI, 554.   [10] *Ibid.,* VI, 564-70.
[11] *Ibid.,* VI, 570-71. "The Heads of a Charge." Without mentioning Lilburne
and Overton by name, this document, as well as the preceding one, calls for their
release.

June 15. The army, asserted Prynne, was being won over to a position it had formerly abhorred, ruling or overriding its own officers to take charge of the king's person, overawing the Parliament, conjuring up a "spirit of Universall Disobedience to Parliaments, Magistrates, and superiours of all sorts." Can such an army, asked Prynne, anticipating progressively exorbitant demands, be "a probable and fitting instrument of redressing those Arbitrary and injurious proceedings . . . of which they now complaine?" [12] On June 22 agitators from Colonel Rich's regiment complained to Fairfax that Lieutenant Hooker was "an enemy to the present iust proceedings of the Army," and asked that he be discharged from his command.[13] It was a warning of the soldiers' rising confidence in their power. On June 23 Fairfax and his officers pressed the House for action on their demands for the exclusion of the eleven members, sounding again the tones of Leveller propaganda, charging the accused members with "such a face of Injustice, Oppression, Arbitrariness, and Tyranny, as we think is not to be parallel'd in any . . . Proceedings of the most arbitrary Courts, against any private Men." [14] Moreover, the privileges of Parliament, "as well as Royal Prerogatives, may be perverted and abused." Acting reluctantly and obliquely under this pressure, the House on June 26 voted the eleven members "liberty to absent themselves from the House." [15]

On June 27 the officers issued from Uxbridge a manifesto strikingly more conciliatory than their violent accusations of June 23. Pledging themselves not to draw nearer to London than their present station, the officers declared their confidence in Parliament's determination to settle the most pressing affairs of the kingdom. Since the eleven members have consented to withdraw, the charges against them need not be immediately pressed.[16] Of these conciliatory accents, written at the point of the army's greatest power, the Levellers were suspicious. From the day of its publication Wildman later dated the officers' defection from the Leveller program. "Let the matter of those seaven proposalls therein be duely weighed . . . ," wrote Wildman, "& doth

---

[12] Pp. 3, 4, 5. Another Presbyterian, in *The Lawfulness of the Late Passages Of the Army* (E 394, 12), June 28, denied that the soldiers had any right to act in the capacity of subjects petitioning Parliament.

[13] *Clarke Papers*, I, 139-40.   [14] Rushworth, VI, 586.

[15] *Ibid.*, VI, 587, 593.   [16] *Ibid.*, VI, 594.

not the whole amount to this? That the Parliament should own them for their Army, and provide them pay, and vote against all opposite forces. There's not the least punctum of *Common iustice* moved to be done before their retreat, not so much as a *Declaration insisted upon against those enslaving presidents of burning petitions . . . no publique vindication of the Army. . . .* All publique good pretended on *June* 23. to be the primary reason of their march to *London,* was thus by *June* 27. in the grave of Oblivion. Doubtlesse the above mentioned and many other foundations of freedome might have been setled in as short a time as the matter of the seaven proposalls, but it seems 4. dayes changed their judgements." [17]

14. Division of Men and Officers

Lilburne's analysis of the march of events is best represented in his postscript to *Ionahs Cry out of the Whales belly,* dated July 16. Since the army "doe not onely dispute the two Houses orders and commands, but also positively disobey them, as unjust, tyrannicall, and unrighteous," the people are now "dissolved into the originall law of Nature." [1] Every man, then, has an equal right with every other to choose representatives to create a new government by mutual agreement. This, insists Lilburne, is the principle of the *Solemn Engagement.* But Lilburne distrusts the officers. The common soldiers, he says, not the officers, were active and resolute in organizing the army; at that time "all or most of the Officers sate still like so many Drones and Snekes." [2] According to the *Engagement* the officers have no more right to determine political policy than the common soldiers; and they must not be permitted, asserts Lilburne, to invade the soldiers' rights. Though the agitators had made every effort to effect a united front with the officers, cracks in the alliance, as Lilburne anticipated, were beginning to appear. In the Northern Association General Sednham Poynts resented the intrusion of agitator or-

---

[17] *Putney Projects* (December 30, 1647) p. 9. The seven proposals Wildman mentions appear in the *Book of Army Declarations,* pp. 67-69. The officers' demands include payment of arrears, recall of Parliament's invitation to desert the army, continuation of the army's status, disposal of reformadoes, declaration against the raising of new forces, disposition of the king's place of residence.

[1] *Ionahs Cry,* p. 13.   [2] *Ibid.,* p. 14.

ganizers from Fairfax' army, and threatened to oppose their political activity with military penalties.[3] Fairfax, however, assured the agitators of the North that the men would have the same privilege of organization as those under his immediate command. On July 16 the agitators urged Fairfax in a representation to march toward London, pressing Parliament to impeach the eleven members, pay arrears, and release Lilburne and his associates from prison.[4] But Cromwell urged negotiation rather than the threat of arms, asserting that what "wee . . . gaine in a free way, itt is better then twice so much in a forc't, and will bee more truly our's and our posterities." As to the army's friends in London, clamoring for their march hither, Cromwell spoke with asperity: "Itt is the generall good of them and all the people in the Kingdome [we ought to consult]. That's the question, what's for their good, nott what pleases them." [5] In his cautions for delay and negotiation Cromwell was ably supported by Ireton, already at work on the Heads of Proposals, but opposed by Joyce, Spencer, Clarke, Chillenden, Tulidah, and the agitators Allen and Sexby. Pleas by Scotton and Chillenden for the release of the prisoners mentioned in the agitators' petition, Lilburne and his friends, were passed over in silence by Cromwell, Ireton, and Rich. Thus appeared a rift between agitators and leaders that was to widen into a chasm in the debates of the momentous November to follow. In the debate of July 16 it is apparent that Lilburne was present in all but voice and body, urging haste upon the reluctant Cromwell, doubting his motives, convinced that only military coercion could expedite his liberation and redress the grievances of his countrymen. This military coercion he expected, nevertheless, to be achieved by the organized might of the common soldiers, bending the officers to their will.[6]

[3] Clarke Papers, I, 145.

[4] Ibid., I, 171-73.

[5] Ibid., I, 193, 209.

[6] The attitude of the chief officers toward the agitators is revealed in a newsletter from headquarters dated July 17. The agitators, says the writer, "now in prudence we admitt to debate . . . considering the influence they have upon the soldiers." Military discipline, if need be, can moderate the fiercest spirits among the agitators; the general is wise in admitting them to their councils, if only to avoid attempts at mutiny. Monarchy, continues the writer, will perhaps "be . . . settled, but not to be hurtfull as formerly." The army, by being so unanimous, is winning the confidence of the king. Clarke Papers, I, 214-16.

15. The *Appeale* of Richard Overton

To stir up commoner sentiment for the army's program, now in significant proportion shaped by the agitators,[1] Overton sent forth on July 17 his remarkable *Appeale*. The path to liberty, argued Overton, now lay in the army's will, not in Parliament's declarations. Like Lilburne before him, he attacks the Commons' crushing of petitions, imprisonment of petitioners; Parliament has forfeited its trust, transformed itself into an anti-Parliamentary body, more tyrannical than the king, some of its members "traytors and rebels to the nature of man." Both king and Parliament are now "dead unto the people," and the only hope lies in the army and the people's own decisions. In appealing to the people from Parliament's authority, Overton addresses the army as representative of the common will to resist tyranny and redress the grievances of the nation. He invokes the united efforts of the soldiers in pursuing their aims with the utmost celerity, emphasizing the burdensome oppression of free-quartering, and the impatience of the citizens.

An Appeale [2] is one of Overton's richest, most timely contributions to Leveller propaganda. Every page shows his awareness, not only of the issues being resolved in the hot crucible of army discussion, but also of the pull and sway of the social forces in conflict. Like Lilburne, he already distrusts the officers, fearful lest they will attempt to usurp the power of the agitators, who alone represent the army. The officers, insists Overton, should serve the army's cause "onely for advise and consultation, not for controll and conclusion," [3] corresponding to the king's function in advising Parliament. Of the army's latest pronouncement Overton is suspicious: Why was it issued only in the name of Fairfax and his Council of War, and not, as formerly, by order of *"Sir Thomas Fairfax with the officers and Souldiers of the Armie"?* [4]

---

[1] Prynne was quick to note the correlation between agitator pronouncements and the theories of his old enemy Lilburne. In *The Totall and Finall Demands already made by . . . the Agitators* (July 21), he reviews the subversive doctrines of *Regall Tyrannie, Birth-Right, The Araignement Of Mr. Persecution,* and shows how they are reflected in the agitators' demands. Prynne warns his countrymen to bestir themselves to avert disaster. Lilburne's "brothers are chief sticklers in the *Armies* Treasonable proceedings."

[2] Document 4 and commentary of the volume, pp. 154-95.

[3] P. 188. Cf. *Book of Army Declarations,* p. 94.   [4] P. 188.

Can it be, he asks, that the soldiers are not "as authoritive as formerly . . . as if they had nothing to doe with the businesse?" He exhorts the soldiers to be on guard against any plot to destroy the power of the agitators, but he is certain of their victory: "I am confident, that it must be the poore, the simple and meane things of this earth that must confound the mighty and the strong." [5] Incorrigible idealists that they were, the Levellers often disclose, as in this sentence, an unrealistic estimate of their own resources. The motives and tactics of their enemies they gauged often with startling accuracy; but the superiority of the enemies' power, if they appraised and acknowledged it in private councils, they never conceded in their manifestoes.

Overton's concept of the nature of man, as set forth in *An Appeale,* probes illuminatingly the root assumptions of his political philosophy. He begins with the premise that man is a rational animal, a product of the creator's planning. Could God create anything perverse, unreasonable, inharmonious? He could not, asserts Overton; he "is not a God of irrationality, and madnesse, or tyranny." Man is naturally a social animal, inclined to *"neighbourhood, cohabitation and humane subsistance,"* observing the golden rule. Any men who would deprive Englishmen of these projections of their true natures are "traytors and rebels to the *nature of man."* Man's rationality is expressed in his laws, not in the letter of the law but in its equity. If laws are not reasonable, they are resistable. Overton's analysis of man as a rational creature, responsive to ideas, amenable to persuasion, impelled by his endowment of reason to seek the perfection of his Creator, explains in part the confidence that he and Lilburne and Walwyn, like Milton and Winstanley, placed in the persuasiveness of their propaganda; like Socrates, they were reluctant to admit that any man's mind could indefinitely resist the appeal of reason and sympathy. The Levellers, then, like all democratic reformers, interpreted the nature of their fellow-citizens in the mirror of their own idealism; placing broad confidence in man's impulse of brotherhood, his good will, his sense of social responsibility; visualizing only spasmodically those depths of depravity and tactics of survival that Hobbes was to delineate with such graphic and terrible ease. To the Levellers man's nature was infinitely responsive and mal-

5 P. 188.

leable, his ascent to perfectibility limited only by ignorance; this concept alone placed them in sharp opposition to the Presbyterians, to whom the natural depravity of man was fixed and unalterable.

16. A Cracking Alliance

The first alliance between Leveller and Independent was now about to be severed. Lilburne, from reports of the debate of July 16, was convinced that Cromwell and Ireton were conspiring with his old enemies Vane and St. John to keep him in prison. Now that the army was in effect the masters of the House, Lilburne could see no reason for his continued imprisonment other than plots of the Independents: *"Why am I kept in prison by them, seeing it is every houre in the day in their power to deliver me if they pleased?"* [1] On July 22 Lilburne wrote to Fairfax reviewing the history of his struggles, thanking Fairfax for efforts on his behalf, but accusing Cromwell and Ireton of obstructing the efforts of the agitators to free him. The special mention of Lilburne in the army's communication of July 21 [2] could have no effect, he claimed, on the action of Marten's committee; it was inserted *"in such a manner that they were sure would doe me no good."* [3] Lilburne emphasizes to Fairfax his propaganda efforts among the common soldiers: "I made a vigorus and strong attempt upon the private Soldiery of your Army, and with abundance of study and paines . . . I brought my just, honest, and lawfull intentions, by my agents, instruments, and interest to a good ripeness, not daring to meddle with the Officers . . . who I had sufficiently tryed." [4] Unless Fairfax can assist him, he will appeal further to the common soldiers, knowing now that Ireton and Cromwell will oppose his release to the end. On July 26, with the release of *Ionahs Cry* and his bitter letters to Cromwell, Lilburne signalized his rupture with the Independent chiefs; henceforth he was to attack them in almost every pamphlet, provoking among his followers in the army the deepest suspicions of Cromwell's motives.

The appearance, nevertheless, of *The Heads of the Proposals* on August 1 must have given some political satisfaction to the

---

[1] *The Iuglers Discovered*, p. 6.   [2] *Old Parliamentary History*, XVI, 161.
[3] *The Iuglers*, p. 5.   [4] *Ibid.*, p. 3.

Leveller leaders. *The Heads* did not, it is true, abolish the negative voices of kings and Lords.[5] With all their faults, however, afterward scrutinized so damningly in *Putney Projects,* they represented Leveller constitutional solutions much more accurately and fully than the ideas of the Independent chiefs. Ireton probably was the penman of *The Heads,* not the author. The twenty-four men appointed by Fairfax to perfect *The Heads* were equally divided between agitators and officers, several of the latter, among them Rainsborough, sympathetic with the Leveller outlook. Even a cursory examination of the document, moreover, shows the infiltration, if not the domination, of the ideas of Lilburne and Overton. The *Proposals* provide for biennial Parliaments, with assurance of freedom of elections, certifying of returns, periodic redistribution of seats, for exemption of commoners from any judicial proceedings by the House of Lords; they declare also for temporary control of the militia by Parliament; the repeal of all religious penalties; for abolition of tithes and the power of ecclesiastical courts; assurance of the right of petition; abolition of the excise on certain consumers' goods; abolition of all monopolies and restraints of trade; the release of imprisoned debtors; the abolition of interrogatories against oneself; the certain meeting of county grand juries.[6] In outlining a secular program for England's reformation, the Levellers had long since taken the lead in the enunciation of these principles. To what extent Ireton and Cromwell had already formulated constitutional convictions, were gradually evolving them in the fiery cross-currents of army debates, or were led by the Leveller theorists to half-hearted consent, are questions unanswerable in the categorical. From the subsequent history of the two factions, it is evident, however, that Ireton was more willing to learn from his adversaries, to relinquish reactionary sentiments, to advance from one revolutionary outpost to another, than the Levellers were prepared to concede. The decision of the chief officers, moreover, though pressed by fears of mutiny, to admit the agi-

---

[5] As late as June 22, in his letter to Cromwell, Lilburne had urged haste in coming to terms with the king as an opponent of Parliament's tyranny. *Ionahs Cry,* p. 8. About July 8-10, when he wrote his *Appeale,* Overton also called for the settlement of kingship, and had nothing in his proposed articles about the abolition of the negative voices of king and Lords.

[6] Rushworth, VII, 731-36; *Book of Army Declarations,* pp. 112-120.

tators to political collaboration with them in shaping England's constitutional destiny, shows a statesmanship and intellectual humility without counterpart in the annals of English warfare.

As the Levellers' own constitutional theories crystallized, however, their scrutiny of the *Proposals* sharpened with suspicion. Months later, in the Putney debates, Ireton and Wildman clashed repeatedly on the efficacy of the *Proposals* as a balm to the nation's troubles. The Independent leaders had doggedly sought a compromise with the existing kingship; the Levellers now wanted none at all. In *Putney Projects* Wildman charged that Ireton had altered the first draft of the *Proposals* in five particulars, all concessions to the king. The king was to have originally no negative voice at all for two Parliaments; this provision, said Wildman, was expunged from the original draft at the king's behest. The royalists had been forbidden except with Parliamentary sanction to hold offices under the king for ten years; this requirement in the final draft was reduced to five. The king was now permitted, moreover, to choose delinquents for his Council of State before the end of the five-year period. Instead of extirpation of the bishops, as in the rough draft, asserted Wildman, the final copy provided only that they were not to have the power to impose civil penalties. A fifth particular was the elimination of the proposal for the sale of bishops' lands.[7] More damning than these compromises, however, in Wildman's opinion, was the underlying assumption of the *Proposals* that the king's will was the source of all authority, superior to all Parliamentary decisions, proceeding from him not only to Lords, but also to all officials of the kingdom. His kingdom and his throne were his personal property. These fundamental assumptions, insisted Wildman, the king's "enslaving principles," were unchallenged in the *Proposals*. Though they did limit the exercise of the king's power, they did not define its nature or declare against its essence.[8] The *Proposals*, though calling for biennial Parliaments, still allowed the king to issue writs of election. This was the highest tyranny, making the calling of Parliaments dependent upon his will. "There is no possible provision for an absolute certainty of the being of Parliaments," wrote Wildman, "while the People shall depend upon Writs or Warrants for elections . . . Why should not one certain day be

7 *Putney Projects* (December 30, 1647), pp. 14-15.   8 *Ibid.*, p. 31.

prefixed, whereupon all the People might meet . . . to elect the Members?" After ten years, according to the *Proposals,* even the control of the militia would return to the king. Moreover, the king was to grant an act of oblivion to all the subjects who have opposed him: the conquerors should humbly petition the forgiveness of the conqueror! Did the king not fight to maintain this principle of his supreme will? "O yee Commons of England!" cried Wildman. "Mistake not, this was the ground of the King's quarrell against the Parliament." [9] The *Proposals* undoubtedly contained the loopholes for royalist absolutism that Wildman visualized; but that the dangers were more theoretical than actual may be discerned in subsequent decades of English history. The *Proposals'* limitation of the king's power, not a blunt denial of its very existence, anticipated the compromises of the future. As always Cromwell and Ireton reached for workable solutions, the Levellers for utopian perfection.

17. For a Purging of the Commons

In late July and early August the military coercion of the Independents, together with the agitation of London Presbyterians, forced a crisis in the struggle for Parliamentary power. On July 26 a mob of reformadoes and apprentices, sympathetic with Presbyterian resistance against the army, invaded both houses of Parliament, threatened violence against the members, and compelled votes reinstating the militia in the hands of the Common Council. Thus frustrated and intimidated, fifty-seven members of the Commons and eight Lords sympathetic to Independency two days later withdrew from London and placed themselves under the protection of Fairfax. Now in full possession of Parliament and the London militia, the Presbyterians prepared to defend the city against the army; but their rash determination gave way before the conviction of military superiority and the strength of Independent sympathies in the suburbs, particularly Southwark, the center of Leveller agitation. On August 6 the army entered London triumphantly, acknowledged the reluctant greetings of mayor and aldermen, restored the absent members to their seats. Despite their apparent victory, a rude awakening awaited the

[9] *Putney Projects,* pp. 18, 28.

Independents. On August 9 the eleven Presbyterian leaders, never formally expelled, took their seats in the Commons, voted in stiff-backed resolution against nulling the votes of July 26-August 6, and helped their comrades win by one vote, 95-94. In the days that followed, their majorities increased as their confidence mounted.[10]

Alert to the fresh Presbyterian successes, the agitators on August 14 addressed Fairfax in a new plea for purging the House of Hollis and his faction. They protested against "the continued destructive designs and dangerous Combinations of perfidious men, formerly Members of Parliament, which constantly blast the fairest hopes and expectations of Peace and Freedom." These men, asserted the agitators, now prevent the true patriots from executing their duties, and should be immediately excluded according to the army's own declarations; they are not fit to remain and "sit judges of their own prodigious Treacheries." [11] On August 18 the army council met at Kingston,[12] drew up a long remonstrance fully supporting the address of the agitators, and ordered a march on London to enforce their demands. Of the presence of the perfidious members, the *Remonstrance* asks, "What a Mock is this to God and Man?" There can be no security for the Parliament, the army, or the kingdom, until they are expelled.[13] This time Cromwell had had enough of legality and negotiations; he favored prompt and vigorous action, and on August 20, not having Fairfax' consent to a military purge, nevertheless ordered a regiment of cavalry to Hyde Park, entered the Commons to cast his vote with officers who were members, and secured an Independent victory.[14] That intimidation, not force, had been the margin of triumph, was of small moment in the perilous course of the army, so long urged by the army radicals.

[10] In this paragraph I have followed Gardiner, *Civil War*, III. The names of the members who fled to the army are in Rushworth, VII, 755.

[11] *The humble Address of the Agitators*, E. 402 (8), pp. 3, 5. Appended is a similar appeal of August 5, signed by fifty-three agitators.

[12] Lilburne afterward wrote that Cromwell at Kingston first began to fear that the agitators were suspicious of his negotiations with the king. *An Impeachment* (Aug. 10, 1649), p. 4.

[13] *Old Parliamentary History*, XVI, 251-73; *Book of Army Declarations*, 129-44.

[14] Gardiner, *Civil War*, III, 351-52.

18. Suspicions and Recriminations: Cromwell and Lilburne

Finding Cromwell unresponsive to his messages, believing himself virtually Cromwell's own prisoner, Lilburne now attacked him with virulent invective. On August 13 Lilburne addressed Cromwell in these words: "It hath been my unhappinesse to be . . . destroyed, by men of guilded outsides, and . . . I must plainly and truly now tell you, I judge you the cheife." In the same letter he begged Cromwell to come within a week to see him in prison, or arrange that Lilburne come to him for a conference. Simultaneously he also threatened Cromwell with a disclosure of important positions held by his relatives in the army, a disclosure, asserted Lilburne, that "would easily pul you as low before you were 3 months older, as I am." In spite of these vehement threats and accusations, Lilburne says his "good thoughts" of Cromwell "are not wholly gone," though "very much shaken." [1] On the 21st Lilburne wrote to Fairfax, scorning the suggestion made at headquarters that he apply to the House of Lords for his freedom, comparing the officers to honest men seeing him set upon by robbers: "though they seeme to pittie him in words, passe by him." [2] On the 26th Lilburne again addressed Fairfax, deploring the officers' speeches on his antagonism to Cromwell, and offering to arbitrate the differences between the two men, Fairfax himself to be the umpire! He again urges Fairfax to secure a report in the Commons from Marten's committee on his case. [3]

In reluctant response to Lilburne's messages, Cromwell on

[1] These passages are in *Two Letters Writ by . . . Lilburne*, p. 7. The pamphlet probably appeared September 18, 1647, though dated by Thomason September 13. Lilburne named seven relatives of Cromwell in important army posts. He declared (p. 8) that Cromwell's "cheife designe, is not the good of the Kingdome . . . but the advancement of himselfe and his own kindred and friends, which will unavoydably destroy him." The real power of the kingdom, says Lilburne, lies not in Fairfax' hands, or the agitators', but in those of Cromwell. The date of this statement is September 16.

[2] *The Iuglers*, p. 10. Lilburne identifies his informant as "Mr. Allen," agitator for Cromwell's regiment, and attacks him as Cromwell's *"Officious and extraordinary creature"* working for Cromwell to corrupt the loyal agitators. This is William Allen, afterward adjutant-general. See Firth's account of him in *Clarke Papers*, I, 432-33.

[3] *Two Letters*, p. 8. How closely he and the agitators were collaborating is revealed in a letter dated by Lilburne August 27, appended to his second edition of *The Iust Mans Iustification*. Titled *To his much honoured friends the Councell of Agitators*, the letter states that on behalf of the agitators Chillenden has asked him to review his case for presentation to the General Council on August 28.

September 6 conferred with him in the Tower. It is regrettable that Lilburne has left no detailed record of this interview, as he was later to do with those of Hugh Peters and Edmond Prideaux. From the brief references that remain, written by Lilburne a month later, we gain the impression that the interview was conciliatory, Cromwell promising to aid the radical leader despite all past fulminations. He apparently voiced the fear, however, that Lilburne if released would take a violently active leadership in army agitation.[4] This fear is too authentically Cromwellian to be doubted, like his suggestion to the officers that Lilburne's release might not be propitious for Lilburne himself. In the upheaving flux of revolutionary change, Cromwell without arrogance played a role that he knew was decisive; he played the role cautiously, knowing well his deficiency in statesmanship, trusting in the main to Vane and Ireton, fearing the excesses of the Levellers, wrestling spasmodically and ineffectively with their ideas. Their power over the soldiers he could gauge with amazing precision, but their ideology seemed strange and remote. Cromwell was therefore not so much concerned with the justice of Lilburne's cause as with the practical political consequences of his release. Though the House acted on September 7 to consider Lilburne's case, on the 8th it was put off "till another Day," on the 10th again postponed, and on the 14th referred again to the committee "to find out some Precedents of this nature and to report to the House." [5] Lilburne felt that his worst fears about Cromwell were

---

[4] *The additional Plea*, in *The grand Plea*, pp. 20, 22. At this point Lilburne interposed an offer to leave England and not return "*so long as the present troubles lasted.*"

[5] *Ibid.*, p. 22; Rushworth, VII, 804, 805, 811. Commons' *Journals*, V, 294, 296, 297, 301. In succeeding weeks Lilburne's case was under almost weekly consideration but deferred from time to time. On October 5 Marten was ordered to report Lilburne's case on the following Saturday (the ninth). On the ninth Marten was directed to report again on the following Tuesday, but on Tuesday the case was deferred again until Friday (the fifteenth). On that day Fiennes' charges against Lilburne were read, and his case referred to another committee, which was ordered to search for precedents and to meet that very afternoon and so from day to day until the case was settled. To this committee, of which John Maynard was chairman, Lilburne was permitted to make a long address on October 20, castigating as before the House of Lords, and denying their right to try or imprison him. On November 1 additions were made to Lilburne's committee, no action apparently having been taken. On November 9, however, the Commons, without passing on his guilt or innocence, allowed him freedom to go abroad each day without a keeper, but required that he return each night to the Tower. Commons' *Journals*, V, 327, 329, 331, 334, 347, 353.

more than confirmed. He wrote later that Nathaniel Fiennes, friend of Cromwell, had made a "most fiery, fierce, and bitter speech" against him in the Commons; and at headquarters he was attacked as both anarchist and communist.[6]

On September 8, in his "Advice to the Private Soldiers," Lilburne intensified his inflammatory accusations of Cromwell and the officers. Whereas previously the strategy of the Levellers had endeavoured to effect a united front against the Presbyterian Parliament, now they made desperate efforts to uphold the agitators against their enemies within the army ranks. Lilburne exhorts the soldiers to call their agitators to an accounting, to elect new ones if they are not satisfied, to beware of the machinations of Cromwell and Ireton, to press for the expulsion of the Presbyterians from the Commons. He voices his fear that "the factious Lordly ends of some great ones" are to use the army and its militant declarations as a bridge to tyranny. Lilburne calls attention to the votes of the Independents for support of tithes; he urges the men to press for arrears, to stand by their declarations for redress of grievances, to agitate for the release of oppressed patriots. "Above all the rest," asserts Lilburne, "be sure not to trust your great officers at the Generalls quarters, no further then you can throw an Oxe." Their strategy, he warns, has been to steal the power "both from your honest Generall, and your too flexible Adiutators," and place it in a corrupt Parliament.[7]

The radicals' suspicions of Cromwell and his negotiations with the king were heightened after September 22, when Marten proposed to the Commons that there be no further addresses to the king. Cromwell and Ireton, however, were reported to have spoken emphatically for further negotiations, Ireton apparently hopeful that the *Heads of the Proposals* were still a sound basis for the settlement of the kingdom.[8] Wildman later insisted that Ireton had declared the feeling of the army to be for further addresses, warning the Commons of the army's opposition if it persisted in cutting off communications.[9] In debate with the Levellers Cromwell did not deny that he had opposed Marten's

[6] *The additional Plea*, in *The grand Plea*, pp. 19, 23.
[7] *The Iuglers*, pp. 10-12.   [8] *Clarke Papers*, I, 230n-231n.
[9] *Putney Projects*, p. 43; *A Cal To All The Souldiers* (E. 412, 10), p. 7.

motion; he insisted, however, that what he had spoken was in his capacity as a Parliament member, not as a representative of the General Council: "What I deliver'd there I deliver'd as my owne sence, and what I deliver'd as my owne sence I am nott ashamed of." [10] Cromwell denied that as an army spokesman he had misrepresented the consensus of the General Council, and Rainsborough reminded the debaters that Cromwell was not present on September 23, when the motion was actually carried to make another address. Ireton, like Cromwell, did not deny that he had favored further addresses in Parliament; but he heatedly denied that he had any design to set up the king. Neither, however, would he destroy him; he would make the best use for the kingdom of both king and Parliament.[11]

19. The Case of Major White

The growing crisis between the radicals and the Independents is nowhere delineated more clearly than in the story of Major Francis White of Fairfax' regiment. On September 9 White was expelled from the General Council for asserting that the sword was now the supreme power of the kingdom. Two days later the officers and soldiers of the regiment demanded an explanation of the General Council for the dismissal of White, their duly elected agitator.[12] In letters to Fairfax White then set forth a justification and elucidation of his beliefs that stamped him as an extreme proponent of Lilburne's principles. Parliament, he maintained, had no legality. The army had the real power in their hands, but by the Engagement they were to use it democratically, the will of the majority to prevail. But "being sensible of what designe was laid by some great men," wrote White, "and knowing how farre short it came of comprehending generall freedome," he had attempted to frustrate the scheme. This scheme, asserted White, was to bring in the king without redressing any real grievances, leaving in his office the control of the militia and the courts.[13] One of the members of Goodwin's

---

[10] *Clarke Papers*, I, 230.

[11] *Ibid.*, I, 232-33.

[12] *The Copy of a Letter Sent to his Excellencie* (E. 413, 17), p. 2. The officers later, however, turned against White and insisted his views were not representative.

[13] *Ibid.*, pp. 1, 5. This letter to Fairfax was written September 23. White's comments on the king anticipate, then, the attacks that the Levellers were to make

congregation had reported that he was the only man in the General Council who stood in the way of such a settlement. White had insisted, moreover, that Fairfax should have no negative voice over the decisions of the General Council; Cromwell himself had admitted that this was the cause of his expulsion. His statement about the supreme power of the sword was in White's view minor and incidental to the powerful forces acting for his removal. The real solution to the constitutional dilemma rested not in the present Parliament, insisted White, and not in the army, but in "a free Parliament equally chosen, with every free man of age having his voice, and that Parliament to have its bounds." [14]

In his letters to Fairfax White stamps himself as an unswerving Leveller, one of the vanguard of fearless constitutional radicals emerging from the white-hot turmoil of army theorizing. A pupil, like all his fellows, of Lilburne and Overton, he was now ready for drastic independent action, his motives, like those of Rainsborough, sustained alone by the idealism of his cause and the fanaticism of the Puritan soldier.[15] He could not compromise with the old social order, an inheritance, as he believed, from William the Conqueror. A new constitution, a sharp break from tradition, with manhood suffrage electing annual or biennial Parliaments, negative voice of king and Lords abolished, Parliament itself bound by a supreme law, these were his insistent premises to the establishment of a binding peace. From such premises long since laid down by Lilburne and Overton, now newly agitated in an atmosphere pregnant with explosion, the first *Agreement* was soon to emerge.

20. New Agitators at Work: *The Case Of The Army*

The election of new agitators, advised by Lilburne on September 8 and effected in five regiments of horse before October

on Cromwell in *Putney Projects* and other tracts for his negotiations with Charles. They indicate that much discussion of this point was taking place among the army radicals. Curiously enough, however, neither Lilburne or Overton had yet criticised Cromwell on his stand for the return of kingship. This is evidence, I believe, that the army radicals were now taking the lead in the shaping of constitutional policy, no longer relying on Lilburne for theoretical leadership.

14 *Ibid.*, p. 14.

15 White proposed a reduction in officers' salaries and an increase of the pay of common soldiers to twelve pence a day. *The Copy of a Letter*, p. 14.

9, stiffened the resistance of the army radicals against Cromwell and instigated the inflammatory manifesto, *The Case Of The Army Truly Stated*.[1] Signed by the agents, as the new agitators styled themselves, on October 9, and presented to Fairfax on the 18th, *The Case Of The Army* gave voice to the extreme discontent of the restless minority of soldier radicals. In biting, recriminatory phrasing it contrasted the demands of the army manifestoes of preceding months with the realities of Parliamentary inaction. "We not only apprehend nothing to have been done effectually, either for the Army or the poore oppressed people of the nation," wrote the agents, "but we also conceive, that there is little probabillitie of any good, without some more speedy and vigorous actings." [2] Partial disbanding is again imminent with no economic grievances redressed; the army is widely separated; monopolies, excise and tithes bear down heavily as ever upon the people. Beyond these old complaints loom new dangers. The machinery of political reconstruction within the army, say the agents, is being sabotaged, with "many discouragements of the Agitators," this contrary to the *Engagement*. "It hath been instilled into them," wrote the agents, "that they ought not to intermeddle with those matters, thereby to induce them to betray the trust the Regiments reposed in them." [3] Moreover the very king against whom they have fought seems now to regain high favor, permitted to see freely his counsellors, his negative voice to be restored, the people again to "depend on his will, for their reliefe in their grievances and oppressions." Meanwhile Parliament has not vindicated the army's honor, or purged itself of the army's enemies. The army must act speedily to effect the passage of a supreme law "unalterable by Parliaments," requiring the successive election of Parliaments at unchangeable intervals, these to be elected by "all the freeborn at the age of 21. yeares and upwards" except, for the first few years, the royalists.

The response of Cromwell and Ireton to *The Case* revealed at once their respect for the new Leveller forces arrayed against them. On October 20 Cromwell made a three-hour speech in the House urging the immediate restoration of monarchy, denying that he or any of his chief officers had had any part in *The Case*

---

[1] Document 5 and commentary, pp. 196-222 of this volume.
[2] P. 199.   [3] P. 202.

Of The Army.[4] On October 23 a letter dated at Putney October 22 appeared in London, purporting to represent the chief officers' hostility to the new agents. Fairfax, said the writer, had declared against *The Case,* but submitted it to the General Council. Even the original agitators had opposed the ideas of the document. In the whole army of twenty-one thousand men, asserted the spokesman, no more than four hundred could be called sympathetic with the positions stated by the new agents in *The Case.* Seditious men who had crept into the regiments to create divisions would be weeded out, and the General Council would publish within a few days a vindication of their actions against the aspersions of the new agents.[5] The promised vindication, however, did not appear. A committee appointed on October 22 wrote no vindication, merely directed its members to read *The Case* carefully and report their findings, good or evil.[6] On October 28 the new agents were present at the General Council, presented a defence of their position,[7] and debated with Cromwell and Ireton, along with Allen, Sexby, and Lockyer. Such serious consideration of the new agents and *The Case Of The Army* by Cromwell, Ireton, and the General Council is a significant revelation of the success of the new Leveller tactics.

21. Birth of a Constitution: The First *Agreement*

Accused of provoking divisions, and aware of the dire need of a constructive constitutional settlement, the new agents in the days preceding October 28 drew up their first draft of *An Agreement Of The People.*[1] This document, the genesis of which we have traced in sixteen months of Leveller agitation, was the culmi-

[4] Gardiner, *Civil War,* III, 381.

[5] *Papers From The Armie* (E 411, 19), pp. 2-5.   [6] Rushworth, VII, 850.

[7] This defence is found in *Two Letters From the Agents of the five Regiments of Horse* (E 412, 6). In restrained, temperate accents, unlike much of the language in *The Case,* the agents refute the charge that they are dividing the army by standing upon the principles of official declarations. A hint that the *Agreement* is in the process of composition appears thus: "We shal speedily give such clear evidence to the whole world of our resolutions to joyn with you, and all the freeborn people of this Nation, to establish immediatly the undoubted principles and rules of equall and just Government, that the mouth of malice it selfe shall be for ever stopped." The *Two Letters* was published on October 28.

[1] Document 6 and commentary, pp. 223-34 of this volume.

nation of their political theorizing, in some respects the most remarkable constitutional innovation of the Puritan Revolution. Extending the idea of the "supreme law" to a broader function, the *Agreement* [2] made not only the convocation of Parliaments and election by manhood suffrage unalterable by the Commons; it gave the sanction of the supreme law as expressed by social compact also to freedom of conscience, freedom from conscription, equality of responsibility under the law. The idea of a mutual compact was undoubtedly an extension of the *Engagement* principle applied now to the whole body of citizens. By placing the supreme representative power directly in the Commons, the *Agreement* by implication destroyed at one stroke the negative voices of king and Lords. The disillusionment of Lilburne and Overton in both king and Parliament now took a positive form: Even Parliament's power must have its bounds. The basic Leveller concept of the people as the supreme source of power emerged as a written social compact anticipating by fourteen decades the structure of the American constitution.

The *Agreement* was the summation of Leveller beliefs, a platform to be their rallying cry for two more years of futile agitation, a document they were to refine and expand but not fundamentally alter. Back of its emergence lay imprisonments, persecution, arrests, religious zeal, Lilburne's intense prison researches, Walwyn's mature historical sense, Overton's infinitely agile mind. The issues of their many pamphleteering battles, the toppling of the bishops, toleration of the sects, freedom of the

[2] Within two weeks after the appearance of *The Case,* the principle of the supreme law was extended in the *Agreement* to protect freedom of conscience and related liberties. In whose mind did this idea first take root? Though well prepared for by the propaganda of Lilburne and Overton, this specific proposal did not, I believe, originate with them or Walwyn. The man on hand most likely to have suggested it was John Wildman, spokesman for the new agents and Lilburne's representative. Though later an apostate to the Leveller cause, Wildman wrote some of the most penetrating social criticism the Leveller party produced, especially in *Putney Projects.* He was probably the main author of *The Case Of The Army* and *A Cal To All The Souldiers.* Since the latter tract appeared on October 29, it must have been written almost simultaneously with the *Agreement.* It contains the following statement: "Joyne and be one with them in heart and hand, with all possible speede in some substantiall and firme AGREEMENT, for just freedom and common right, that this nation may no longer flote upon such wavering uncertain and sandy foundations of Government." Wildman warns the people to secure in the Agreement "a firme establish't certainty of all particulars . . . conducing both to the prosperity and safety of the People."

press, the treatment of prisoners, and court and jail rights of citizens, the prerogatives of the Lords over commoners, interpretation of ancient charters, the supremacy of the Commons, the limitations of their power over commoners, manhood suffrage, rotten boroughs, the prerogatives of kings, the right of revolution by social compact, the application of the law of nature, the redress of economic grievances, the restraints of trade and commerce, the nature of martial law, the citizenship rights of soldiers —all these issues had found a place in their restless, searching propaganda. From these issues had sprung the determined pressure for military coercion, the organization of the General Council, the army's democratic manifestoes, and now the *Agreement* as the organ of deliverance.

Committed by conviction to a modification, not an abolition, of England's traditional structure, Cromwell and Ireton found it impossible to accept the drastic departure of the *Agreement*. When the document was read for the first time at Putney, on October 28, Cromwell's opposition, often veiled and enigmatic, found voice in ominous directness. The *Agreement* embodied, he asserted, "very great alterations of the very Governement of the Kingedome, alterations from that Governement that itt hath bin under, I beleive I may almost say since itt was a Nation." [3] The document possessed, indeed, the virtue of plausibility; but so might any other scheme that any man of the forty present might have conceived. If the *Agreement* were accepted, why might not any other equally plausible plan be proposed tomorrow, and thus many more, breeding confusion and civil war? More than plausibility, more than desirability, insisted Cromwell, they needed a plan that "the spiritts and temper of the people of this Nation are prepared to receive and to goe on alonge with." [4] A practical middle step, adapted to the traditional structure, not a sudden leap into the world of a strange new model, however noble, was to Cromwell the wiser goal of their deliberations. In the path of the Agreement there were "very great mountaines." Was the army not bound to obey Parliament? To what degree was the army free to accept or champion such a plan? In Cromwell's mind it was "a very great jumpe" out of their engagements

[3] *Clarke Papers,* I, 236.
[4] *Ibid.,* I, 237.

to the country;[5] he did not accept, it was plain, the Lilburnian theory of the country being dissolved into a state of nature, with any one free to propose a mutual compact for the collective settlement of the constitutional dilemma. Notwithstanding his blunt hostility to the *Agreement* Cromwell sounded the note of conciliation. More than all else he dreaded divisions; he exhorted them: "I shall desire this, that . . . wee may have free discourses amongst ourselves . . . and you will bee able to satisfie each other." As for himself, he would accept whatever plan they could agree upon; rather than be an obstacle, indeed, to such unity, he would lay down his commission and his life.[6]

In the pauses of the debate, between the spoken lines, one catches the Levellers' suspicions of Cromwell's negotiations with the king. Whatever dangers lay in the projection of the *Agreement,* argued a Bedfordshire Leveller, more menacing dangers impended in the settlement with the king. Sensing these suspicions, Cromwell felt impelled, indeed, to deny that he had any agreement with the king, pronouncing himself "as free from Engagements to the Kinge as any man in all the world." He was willing, he affirmed, to be persuaded; he and Ireton were not "wedded and glewed to formes of Governement." He granted that "the foundation and supremacy is in the people, radically in them." As he was not bound to the king, so he was not obligated to support the House of Lords.[7] Let men say what they would, he knew the integrity of his own spirit.

In his antagonism to the Leveller utopia Cromwell spoke well for the forces arrayed against the radicals. He possessed, it is true, the conservative's fear of a violent rent in the traditional structure. But this fear was less a factor in his opposition than his realistic appraisal of the economic power of the Presbyterians and the national sentiment, both Puritan and royalist, for the continuity of the monarchy. An immature, uncertain grappler with political theory, Cromwell knew better than the Levellers the inexorable timing of history. Whereas they spoke for the future, and made ready to take the great leap, taking no thought, as Rainsborough said, for the opposition of unrighteousness, Cromwell looked into men's faces, appraised the power of London

5 *Clarke Papers,* I, 269.   6 *Ibid.,* I, 251.   7 *Ibid.,* I, 248-249, 277, 278.

wealth, the sway of the Presbyterian clergy, the magic of the king's name, the insistent pressure of the wealthy nobles allied to the Independent cause. With the rise of his military powers, Cromwell had ridden the crest of the revolutionary tide sweeping his army to a mighty democratic decision, a sharp cleavage from the political assumptions of both the commercial and the feudal classes. To strengthen his army, to sharpen the zeal of his sectarian soldiers, he had encouraged the robust freedom of the meetings of minds, of free speech at council and campfire. But now he must turn back. The tide of agitation had carried them, he thought, to the brink of disaster. As Ireton said, the danger of passive obedience to Parliament was now less than the folly of disobedience and the breaking of their pledges. In months to come, it is true, in the long agony of a second war, Cromwell was to take the bold revolutionary step he now distrusted. But in October, 1647, he wanted a compromise constitutional settlement, one acceptable, he knew, to the Independents and large numbers of the Presbyterians. In attempting to unite all factions, as Sexby pointed out, Cromwell and Ireton had pleased no one. Yet Cromwell was aware that to satisfy the Levellers, vociferous minority that they were, even among army ranks, would be a fatal defiance of national forces and preponderant English sentiment.[8]

Felicitous and gifted in the phrasing of abstract theory, Ireton now advanced his first deep objection to the new document. The *Agreement* embodied, he asserted, the breaking of the army's engagements to Parliament. Such covenants are the foundation of justice itself, the means by which men assure each other the continued possession of their property and privileges. A man is bound in some degree to keep even an unjust covenant. If he finds it impossible to keep it to the letter, he is bound to satisfy its demands as far as is humanly possible. For men to break covenants unilaterally, asserted Ireton, is to establish the principle of revolutions, of destroying commonwealths at will. If men may

---

[8] The Bedfordshire Leveller, plainly pessimistic of collaboration with the Independent leaders, asked that those who supported the *Agreement* might proceed in their efforts to secure its acceptance without the opposition of the Independents. He hoped there would "bee noe hinderances to hinder the people in a more perfect way." If the Independents could not favor the *Agreement*, he said, in effect, would they desist from active hostility? To this question Ireton and Cromwell made no response. *Clarke Papers*, I, 252.

break a covenant, he asked, why may not your *Agreement,* if established, be broken in the same manner? Because the *Agreement* accepts the principle of covenant breaking, Ireton believed it a dangerous precedent. The army's declarations, he continued, have insisted that Parliament recognize the people as the source of all power, and when the army thought this fundamental principle violated, it has refused to obey Parliament. To assume, however, said Ireton, that the army has a right to disobey Parliament on any issue it felt unjust, is "the abuse and misapplication of those thinges the Army hath declar'd." This assumption has now "led many men into a great and dangerous errour and destructive to all humane society." [9]

The Levellers and agitators, led by Wildman, objected vehemently to the arguments of both Ireton and Cromwell. To the qualifications of a middle ground, the practical cognizance of obstacles, the compromise of ideology with reality, the Levellers juxtaposed the logical extremes of the democratic position. The issue first to be resolved, asserted Wildman, was the honesty or dishonesty, the justice or injustice of the *Agreement,* not the army's previous engagements. If the *Agreement* is only common right and freedom, then it is just and right that the soldiers renounce their former covenants, which they had made with more limited understanding than they now possess. Wildman denied that there was any fundamental contradiction between the army's engagements and the *Agreement;* but he answered Ireton's arguments by denying that the men were bound to obey unjust covenants. The issue of engagements, explored with tenacious thoroughness by Ireton, Wildman tried unsuccessfully to postpone in favor of an immediate consideration of the *Agreement* itself. If a treaty between the king and Parliament were imminent, "a few dayes may bee the losse of the Kingedome," with none of the people's grievances redressed, and the army's declarations nullified.[10] Rainsborough also urged haste, fearing impending destruction to their common purposes. As for Cromwell's fear of "great alterations" he had no concern at all: All the good laws of England had once been innovations; all of them had reduced the power of king and Lords, after long "scufflinges betweene the honest men of England and those that have tyranniz'd over them."

[9] *Clarke Papers,* I, 242, 263, 267, 268.   [10] *Ibid.,* I, 241, 261, 264.

On the point of difficulties and obstacles Rainsborough spoke with eloquent bitterness. Had they counted the cost, the difficulty, when they had taken up arms against the king? They were bound, he offered, not by difficulties, but by justice. Though death lay ahead, and the sea on three sides, they should unflinchingly carry on. Whatever great leap the *Agreement* called for, he would have no fear: "When I leape I shall take soe much of God with mee, and so much of just and right with mee, as I shall jumpe sure."[11]

The debate of October 28 closed with the appointment of a committee to consider the army's engagements and an agreement to hold a prayer meeting the following day. "Cromwell in difficulties," writes Professor Firth, "generally moved for a Committee; Goffe invariably proposed a prayer-meeting." [12] Though Cromwell had emphatically seconded Goffe's motion, he was aware that the Levellers trusted reason more than prayer, aware, too, that they were especially suspicious of the prayers of Independents. When both Buffe-coate and Pettus seemed to resent postponement of action by a single day, neither they nor any of the Levellers seconding the proposal for a prayer meeting, Cromwell turned on them angrily: "I hope wee know God better then to make appearances of Religious Meetings as covers for designes for insinuation amongst you." They were sincerely seeking, he continued, "to recover that presence of God that seemes to withdraw from us." One of the chief differences between them and the supporters of the *Agreement,* he asserted, was the agitators' attitude toward seeking God. He would not urge them to join the prayer meeting; but if they came, they would be welcome; meanwhile, he hoped they should "thinke fitt to see what God will direct you to say to us." [13] Thus clashed and revolved an endless pattern of the Puritan temper, mysticism and rationalism compounded in a thousand shades and blendings, giving birth to the fanatical courage of Harrison, the gentleness of Saltmarsh, the revolutionary idealism of Lilburne, Harrington, and Winstanley, the enigmatic character of Cromwell. Among the Independents, the virtues of sainthood and religious tolerance loomed pre-eminent; among the Levellers, those of social redemption.

11 *Clarke Papers*, I, 246, 271.　　12 *Ibid.*, I, lxxiv.　　13 *Ibid.*, 258-59.

22. The Crucial Debate: Dilemma of the Suffrage

Complying with Cromwell's invitation, the Levellers attended the prayer meeting on the morning of October 29. The debate that followed, in an ideological sense the most crucial and remarkable of the Civil War, illuminates as no other the sharpening divisions between Leveller and Independent. The Levellers, mature but unrealistic democrats, reasoned for political privileges almost three centuries remote from actuality in their native land; the Independents, theocrats tinged with democratic persuasions, were driven to defend the rights of property against the encroachments of the belligerent democratic surge.

Reluctantly yielding to the reading of the *Agreement* before a resolution of the army's engagements, Ireton immediately attacked the first clause of the *Agreement,* the provision for manhood suffrage. To give every man a vote, he asserted, would tend to destroy the most fundamental element of the constitution, property itself. The propertyless men in the kingdom were in the majority (outnumbering the property-owners, Rich said later, five to one). "Why," asked Ireton, "may nott those men vote against all propertie?" [1] Only those should vote, he maintained, who had a fixed freehold interest in land or house worth forty shillings a year in rent, according to the prevailing law. The protection of property was of paramount importance in a land of freedom. Everyone had the same privilege of gathering wealth and owning property; everyone had the same protection of the law. To justify manhood suffrage, insisted Ireton, you must resort to the law of nature; but by nature's law there is no fixed property: Everyone is entitled to whatever goods are necessary to sustain himself. Having shown the implications of the Leveller position by the law of nature, Ireton made no attempt to justify his stand against manhood suffrage on religious grounds. The right of property and suffrage "descends from other thinges." The Bible lays down not particulars but generals; he would not attempt to resolve the question by appeal to Biblical teachings. He knew only that the proposal nullified the fundamental constitution of the kingdom.

Ireton's refusal to test his stand on the suffrage by his religious

[1] *Clarke Papers,* I, 306, 314.

concept is a significant illumination of the character of the Independent. Both Cromwell and Ireton sincerely sought the guidance of divine revelation, a process that opened their minds on occasion to the persuasions of men less humble but more rational than they. Yet, as I have shown elsewhere,[2] Cromwell and Ireton threw off at critical moments all appeal to divinity, resolving the issue by a realistic appraisal of forces and opinion remote from mystical concepts. Thus it was in the debate on manhood suffrage. Though Ireton had said on October 28 that he would be willing to destroy king, Lords, and property if God directed, he returned the next day to argue from the training of his economic background against the suffrage of propertyless men. When Cromwell said to Rainsborough, "Noe man says that you have a minde to anarchy, butt the consequence of this rule tends to anarchy, must end in anarchy," he made no mention of the divine light in justifying his position. Quoting Paul, Cromwell said that forms of government were but "drosse and dung in comparison of Christ"; but in his argument against the *Agreement* he spoke as an Englishman attached to the ancient forms. As men of property, then, he and Ireton argued, seeking a constitutional solution that would protect the rights of men like themselves. Religious enthusiasm they directed to liberty of conscience and the virtues of holy living; realism they applied to forces of battle, to power politics, and questions of constitutional settlement.

Not property, replied Rainsborough, but reason, qualifies a man to vote, and reason is the endowment of the humblest man of England. To deny a man the suffrage is to deny him the privilege of using his reason. "I doe nott finde any thinge in the law of God," asserted Rainsborough, "that a Lord shall chuse 20 Burgesses, and a Gentleman butt two, or a poore man shall chuse none. I finde noe such thinge in the law of nature, nor in the law of nations."[3] Only in English law could he find such inequality, and if the people were the source of all power, why could they not change it? How had it happened that the franchise was the property of some men and not others? "The law of the land in that thinge is the most tyrannicall law under heaven, and I would faine know what wee have fought for."[4] Certainly, added Rains-

---

[2] In *Milton and the Puritan Revolution*, Chapter V.
[3] *Clarke Papers*, I, 304.　　　　[4] *Ibid.*, I, 311.

borough, they have not fought for an old law to which none of them had ever given consent. To the charge that manhood suffrage would destroy property, Rainsborough answered with bitter scorn: "I wish you would nott make the world beleive that wee are for anarchy." [5] The purpose of government, he asserted, was to preserve people as well as property. Is not a person more valuable than property? Colonel Rich feared that the people would vote a law enacting "an equality of goods and estate." He feared also that the people would sell their votes to the highest bidder, with dictators triumphing, as in ancient Rome.[6] Against these fears Rainsborough painted the evils of the rich triumphant. They could vote to enslave the four-fifths without the suffrage: "One parte shall make hewers of wood and drawers of water of the other five." [7] In the debate of the 29 Rainsborough was easily the most nimble and effective debater for the Levellers, answering *reductio ad absurdum* and *ad hominem* in kind, combining with scorn and irony an appeal to first principles, crystallizing in a few sallies the culminating democratic implications of the Leveller propaganda.

In this debate, as in later pamphleteering warfare, the Levellers found it difficult to combat the charge of property annihilation. Though they were not believers in economic democracy, they did wish to reduce the political power of the propertied classes and enlarge the political strength of the poor. Whereas Rainsborough dismissed the charge of anarchy with angry scoffing, saying, "Sir I see, that itt is impossible to have liberty butt all propertie must be taken away," Pettus replied in a serious defence, asserting that he wished to keep property while destroying king and Lords. Would not property indeed be safer when everyone had a share in the government? The *Agreement,* indeed, was "the onely meanes to preserve all propertie." [8]

It is difficult to doubt the sincerity of the Leveller concern for property as voiced by Pettus. Though they suffered from monopolies and many other economic restrictions, the Levellers were not, by and large, among the economically disinherited. Many of them were property owners, traders, shopkeepers, making their living from England's expanding commerce, prosperous enough to agitate for votes and free speech as first needs rather

[5] *Clarke Papers,* I, 309.   [6] *Ibid.,* I, 315.   [7] *Ibid.,* I, 320.   [8] *Ibid.,* I, 325, 312.

than bread and raiment. Walwyn was a successful merchant, Prince a cheesemonger, Overton a printer, Lilburne at one time a brewer. To Gerrard Winstanley, indeed, the futility of the Leveller program lay in its preservation, by and large, of existing economic patterns. Until the twin evils of buying and selling were annihilated, he thought, and goods produced and distributed by community labor, there would be no freedom. "A thing called *An Agreement of the People* . . .," he declared, "is too low and too shallow to free us at all." [9] To separate their cause from the lowly Diggers, and combat the independent accusations, the Levellers inserted in later *Agreements* a clause against communism and the levelling of estates. Accused as a communist and anarchist, Walwyn replied in his *Defence* that he wished only those reforms that would allow every one who labored in so plentiful a land as England to earn a comfortable subsistence.[10] However inaccurate the Independent charges of communism and anarchy, they found everywhere receptive believers, representing a political strategy proved by time and sustained by ineradicable superstitions.[11]

Underlying the debate on property and suffrage loomed a deeper issue, to be faced, as the months passed, more and more realistically by both Leveller and Independent. Now that defeat of the enemy impended, antagonistic forces among the conquerors, as in all wars, sought to direct to their own ends the fruits of victory. The Independents sought a compromise with the traditional monarchy, enlarged religious freedom, and the *status quo* in economic processes; the Levellers, however, now aimed at a deeper cleavage from the old order, the enfranchisement of the many poor. "There are many thousands of us souldiers," said Sexby, "that have ventur'd our lives; wee have had little propriety in the Kingedome as to our estates, yett wee have had a birthright . . . I doe thinke the poore and meaner . . . have bin the meanes

[9] *More Light Shining in Buckingham-shire* (E. 548, 33), p. 16.

[10] *Walwyn's Just Defense,* 1649, p. 24. Cf. my *Milton in the Puritan Revolution,* Chapter VI.

[11] Only a few weeks after the debates, on November 22, the Independents issued their *Declaration By Congregationall Societies,* attacking communism and polygamy, upholding on Biblical grounds the rights of property and the virtues of buying and selling. God himself, maintained the *Declaration,* had decreed inequalities in ownership. Walwyn believed this pamphlet to be an attempt to discredit him as one of the leaders of the Levellers.

of the preservation of this Kingedome." [12] This statement Rainsborough emphasized with a caustic thrust: "I would faine know what the souldier hath fought for all this while? Hee hath fought to inslave himself, to give power to men of riches, men of estates, to make him a perpetuall slave." [13] When gentlemen differ among themselves, he asserted, they conscript poor men to fight their wars for them. But freeholders are not thus pressed.

To Ireton, on the contrary, the war had been prosecuted for a more realistic, immediate purpose; assuredly it had not been fought to grant suffrage to the poor. They had fought, he insisted, against absolutism, against the conception that "one man's will must bee a law." Other men had fought that they might have Parliament's protection, protection of their business, their livelihood, their efforts to acquire property. Though not all men had an equal stake in this protection, everyone had some interest in it. Why, asked Ireton, should we go further? Why should we go on to plead for privileges by the law of nature that are opposed to the constitution? [14] Like all the Puritan reformers, Ireton and Cromwell had swum with the current of reform impelled by the energy of individualistic search for truth; now they wished to stop, to dam up the tide, to set a barrier before those goals to which their own had been signposts and signals.

23. Waning of Agitator Power

The debate of October 29 closed indecisively, no vote, so far as the Clarke records show, having been taken on the crucial issue.[1] Rainsborough favored a general rendezvous to determine the wishes of the whole army, and Cromwell proposed a committee to work out a compromise, suggesting that copyholders, or some copyholders, might be admitted to the suffrage. He said emphatically that he had not heard Ireton's arguments refuted, "nott in a parte to my knowledge, not in a tittle," but he wished to "bringe thinges to an understanding." Though Cromwell's proposal of a committee was finally accepted, the Levellers were uneasy. Everard voiced the suspicions of some that the debates

---

[12] *Clarke Papers*, I, 323.   [13] *Ibid.*, I, 325.   [14] *Ibid.*, I, 327.
[1] The Levellers afterward declared, however, that a vote had been taken, with only three voices dissenting from their clause on manhood suffrage. See p. 61.

were prolonged intentionally by the Independents, that meanwhile they held meetings secretly to contrive against the agitators and their proposals. When Ireton accused the agitators of promoting dissensions in the army, particularly the publication of *The Case of the Army,* an agitator replied that the soldiers themselves, being highly dissatisfied, had stirred the agitators to action.[2]

The committee suggested by Cromwell met the next day, October 30. Of the Leveller spokesmen Rainsborough and Sexby were present, Wildman significantly absent. The suffrage clause of the *Agreement* was apparently not settled by the committee to the satisfaction of either group; members of the Commons, according to the new wording, were to be distributed "according to some rule of equality of proportion, soe as to render the House of Commons as neere as may bee an equall Representative of the whole body of the people that are to Elect." [3] The hand of Ireton is here plainly evident, as in other elaborations of the original *Agreement* clauses. The changes made correspond in the main to *The Heads of the Proposals.* The delicate question of the suffrage was deferred to a future settlement.

In the days that followed the proponents of the *Agreement* gradually lost ground in their efforts to secure an acceptance of their proposals by the highest officers. On November 1, when the debate turned to the abolition of the negative voices of king and Lords, and feeling ran high against the king, Cromwell warned the Council that whatever they might conceive had to be presented to Parliament; that Parliament should then secure acceptance from the king. As for disorders in the army, he was resolved to impose military sanctions; he would not allow rendezvous to instigate disobedience to Fairfax.[4] That Cromwell made this threat, which he afterward crystallized in action, shows that he felt the power of the Levellers was waning. On November 8, after again attacking the suffrage clause of the *Agreement* as tending to anarchy, he succeeded in getting a motion passed for the officers and agitators to return to their regiments until time for a general rendezvous.[5] Meanwhile the number of Leveller sympathizers on the constitutional committee was declining. On November 9 a large committee was appointed again to consider

---

[2] *Clarke Papers,* I, 346, 328, 332, 342-43, 349.   [3] *Ibid.,* I, 365.
[4] *Ibid.,* I, 371.   [5] *Ibid.,* I, 412, 413.

the engagements of the army and the *Agreement,* and "to consider how farre any thing contain'd in the same are consistent with the said Engagements and Declarations." [6] On November 11 Harrison bluntly called the king "a Man of Bloud", denounced their engagement to him, and demanded his prosecution. To this ominous forecast of his own, and Ireton's, attitude toward the king, Cromwell replied with Biblical instances of murderers whose lives were spared.[7] On November 14, apparently to offer to the soldiers an alternative to the *Agreement,* a manifesto was drawn by the Council and Fairfax, stating the desires of the army. In this manifesto the Council formally disengaged itself from any attempt to effect a constitutional settlement except through Parliamentary channels. Attached to the manifesto was a pledge of loyalty to Fairfax and the Council, which each soldier was to be asked to sign.[8] This action of the Council, taken after the agitators had been withdrawn, was a symbol of Leveller defeat, a symbol, too, of the ascendancy of military discipline over the tenuous democratic organization of the soldiers as citizen legislators.

Leveller analysis of Independent strategy in the Putney debates appears most fully in *A Copy of a Letter Sent by the Agents of severall Regiments,*[9] which is dated November 11, and according to Thomason was scattered up and down the streets of London by the agitators. According to *A Copy* the agitators had won a vote in the affirmative (three voices dissenting) on the crucial issue of manhood suffrage (October 30),[10] but all had been referred to

---

[6] The Independents of London and Parliament were now making a concerted effort with Cromwell and Ireton to combat the *Agreement.* On November 9 the Commons branded *The Case Of The Army* and other papers presented by the agitators (which evidently included the *Agreement*) as "destructive to the Privileges of Parliament, and *the Fundamental Government of this Kingdom.*" Rushworth, VII, 867, 887.

[7] *Clarke Papers,* I, 417. [8] Gardiner, *Civil War,* IV, 22.

[9] E. 413 (18). The same pamphlet appeared the next day as *A Letter sent from several Agitators of the Army* (E. 414, 8).

[10] Did the vote on manhood suffrage actually take place? About it one can reach only one of two conclusions. Either Clarke omitted the vote from the record (by instruction), or no such vote was taken. If no vote was taken, then the Levellers deliberately falsified the facts in their letter of November 11. If the vote was taken, then Clarke omitted the most vital point of the debate. That manhood suffrage was still an issue on November 8, when Cromwell condemned it as anarchy, is proved by both the Clarke record and *A Copy of a Letter.* On this point the two sources agree.

a committee. At the next meeting (November 1), said the agents, *"a Declaration* was offered to the Councell, wherein the Kings corrupt interest was so intermixed, that in a short time, if he should so come in, he would be in a capacitie to destroy you, and the people." Protesting against this, the Levellers wished a debate on whether *any* power should be given the king.[11] Agreeing to a debate on this topic, Cromwell had appointed "munday last" (November 8) for that purpose: "But when they met they wholly refused, and . . . spake very reproachfully of us and our Actions, and declared against that which was past by the Councell before, *Concerning the voyces of those in Election, which have not fortie shillings by the yeare free-hold."* The next day (November 9), continued the agents, Cromwell and Ireton refused further to discuss the question and dissolved the Council for two weeks. Though agreeing to a rendezvous, they insisted on dividing the army in three parts. "Thus," add the agents, "you may observe the strange unconstancy of those who would obstruct our wayes." This opposition, nevertheless, they had expected; they urge the soldiers not to be dismayed, since these same great officers opposed their first petitions against disbanding.

24. Leveller Sallies and Counter-Attacks

While the Independents had been emasculating the *Agreement,* the Leveller propaganda tracts, their sharpest, most effective weapon, had struck blow after blow at the opposing forces. Appearing on October 29, *A Cal To All The Souldiers,* probably the product of Wildman's pen, had anticipated but minimized the danger of martial discipline as an attack on the *Agreement.* Reflecting Lilburne's own attitude toward Cromwell, *A Cal* is bitterly pessimistic about the sincerity of the two leaders. "One of the surest markes of deceivers," wrote Wildman, "is to make faire, long and eloquent speeches." Distrust these speeches, he advised. Cromwell and Ireton "doe earnestly and palpably carry

[11] The agents declare that the Council had agreed upon a letter to Parliament voicing Leveller wishes, but that Ireton threatened to leave the Council if it were not recalled. This must have been November 5 or 6, when, according to Rushworth, the Council met. *Clarke Papers* as edited by Firth have no verbatim record of the meetings of November 5 and 6, and make no mention of the letter to Parliament or Ireton's threat. Nor has Rushworth himself left any comment on these two meetings.

on the Kings design." Furthermore, do not be "frighted by the word *ANARCHY,* unto a love of *Monarchy,* which is but the gilded name for *Tyranny.*" [1] On November 4 appeared *Proposalls From Nine Regiaments of Horse,* a reprint of the main portions of the agitators' *Agreement.* [2] On November 5 was published another edition of the *Agreement,* titled *A Declaration From The severall Respective Regiments in the Army, to all Free-born Commons.* [3] On November 9 the Levellers sent forth *An Alarum To The Headquarters,* an earnest plea with the Independents to face the implications of their war against the king. Though written by a more moderate, conciliatory Leveller than Wildman or Lilburne, *An Alarum* left no point unattacked in examining the Independent position. "As a fore you went a King catching," says the writer, "now yee will goe a King courting . . . This must not be, you will ruine us." Now, having conquered him, let us proclaim him no king, and let us not "retain his insolent heathenish lawes." The people wish no longer to be "King-ridden & Priest-ridden fools." The emphasis in the *Alarum* is the contradiction between conquering the king, and then, not only restoring him, but asking for his forgiveness, "as though the Right, Title and power over us free Commoners, did run . . . in the vaines, . . . loyne, and in the bloud, of our insolent usurpers." With the king, insists the author, there can be no compromise: "Make us free now for ever, or absolute slaves, villens, and vassals." If the Independents will face the issue, and resolve it against the king, they will find among the people and common soldiers hearty support "to shake and tumble downe that mountain of dishonour and oppression." [4]

25. Corkbush Field: Doom of the First *Agreement*

The rendezvous at Corkbush Field on November 15 witnessed the doom of the first *Agreement.* Contrary to the wishes of the Levellers, Fairfax had ordered only one-third of the army to appear at the Corkbush rendezvous. Though he did not reject

---

[1] E. 412 (10), pp. 4, 7, 6.   [2] E. 412 (23).   [3] E. 412 (29).
[4] E. 413 (10), pp. 2, 3, 4. On November 11 Lilburne made a new plea for his vindication and total freedom, distributing *For every Individual Member of the Honorable House of Commons* (E. 414, 9) at the door of the House itself. On November 23 he sent forth another plea to the Commons, titled *A new complaint of an old grievance* (E. 426, 25).

Rainsborough's proffer of a copy of the *Agreement,* Fairfax spoke to each regiment "very gallantly," urging them to sign the pledge *he* had distributed among them. Without avail Colonel Eyre and Major Scott exhorted the men to stand by the *Agreement.* The soldiers' voices spoke for Fairfax. Contrary to order, Harrison's and Lilburne's regiments appeared at the rendezvous and proved the most intransigent. On the way to Corkbush Lilburne's regiment had driven away all of their commissioned officers except William Bray; they appeared flaunting copies of the *Agreement* from their hats.[1] Though Harrison's regiment was soon quieted, Lilburne's remained in a mutinous mood until Cromwell, after shouts of admonition, dashed among the men with drawn sword and restored order. Throwing down their documents, the soldiers begged for mercy. Selecting three of the leaders, Cromwell had them tried by court-martial on the field; when found guilty, the three men drew lots to select the comrade to be executed. As Arnold sank to the ground after the fatal shots, the men on the field had learned their lesson. The resolute discipline of war had dissolved their attempts at a democratic compact. Cromwell's timely deed had restored order in a mutinous army.[2] In his letter to Manchester Fairfax spoke of the outcome with satisfaction, acknowledging God's favor "in making these poor Men so unanimous" in ideas of settlement. Further, "they profess likewise an absolute Submission and Conformity to the antient Discipline of the Army." The *Agreement,* wrote Fairfax, had much inflamed the soldiers "towards Mutiny and Disobedience." But the men at heart were sound enough; they had been "merely cozened and abused with fair Pretences of those Men which acted in the *London* Councils. "Many copies of the *Agreement,* continued Fairfax, had been "dispersed among the Soldiers, thereby to engage them; but, blessed be God, all proved ineffectual." [3] The regiments had parted composed and satisfied, after having signed the engagement he had presented to them. Thus Fairfax. What Cromwell and Ireton concluded we have no record to resolve. In the perspective of history, we can be certain, however, that the Levellers' hopes for a constitutional settlement by their first *Agreement* were shattered at Corkbush Field. They had been unable to win de-

1 Rushworth, VII, 873-74.   2 Gardiner, *Civil War,* IV, 23.
3 *Old Parliamentary History,* XVI, 333-36.

cisively even the rank and file of the army to their cause. How much their defeat stemmed from the inadequacy of their numbers, and how much from the pressure of martial discipline exerted by Cromwell, are questions pertinent but unanswerable.

26. Lilburne Assails Martial Law

In the weeks that followed the execution at Corkbush Field, the Levellers hurled more imprecations at the Independent leaders, meanwhile shifting their center of agitation from the army to London. On November 23 they presented to Parliament a petition for the *Agreement*.[1] On December 2 Lilburne arraigned as illegal the close committee of Lords and Commons to examine the London agents.[2] On December 8 John Harris sent forth *The Grand Designe,* reviewing the machinations, as he conceived them, of Cromwell and Ireton, and interpreting Cromwell's negotiations with the king as the selfish seeking of power. After repeating Lilburne's charges of Cromwell's appointing his friends and relatives in key military posts, and of supporting only those men in Parliament who would follow his directions, Harris berates Cromwell for his opposition to the *Agreement*.[3]

The deepest resentment of the Levellers, however, was now directed at the court-martialling of soldier Levellers. In late November or December Lilburne had written *A Defence for the honest Nownsubstantive Soldiers of the Army, against the proceedings of the Gen. Officers to punish them by Martiall Law.*[4] On December 14 appeared *Englands Freedome, Souldiers Rights,*[5] probably written by Lilburne himself. The significance of these two documents rests not alone on the stirring events of 1647; they are pertinent wherever armies are composed of citizens with traditional privileges. The more widespread the democratic habits and convictions of citizen soldiers, the more difficult the

[1] Document 7 and commentary, pp. 235-41 of this volume.

[2] *A Defiance to Tyrants,* January 28, 1648 (E. 520, 30); Rushworth, VII, 888, 915.

[3] E. 419 (15), no pagination. Harris reprints and defends two main clauses of the *Agreement.*

[4] Reprinted complete in this volume (pp. 243-47) from *The peoples Prerogative,* pp. 42-44. Thomason did not apparently collect it as a separate publication, though it must have appeared as such.

[5] Document 8 and commentary, pp. 242-58 of this volume.

adjustment to the authoritarian practices of army discipline. Who could place his finger on the delicate, shifting line between the duty of the soldier and the privileges of the citizen? Lilburne resolved the question, as was his wont, by appeal to the documents, some venerable, others recent indeed. Martial law, he maintained, was not applicable in time of peace to soldiers; much less, then, was it applicable to Will Thompson, who had been cashiered from the army and was now, in his own words, "a free Commoner." Moreover, asserted Lilburne, quoting the *Engagement* of June 5, by mutual agreement the army was now functioning in an extraordinary manner, unique in warfare. The discipline of war, even had war existed, had been nullified by the *Engagement.* Had they not agreed not to disband until their demands were met? This implied, insisted Lilburne, that no man or officer could be cashiered. When Fairfax signed the *Engagement,* he had given "away all his power of exercising Martial Disciplin." By compact the army was now a democratic organization, governed by the General Council, no longer subject to the rules of war.

27. Cromwell and Ireton on New Ground

Although Cromwell and Ireton had stubbornly defended the return of limited kingship as described in *The Heads of the Proposals,* events were now forcing them inexorably to a reversal of their position and substantial agreement with the Leveller concept of annihilating the negative voice. Only three or four days after Corkbush Field Ireton remarked, according to Huntington, that since a treaty between Parliament and the king seemed imminent, he hoped *"we might with a good conscience fight against them both."* [1] About November 21 Cromwell intercepted a letter showing Charles' preference for Scottish support as opposed to that of the army. "Finding we were not likely to have any tolerable terms from the King," Cromwell reportedly said later, "we immediately, from that time forward, resolved his ruin." By November 28 Cromwell had swung over to the Leveller position; on the 29th he informed Berkeley that he could no longer see him, "it being very dangerous to both." [2] Several weeks later, at a

[1] *Sundry Reasons inducing Major Huntington to lay down His Commission* (August 2, 1648), in *An Impeachment Of High Treason,* p. 59.

[2] Gardiner, *Civil War,* IV, 29, 34.

prayer meeting of the officers, when Cromwell, Ireton, Tichborne, Hewson, and Peters "pray'd very fervently and pathetically . . . from Nine in the Morning till Seven at Night," it was resolved that "the King should be prosecuted for his Life as a Criminal Person." [3] On January 3 Cromwell supported Sir Thomas Wroth's motion: "to lay him [Charles] by, and settle the Kingdom without him: He cared not what Form of Government they set up, so it were not by Kings and Devils." On November 5 Cromwell had opposed the Vote of No Addresses, but now he declared that Parliament "should govern and defend the Kingdom by their own Power and Resolution, and not teach the People any longer to expect Safety . . . from an obstinate Man, whose Heart God had hardened." If they yielded to the king, continued Cromwell, the Commons could expect "to find his future Government of them insupportable, and fuller of Revenge than Justice." He warned that Parliament should act decisively against Charles; otherwise the mood of despair might teach the army "to seek their Safety by some other Means." Ireton also spoke ominously for the army, saying that the soldiers "would never forsake the Parliament, unless the Parliament forsook them first." [4]

For this bold change of front Cromwell's motives still escape the light of certainty. To trace their outlines is less difficult than to gauge their weight in the scales of a mighty decision. The pressure of evidence, it is true, culminating in the intercepted letter, had apparently convinced Cromwell and Ireton that, whatever the king's professed compromises, his pledged word was valueless. Without the positive assurance that Charles would abide by his engagements to them, the Independent leaders visualized not only the old tyrannies but also criminal charges against them in the offing. After the many glorious battles won against him, were they now to risk such ignominy at his hands? Such had been the Leveller questioning; thus had spoken Harrison and Rainsborough; thus now spoke Cromwell and Ireton. Cromwell's desire to unify the army so far as possible, without yielding to the *Agreement*, was undoubtedly another compelling motive. After Corkbush Field representatives of two-thirds of the army had assured Crom-

---

[3] Clarendon, *The History of the Rebellion* (3 v., London, 1707), Vol. III, Part I, p. 93; Rushworth, VII, 943.
[4] *Old Parliamentary History*, XVI, 491, 492.

well that despite the execution of the mutineer, the Levellers were resolved to win over the whole army or divide it and do battle, seeking help wherever they could. Whatever the actual danger, Cromwell and Ireton were impressed; they resolved, partly through the persuasions of Hugh Peters, "if we cannot bring the Army to our sense, we must go to theirs." [5] Without a unified army, indeed, Cromwell knew that his influence was a diminishing force. The king was no longer a potential ally; the Independents in Parliament were divided; the Levellers were now fiercely hostile. Almost unanimously the Presbyterians now stood for the king against their former allies, the Independents. Moreover, the army leaders faced now a sharply rising tide of royalism, accelerated by resentment against free quarter, by excessive taxation, scanty harvests, repression of Christmas games, plays, amusements. Heedless of censorship, royalist newspapers abounded; pamphlets for the king flowed from the presses.[6] Spontaneous riots burst out. In defiance of the Puritan Parliament, Londoners filled the theatres to overflowing. As war weariness spread over the land, "the king's health!" was the toast of rich and poor. In his long labors to come to terms with Charles, Cromwell had been acutely aware, as always, of the strange magic of the king's name in the minds of the people; but now with an army unified in its antagonism to the king, he was ready to defy the sentiment of the nation.

In throwing their forces against the king, Cromwell and Ireton sought to bring him to judgment without first constructing a new constitution. To the Levellers this was unthinkable. The principal aim, they thought, was not to bring the king to trial, but to effect the signing of a social compact by which the government thereafter, king or no king, should be sustained and limited by a larger proportion of the population than had hitherto been influential in its decisions. The *Agreement* had not mentioned the monarch. In placing all power in the Commons, however, it had so effectively nullified both the king's power and the Lords' that the existence of either was no longer an issue of consequence. The Levellers were glad to welcome Cromwell as a king-hater; but they distrusted his motives. Lilburne afterward wrote that in his opin-

---

[5] Berkeley, *Memoirs*, in Maseres, *Select Tracts* (2 v., 1815), II, 385.
[6] Cf. my analysis of royalist pamphlets in *Milton in the Puritan Revolution*, pp. 189-93.

ion Cromwell and Ireton had made their decision in order to regain the good will of the Leveller faction; they needed Leveller support to fight a new war against the king and "to preserve their own greatness." But this new war they were to prosecute "without giving or offering unto the people the least valuable consideration for all the blood they have already lost." [7] By *consideration* Lilburne meant, of course, assurance of a more democratic regime than had existed under Charles. Having no substitute for Charles, Cromwell and Ireton might easily become, thought the Levellers, greater tyrants than the king himself. In the fall of 1648, it is true, the Independent leaders were to turn seriously to the *Agreement* as a possible solution; but as before, after changing some of its vital provisions, they were to reject its function as a social compact by presenting it to the Commons for approval and promulgation.

Sent forth on December 30, *Putney Projects* attacked the Independent chiefs for a position that they had already in substance relinquished. By this time Cromwell and Ireton were committed by conviction to the trial of Charles if not to the abolition of kingship itself. The main aim of the pamphlet was to discredit Cromwell and Ireton not on this score alone, however, but also to stamp them as hypocritical traitors to the purposes of the army's own declarations. Relying upon dozens of quotations from the *Book of Army Declarations,* Wildman attempted to prove that Ireton and Cromwell had repudiated pledges made mutually with the whole army, beginning with the *Engagement* of June 5. When the people, wrote Wildman, were "filled with living hopes of perfect freedome from all kinds of tyranny or oppression," then "what fiery zeale and burning indignation did these our seeming Saviours breath forth against the invaders of our native freedome, and obstructors of their speedy settlement?" [8] They spoke out against the faction of Hollis and Stapleton; they supported the soldiers' petitions; they joined with them at New Market and Triploe Heath. "Now O yee Commons of England," exclaimed Wildman, "behold these your great Commanders thus cloathed with the glorious garment of their Declarations. . . What Eagle eye could at first discerne, that this glorious cloathing was but

---

[7] *The peoples Prerogative* (February 17, 1648), pp. 58-59.
[8] *Putney Projects,* p. 4.

painted paper? What jealous heart imagined that these promising Patriots were only sweet mouthed courtiers?" [9] After threatening Hollis and his faction, at the last moment they had not only drawn back, refused to purge the House, been content with vague promises; they had negotiated privately with the king, allowed royalist courtiers to come and go at will, all the while attacking Hollis for the same treasonable intercourse with the chief enemy of Parliament.[10] Analyzing motives only from the vantage point of radical ideology, Wildman attacked Cromwell without full comprehension of his political values. In Cromwell's mind the Leveller program was a solution to be shunned as doggedly as absolutism itself. What Wildman stamped, therefore, as arrant hypocrisy, was to Cromwell only the tactical recognition of conflicting political forces that he felt must be merged and reconciled in a moderate constitutional adjustment. He was determined to avoid extreme solutions, whether reactionary or revolutionary. Cromwell had signed the army declarations not because he accepted their democratic implications, or the validity of the fiery Leveller propaganda that had roused the soldiers to action, but because he wished to hold the army together. Unfamiliar with the ardent theorizing of the Levellers, distrustful of utopian planning, Cromwell adjusted his convictions readily to the flow and pressure of forces. The Levellers, on the other hand, idealists that they were, strove to fit men's minds and energies and the might of the army into their blueprints of perfection.

28. The January Crisis

Having had partial freedom from his Tower cell since November 9, Lilburne was meanwhile engaged in organizing and promoting a great new petition, a remarkable constitutional document,[1] destined, like its predecessor of March, 1647, to incur the deep hostility of the Commons.[2] On January 17 Lilburne and Wild-

[9] *Ibid.*, p. 6.

[10] Wildman reviews Cromwell's change of position in *Truths triumph* (pp. 7-8), offering the conjecture that the Scots had outbid Cromwell and Ireton by assuring the king more royal power than the army leaders. This necessitated Cromwell's reversal of policy. "I cannot imagine," he concluded, "that so great a turne [as Cromwell's], should be upon any other then a private interest."

[1] Document 9 and commentary, pp. 259-72 of this volume. *The mournfull Cries* (Document 10, pp. 273-78), was issued mainly to promote the petition.

[2] On January 19 a copy of the petition was presented to the House by Lilburne (at their command). On January 20 the House referred it to a committee and or-

man addressed a meeting at a private home in Wapping, one of many such meetings arranged by the Levellers in preparation for their appeal. As the petition shows, the radicals were now in a desperate mood. Their organization of agitators had fallen apart, its demise hastened by the opposition of the officers, the execution of Arnold, and the abandonment of the General Council as a representative body of the army. In the Commons, still unpurged of men the Levellers had denounced as traitorous, Presbyterians and conservative Independents dominated legislation, fearful both of the New Model army and the surge of royalism.[3] Much disillusionment as they felt in the Commons, it was now the only visible authority to which the Levellers could appeal. In the meeting at Wapping, therefore, Wildman and Lilburne voiced the necessity for the new petition; they also apparently harangued their followers with some violent imprecations against Lords and Commons, and warnings of imminent disorders. Wildman anticipated "a suddain confusion . . . if a speedie settlement were not procured." He declared that "the poor did gather together in troops of 10. 20. 30. in the Roades, and seized upon Corne as it was carrying to market, and devided it among themselves before the owners faces telling them they could not starve."[4] Lilburne spoke also for an appeal to the Commons, saying that though it was "sufficiently corrupted," its toppling would *bring in such a present Inundation of misery and confusion . . . that there would be nothing in the eye of Reason, but cutting of throats . . . and the longest Swords to be Judges of all."* In this confusion, declared Lilburne, the Levellers themselves might be destroyed. He wanted to preserve the integrity, the "interest and being" of the Commons (especially since they had declared against both the king and the Scots), *"yet in such a way, That they might not invassalize the people."* [5]

dered it to "prevent any Assemblings or Actings upon the said petition." *Commons' Journals*, V, 438.

[3] In *The Royall Quarrell* (February 9), John Harris described the conservative reaction thus: "Now we plainly see the *Reall Presbyter* and *Reall Independent* party, over-awed by the *Royall Presbyter* and *Royall Independent*."

[4] *Truths triumph* (January 18), p. 4. Wildman "conceived no other probable way of *preventing a new warre* with the *Scots* . . . but by uniting the people in the principles of *common right and freedome*. Hence the necessity, he said, for a nation-wide distribution of the petition.

[5] *An Impeachment Of High Treason Against Oliver Cromwell* (August 10, 1649), p. 14.

Lilburne's preference of even a reactionary Commons to an impending dictatorship was undoubtedly sincere. The procedure of petitioning symbolized to him the power of ancient, accepted custom. Though the *Agreement* had evolved from the slow formulation of his political premises, the petition, rooted as it was in traditional processes, was a weapon of agitation more congenial to Lilburne's political temperament than the concept of a new constitution. More fully than any of his radical contemporaries, Lilburne recognized the libertarian overtones of traditional procedures; more effectively than any other he turned documentary interpretation to his own purposes. Partly for this reason the prospect of a military dictatorship he visualized with dismay. With king, Lords, and Commons, however tyrannical, had grown up intermingling patterns of common rights and privileges, some of them centuries old; liberties, said Lilburne, still not understood by the people, nor the means of preserving them. If the army leaders were to destroy the Commons, substituting only the power of their swords, this complex growth of safeguards and privileges would be swept away.

On January 18 George Masterson, minister at Shoreditch, who had attended the meeting the night before, gave information [6] to the Lords of the speeches of Wildman and Lilburne and their intention to distribute many thousand copies of the petition. After a conference with the Lords, the Commons repealed its former order allowing Lilburne liberty, and ordered him again committed to the Tower. Appearing at the bar of the House the next morning, January 19, Lilburne was brought face to face with his accuser and permitted to make three speeches in answer.[7]

Less tedious in documentation than his pamphlets, Lilburne's long speech before the House delineates with persuasive clarity his diagnosis of the march of events; it illuminates also the mainsprings of his political idealism. After a full account of his part in writing and promoting the petition (and a most revealing description of Leveller organizational methods), Lilburne defended the principles of the petition as "a salve to heal and cure all our

[6] Masterson's account appeared in *The Triumph stain'd* (February 10) and again in *A Declaration Of some Proceedings* (February 14).

[7] Rushworth, VII, 969; Commons' *Journals*, V, 437-38. One of the speeches was an hour and a half long. *A Whip for the present House of Lords* (February 27, 1648), p. 21.

sores and diseases, and to knit the hearts together of all ingenuous men, in every faction or interest." Outlining objections to the petition that had been voiced in his meetings, Lilburne spoke realistically of the sentiment for the king. The people, some objectors had asserted, favored the king more than Parliament. This was true, Lilburne had granted, but for what reason? He condemned not the people, but the miseries under which they labored: "Their burthens are greater now then before, and are likely to continue without any redresse . . . for all the bloud and treasure they had spent for their liberties and freedoms." Should one refuse to help his neighbors because they did not understand their dangers, or sought the wrong way out of their plight? This justified instead a more energetic appeal to their reason *"and prosecuting of some universall just things to ease them, and for the future to secure them."* In the petition lay the healing of all their wounds. Even if men would be slaves, if "our friends, our Countrymen, our brethren, were ready to perish, and in their sottishness were ready to be destroyed," he would not accede to their slavery or destruction. To do so, asserted Lilburne, would be to repudiate "the great end wherefore God sent man into the world . . . that he should do good in his generation."⁸ If a neighbor were drowning himself, should a man stand aloof? If a neighbor's house were burning, and his own likely to burn with it, should a man stand aloof even though the neighbor refuses assistance? Having thus given religious and social justification for his political agitation in the face of great odds, Lilburne dwelt for a few minutes on the central contradiction outlined in *Putney Projects,* attacked the Lords for their subversion of fundamental liberties, and concluded with a bitter charge against Cromwell as the chief apostate to the cause of freedom.

The speaker of such sentiments, self-depicted agitator and organizer, was too dangerous a man to remain long at large. After long debate, Lilburne was committed to the Tower *"for treasonable and seditious practices against the State."* Supported by a crowd of about a hundred radicals at the door of the Commons, Lilburne attempted to challenge the validity of his warrant. Finding the speaker had already gone home (it being late enough for candles to be lighted), the sergeant allowed Lilburne to depart,

⁸ *An Impeachment,* pp. 21, 25, 23; *A Whip for the . . . Lords,* pp. 11-26.

having his word that he would appear the next morning. On the following day, January 20, when the speaker refused to change the warrant, a riot ensued between Lilburne's followers and soldiers called in to execute the House's order. When the mob was finally quelled, Elizabeth Lilburne standing in front of her husband to protect him from musket butts, Lilburne was again lodged in the Tower.[9]

The January imprisonment of Lilburne and Wildman threw again into bold outline the constitutional privileges in which the Leveller leaders had repeatedly sought refuge. Both Lilburne and Wildman pointed out that Masterson's verbal charges had no validity in law. Wildman objected that he had not been arraigned in the customary manner, that is, before a justice of the peace, where he would have had the benefit of traditional legal procedures. The warrant itself, charged the radicals, was illegal. Parliament had no power to imprison any man *"untill the pleasure of the House bee further signified."* Furthermore, asserted Wildman, it was illegal to charge a man merely with *"treasonable and seditious Practices against the State."* [10] Not the general but the specific charge of treason, a type of treason already defined by statute, was the requirement of a legal warrant utterly disregarded by the Commons. To demonstrate his point, Wildman elaborated with brilliant use of precedents on the concept of treason, arguing that the intent to levy war against the state is not treason: *"There must be levying warre in facto, actually* before it be *treason."* [11] Certainly in addressing an audience about a petition he and Lilburne had violated no statute. Could the Commons write its own definition of treason to fit a particular situation, and punish accordingly? *"Penalties,"* Wildman answered, 'are to perswade to the *keeping* of *known lawes,* not of *Lawes coniectural, ambiguous,* and to be taken by *consequence."* [12] Behind the protest of Wildman and Lilburne lay their old complaint against the arbitrary use of the legislative power, the Parliament men, as Wildman said, instead of abiding by the statutes, keeping the law within their own breasts. Reverting to the main principle of the *Agreement,* Wildman wrote, "I beleeve the freedomes of this Nation will never be secure, untill the extent of the power and trust

---

[9] *A Whip for the present House of Lords,* pp. 23-26.
[10] *Truths triumph,* p. 10.   [11] *Ibid.,* p. 16.   [12] *Ibid.,* p. 16.

of the peoples representatives, and the peoples reservations to themselves be clearly declared." [13]

29. New Blows at Cromwell

Lilburne's new imprisonment impelled him to more furious pamphleteering than ever. On January 28 he sent forth his *Defiance to Tyrants,* reprinting his attack of December 2 [1] on the close committee of Lords and Commons to examine the London agents, and appending a denunciation of the Committee for Plundered Ministers for their attempts to collect tithes by law. On February 14 he published *The peoples Prerogative and Priviledges,* a long collection of soldiers' petitions and libertarian documents, some of them his own, interspersed with new attacks on the Grandees. As in previous pamphlets, he berates Parliament members for "sharing (as daily they doe), the Common wealths money amongst themselves." Already he fears "an everlasting Parliament." Reprinting *Englands Freedome, Souldiers Rights,* he denounces the officers again for using martial law against the civil demands of common soldiers. The "new factionated Independents" he fears more tyrannical than "the Episcopalls of old": They set their "Beagles and Cur-doggs" on any man who wants to enlighten the people. But Lilburne's bitterest condemnations he reserves for Cromwell, on whose account he can never again, in matters of state, trust "father, brother, or any other relations *I* have in the world." Though new tyrants now appear, Cromwell in the lead, he does not fear them; though slavery has already crossed the threshold, he will supply his friends with "some weapons to keep it out of the kitchine and Hall." [2] On February 27 Lilburne answered *A Declaration Of some Proceedings* with *A Whip for the present House of Lords,* reviewing the history of the January petition, claiming that it "struck at the very root of all that tyranny," and blaming the instigation of the Civil War on the Lords for their refusal to concur in settling the militia. He denounces their desire to have not only "arbitrary power in-

[13] *Truths triumph,* p. 11.

[1] E. 520 (30). I have found no mention in Thomason of the original pamphlet of December 2. The edition of January 28 Lilburne later reprinted in *The peoples Prerogative,* pp. 67-76.

[2] "Proem" at beginning of pamphlet; p. 67.

herent in themselves, for life, but also to have it hereditary to
their sonnes, and sonnes sonnes, for ever, be they Knaves or *Fools.*"
Though for his part they may keep their dignities and their estates, the kingdom will never be free until their power is plucked
up, roots and all.[3] In *The Prisoners Plea for a Habeas Corpus*
(April 4),[4] after reviewing the documents that should by law have
assured him this protection (and for which the lawyers he had
consulted were afraid to initiate proceedings), Lilburne returned
to his attack on Cromwell and Ireton with the most violent, un-
measured invective he had yet resorted to. A worse tyrant than
Strafford; a thief of the country's funds; a murderer of the soldier
Arnold at Corkbush Field, since he had arbitrarily applied martial
law in time of peace—these intemperate accusations against Cromwell, unworthy of Lilburne's more generous moments, suggest the
scope of his desperation.

30. A New Army Manifesto

In the months that followed, when royalist uprisings in England appeared imminent, and the Scots threatened invasion from
the North, the Levellers essayed no further petitioning of the
House. They did, however, briefly though ineffectually instigate
the army to draw up a plea to Parliament. Written sometime in
April, the *The Armies Petition* appealed for many of the reforms
laid down in the January petition. Subordinating the idea of
the *Agreement,* though incorporating its main provisions, the
soldiers omitted the demand implying manhood suffrage, which
had caused so much controversy in the Putney debates. Instead
they asked that possessors of land held by copyright "may purchase themselves freeholders" at prices determined by the state,
the soldiers also demanded that "the antient and almost anti-

[3] Pp. 13, 17.

[4] E. 434 (19). On April 19, and again on April 25, Lilburne petitioned the
judges of the Kings Bench for a writ of *habeas corpus*. The writ was finally
granted after Lilburne had consented to act through counsel, a procedure much
against his convictions. At the same time he made an issue of *habeas corpus* by
inducing other prisoners, Richard Woodward, Mary Collens, and William Thompson, to petition for the same right. On May 8 Lilburne finally appeared before
the Kings Bench, made a long defense of himself (his attacks on the Lords interrupted and forbidden by the justices), but was recommitted to the Tower. *The
Prisoners mournfull cry* (E. 441, 17), May 9, 1648; *The Lawes Funerall* (E. 442, 13),
May 15, 1648.

quated badge of slavery, that is, all base Tenures of Lands, as by
Copyes and Fines at will, by oathes of fealty, homage, &c. . . . be
taken away." Their engagements as soldiers, asserted the petitioners, bound them to the fulfilment of the aims they were now again
presenting. Though grateful for Parliament's Votes of No Addresses, the soldiers declared that no settlement for common justice had followed. "We see the oppressions of the people," they
wrote, "as far from being removed or lessened, as if our ransome
cost no blood." [1] On April 24 soldiers of several regiments met
at St. Albans to discuss ways and means of securing subscriptions
to their petition in the army. Colonel Rich's regiment had already
selected an agitator from each troop. Several officers, however,
among them Captains Brown, Cladman,[2] and Packer, rushed into
the meeting and carried off the whole group as prisoners to Windsor. When two men of Rich's regiment presented a petition to
Fairfax for the release of their agents, they were, according to the
Leveller account, released only after threats of death, with no
satisfaction given for the freeing of their comrades. Thus the
chief officers met the threat of a new organization of the agitators;
they were resolved not to allow again the growth of organized
representation of the soldiers in the political decisions of the army.
The incident points to the decline of Leveller effectiveness in
army ranks. The movement that only a few months before had
forced the chief officers to debate a democratic constitution had
now dwindled to a single manifesto easily brushed aside.

31. Prayers and Tears: New Resolutions

On April 29, 30, and May 1 the officers of the army held meetings at Windsor to analyze their position in the midst of impending uprisings and the frustration of their hopes for a constitutional
reconciliation of all factions.[1] If royalist risings seemed imminent,
the complaints of the agitators were ominous of heightened dissatisfactions within the ranks. In such a crisis the prayerful searching of souls, thought William Allen, drew all hearts together,
purging, healing, crystallizing purpose and shedding light. Many

---

1 *The Armies Petition*, May 3, 1648 (E. 438, 1), pp. 5, 4, 6, 7.
2 I can find no officer listed by this name. The soldiers may refer to Captain
John Gladman.
1 Gardiner, *Civil War*, IV, 118.

years later, in the heaving distractions of 1659, he described for the edification of his countrymen the famous prayer meeting at Windsor eleven years before. "We were . . . filled with a spirit of great jealousy and divisions amongst ourselves . . . ," wrote Allen, "some of us judging it a duty to lay down arms, and quit our stations." In the prayer meeting Cromwell "did press very earnestly on all . . . to a thorough consideration of our actions as an army . . . to see if any iniquity could be found in them; and what it was, that if possible we might find it out, and so remove the cause of such sad rebukes as were upon us." On the third day of prayer, after long self-laceration, the officers were "led to find out the very steps . . . by which we had departed from the Lord, and provoked him to depart from us." These steps, continued Allen, the roots of their wrongdoing, they "found to be those cursed carnal conferences, [which] our own wisdom, fears, and want of faith, had prompted us the year before to entertain with the king and his party." Convinced of their heavy sins, "able hardly to speak a word to each other for bitter weeping," the officers "were also helped with fear and trembling to rejoice in the Lord." Finally they resolved, none dissenting, "to call Charles Stuart, that man of blood, to an account for that blood he had shed . . . against the Lord's cause and people in these poor nations." [2] Though the historian might wish for the account of a less mystical observer, Wildman, Ludlow, Rainsborough, or Ireton himself, to corroborate or qualify Allen's narrative, the import of the event is clear enough. Months before Cromwell's mind had at least partially settled on the course to which the prayer meeting now committed him. The meeting, however, unified the spirit of the officers and gave some reassurance to the men who still clamored for a new constitution. Henceforth the army would drive straight to its goal, despite the convictions of many Independents, who, Vane among them, had voted on April 28 to settle the traditional monarchy. [3] As the king was to most Englishmen the symbol of royalism, obscuring realities difficult to discern, he had become to this strange Puritan army the image, the concentration, of all the war's evils: death, destruction, horror, frustration of their civil hopes. That Charles was

[2] Somers' *Tracts,* edited by Sir Walter Scott (13 v., London, 1811), VI, 500, 501.
[3] Gardiner, *Civil War,* IV, 116.

the chief obstruction to the shaping of a new England was a simplification much easier to grasp than the complex play of forces, the political and economic realities of a changing England.

32. The Second Civil War: Cromwell Triumphant

In the five months that followed, from May 1 to October 4, the New Model Army, in a series of relentless, bitter battles, unrelieved by the magnanimity that had often lightened the burdens of the first Civil War, crushed its enemies within and brought the armies of Scotland to surrender. On May 1 Cromwell was dispatched to put down a revolt in Wales. On May 3 Parliament received sharp demands for the Presbyterianizing of England, the suppressing of sectaries, and the disbanding of the army. On June 1, to quell the rising in Kent, Fairfax met and defeated a royalist army of about ten thousand men. Two weeks later, after a fierce but unsuccessful attempt to storm the defences of Colchester, Fairfax laid siege to the city. On July 6 Hamilton's army crossed into England and occupied Carlisle. A few weeks later, on August 17, Cromwell defeated Hamilton and his English allies at the battle of Preston, forcing them into ignominious retreat and surrender of their remnants on August 25. The next day, after long and bitter privation, Colchester surrendered to Fairfax. On August 30 a sudden storm off the coast forced the royalist fleet to desist from attack and seek refuge in neutral waters. By early October both Berwick and Carlisle had capitulated to Cromwell, who entered Edinburgh on October 4.[1] In a military sense the New Model army was now master of England, Scotland, and Wales. But the country was not pacified. Under the threat of force the population waited uneasily the march of events, at heart more staunchly royalist than ever. In social concepts and political awareness, the men of the army had leaped ahead of their fellows many decades. In the England of the seventeenth century, they were a nineteenth-century anomaly, their antagonism to monarchy incomprehensible, their ideas of a new order strange and remote.

[1] I have here followed Gardiner, *Civil War*, IV, 118-230.

33. A New Compact of the People

Frustrated in their latest appeals both to Parliament and the army, the Levellers in early August turned again to the concept of the *Agreement* as means to organize the resistance of their followers and channel dissatisfactions into agitation for their utopian blueprint. On August 3 appeared *A New Engagement, or, Manifesto,* declaring the necessity of a mutual resolution of many thousands "to labour for a speedy establishment of a Just and Equall Government." Because "all present Authorities" have perverted the purposes of government, the engagers are constrained to appeal to all their faithful fellow-countrymen to proceed with a constitutional settlement, the end of which is not to divide but unify. After reviewing the standing oppressions, and the defections of both Parliament and the army, the manifesto outlines the new national plan. With the dissolution of the present Parliament, the Commons members are to be elected biennially by manhood suffrage. On the day of the first such election the people are to sign a mutual compact "wherein the bounds, limits and extent of their trust shall be clearly expressed," and the powers of the Commons clearly defined. The Commons is not to have the power to bind "any man in matters of Religion, or in the way of Gods Worship"; nor may it conscript men for fighting on land or sea. After this brief statement of the principles of the first *Agreement,* the manifesto lists thirteen specific reforms to which the signers engage themselves; these reforms are in the main the ones represented in the petitions of March, 1647, and January, 1648. The stirring march of history, however, has forced the Levellers to new demands: No official, military or civil, is to hold office more than two years; Parliament's committees with judicial functions are to be dissolved; all statutes and ordinances are to be examined and revised, "especially, that mens lives be more precious then formerly"; the protection of *habeas corpus* is in no event to be delayed; children are to be trained to useful employment; Ireland is to be reduced to tranquillity by peaceful means if possible.[1] Thus did the Levellers combine in the August manifesto the main concepts of their petitions with the central idea of

---

[1] Thomason broadside 669 f. 12 (97), August 3, 1648.

their *Agreement,* a compact emanating from the people themselves, a "law paramount" securing fundamental privileges from destruction or abridgment, limiting and defining the powers of the Commons. In no earlier manifesto had this coalescence taken place; nor did petition and *Agreement* unite again in a similar proclamation until the third *Agreement* in May, 1649.

34. On the Home Front: Presbyterian Strategy and Leveller Doubts

While Cromwell was prosecuting the Second Civil War with his usual thoroughness and dispatch, the Presbyterians of Parliament had been gaining confidence and power with amazing rapidity. As the army's hate for the king mounted, and their determination to bring him to judgment crystallized, Parliament's sentiment veered more sharply than ever toward reconciliation. By this time the Presbyterian majority had a much deeper fear of the Independent radicals than of any excesses of kingship, even those of Charles I. As early as June they had voted to allow the eleven members (excluded by military pressure the previous August) to return to their places; [1] on August 11, Holles, their leader, so hated by the Leveller faction, took his seat again in the Commons. On July 3 a great debate took place in the Commons on the issue of a treaty with the king. "He that draws his Sword upon the King," said Scott, "must throw his Scabbard into the Fire." [2] But the royalist sentiment was not to be denied. On August 24 the Commons voted to repeal their vote of No Addresses of January 3, thus opening the way to formal communications with the king. Meanwhile (August 8) they had reminded the Scots that on several occasions they had declared *"That they will not alter the Government by King, Lords, and Commons."* [3] Petitions for kingship and Presbyterianism were more numerous and insistent, and certainly more exact indicators of public sentiment, than the statements of Levellers or Independent radicals.

The Levellers watched the growth of royalist power with grave uneasiness. Intensely as they hated Cromwell and Ireton, they even more deeply dreaded the prospect of a Presbyterian victory,

[1] *Old Parliamentary History,* XVII, 212.
[2] *Ibid.,* XVII, 276.   [3] *Ibid.,* XVII, 377.

with the inevitable persecution of sects and annihilation of their political hopes. When, therefore, the Presbyterians secured Lilburne's release from prison on August 1,[4] hoping thereby to gain his support in discrediting Cromwell, Lilburne disappointed them. On August 2 Major Huntington presented to the House his *Sundry Reasons* for retiring from the army, a document containing in the main the Levellers' own analysis of Cromwell's strategy, and concluding with the affirmation that Cromwell believed it "lawful to play the knave with a knave." [5] Though repeatedly solicited (according to his own evidence), to join with Huntington in impeaching Cromwell, Lilburne rebuffed the Presbyterian offers. "I then by my absolute freedom was a little up," wrote Lilburne later, "and could have at my pleasure been revenged of him, . . . either by [causing] divisions in his Army, which was . . . then in my power; or by *joyning in impeaching him with Major* Huntington . . . yet I scorned it, and rather applyed my hand to help him up again, as not loving a Scotch Interest." [6] On the second day of his freedom, August 3, Lilburne wrote Cromwell a letter assuring him support "for all your late severe hand towards me." Carried by Sexby to Cromwell, the letter was "not a little welcome," and Lilburne was encouraged to seek out Cromwell in the North. From this conference, of which unfortunately no record remains, Lilburne returned to London with some assurance that Oliver was now open to Leveller convictions. The Levellers immediately busied themselves with the great petition of September 11, stressing the guilt of the king and announcing radical support of the army. Though the London Independents did not support the September petition, the Levellers evidently believed it had the approval of Cromwell and Ireton, Lilburne declaring it *"was no small piece of service to Cromwel and his great Associates."* [7] Resolved as they were to bring the king to trial despite all opposition, the Independents welcomed the support of the king-hating Levellers; they were prepared, moreover, as events were to demonstrate, to accept more fully than in the Putney de-

---

[4] Sir John Maynard made a speech August 1 on his behalf (*Old Parliamentary History*, XVII, 349). On the same day a petition for Lilburne's release was presented, signed by more than ten thousand people (E. 457, 19).

[5] *An Impeachment Of High Treason*, p. 60.

[6] *The Legall Fundamentall Liberties* (1st ed.), p. 28.

[7] *The Legall Fundamentall Liberties* (1st ed.), p. 29.

bates the fundamental positions of the radical chiefs. The Levellers, on the other hand, grasped at the opportunity, however tenuous, of directing the might of the army toward the constitutional policy on which their hopes were centered.

35. The Petition of September

The September petition,[1] though not promoted on a national scale, or with such zealous activity as the document of January, marked one of the high tides of Leveller agitation. In their opening paragraphs the petitioners attempt to show that a break with both king and Lords is inherent in the Parliament's own declarations, in its own defiance of the king's authority, and the non-concurrence of the Lords. Phrasing in a conciliatory tone, appealing to reflection and reason, the argument assumes a persuasive validity which few pamphlets of the day could equal. In a national sense the Levellers were attempting to unite the forces of wavering Parliamentarians and Independent army chiefs with their own; hence they speak praise for the army and urge the vindication of its declarations. By means of such a popular front, which the Independents also recognized as an expedient procedure, the Levellers hoped to channel the victories of Parliament over the king into a democratic triumph. In the long run this strategy was doomed to failure, even had the Levellers and Independents achieved unanimity. The Independents, backed by the army, and the Levellers, masters of propaganda processes, exerted power and achieved an influence out of all proportion to their numbers. Before the accumulated forces of economic pressure and political opinion, enhanced by revered traditions, the power of both factions, whether soon or late, was certain to crumble.[2]

36. The Second *Agreement:* A New Alliance

As the Second Civil War drew to a close in the autumn of 1648, Cromwell and Ireton were again faced with the responsibility of attempting a constitutional settlement. They were now

[1] Document 11 and commentary, pp. 279-90 of this volume.

[2] *A Full Answer To The Levellers Petition* (September 19, 1648) accused the Levellers of "labouring to make *Kings, Queens, Princes, Dukes, Earles, and Lords,* with themselves fellowes at football, and equall to the poorest Peasant, a desire against all Law, and president of all Countries and Ages."

absolutely determined upon one Leveller plank of 1647, that of bringing the king to judgment and destroying the negative voice of him and his successors. To what extent Ireton had swung over to the Leveller demands for manhood suffrage remains uncertain; but his long defense of the sovereignty of the people in the army *Remonstrance* of November 16 leaves no doubt that he was a much more thoroughgoing democrat than in the Putney debates, twelve months past, when he had strenuously upheld the right of property owners alone to guide the nation's destiny. The indecision of Cromwell and Ireton in the preceding autumn, when their delay had allowed Charles to rally new forces to his banner; the necessity for a whole new series of battles when they thought the war won; their bitter experience with Charles' tactics in negotiations; the Leveller and half-Leveller convictions of Harrison, Rainsborough, and many other officers voiced boldly in army councils month after month; their court-martialing of respected soldiers for Leveller demonstrations; the royalist assassination of Rainsborough at the war's very end—all these had wrought changes of democratic significance in the leadership of the army, to a greater extent, of course, in Ireton the theorist than in Cromwell the commander. On Fairfax, who listened patiently and tolerantly to all views, and retained Leveller confidence long after Lilburne's bitter denunciations of Cromwell, the ideas of the Levellers apparently made no impact whatever; he remained a serene, moderate, aristocratic warrior, content with England's ancient government by king, Lords, and Commons. But on the Puritans Ireton and Cromwell the fierce ideological conflicts of the war had set their mark.

Certain it is, whether motives ideological or tactical were decisive, Cromwell and Ireton made overtures for Leveller support in the autumn of 1648. Distrusted by Fairfax, roundly hated by the Parliament's Presbyterian majority, the two army leaders turned to the indefatigable Levellers as allies of no mean consequence in their destruction of the *status quo*. At Cromwell's suggestion the Independents of London in November engaged in conversations with the Levellers about a constitutional settlement.[1] The *Remonstrance* of November 16 bears strong evidence

[1] In September or October Lilburne and his friends had written to Cromwell voicing their conviction of his understanding of *"the principles of a just Govern-*

of Leveller influence, especially in the concluding passages, which call for an *Agreement of the People* as the basis of constitutional settlement.[2] This statement alone represents a signal victory of the Levellers in army councils, though, as will appear later, the officers at heart may have had no intention of actually allowing the *Agreement* to be circulated for subscriptions. Consistent with Leveller demands, the *Remonstrance* calls for annual or biennial Parliaments, "an equal Representative of the whole People electing," [3] an elective monarchy,[4] restriction of Parliament's power to abolish basic freedoms, redress of grievances mentioned in the Petition of September 11. True it is that the *Remonstrance* would have had settlement by the *Agreement* effected only "after public Justice," that is, after the trial of the king. This provision was to break in pieces the last alliance of Leveller and Independent: The Levellers not only distrusted the promises of the officers to effect such a settlement after "public Justice"; they denied the constitutionality of a Parliamentary purge before the *Agreement* had been signed.

The collaboration of the Leveller and Independent on the second *Agreement* began with a meeting at the Nags-head Tavern probably in early November, the Levellers being represented by Lilburne and Wildman. When the Independents pressed for immediate trial and execution of the king, Lilburne replied that the army could be trusted with such power no more than the king,

---

ment," evidently referring to the growth of Leveller ideas at army headquarters. Cromwell's response to this was a suggestion to the Independents of London that they confer with Lilburne and his friends. See *Legal Fundamental Liberties* (second edition), pp. 32-33.

2 *Old Parliamentary History*, XVIII, 234. On November 15, at the Nags-head Tavern, the committee of four Independents and four Levellers had agreed that constitutional settlement by an *Agreement* should be incorporated "if it may be" in the *Remonstrance*. This is evidence that the *Agreement* sections of the *Remonstrance* were incorporated the very day of its presentation to the Council of Officers (November 16). See *Legal Fundamental Liberties* (second edition), p. 34.

3 It is significant that the *Remonstrance* makes no restriction on the suffrage, which Ireton had supported so strongly in the long debates at Putney. Meanwhile, however, the Levellers had retreated from their original position. No longer did they demand manhood suffrage. In the *Agreement* of December 15 (p. 297) servants and beggars were forbidden to vote. Nor could those men vote who were "receiving wages from any particular person."

4 This was probably not a Leveller suggestion. The Levellers cared little how a monarch was selected so long as he was shorn of his veto power. The suggestion anticipates a provision in the *Instrument of Government* by which the Council of State was to elect Cromwell's successor.

that a military tyranny could easily become a greater menace than
Charles himself. First there must be a constitutional settlement
by means of an *Agreement*. Though "desperately cholerick" at
this stand, said Lilburne, the Independents finally agreed to the
appointment of a committee of eight, four Independents and four
Levellers, to frame the main articles of an *Agreement*. At a meeting at the Nags-head on November 15 the committee unanimously agreed upon a method of constitutional settlement: A constitutional convention was to be called, the members to consist
of representatives from each county of England and the army,
this group of representatives to have no legislative power, their
function being merely to frame an *Agreement* for submission to
the "well-affected" people.[5]

Later meeting with Ireton and his officers to protest some of
the statements in the *Remonstrance,* Lilburne found that the
army leaders were still resolved to let no constitutional settlement
interfere with a speedy trial of the king; whereupon Lilburne and
his colleagues departed, certain that any further consultations
were useless. But Harrison, hybrid that he was of mystic, democrat, and tactical realist, was not content at this juncture to accept
a break in the tenuous alliance of Leveller and Independent. In
conference with Lilburne later, he readily admitted that the army
leaders had betrayed the cause of the people and broken their
own declarations; but he pleaded the present desperate necessity
of trying the king before Parliament could conclude a treaty with
him. Faced with this dilemma, Lilburne was not at a loss for a
constructive alternative to a constitutional convention, now admittedly impractical in the race with time. The Levellers therefore proposed the framing of an *Agreement* by a committee of
sixteen, four members each to represent the army, the London
Independents, the Independents of Parliament, and the Levellers;
this committee could act immediately, no appeal to be made from
its phrasing of the *Agreement;* it could be presented promptly for
signatures in all parts of England. When Harrison carried this
proposal to headquarters, Ireton "did absolutely and heartily
agree" to it; so that there seemed no barrier to the acceptance of
the *Agreement* by all groups represented. In spite of some delay
in securing attendance of its busy members, the committee of six-

---

[5] *Legal Fundamental Liberties* (second edition), p. 34 (p. 413 of this volume).

teen finally concurred upon the provisions of the *Agreement,* at which point the Levellers considered their great work accomplished. Now the *Agreement* would be distributed in printed form for signatures of soldiers and citizens. In this assumption, however, the Levellers were sorely disillusioned. Instead of presenting it for signatures, the officers began to debate and conclude upon the articles of the *Agreement,* a procedure which Lilburne bitterly denounced. "I took my leave of them," he afterward wrote, *"for a pack of dissembling, jugling Knaves . . . for there was neither faith, truth nor common honesty amongst them:* and so away I went to those that chose and trusted me, and gave publikely and effectually . . . an exact account how they had dealt with us, *and cozened and deceived us."* [6] He then published the copy of the *Agreement* as framed by the committee of sixteen, prefixed a letter to it signed, curiously enough, *AN,* and secured its distribution on December 16, 1648.[7]

Whether Ireton's consideration of the *Agreement* and debates with the Levellers were only a ruse to prevent timely Leveller opposition, as Lilburne later believed, lie still unresolved among history's many obscurities. But on November 29, in sending his message through Harrison that he would accept whatever draft of the *Agreement* that the committee of sixteen should frame, Ireton won Lilburne's reluctant acquiescence to the army's march on London. On December 1 the army entered the city. On December 6 Colonel Pride purged the Commons of its Presbyterian majority. By December 10, four days after military dictatorship had begun, the draft of the *Agreement* was completed. Then, on December 11, Ireton submitted it to the Council of Officers, an action considered by Lilburne a gross violation of Ireton's promise.[8] Now that the dictatorship was a reality Ireton paid less

---

[6] *Legal Fundamental Liberties,* p. 39. For this whole account in Lilburne's words, see pp. 411-24.

[7] Document 12 and commentary, pp. 291-303 of this volume.

[8] Gardiner concludes that Lilburne misunderstood Ireton's message, adding (*Civil War,* IV, 262) that "it seems hardly possible that Ireton should have proposed to bind his brother officers to the details of a scheme on which their opinion had not been taken." Lilburne, however, is particularly emphatic on his clear understanding of Ireton's message (p. 417). Did Harrison intentionally misrepresent the tone of Ireton's message to Lilburne? Or did Ireton impulsively give the assurance Lilburne describes, then realize the untenable nature of his position? Ireton made no response to Lilburne's charge that he had agreed to accept without alteration the committee's draft of the *Agreement.*

deference to Leveller agitation; at the same time he may have
felt a greater concern than before the purge for securing the approval of his fellow-officers. Lilburne, Wildman, and Overton
were, nevertheless, admitted to the debates to defend the committee's *Agreement*. On December 14 the debate, to which Independent spokesmen were also invited, hinged on the *Agreement's* reservation of any Parliamentary power to limit freedom
of conscience. From the flood of Independent pamphlets favoring
extreme toleration in 1644-46, one would have expected no dissent with the Levellers on this crucial issue. John Goodwin, indeed, spoke positively for unlimited toleration, taking issue vigorously with Ireton himself.[9] But Nye sided with Ireton for official
restriction on liberty of conscience, Hugh Peters suggested a later
debate on the crucial issue, and Parker straddled the toleration
fence.[10] The army officers in general supported the original phrasing of the *Agreement,* with Ireton only persistently attacking it
on the basis of Old Testament precedent, which he claimed justified the active interference of the magistrate in matters of conscience. Without such a restriction, men would be free "to practice idolatry, to practice atheisme, and any thinge that is against
the light of God." [11] But Captain Clarke's opinion was far more
representative than that of Ireton: "Noe man or Magistrate on
the earth hath power to meddle in these cases. As for meum and
tuum, and right betweene man and man hee hath right, butt as betweene God and man hee hath nott." [12] Though the conference of
December 14 ended with the issue still undecided, it was later (December 21) resolved in Ireton's favor. By this time Lilburne and
his followers had withdrawn from the discussions of the officers'
Agreement, convinced that further attendance was useless. On
December 28 they wrote conciliatory protests to Fairfax entitled
A Plea For Common-Right And Freedom, deploring the officers'
position on freedom of conscience, "the tedious disputes and con-
tests" held about "things so essential unto our Freedom, as without which we account the Agreement of no vallue." The Levellers
suggested to Fairfax a debating procedure for the General Council: recognition by the chair, agreement on the number of times

9 *Clarke Papers,* II, 74, 115-18.
10 *Ibid.,* II, 100, 124 (Parker), 89-91 (Peters), 102-111 (Nye).
11 *Ibid.,* II, 98.   12 *Ibid.,* II, 95.

any person might speak, agreement on the number of officers to make up the Council, rejection of any military veto of their conclusions, the elimination of known enemies of tolerance.[13] The ideas of *A Plea* show the Leveller dissatisfaction not only with Ireton's long and frequent speeches, but also with his domination of Council membership. But the style of the address is moderate and restrained. Though the Levellers may already have despaired of gaining their ends through the chief officers, they were not yet ready to denounce them to the world.

37. The Officers Test the *Agreement*

In the tumultuous days that followed Pride's Purge, when the king's fate still hung in the balance, the officers proceeded steadily with debates on the Leveller *Agreement,* which they regarded indisputably as the foundation of the impending constitutional settlement. Meetings to discuss the *Agreement* were held on December 14, 16, 18, 21, 26, 29, January 6, 8, 10, 11, 13.[1] On January 13 the officers evidently reached agreement on all disputed points; the petition preceding the officers' *Agreement* is dated January 15, just two weeks before the king's execution. Though one hundred seventy-four officers attended one or more of the debates, fifty was a good attendance. At the crucial discussion of December 14, when Levellers and Independents were admitted, forty-two officers were present; on December 16, thirty-two; on December 21, fifty-two; on December 29, when Elizabeth Poole was questioned, fifty-six.[2] Though Lilburne apparently did not attend after December 14 (since he published the committee's *Agreement* the next day), Walwyn and Wildman [3] were present on December 18. Cromwell was present only on December 29; he engaged in none of the discussions on liberty of conscience. Significantly enough, he was present on December 15, when a committee of seven was appointed "to consider of the best ways and grounds for the speedy bringing of the King to Justice." [4]

The long, minute examination given the *Agreement* by the officers (Fairfax himself often in the chair) exemplifies the persua-

---

[13] E. 536 (22), pp. 3, 4, 5. The *Plea* is signed by Lilburne, Overton, and fourteen others, Wildman and Walwyn not included.

[1] *Clarke Papers,* II, 73-186.   [2] *Ibid.,* 270-81.
[3] *Ibid.,* II, 282.   [4] *Ibid.,* II, 132.

siveness of Leveller constitutional concepts. On this short document the officers hung their faith. When, on January 13, Erbury denounced the *Agreement* as like to prove "an Hellish thinge, and altogether tending to disagreement," adding later that "a dozen or 24 may in a short time doe the kingdome as much good as 400 that sitt in the Parliament in 7 yeares," Ireton spoke in staunch defense of the *Agreement*. Its virtue, he argued, was that it would prevent oppressions by taking away power that hitherto had been used tyrannically. Meanwhile the *Agreement* did not substitute an alternative authority; its function was "a paring off of those unnecessary advantages which power in this Kingdome formerly had, and is still apt to have, whereby itt may oppresse." [5] Not only did it take away the king's power and the Lords', but it defined and limited the power of the Commons itself. Hitherto, argued Ireton, nothing had contributed to more discord than controversy among "those severall Competitors to the Legislative power of the Kingedome, Kinge, Lords, and Commons." [6] If the *Agreement* could resolve this controversy, then it would achieve a settlement of lasting efficacy. Concurring with Ireton that the *Agreement* would effect a settlement, Sir Hardresse Waller urged the desperate need for haste. "If there bee nott neede of an Agreement now," he said, "there never was since the sons of men were uppon earth. . . . I am sure there needes somethinge to goe out from you. You promised itt in your Remonstrance. Wee are now gott into the midst of January. . . . You have lost two monthes." [7] Denying, like Ireton, that the *Agreement* was a means to give themselves power, as their detractors had charged, Harrison declared that the *Agreement* was the crystallization of their noblest aspirations: "Itt is nott an Agreement amongst men that must overcome the hearts of men; itt shall nott bee by might, nor by strength, butt by his spiritt. Now this Agreement doth seeme to mee to bee a fruite of that spiritt." [8] In their petitionary preface to the *Agreement* (p. 335), the officers call the *Agreement* "*a perpetual witness of our real intentions and utmost endeavours*

---

[5] *Ibid.*, II, 175, 177, 179.

[6] *Ibid.*, II, 179. Ireton (*Clarke Papers*, II, 171) wanted the dissolution of the Rump written into the *Agreement*. If this were done, he said, the people would be more likely to accept the new constitutional settlement. Nothing more conclusively proves Ireton's attachment to the *Agreement*.

[7] *Ibid.*, II, 181.   [8] *Ibid.*, II, 184.

for a sound and equal Settlement." Cromwell's own private thoughts about the *Agreement* are veiled in mystery; he trusted to Ireton, realizing that his forte was not the shaping of constitutions. But of the intentions of the officers who based their hopes on it there can be no reasonable doubt.

Presented to the Rump on January 20, the *Agreement* [9] lingered there unnoticed and finally perished. Of this Lilburne was suspicious. Was not the Rump the creature of the army? But the Rump was as determined a body of men as ever sat at Westminster; and their failure to act on the *Agreement* may have been the consequence more of a resolution to retain their own power than of the officers' failure to insist upon its release for the people's approval. The Rump's ratification of the *Agreement* would have been the signature to its own death warrant. For over three years the Rump was to resist every hint from Cromwell and his officers that it dissolve itself and give way to a new Parliament.

38. Attacks and Vindication

Meanwhile the pamphlets of both friends and foes of the Levellers revealed the fascination with which the image of the *Agreement* had stamped men's minds, a fascination that a year before would have seemed remote and improbable. No one realized the gains the Levellers had made more clearly than William Prynne. In his remarkable speech of December 5, only the day before Pride's purge, Prynne contrasted the Commons' condemnations of the *Agreement,* and the army's execution of a soldier agitator, with the army's new resolution, according to the Remonstrance, to settle upon the country the constitution they had formerly condemned. To the Levellers Prynne correctly traced the agitation against the king that had now crystallized in the army's determination to bring him to judgment. The radicals Prynne attempted to link with the Papists, calling their *Agreement* "this Stratagem of the Jesuits to blow up this and future Parliaments." [1] On December 21, less than a week after *Foundations of Freedom* appeared, an anonymous author sent forth *No Papist nor Presbyterian,*[2] a memorable pamphlet approving the new constitution

[9] Document 16 and commentary, pp. 331-54 of this volume.

[1] *Old Parliamentary History*, XVIII, 436-37.

[2] Document 13 and commentary, pp. 303-10 of this volume. On December 19 John Vernon supported the Leveller tolerationist stand in *The Swords Abuse Asserted* (E. 477, 3).

and recommending toleration of the Catholics as one of its chief
tenets. Working independently of the Levellers, though sympathetic with their program, Lieut. Col. John Jubbes published on
December 22 *Several Proposals For Peace & Freedom by an Agreement of the People,*[3] a manifesto rich in felicitous phrasing and
ideological pertinence. On December 26 William Ashurst answered *Foundations of Freedom* with his *Reasons Against Agreement with a late Printed Paper.*[4] Even Popery itself, asserted
Ashurst, was allowable by the *Agreement*; no such dangerous
document would be acceptable to soldiers and ministers, much
less to peers and king.

In January and early February pamphlets abounded with propaganda that one year before could have been found only in Leveller tracts; and the conservatives, both Independent and Presbyterian, had cause for their cries of alarm. On January 1 the officers
sent forth *A New-Years Gift,* a proclamation addressed not to
Parliament but to the nation, announcing their support of *Agreement* principles.[5] On January 2 John Goodwin published his
Right and Might well met, justifying the army's course of action
with Prynne's former democratic pronouncements and the dubious logic of necessity.[6] On January 5 the House asked Fairfax
to proceed against "scandalous and unlicensed Pamphlets." [7] The
king was now the target of Independent abuse. "Hath not the
King beene a corrupt fountaine, poisoning every stream and rivo-
let he hath had access to?" asked John Redingstone, in *Plain
English* (January 12).[8] In less violent terms *The Peoples Right
Briefly Asserted* (January 15) [9] repeated Redingstone's thesis, bas-
ing its contentions on the democratic principle, as did the officers
in presenting their *Agreement* on January 20. Warned by the
ordinance of January 5, the Levellers on January 18 issued their
petition for freedom of the press.[10] On January 27 appeared a
royalist condemnation of the *Agreement,* declaring it sinful for
any subject to agree to alter the established government.[11] After

---

[3] Document 14 and commentary, pp. 311-12 of this volume.
[4] E. 536 (4).　　　　　　[5] E. 536 (24).　　　　　　[6] E. 536 (28).
[7] Rushworth, VII, 1384.　　　　[8] E. 538 (4).　　　　[9] E. 538 (13).
[10] Document 15 and commentary, pp. 322-30.
[11] *An Appendix to the Agreement for the People,* E. 540 (10). On February 16
sixty-three Essex ministers signed a petition against the *Agreement* (E. 546, 11).
On March 6 fifty-four Lancashire ministers presented a similar petition (E. 546,

the execution of the king on the 30th, presses turned more fiercely than ever, rushing forth pamphlets for and against the democratic ideas now crystallized in justifications of revolution. On February 5 John Warr published his philosophical *The Privliedges* [sic] *Of The People*, defining liberty as the gradual and fearless extension of man's innate reason and righteousness, and deploring the intellectual corruption that has hampered the full social fruition of man's best self.[12] On February 7, replying to the attacks of William Ashurst, William Cockayne defended *Agreement* principles in his *Foundations Of Freedome* [sic] *Vindicated*.[13] A week later, on February 13, appeared Milton's *The Tenure of Kings and Magistrates*, a tract filled with the democratic assumptions that the Levellers had propounded two years before in *Regall Tyrannie*.[14]

39. By the Might of a Few: A King Falls

In the critical days of the king's trial preceding January 27, 1649, when Charles' death warrant was finally signed by sixty-seven judges, Cromwell had been busy steeling the nerves of the hesitant. As for himself, he had fully resolved all his doubts, those doubts about bringing the king to judgment that only a short twelve months before had brought upon him the condemnation of the Leveller faction of his army. On January 30, amid the anguished hush of the onlookers, Charles ascended the scaffold with superb dignity and inflexible courage. After laying his head upon the block, and speaking a last prayer, he gave the signal for the ax to strike. The blade flashed and fell. A moan, a rumble of horror and fierce resentment rose from the throng around the scaffold. Thus perished, according to the death warrant, "a tyrant, traitor, murderer, and public enemy to the good people of this nation." [1] He had been charged "in the behalf of the Commons of England assembled in Parliament and the good people of England." [2] But how many of England's good people wanted Charles' blood? "It is a lie," Lady Fairfax had cried out, from the gallery

27), complaining that the *Agreement* would turn the people into "an Anarchy, or jumbled multitude . . . without distinction or order."

[12] E. 541 (12).   [13] E. 541 (25).
[14] Cf. *Milton in the Puritan Revolution*, pp. 209-19.
[1] Gardiner, *Civil War*, IV, 308.   [2] *Ibid.*, IV, 300.

of the courtroom; "not half, nor a quarter of the people of England. Oliver Cromwell is a traitor." [3]

The execution of Charles and the abolition of kingship, we must grant with Lady Fairfax, were carried out in defiance of even middle-class public opinion. They were the acts of a fanatical minority of Independents. Ideologically, however, the trial of Charles and the abolition of kingship were the product of Leveller propaganda. The Levellers had been the first, in their *Remonstrance Of Many Thousand Citizens,* to attack kingship as an institution. "The continuall Oppressours of the Nation, have been Kings . . . none but a King could doe so great intollerable mischiefes." [4] The Commons should show the people "the intollerable inconyeniences of having a *Kingly Government";* [5] it should declare Charles an enemy of the state. In their agitation of 1647 the Levellers had driven this lesson fiercely home; they had flooded the army with their propaganda, derided Cromwell for his negotiations with Charles. In *Putney Projects* John Wildman had laid bare the false position of fighting a king in the name of a king. The king "arrogates to himself," said Wildman, "a superiority to all lawes, and an exemption from all the censures and penalties which are the strength, vigour, and life of the lawes." [6] Not the people, but the king, according to his claim, was the original of all law and the creator of all privileges, tenures, lordships. Against these propositions the soldiers, said Wildman, had fought many battles. Gradually the theses of Wildman's analysis had become accepted, not only by the common soldiers and the radical officers, but by Ireton himself. In its attack on kingship the *Remonstrance* of November, 1648, reads like a Leveller manifesto.

By the might of the army the Independents had now transformed into reality constitutional measures long advocated by their teachers, the Levellers. On January 30, returning to their labors after the execution of Charles, the Commons passed for the third time "an Act for prohibiting the proclaiming of any Person to be King of *England, Ireland,* or the Dominions thereof." [7] On February 6 the House voted "That the House of Peers in Parliament is useless and dangerous, and ought to be abolished; and that

---

[3] Gardiner, *Civil War,* IV, 300.   [4] P. 5.
[5] P. 6. The author calls kings the "originall of all Oppressions."
[6] P. 19.   [7] *Old Parliamentary History,* XVIII, 546.

an Act be brought in to that purpose." [8] On occasions the Levellers had been harshly treated for petitioning the House as the "supreme Authority." But already, on January 4, the House had voted itself this dubious power and declared the original of all power to be the people themselves. On February 13 John Milton, soon to be nominated the pamphleteering spokesman of the new republic, justified in *The Tenure* the execution of Charles with expressions of democratic principles anticipated almost wholly in Leveller pamphlets of the past three years. The Independents had even adopted in part the Leveller *Agreement,* recommending its first principles as the basis of England's new government.

40. The Levellers: "Liberty in Name Only"

But the Levellers were not satisfied. The name of liberty they had gained, but not, they thought, its substance. "The change be onely Notionall, Nominall, Circumstantiall," they afterward wrote, "whilst the reall Burdens, Grievances, and Bondages, be continued, even when the Monarchy is changed into a Republike." The first Leveller protest against the Commons, as we have seen, was the Petition of January 18 on restrictions of the press; their second, which appeared February 26, was *Englands New Chains Discovered.* After analyzing the differences between the officers' *Agreement* and their own, the Levellers enumerate their further dissatisfactions with the Independent regime. The Commons have not redressed any economic grievances: removed tithes or excise, abolished monopolies or patents, lightened the prison burdens of honest debtors, reformed the courts and cut down legal fees, reduced the allowances of army officers, abolished or reduced freequarter. Moreover, the House has caused to be erected a special court in which the right of trial by jury is repudiated and ordinary legal privileges overruled; this is a "practise whereof we cannot allow of, though against open and notorious enemies." Such a special court might easily be turned tomorrow against the friends of freedom. Then, too, the Commons have passed an act for conscripting seamen, a measure contradictory to the *Agreement* submitted by the officers; they have imposed a censorship "to gag us from speaking truth, and discovering the tyrannies of bad men";

[8] *Ibid.,* XVIII, 553.

they have treated petitioners with anger and contempt; they have forbidden common soldiers to petition the House. Finally, the House has erected a Council of State possessed with extraordinary powers. In this Council, warns Lilburne, lie the seeds of tyranny.[9] He closes with a series of admonitions, repeating the persistent Leveller demands of the Petition of September 11.

The publication of *Englands New Chains Discovered* marks the beginning of the final break between Leveller and Independent. In 1647, after long debates and much pamphleteering, the Levellers had apparently won no concessions from the army leaders. But by the autumn of 1648 the Independents found themselves ready to cooperate with the Levellers in the formation of the new constitution. In a year's time they had gained new respect for Leveller ideas. Left-wing Independents, like Marten and Ludlow, were sympathetic with Leveller aims, but in the Commons right-wing Independents predominated, as in the army. Once in power the Independents turned more and more to the leadership of Cromwell, who had never really understood and sympathized with the democratic aspirations of Lilburne, Overton, and Walwyn. In the shadow of a military dictatorship, the new government leaned inevitably upon repressive measures, grew daily less sympathetic with the radical ideology that had helped them gain power.

41. Propaganda Sallies Against the Republic

With each passing week the Levellers watched the Independents warily and uneasily, unwilling to voice either their most sanguine hopes for reform or most bitter fears of onrushing tyranny. Without the might of Independent swords the Levellers knew they could accomplish nothing. In their last discussion with the army leaders Overton had prophetically pointed to the crisis faced by the two revolutionary parties: "God hath made you instruments of libertie. In matters of Religion that's preferr'd by us

[9] On February 26 Lilburne appeared with a number of followers at the Commons, requested and received permission to speak to the House. Fearing that they should be prevented from securing subscriptions, said Lilburne, and *"so be frustrated in that benefit or relief that we justly expect from you,"* the Levellers had resolved to present it to the House and publicly acknowledge *Englands New Chains Discovered* as their own. Lilburne's brief address to the Commons is printed at the end of this pamphlet. Commons' *Journals,* VI, 151.

before life . . . If you cannott agree uppon itt, then I shall conclude for my parte, never to expect freedome whiles I live." [1]
Hence the long delay of the Levellers in breaking their tenuous
bonds with the "Grandees." But every day saw the Independent
republic more firmly entrenched, and Leveller power declining.
The Levellers' old associates among the parties of the left, whether
from fear or conviction, hastened to support the new order. Many
common soldiers, it is true, and a few officers were still as suspicious as the Levellers of Cromwell's intentions. But in the House
only Marten, Scott, and Ludlow could be considered sympathetic
to the Leveller program; the body of the Rump Independents
gagged at the thought of the Leveller *Agreement*. Long since, as
early as March, 1647, the Independent congregations of London
had begun to disassociate themselves from Leveller petitions.
Even leading members of the Baptist churches, where Lilburne,
Overton, and many other Levellers had learned their first tolerationist radicalism, were preparing to take their stand with the
right-wing Independents. From all these groups the Levellers had
elicited support, reluctant, enthusiastic, or half-hearted. But now
that the Independents were safely in control of government revenues and offices, they secured many defections from the left, even
of the brilliant Leveller, John Wildman.

Recognizing these formidable weights in the balance, and seeing their old suspicions daily confirmed, the Levellers were preparing a revolutionary attack on the new republic, using the army
as the spearhead. True to their propaganda habits, they plied at
once weapons of conciliation and muckraking exposure. By mid-
February they had begun to agitate in the army for the election
of new agents and the formation of a new General Council.[2] On
February 22 a soldier petition to Fairfax inspired a fiery attack
on the Levellers in the Council of Officers, Hewson saying, *"We
have had tryal enough of Civil Courts, we can hang 20. before they
will hang one."* [3] The Council of Officers were resolved to halt
army propaganda by civilians; they directed Cromwell and Ireton
to ask Parliament to pass the necessary measure.[4] *Englands New
Chains* on February 26 was the Levellers' last conciliatory appeal;
they still withheld their heaviest fire against Cromwell and Ireton.

[1] *Clarke Papers*, II, 92.   [2] Gardiner, *Commonwealth and Protectorate*, I, 34.
[3] *Hunting of the Foxes*, p. 368 of this volume.   [4] *Clarke Papers*, II, p. 192.

In the army fiery spirits were meanwhile at work. On March 1 eight troopers laid a manifesto before Fairfax, declaring their share in the authorship of *Englands New Chains,* denouncing the High Court of Justice, the Council of State, and restrictions on the common soldiers' right of petition. "We are English Soul-diers," asserted Ward and his fellows, "engaged for the Freedoms of *England;* and not outlandish mercenaries, to butcher the people for pay . . . It hath been a principle by you asserted and avowed, that our being Souldiers hath not deprived us of our Right as Com-moners, and to Petition the people in Parliament, we do account in the number of our Birthrights." [5] For this bold pronounce-ment the soldiers were brought before a court-martial and five of them sentenced to dishonorable dismissal. On March 6 the soldiers were required to mount their horses with their faces tailward, and their swords were broken over their heads in token of military disgrace. On March 21 Richard Overton [6] spoke for the army mal-contents in *The Hunting of the Foxes,* one of the most incisive, illuminating tracts of the civil war period. No Leveller tract more clearly outlines the failure of Cromwell's army to fuse military discipline and democratic citizenship. The troopers unqualifiedly condemned the officers and their whole new order. "Are they not above the Parliament?" they asked. "They have even a Negative Voice thereover . . . We were before ruled by King, Lords, and Commons; now by a General, a Court Martial, and House of Commons; and we pray you what is the difference?" [7]

With the publication of *The second Part of Englands New Chaines* [8] (March 24), the Levellers again dramatized their utter disillusionment with the Independent leaders. For the second time in three days the radicals opened their biased conception of the history of Independent political strategy, painting their ene-mies as knaves and hypocrites, holding up the discrepancies be-tween army declarations and officer tactics. The truth was, of course, that the declarations of the army, quoted constantly by the Levellers, represented largely the sentiments of the soldiers,

[5] *Hunting of the Foxes,* pp. 372-73.

[6] The bold satirical style, the striking metaphors and similes, the logical para-graphing, the penetrating intellectual thrusts all point to Overton's authorship.

[7] *Hunting of the Foxes,* p. 371.

[8] The whole pamphlet is reprinted in my *Milton in the Puritan Revolution,* pp. 399-415.

not those of the officers; they had been drawn up in the main by Ireton in moments of crisis, with mutinies impending, with the common soldiers roused and organized by the Levellers to a pitch of desperate resolution. No one could deny, however, that the officers had assented to the declarations; the Levellers' propaganda centered endlessly on the officers' renunciation of their declared political positions. "They have already lost the affections of all People," charged the authors of *The second Part*, "and are onely supported by *their present strength*" to advance "a few lofty and imperious mens *designes*." [9] The chief specific charges against the Independents were as follows:

1. They had engaged in repeated intercourse with the king, even submitting constitutional proposals for him to ratify and change.
2. They had violated the Engagement by bringing into the General Council officers not selected to sit, thus overpowering the representatives of the common soldiers.
3. The officers had very much opposed the *Agreement* of November, 1647.
4. After securing the king, they had turned against those favoring the *Agreement,* shooting one soldier to death, and arresting Col. Rainsborough, Major Scott, Col. Ayres, Major Cobbett, and Captain Bray for speaking on behalf of the *Agreement*.
5. They had removed Rainsborough from his position in the army, fearing his opposition, and allowed him only a titular command at sea. They had sent Rainsborough to the dangerous service at Pomfret, where he was killed, and whither he had been unwilling and reluctant to go.
6. They had threatened soldiers who had petitioned that Major Reynolds might serve as the successor to Major Huntington.
7. They had rejected Major White as the candidate for the lieutenant-colonelcy, notwithstanding White's notable services against the Scots, in which engagements he had acted as both major and lieutenant-colonel.
8. Notwithstanding their hatred of the Levellers, they had

9 *Milton in the Puritan Revolution*, pp. 410-11.

sought an alliance with them in order to gain power; urging their followers to support the petition of September 11, 1648, as the basis of an *Agreement of the People*.

9. Their abolition of king and Lords, declaration of the supreme power inherent in the people, setting up of the high court of justice and council of state—all were only means to gain power.

10. They had set up a strict censorship of the press.

11. They had rebuked a member of the House for his religious opinions, thus setting at naught their professions of toleration.

12. They had forced worthy soldiers to ride their horses with their faces turned backward in token of disgrace, and dismissed them dishonorably, all for the act of petitioning.

13. They have at various times substituted martial law for civil justice.

14. They are driving toward one aim: a dictatorship of a single person.

Filled with such bitter accusations, provocative of mutiny and disorder, *The second Part* struck at the very existence of the new government. The Independents had no choice but to resolve the dispute by suppression. On March 24 the Rump declared the pamphlet contained "much false, scandalous, and reproachful Matter." Further, it was "highly seditious . . . destructive to the present Government . . . tended to Division and Mutiny in the Army." The authors they declared "guilty of High Treason, and should be proceeded against as Traitors." [10]

42. Four Leaders under Arrest

Accordingly, on March 28, between four and six in the morning, troops of horse and foot surrounded the homes of Lilburne, Walwyn, Prince, and Overton, roused them roughly from their beds, and carried them off to Whitehall, there to await questioning by the Council of State. The story of their arrest and subsequent examination is told vividly by Lilburne, Prince, and Over-

[10] *Old Parliamentary History*, XIX, 91.

ton, in *The Picture of The Councel of State,* published only six days later. The dramatic situation was ideal for propagandistic effect, and the Levellers promptly identified the principle of political justice with their own sufferings at the hands of the Grandees. Each of the four men refused to answer interrogatories that would have incriminated himself; of the four men Walwyn was the least aggressive, Lilburne and Overton the most defiant and voluble, denying the legality of both the Rump and the Council of State. Lilburne was permitted to make a long speech pointing out that it was not in the power of Parliament to execute the laws, denying the power of the Council to imprison him in a military prison, and threatening to burn the very military prison they should consign him to. Looking fixedly at Cromwell, Lilburne said, *"I* must be plain with you, *I* have not found so much Honour, Honesty, Justice, or Conscience, in any of the principal Officers of the Army, as to trust my life under their protection, or think it can be safe under their immediate fingers." [11] After Overton, Prince, and Walwyn had been questioned, Lilburne put his ear to the door of the chamber: "I . . . heard *Lieutenant General Cromwel* (I am sure of it) very loud, thumping his fist upon the *Councel Table,* til it rang againe, and heard him speak in these very words, or to this effect; *I tel you Sir, you have no other Way to deale with these men, but to break them in pieces*; and thumping upon the *Councel Table* againe, he said Sir, *let me tel you that which is true, if you do not breake them, they will break you; yea, and bring all the guilt of the blood and treasure shed and spent in this Kingdom upon your heads and shoulders; and frustrate and make voide all that worke, that with so many yeares industry, toile and paines you have done, and so render you to all rationall men in the world, as the most contemptiblest generation, of silly, low spirited men in the earth."* [12] Despite any exaggeration these lines may contain, they are too authentically Cromwellian to be discounted, reflecting, as they do, Cromwell's known attitude toward the Levellers both before and after this incident. Little as he understood the far-reaching significance of Leveller ideology, Cromwell's analysis of the play of forces was seldom wanting. For almost two years he had been forced into an awareness of the power of Leveller propaganda over the minds of his

11 *The Picture,* p. 13.   12 *The Picture,* pp. 14-15.

soldiers. Now he sensed that imminence of danger that unfailingly aroused him to action, a danger this time to the new government, frankly upheld by force against the will of most Englishmen. There sat Ludlow, moreover, a doubtful follower, recommending bail for the four Levellers. Cromwell's only recourse was a measure he used reluctantly but repeatedly, the blunt action of repression. His will swayed the Council, and the four Levellers were ordered imprisoned. No sign of Independent strategy more clearly illuminates the fundamental respect with which Cromwell and the new government held Leveller opposition.

Though confined in the tower the next day, Overton, Prince, and Lilburne immediately began composition of their testimony, sent it to friendly printers. Successfully eluding the military censorship, the printers sent forth *The Picture* six days later. Meanwhile, the four leaders had been visited by the Baptist preacher Richardson, who tried to sway them to a more conciliatory attitude toward the new regime. The four Levellers in turn appealed to Richardson's conscience not to desert the cause to which he had formerly shown himself sympathetic. Finally, "to let him know (as one we judged honest, and our friend) we were men of reason, moderation, . . . sought nothing particularly for ourselves," [13] Lilburne and his followers offered to end all opposition if the Independents would press their *Agreement of the People,* changing it according to Leveller stipulations. Or, said they, if this seemed unreasonable, let their differences be resolved by debate and arbitration: "If they judge our exceptions against their Agreement (or any one of them) irrational, let them chuse any 4. men in England, and let *Cromwel and Ireton be* 2. *of them,* and take the other 2. where they please, in the whole nation, and we 4. now in prison, will argue the case in reason with them, and if we can agree, there is an end, as to us, and all our interest, but in case we cannot, let them (said we all) chuse any 2. members of the House of Commons, and we will chuse 2. more, *viz.* Col. *Alex. Rigby,* and Col. *Henry Martin,* to be final umpires betwixt us, and what they, or the major part of them determine, as to us (in relation to an *Agreement*) and all our interest in the whole land, we will acquiesce in, be content with, and stand to without wavering: and

[13] *The Picture,* p. 21.

this we conceive to be as rational, just, and fair, as can be offered by any men upon earth: and I for my part, say and protest before the Almighty, I will yet stand to this, and if this will content them, I have done." [14]

43. Crest of a Movement: The Third *Agreement*

From their prison cells the four Leveller leaders now sent forth the summation of their constitutional strivings, the third *Agreement Of The People* (May 1, 1649).[1] A synthesis of the original *Agreement* principles and the leading ideas of their great petitions, this document represented to the radicals the ultimate scope of their political aims, the highest reach of their social aspirations, their most mature analyses of the critical issues of the Civil War, issues now only temporarily resolved, they thought, in the harsh pressures of a military tyranny.

In sending forth the third *Agreement,* the Levellers really brought to a conclusion the growth and development of their constitutional ideas. Their energies henceforth they directed either to denunciations of the new regime or to repetitions of their *Agreement* principles. On July 17 Lilburne urged his comrades in every county to choose two agents and send them to London to confer upon a constitutional settlement by the *Agreement*.[2] By this time Lilburne was willing to throw his strength to Prince Charles if Charles would make a compact with the people according to *Agreement* principles.[3] On September 21 the Levellers presented another *Remonstance Of many Thousands of the Free-People of England,* recapitulating the demands of the three great petitions and the third *Agreement,* but extending in no significant particular their basic concepts. If the *Remonstrance* was signed, as the authors declare, by 98,064 hands, the Levellers had stirred an immense popular response, their agitation enhanced, of course, by prevalent resentment against the new republic.[4] In an ideological sense, however, the movement had come to fruition in the preceding May.

14 *The Picture,* p. 22.

1 Document 19 and commentary, pp. 397-410 of this volume.

2 *An Impeachment,* p. 7.

3 *Ibid.,* p. 8. The prince may be supported, says Lilburne, "a thousand times more justly" than the military dictatorship of the Independents.

4 E. 574 (15).

44. Mutiny and Repression

Against men of few economic resources, such as the Levellers represented, the tactics of repression were certain to be immediately efficacious. Resourceful as always, however, the radicals were able, in the days preceding and following publication of the *Agreement,* to evoke violent agitation among their followers both in London and the army. On April 18 a petition signed by ten thousand hands had demanded the release of Lilburne, Walwyn, Prince, and Overton. "We are perswaded in our Consciences" wrote the petitioners, "the greatest crime . . . for which they are thus molested is, *That they have uncessantly* [sic] *endeavoured to induce the Army to the real performance of those many good things they engaged for . . . And . . . to reduce the Military power to a real subordination to the Civil Authority."* [1] Disregarding the House's rebuke of the "scandalous and seditious Suggestions" of their husbands, Leveller wives then presented a sharp petition of their own, only to be told that the business was "of an higher Concernment than they understood." The House desired them to tend to their own affairs, and "meddle with their Housewifery." [2] On April 25 the radicals scattered abroad on the streets an inflammatory appeal to officers and soldiers, charging that the highest officers were committing treason in establishing their ascendancy over the Parliament, the Council of State, and all the men of the army. The fiery exhortation concluded with an appeal to elect agitators again and form a representive Council, or face a perpetual bondage.[3]

The execution of Robert Lockyer on April 27 crystallized anew the desperation of the Levellers and the resolution of Cromwell and Ireton to meet resistance with suppression. On April 24 thirty of the men in Captain Savage's troop refused, in a dispute over pay, to march to a rendezvous at Mile End Green. Obdurate against all argument until Fairfax and Cromwell appeared at their quarters next morning, the thirty men reluctantly submitted. On the 26th six of them were sentenced to death by a court-martial sitting at Whitehall. Upon Crom-

---

[1] Thomason broadside 669 f. 14 (27), April 17, 1649.
[2] *Old Parliamentary History,* XIX, 107.
[3] E. 551 (21). A single small sheet without title or date, marked by Thomason "A Libbell."

well's plea, five of the six were pardoned; Robert Lockyer alone on April 27 [4] was marched before the squad of execution. A young veteran of the loftiest motives, his mind attuned to the extreme democratic idealism of army Levellers, Lockyer died with the fearless zeal of a martyr, in his last moments admonishing the firing squad for obeying the murderous commands of their officers. His funeral on the 29th was the occasion of a solemn demonstration. The hero's riderless horse advanced before the body. Thousands of silent men and women wearing black and sea-green marched behind the coffin, on which, beneath Lockyer's sword, lay sprigs of rosemary stained with blood. In all the procession there was no outcry, no grim threat, no sound save for marching feet and the call of soldiers' trumpets.[5]

The unhappy prospect of invading Ireland or retiring from the army (with no grievances redressed), coupled with the inflammatory appeals of their leaders, now provoked the military Levellers to serious mutiny. On May 2 all but two troops of the regiments of Scropes and Ireton refused to march farther toward Ireland until their political demands had been satisfied. On May 6 William Thompson, agitating without leave in his old regiment, led away several troops of fiery spirits and issued a denunciation of the new regime.[6] The next day, May 7, *The Moderate Intelligencer* reported that "Here comes news that some of the horse in the West are still in discontent, and will not endure that L. Col. *Lilburn* and those with him, remain in prison, nor that things goe on as they doe, but will have the agreement of the people goe forward." [7] By May 11 the forces

[4] On April 27, probably after Lockyer's execution, Lilburne and Overton addressed a letter to Fairfax, denouncing the use of court-martial in time of peace, and pleading for the lives of the six men. Even, as appears doubtful, Fairfax even glanced at this appeal before the fatal volleys, it would have had not the slightest effect. Though much more trusted than Cromwell by the Levellers, Fairfax was less inclined the leniency than Cromwell in all such decisions. *The Copie of a Letter* (669 f. 14, 23), dated by Lilburne and Overton April 27.

[5] Gardiner, *Commonwealth and Protectorate*, I, 52.

[6] *Ibid.*, I, 54; *The Levellers Remonstrance* (E. 555, 2).

[7] E. 555 (3). On May 9 the four leaders were forbidden visitors except families and servants; on May 12 they were placed in separate cells and forbidden all intercourse, the authorities evidently considering their agitation the prime instigation of the growing mutiny. Commons' *Journals*, 205, 208. An apprentice petition for the four leaders (669 f. 14, 8), which appeared in May 9, was attacked by apprentices hostile to the Levellers on May 15 (*The Resolved Apprentices*, 669 f. 14, 32). Another apprentice broadside in May championed the four leaders again (*To The Supreme Authority*, 669 f. 14, 31).

of the mutineers had increased to six hundred men; by May 14 to twelve hundred. On the 12th, when Cromwell addressed his men near Andover, saying that *"as he had often engaged with them against the common Enemy of this Nation, so was he resolved still to persist therein, against those Revolters . . . called . . . Levellers,"* many of the men were openly rebellious at the prospect of tracking down their former comrades.[8] The persuasions of martial discipline, however, overwhelmed all sentiment. Shortly after midnight on the 14th, Cromwell and his men surprised and routed the Leveller forces near Burford. On the 17th, after dogged resistance against odds, William Thompson was shot to death, and the mutiny was at an end.

45. In the Time-Stream of History

If it is true, as Charles Beard writes, that "history is the interplay of *ideas* and *interests* in the time-stream," the Leveller movement derives its essential significance from its promulgation of ideas, and not from the pressure of its interests. The economic disadvantages of the lower middle class, from which sprang the large body of Leveller followers, cannot of course be disassociated from the urgent cries of their petitions or the demands of their manifestoes. Nor can the superiority of their economic status to roughly one-half of England's population, whose only brilliant spokesman was Gerrard Winstanley, be considered a remote irrelevance in their effectual disregard of Winstanley's premises. Nevertheless, the ideas of the Levellers were destructive to the dominant economic and political interests of their day, to the landed Anglicans, the Presbyterian business men, the Independent intellectuals. Against these interests they struggled mightily, upheld by the energy of fanaticism, heedless of retaliation, family disasters, imprisonment, military coercion, court-martial executions.

[8] *The Declaration of Lieutenant-Generall Crumwel Concerning the Levellers* (E. 555, 12). On August 29, in *An Outcry of the Youngmen and Apprentices of London*, ten Leveller agents directed an appeal to the private soldiers ("more especially") who helped to defeat their comrades at Burford. *An Outcry* vehemently attacks the officers and urges the common soldiers to support the *Agreement* in cooperation with the Levellers of London. The ten agents announce their hope "to methodize all our honest fellow Prentises, in all the Wards of *London*, and the out-Parishes, *to chuse out their Agents to joyn with us or ours:* to write Exhortative Epistles, to all the *honest hearted freemen* of England, in all the particular Countries thereof, to erect severall *Councells amongst themselves.*"

The unique intellectual circumstances of the Puritan Revolution, together with the inexhaustible vitality of the printing press, account in part for the dramatic but short-lived victories of the Leveller faction. The whole impetus of the Reformation, carried to full tide in 1642-49, was ideological rather than ceremonial. In reading the Bible, every literate Puritan grappled with ideas, wove them with burning assurance into the fabric of his mind, his spirit sustained by the fervor of an explorer standing at the gateway of a new land. In the Puritan's psychology the transition from religious to political ideas required no uncertain gropings; his intellectual test was Biblical, his practical test the hard anvil of application. To the Puritan an idea was often so explosively real, so impregnated with religious responsibility, that he could not evade its consequence, were it contempt, a cell, a pillory, a scaffold. Often humorless and intolerant, he could not comprehend a Montaigne's amused skepticism, a Hobbes' cynicism, a Bacon's cold detachment. Once released from rigid Calvinism, such a mind was fertile seed ground for the growth of Leveller notions. The new pamphlet magic, now for the first time fully exploited, found its way into every literate home; as never before in any land, the printing press magnified a thousand fold the persuasion of ideas. Milton pictured the English "sitting by their studious lamps, musing, searching, revolving new notions and ideas wherewith to present, as with their homage and their fealty, the approaching reformation: others as fast reading, trying all things, assenting to the force of reason and convincement." [1] Samuel Hartlib, too, saw the infinite power of the press: "The art of printing will so spread knowledge, that the common people, knowing their own rights and liberties, will not be governed by way of oppression; and so, by littlle and little, all kingdoms will be like Macaria." [2] Possessing limitless confidence in the persuasion of the written word, the Leveller exploited the power of propaganda more imaginatively and extensively than any pamphleteers of their generation.

Shaped by an era of fluid intellectual strivings, the Leveller leaders possessed peculiar talents for the scattering of ideas in relentless contempt for safety and security and the forces arrayed

[1] *Areopagitica, Prose Works*, II, 91-92.
[2] *A Description of the famous Kingdom of Macaria*, 1641, in *Harleian Miscellany*, I, 584.

against them. In Lilburne's personality a fanatical courage and mystical faith were blended with endless energy, ready speech, boundless self-assurance; he constantly identified and dramatized himself as the spokesman of true liberty and victim of unnatural tyranny. Less pre-occupied with documents than Lilburne, more subtle and flexible in thought and style, gifted with a rare sense of humor and satire, Overton was also fiercely courageous, a man heedless of family sufferings, infinitely zealous, undaunted by disaster. Genial, tolerant, conciliatory, less combative and extreme in opposition than his friends, Walwyn was in some respects the most mature and seasoned theoretician, but older than they, less energetic, more prosperous. Of the three men, Lilburne came to his democratic convictions slowly and laboriously, Walwyn and Overton apparently in easy leaps, each of them fitted intellectually and temperamentally to the adoption of extreme positions.

If the Leveller leaders anticipated the shaping of American constitutional patterns, they also delineated with arresting skill and comprehensiveness the foundational ideology of the democratic impetus. In spite of the hostile pressure of interests, the pay and position of officers, the prestige of kingship, the power of the rich and able among Independents and Presbyterians, they did not for a moment doubt the ultimate triumph of their concepts. Their primary principle was a belief in the inevitable, ultimately resistless power of ideas, of man's response to reason and persuasion. In extending this principle to military, political, and religious organization, the Levellers traced the thought patterns of three centuries of their successors, among them Jefferson, Paine, Lincoln, Whitman, Emerson, Bellamy, George, Altgeld, George Norris, Steffens. If the belief in man's response to reason is irrational, together with the psychological premises that sanction it, then the Leveller ideas are a delusion destined to be dispelled with perennial inevitability.

Like all idealists of democratic persuasions, the Levellers exaggerated the power of their propaganda and failed to evaluate the strength of the tenacious forces arrayed against them. Calculating thus inaccurately, they lacked a sense of their position in the time-stream of history. On their basic principles, however, still vehemently damned and asserted, the final judgment of history is yet to be formulated.

A REMONSTRANCE OF MANY THOUSAND CITIZENS

[Richard Overton]

Appeared July 7, 1646. Reprinted from a photostat copy of the original pamphlet in the McAlpin Collection of Union Theological Seminary.

The imprisonment of John Lilburne and his treatment by the House of Commons were the rallying point of agitation from which evolved the principles of the *Remonstrance,* the most revolutionary tract that the Puritan Revolution had hitherto evoked. For the first time the Levellers speak confidently for the people at large, assuming a unanimity that actually did not exist between Leveller aims and the sentiment of the lower middle class, making the hero Lilburne the embodiment of surging democratic demands.

Bold and bitter denunciation not only of Charles but of kingship itself, such as appears in the *Remonstrance,* is new to Leveller propaganda, though antagonism to monarchy had appeared in earlier tracts. This bold attack may have been inspired in part by Henry Marten, most ardent king-hater among the Independents, who was a friend of the Leveller leaders and had been highly praised by Walwyn in *Englands Lamentable Slaverie.* In its bitterness toward kingship the *Remonstrance* anticipates *Regall Tyrannie,* Wildman's *Putney Projects,* and Milton's defiant republicanism. For the first time, indeed, appears the bold thesis that England would be happier without any king, an assumption that expanded with explosive power in the victorious marches of Cromwell's army and amid the frontier pressures of the American colonies. Since the Conquest, runs the argument of the *Remonstrance,* kings have been the nation's chief oppressors; indeed they have been the "originall of all Oppressions." The Civil War was the product of such actions, and "none but a King could doe so great intollerable mischiefes" as the English have suffered; yet the very name of king has proved a snare and a delusion, "as if it were impossible for any Nation to be happy without a King." In spite of these facts, after having declared his whole reign to be "one continued act of the breach of the Law," the Commons still acknowledges Charles as its rightful sovereign, begging him to return, instead of declaring him an enemy and confiscating his property and revenues.

As the king's power must be destroyed, so must that of his creatures, the Lords, who in no way represent the will of the people. Power is really lodged in the Commons; yet the Commons sends its bills to the Lords "to importune their assent." Such action is "a most gross absurditie"; the Lords either have or have not a negative voice, and the Commons should declare their constitutional status. Meanwhile the Lords, "thrust upon us by *Kings*," and even freed by their titles from equal responsibility before the law, imprison commoners at will upon their own authority. Such tyranny cannot be endured; its prevention in the future must be certain and sure. The Commons must make "a Law against all kinds of *Arbitrary Government,* as the highest capitall offence against the *Common-wealth*." No one then can have an excuse for tyranny, the law being plain before him. This suggestion of constitutional guarantees and the hint that the Commons itself has been tyrannical foreshadows, like other statements we have noted, the Leveller appeal from the Commons to the army and the crystallization of their *Agreement* principles.

Through the *Remonstrance* runs the assumption of the Commons' accountability to the people, with the Leveller authors acting as spokesmen of the people and therefore legitimate judges of the Commons' conduct of the political war. Not content, then, with nullifying of the power of king and Lords, and the assurance of a protective law against all arbitrary proceedings, the authors of the *Remonstrance* name the specific grievances that must be redressed, thus anticipating the platforms of their famous petitions. Men must not be forced to answer interrogatories against themselves. The presses, now free only to the Presbyterians, must be open to all. No one must be questioned about his religious convictions; not even the Commons, indeed, has any right to "conclude the People in matters that concerne the Worship of God." (It is notable on this point that the Levellers do not even except the hated Papists.) Imprisonment for debt must be abolished, and the conscription of soldiers and sailors, a biting tyranny indeed, must be obliterated. Merchant monopolies must be destroyed, and the oppressive customs. The poor must be succored with open hand: *"Yee are Rich, and abound in goods, and have need of nothing; but the afflictions of the poore; your hunger-starved brethren, ye have no compassion of."* Finally, the Commons should set times and places for the annual elections of Parliament members, no writs or summons to be issued. If this is done, "then Wee shall not doubt to be made absolute *Free-men* in time, and become a just, plenteous and Powerfull Nation."

Undoubtedly the *Remonstrance* was written in the main by Richard Overton, whose satirical tone, orderly thought development, and styptic phrasing are particularly evident in the first thirteen pages. The style and loose arrangement of thought in the last seven pages, however, show traces of Walwyn's hand. As I have pointed out elsewhere, the *Remonstrance's* characterization of Magna Charta as "but a beggerly thing" is more characteristic of Walwyn than Overton, who a few months later inserted praise of Magna Charta in *An Arrow Against All Tyrants.* Moreover, emphasis on relief of the poor and imprisonment for debt is far more typical of Walwyn than Overton. The analysis of the Presbyterians as preferring kingship and Lords to the extension of their principles to logical democratic ends appears, so far as I know, nowhere else in Leveller tracts. Of the three Leveller leaders Overton had written most fully and comprehendingly of Presbyterian psychology, but of their economic and political grand strategy nothing at all. I assume, therefore, that there was collaboration in ideas among Overton, Marten, and Walwyn, with Overton as the most versatile stylist taking the lead in the actual composition, and Walwyn adding passages to Overton's manuscript.[1]

[1] Pease (*The Leveller Movement,* p. 153) suggests that Marten may have been the author of the *Remonstrance.* The passages in the tract that do not instantly suggest Overton are those in italics on pp. 119-20, and parts of pp. 124-30. If Marten supplied phrases as well as ideas, I believe they are found on pp. 118, 119, and 120, the analysis of Presbyterian strategy.

A
REMONSTRANCE

OF

Many Thousand Citizens, and other Free-born

PEOPLE of ENGLAND,

To their owne House of

COMMONS.

Occasioned through the Illegall and Barbarous Imprisonment
of that Famous and Worthy Sufferer for his Countries
Freedoms, Lievtenant Col.

JOHN LILBURNE.

*Wherein their just Demands in behalfe of themselves and the
whole Kingdome, concerning their Publike Safety, Peace and
Freedome, is Expres'd; calling these their Commissioners in
Parliament to an Account, how they (since the beginning of
their Session, to this present) have discharged their Duties to
the Universallity of the People, their Soveraigne LORD, from
whom their Power and Strength is derived, and by whom (ad
bene placitum,) it is continued.*

Printed in the Yeer.   1646.

A

REMONSTRANCE

OF

Many Thousand Citizens, *and other* Free-borne *People of* England, *to their owne House of C O M M O N S .*

WEE are well assured, yet cannot forget, that the cause of our choosing you to be *Parliament-men,* was to deliver us from all kind of Bondage, and to preserve the Common-wealth in Peace and Happinesse: For effecting whereof, we possessed you with the same Power that was in our selves, to have done the same; For wee might justly have done it our selves without you, if we had thought it convenient; choosing you [as Persons whom wee thought fitly quallified, and Faithfull,] for avoiding some inconveniences.

But ye are to remember, this was only of us but a Power of trust, [which is ever revokable, and cannot be otherwise,] and to be imployed to no other end, then our owne well-being: Nor did wee choose you to continue our Trust's longer, then the knowne established constitution of this Commonly-wealth will justly permit, and that could be but for one yeere at the most: for by our Law, a Parliament is to be called once every yeere, and oftner (if need be,) as ye well know. Wee are your Principalls, and you our Agents; it is a Truth which you cannot but acknowledge: For if you or any other shall assume, or exercise any Power, that is not derived from our Trust and choice thereunto, that Power is no lesse then usurpation and an Oppression, from which wee expect to be freed, in whomsoever we finde it; it being altogether inconsistent with the nature of *just Freedome,* which yee also very well understand.

The History of our Fore-fathers since they were Conquered by the *Normans,* doth manifest that this Nation hath been held in bondage all along ever since by the policies and force of the Officers of Trust in the Common-wealth, amongst whom, wee always esteemed Kings the chiefest: and what (in much of the former-time) was done by warre, and by impoverishing of the People, to make them slaves, and to hold them in bondage, our latter Princes have endeavoured to effect, by giving ease and wealth unto the People, but withall, corrupting their understanding, by infusing false Principles concerning Kings, and Government, and Parliaments, and Freedoms; and also using all meanes to corrupt and vitiate the manners of the youth, and strongest prop and support of the People, the Gentry.

It is wonderfull, that the failings of former Kings, to bring our Fore-fathers into bondage, together with the trouble and danger that some of them drew upon themselves and their Posterity, by those their unjust endevours, had not wrought in our latter Kings a resolution to rely on, and trust only to Justice and square dealing with the People, especially considering the unaptnesse of the Nation to beare much, especially from those that pretend to love them, and unto whom they expressed so much hearty affection, (as any People in the world ever did,) as in the quiet admission of King *James* from *Scotland*, sufficient, (if any Obligation would worke Kings to Reason,) to have endeared both him and his sonne King *Charles,* to an inviolable love, and hearty affection to the *English Nation*; but it would not doe.

They choose rather to trust unto their Policies and Court Arts, to King-waste, and delusion, then to Justice and plaine dealing; and did effect many things tending to our enslaving (as in your First *Remonstrance;* you shew skill enough to manifest the same to all the World:) and this Nation having been by their delusive Arts, and a long continued Peace, much softened and debased in judgement and Spirit, did beare far beyond its usuall temper, or any example of our Fore-Fathers, which (to our shame,) wee acknowledge.

But in conclusion, longer they would not beare, and then yee were chosen to worke our deliverance, and to Estate us in naturall and just libertie agreeable to *Reason* and common *equitie*; for whatever our Fore-fathers were; or whatever they did or suffered, or were enforced to yeeld unto; we are the men of the present age, and ought to be absolutely free from all kindes of exorbitancies, molestations or *Arbitrary Power,* and you wee choose to free us from all without exception or limitation, either in respect of Persons, Officers, Degrees, or things; and we were full of confidence, that ye also would have dealt impartially on our behalf, and made us the most absolute free People in the world.

But how ye have dealt with us; wee shall now let you know, and let the *Righteous GOD judge between you and us*; the continuall Oppressours of the Nation, have been Kings, which is so evident, that you cannot denie it; and ye yourselves have told the King, (whom yet you owne,) *That his whole 16. Yeeres reigne was one continued act of the breach of the Law.*

You shewed him, *That you understood his under-working with* Ireland, *his endeavour to enforce the Parliament by the Army raised against* Scotland, *yee were eye-witnesses of his violent attempt about the* Five Members; *Yee saw evidently his purpose of raising Warre; yee have seen him engaged, and with obstinate violence, persisting in the most bloody Warre that ever this Nation knew, to the wasting and destruction of multitudes of honest and Religious People.*

Yee have experience, that none but a King could doe so great intollerable mischiefes, the very name of King, proving a sufficient charme to delude many of our Brethren in *Wales, Ireland, England,* and *Scotland* too, so farre, *as to fight against their own Liberties,* which you know, no man under heaven could ever have done.

And yet, as if you were of Counsell with him, and were resolved to hold up his reputation, thereby to enable him to goe on in mischief, you maintaine, *The King can doe no wrong,* and apply all his Oppressions to *Evill Counsellors,* begging and intreating him in such submissive language, to returne to his Kingly Office and Parliament, as if you were resolved to make us beleeve, hee were a God, without whose presence, all must fall to ruine, or as if it were impossible for any Nation to be happy without a King.

You cannot fight for our *Liberties,* but it must be in the Name of *King* and *Parliament*; he that speakes of his cruelties, must be thrust out of your House and society; your Preachers must pray for him, as if he had not deserved to be excommunicated all Christian Society, or as if yee or they thought God were a respecter of the Persons of Kings in judgement.

By this and other your like dealings, your frequent treating, and tampering to maintaine his honour, Wee that have trusted you to deliver us from his Opressions, and to preserve us from his cruelties, are wasted and consumed (in multitudes) to manifold miseries, whilst you lie ready with open armes to receive him, *and to make him a great and glorious King.*

Have you shoke this Nation like an Earth-quake, to produce no more than this for us; Is it for this, that ye have made so free use, & been so bold both with our Persons & Estates? And doe you (because of our readings to comply with your desires in all things) conceive us so sottish, as to be contented with such unworthy returnes of our trust and Love? No; it is high time wee be plaine with you; *WEE are not, nor SHALL not be so contented;* Wee doe expect according to *reason,* that yee *should* in the first place, declare and set forth *King Charles* his wickednesse openly before the world, and withall, to shew the intollerable inconyeniences of having a *Kingly Government,* from the constant evill practices of those of this Nation; and so to declare *King Charles* an enemy, and to publish your resolution, never to have any more, but to acquite us of so great a charge and trouble forever, and to convert the great revenue of the Crowne to the publike treasure, to make good the injuries and *injustices* done heretofore, and of late by those that have possessed the same; and this we expected long since at your hand, and untill this be done, wee shall not thinke our selves well dealt withall in this originall of all Oppressions, to wit *Kings.*

Yee must also deal better with us concerning the L*ords,* then you have done? Yee only are chosen by Us the People; and therefore in you onely is the Power of binding the whole Nation, by making, altering, or abolishing of Lawes; Yee have therefore prejudiced Us, in acting so, as if ye could not make a Law without both the Royall assent of the King (*so ye are pleased to expresse your selves,*) and the assent of the Lords; yet when either King or Lords assent not to what you approve, yee have so much sense of your owne Power, as to assent what yee thinke good by an Order of your owne House.

What is this but to blinde our eyes, that Wee should not know where our Power is lodged, nor to whom to aply our selves for the use thereof; but if We want a *Law,* Wee must awaite till the *King* and *Lords* assent; if an Ordinance, then Wee must waite till the *Lords* assent; yet ye knowing their assent to be meerly formall, (*as having no root in the choice of the People, from whom the Power that is just must be derived,*) doe frequently importune their assent, which implies a most grosse absurditie.

For where their assent is necessary and essentiall, they must be as *Free* as you, to assent, or dissent as their understandings and

Consciences should guide them: and might as justly importune you, as yee them. Yee ought in Conscience to reduce this case also to a certaintie, and not to waste time, and open your Counsells, and be lyable to so many Obstructions as yee have been.

But to prevaile with them (enjoying their Honours and Possessions,) to be lyable, and stand to be chosen for Knights and Burgesses by the People, as other the Gentry and *Free-men* of this Nation doe, which will be an Obligation upon them, as having one and the same interest: then also they would be distinguished by their vertues, and love to the *Common-wealth,* whereas now they Act and Vote in our affaires but as intruders, or as thrust upon us by *Kings,* to make good their Interests, which to this day have been to bring us into a slavish subjection to their wills.

Nor is there any reason, that they should in any measure, be lesse lyable to any Law then the Gentry are; Why should any of them assault, strike, or beate any, and not be lyable to the Law, as other men are? Why should not they be as lyable to their debts as other men? there is no reason: yet have yee stood still, and seen many of us, and some of your selves violently abused without repairation.

Wee desire you to free us from these abuses, and their negative Voices, or else tell us, that it is reasonable wee should be slaves, this being a perpetuall prejudice in our Government, neither consulting with *Freedome* nor *Safety*: with *Freedome* it cannot; for in this way of Voting in all Affaires of the *Common-wealth,* being not Chosen thereunto by the People, they are therein Masters & Lords of the People, which necessarily implyes the People to be their servants and vassalls, and they have used many of us accordingly, by committing divers to Prison upon their owne Authority, namely *William Larner,* Liev. Col. *John Lilburne,* and other worthy Sufferers, who upon Appeale unto you, have not beene relieved.

Wee must therefore pray you to make a Law against all kinds of *Arbitrary Government,* as the highest capitall offence against the *Common-wealth,* and to reduce all conditions of men to a certainty, that none hence-forward may presume or plead any thing in way of excuse, and that ye will leave no favour or scruple of Tyranicall Power over us in any whatsoever.

Time hath revealed hidden things unto us, things covered over thick and threefold with pretences of *the true Reformed Religion,* when as wee see apparently, that this Nation, and that of *Scotland,* are joyned together in a most bloody and consuming Warre, by the waste and policie of a sort of *Lords* in each Nation, that were male-contents, and vexed that the *King* had advanced others, and not themselves to the manageing of State-affaires.

Which they suffered till the King increasing his Oppressions in both Nations, gave them opportunity to reveale themselves, and then they resolve to bring the King to their bow and regulation, and to exclude all those from managing State-affaires that hee had advanced thereunto, and who were growne so insolent and pre-sumptuous, as these discontented ones were lyable to continuall molestations from them, either by practices at Counsel-table, High-Commission, or Starre-chamber.

So as their work was to subvert the *Monarchiall Lords* and *Clergy,* and therewithall, to abate the Power of the King, and to Order him: but this was a mighty worke, and they were nowise able to effect it of themselves: therefore (say they,) the generallity of the People must be engaged; and how must this be done? Why say they, wee must associate with that part of the *Clergy* that are now made underlings, and others of them that have been op-pressed, and with the most zealous religious Non-conformists, and by the helpe of these, wee will lay before the Generalitie of the People, all the *Popish Innovations in Religion, all the Oppres-sions of the Bishops and High-Commission, all the exorbitances of the Counsell-board, and Star-chamber, all the injustice of the Chancery, and Courts of Justice, all the illegall Taxations, as Ship-mony, Pattents, and Projects,* whereby we shall be sure to get into our Party, the generalitie of the Citie of *London,* and all the considerable substantiall People of both Nations.

By whose cry and importunity we shall have a *Parliament,* which wee shall by our manifold wayes, alliant, dependant, and relations soone worke to our purposes.

But (say some) this will never be effected without a Warre, for the King will have a strong party, and he will never submit to us; 'tis not expected otherwise (say they) and great and vaste sums of money must be raised, and Souldiers and Ammunition must be had, whereof wee shall not need to feare any want: for what will not an opprest, rich, and Religious People doe, to be delivered from all kinds of Oppression, both *Spirituall* and *Temporall,* and to be restored to *purity* and *freedome* in Religion, and to the just liberty of their *Persons* and *Estates?*

All our care must be to hold all at our Command and dispos-ing; for if this People thus stirred up by us, should make an end too soon with the King and his party, it is much to be doubted, they would place the *Supreme Power* in their House of *Commons*, unto whom only of right it belongeth, they only being chosen by the People, which is so presently discerned, that as wee have a care the King and his Lords must not prevaile; so more especially, wee must be carefull the *Supreme Power* fall not into the Peoples hands, or House of *Commons*.

Therefore wee must so act, as not to make an end with the King and his Party, till by expence of time and treasure, a long, bloody and consuming War, decay of trade, and multitudes of the highest *Impositions*, the People by degrees are tyred and wearied, so as they shall not be able to contest or dispute with us, either about *Supreame* or *inferiour Power*; but wee will be able, afore they are aware, to give them both Law and Religion.

In Scotland *it will be easie to establish the* Presbyteriall *Government in the Church, and that being once effected, it will not be much difficult in* England, *upon a pretence of uniformity in both Nations, and the like, unto which there will be found a Clergy as willing as wee, it giving them as absolute a Ministery over the Consciences of the People, over the Persons and Purses, as wee our selves aime at, or desire.*

And if any shall presume to oppose either us or them, wee shall be easily able by the helpe of the Clergy, by our Party in the House of Commons, *and by their and our influence in all parts of both Nations, easily to crush and suppress them.*

Well (saies sume) all this may be done, but wee, without abundance of travell to our selves, and wounding our owne Consciences, for wee must grosly dissemble before God, and all the world will see it in time; for wee can never doe all this that yee aime at, but by the very same oppressions as wee practised by the King, the Bishops, and all those his tyranicall Instruments, both in Religion, and Civill Government.

And it will never last or continue long, the People will see it, and hate you for it, more then ever they hated the former Tyrants and Oppressours: were it not better and safer for us to be just, and really to doe that for the People, which wee pretend, and for which wee shall so freely spend their lives and Estates, and so have their Love, and enjoy the Peace of quiet Consciences?

For (say they) are not Wee a L O R D , *a Peere of the Kingdom? Have you your Lordship or Peerage, or those Honours and Priviledges that belong thereunto from the love and Election of the People? Your interest is as different from theirs, and as incon-*

sistent with their freedoms, as those Lords *and* Clergy *are, whom wee strive to supplant.*

And therefore, rather then satisfie the Peoples expectations in what concernes their Freedoms, *it were much better to continue as wee are, and never disturbe the King in his* Prerogatives, *nor his* Lords *and* Prelates *in their* Priviledges: *and therefore let us be as one, and when wee talke of Conscience, let us make conscience, to make good unto our selves and our* Posterities *those Dignities,* Honours *and* Preheminencies *conveyed unto us by our Noble* Progenitours, *by all the meanes wee can; not making questions for Conscience sake, or any other things; and if wee be united in our endeavours, and worke wisely, observing when to advance, and when to give ground, wee cannot faile of successe, which will be an honour to our Names for ever.*

These are the strong delusions that have been amongst us, and the mystery of iniquity hath wrought most vehemently in all our affaires: Hence it was that Strafford *was so long in tryall, and that he had no greater heads to beare his company. Hence it was that the King was not called to an account for his oppressive Government, and that the treachery of those that would have enforced you, was not severely punished.*

That the King gained time to raise an Army, and the Queene to furnish Ammunition; that our first and second Army was so ill formed, and as ill managed; Sherburn, Brainford, Exeter, *the slender use of the Associate Counties, the slight garding of the sea,* Oxford, Dennington, *the West Defeate, did all proceed from (and upon) the Mystery of Iniquity.*

The King and his Party had been nothing in your hands, had not some of you been engaged, and some of you ensnared, and the rest of you over-borne with this Mystery, which you may now easily perceive, if you have a minde thereunto, that yee were put upon the continuation of this Parliament, during the pleasure of both Houses, was from this Mystery, because in time these Politicians had hopes to worke, and pervert you to forsake the common Interest of those that choose and trusted you to promote their unjust Designe to enslave us; wherein they have prevailed too too much.

For Wee must deale plainly with you, yee have long time acted more like the *House of Peers* then the *House of Commons:* Wee can scarcely approach your Door with a Request or motion, though by way of Petition, but yee hold long debates, whether Wee break not your *Priviledges;* the *Kings,* or the *Lords* pretended *Prerogatives* never made a greater noise, nor was made more dreadfull then the Name of *Priviledge of the House of Commons.*

Your Members in all Impositions must not be taxed in the places where they live, like other men: Your servants have their *Priviledges* too. To accuse or prosecute any of you, is become dangerous to the Prosecutors. Yee have imprisonments as frequent for either Witnesses or Prosecutors, as ever the *Star-chamber* had, and yee are furnished with new devised Arguments, to prove, that yee onely may justly doe these grosse injustices, which the *Starre-Chamber, High-Commission,* and *Counsell-board* might not doe.

And for doing whereof (whil'st yee were untainted,) yee abolished them, for yee now frequently commit mens Persons to Prison without shewing Cause; Yee examine men upon *Interogatories* and *Questions* against themselves, and Imprison them for refusing to answere: And ye have Officious servile men, that write and publish Sophisticall Arguments to justifie your so doing, for which they are rewarded and countenanced, as the *Starre-Chamber* and *High-Commission*-beagles lately were.

Whilst those that ventured their lives for your establishment, are many of them vexed and molested, and impoverished by them; Yee have entertained to be your Committees servants, those very prowling Varlets that were imployed by those unjust Courts, who took pleasure to torment honest conscionable People; yet vex and molest honest men for matters of Religion, and difference with you and your *Synod* in judgement, and take upon you to determine of Doctrine and Discipline, approving this, and reproaching that, just like unto former ignorant pollitick and superstitious Parliaments and Convocations: And thereby have divided honest People amongst themselves, by countenancing only those of the *Presbitry,* and discountenancing all the Separation, *Anabaptists* and *Independents.*

And though it resteth in you to acquiet all differences in affection, though not in judgement, by permitting every one to be fully perswaded in their owne mindes, commanding all Reproach to cease; yet as yee also had admitted *Machiavells* Maxime, *Divide & impera,* divide and prevaile; yee countenance onely one, open the Printing-presse onely unto one, and that to the *Presbytry,* and suffer them to raile and abuse, and domineere over all the rest, as if also ye had discovered and digested, That without a powerfull compulsive *Presbytry* in the Church, a compulsive mastership, or Arristocraticall Government over the People in the State, could never long be maintained.

Whereas truely wee are well assured, neither you, nor none else, can have any into Power at all to conclude the People in matters that concerne the Worship of God, for therein every one of us ought to be fully assured in our owne mindes, and to be sure to Worship him according to our Consciences.

Yee may propose what Forme yee conceive best, and most available for Information and well-being of the Nation, and may perswade and invite thereunto, but compell, yee cannot justly; for ye have no Power from Us so to doe, nor could you have; for we could not conferre a Power that was not in our selves, there being none of us, that can without wilfull sinne binde our selves to worship God after any other way, then what (to a tittle,) in our owne particular understandings, wee approve to be just.

And therefore We could not referre our selves to you in things of this Nature; and surely, if We could not conferre this Power upon you, yee cannot have it, and so not exercise it justly; Nay, as we ought not to revile or reproach any man for his differing with us in judgement, more then wee would be reviled or reproached for ours; even so yee ought not to countenance any Reproachers or revilers, or molesters for matters of Conscience.

But to protect and defend all that live peaceably in the Commonwealth, of what judgement or way of Worship whatsoever; and if ye would bend your mindes thereunto, and leave your selves open to give eare, and to consider such things as would be presented unto you, a just way would be discovered for the Peace & quiet of the land in generall, and of every well-minded Person in particular.

But if you lock up your selves from hearing all voices; how is it possible you should *try all things.* It is not for you to assume a Power to controule and force Religion, or a way of *Church Government,* upon the People, because former Parliaments have so done; yee are first to prove that yee could have such a Power justly entrusted unto you by the People that trusted you, (which you see you have not,) we may happily be answered, that the Kings Writt that summons a Parliament, and directs the People to choose Knights and *Burgesses,* implyes the Establishment of Religion.

To which wee answere, that if Kings would prove themselves Lawfull Magistrates, they must prove themselves to be so, by a lawfull derivation of their Authority, which must be from the voluntary trust of the People, and then the case is the same with them, as between the People & you, they as you, being possessed of no more Power then what is in the People justly to intrust, and then all implications in the Writts, of the *Establishment of Religion,* sheweth that in that particular, as many other, we remain under the *Norman* yoke of an *unlawfull Power,* from which wee ought to free our selves; and which yee ought not to maintaine upon us, but to abrogate.

But ye have listned to any Counsells, rather then to the voice of us that trusted you: Why is it that you have stopt the Presse; but that you would have nothing but pleasing flattering Discourses, and go on to make your selves partakers of the *Lordship over us,* without hearing any thing to the contrary: yea, your *Lords* and *Clergy* long to have us in the same condition with our deluded brethren, the *Commons of Scotland,* where their understandings are so captivated with a Reverend opinion of their *Presbytry,* that they really beleeve them to be by *Divine Authority,* and are as zealous therein, as ever the poore deceived Papists were.

As much they live in feare of their thunder-bolts of Excommunication, and good cause they have, poor soules, for those *Excommunications are so followed with the civill Sanction, or secular Power, that they are able to crush any opposer or dissenter to dust, to undoe or ruine any man: so absolute a Power hath their new* Clergy *already gained over the poore People there, and earnestly labour to bring us into the same condition, because if wee should live in greater Freedome in this Nation, it would (they know,) in time be observed by their* People, *whose understandings would be thereby informed, and then they would grow impatient of their thraldome, and shake off their yoake.*

They are also in no lesse bondage in things Civill, the Lords and great Men over-rule all, as they please; the People are scarce free in any thing.

———— Friends, these are known Truths. ————

And hence it is, that in their Counsells here, they adhere to those that maintaine their owne greatnesse, and usurped rule over us, lest if wee should bare possesse greater liberty, then their vassalls the People *in* Scotland, *they might in short time observe the same, and discharge themselves of their Oppressions.*

It is from the mystery of iniquity, that yee have never made

that use of the People of this Nation, in your warre, as you might
have done, but have chosen rather to hazard their coming in,
then to Arme your owne native undoubted friends; by which
meanes they are possessed of too many considerable strengths of
this Nation, and speak such language in their late published
papers, as if they were not payed for their slow assistance.

Whereas yee might have ended the Warre long ere this, if by
Sea or Land you had shewed your selves resolved to make us a
Free-People; but it is evident, a change of our bondage is the
uttermost is intended us, and that too for a worse, and longer;
if wee shall be so contended, but it is strange you should imagine.

But the truth is, wee finde none are so much hated by you, as
those you thinke doe discerne those your purposes, or that apply
themselves unto you, with motions tending to divert you from
proceeding therein: for some yeers now, no condition of men can
prevaile with you, to ammend any thing that is amisse in the
Common-wealth.

The exorbitances in the *Cities Government,* and the strivings
about *Prerogatives* in the *Major* and *Aldermen,* against the *Free-*
doms of the *Commons,* (and to their extreme prejudice,) are returned to the same point they were at in *Garrawayes* time, which
you observe, and move not, nor assist the *Commons*; Nay, worse
then in his time, they are justified by the *Major,* in a book published, and sent by him to every *Common-Counsell-man.*

The oppression of the *Turky Company,* and the *Adventerers*
Company, and all other infringements of our Native Liberties
of the same nature, and which in the beginnings of the Parliament, yee seemed to abhominate, are now by you complyed
withall, and licensed to goe on in their Oppressions.

Yee know, the Lawes of this Nation are unworthy a *Free-*
People, and deserve from first to last, to be considered, and seriously debated, and reduced to an agreement with common *equity,*
and *right reason,* which ought to be the Forme and Life of every
Government.

Magna Charta it self being but a beggerly thing, containing
many markes of intollerable bondage, & the Lawes that have been
made since by Parliaments, have in very many particulars made
our Government much more oppressive and intollerable.

The *Norman* way for ending of Controversies, was much more
abusive then the *English way,* yet the *Conquerour,* contrary to his
Oath introduced the *Norman* Lawes, and his litigious and vexatious way amongst us; the like he did also for punishment of

malefactours, Controversies of all natures, having before a quick and finall dispatch in every hundred.

He erected a trade of Judges and Lawyers, to sell Justice and injustice at his owne unconscionable rate, and in what time hee pleased; the corruption whereof is yet remaining upon us, to our continuall impoverishing and molestation; from which we thought you should have delivered us.

Yee know also, Imprisonment for Debt, is not from the beginning; Yet ye thinke not of these many Thousand Persons and Families that are destroyed thereby, *yee are Rich, and abound in goods, and have need of nothing; but the afflictions of the poore; your hunger-starved brethren, ye have no compassion of*; Your zeal makes a noise as farre as *Argiere,* to deliver those captived Christians at the charge of others, but those whom your owne unjust Lawes hold captive in your owne Prisons; these are too neere you to thinke of; Nay, yee suffer poor Christians, for whom Christ died to kneel before you in the streets, aged, sick and cripled, begging your halfe-penny Charities, and yee rustle by them in your Coaches and silkes daily, without regard, or taking any course for their constant reliefe, their sight would melt the heart of any Christian, and yet it moves not you nor your *Clergy.*

Wee intreat you to consider what difference there is, between binding a man to an Oare, as a *Gally-slave* in *Turkie* or *Argiere,* and Pressing of men to serve in your Warre; to surprize a man on the sudden, force him from his Calling, where he lived comfortably, from a good trade; from his dear Parents, Wife or Children, against inclination, disposition to fight for a Cause hee understands not, and in Company of such, as he hath no comfort to be withall; for Pay, that will scarce give him sustenance; and if he live, to returne to a lost trade, or beggery, or not much better: If any Tyranny or cruelty exceed this; it must be worse then that of a *Turkish Gally-slave.*

But yee are apt to say, What remedy, men wee must have? To which we answer, in behalfe of ourselves, and our too much injured Brethren, that are Pressed; That the *Hollanders* our provident Neighbours have no such cruelties, esteeming nothing more unjust, or unreasonable, yet they want no men; and if ye would take care, that all sorts of men might find comfort and contentment in your Government, yee would not need to enforce men to serve your Warres.

And if yee would in many things follow their good example, and make this Nation a *State,* free from the Oppression of *Kings,* and the corruptions of the Court, and shew love to the People in the Constitutions of your Government, the affection of the People, would satisfie all common and publike Occasions: and in many particulars wee can shew you a remedy for this and all other inconveniences, if wee could find you inclinable to heare us.

Yee are extreamely altered in demeanour towards us, in the beginning yee seemed to know what Freedome was; made a distinction of honest men, whether rich or poor, all were welcome to you, and yee would mix your selves with us in a loving familiar way, void of Courtly observance or behaviour.

Yee kept your Committee doores open, all might heare & judge of your dealings, hardly ye would permit men to stand bareheaded before you, some of you telling them, ye more regarded their health, and that they should not deem of you, as of other domineering Courts, yee and they were one, all *Commons* of *England*; and the like ingenious carriage, by which ye wanne our affections to that height, that ye no sooner demanded any thing, but it was effected; yee did well then, who did hinder you? *the mystery of iniquity*, that was it that perverted your course.

What a multitude of precious lives have been lost? What a masse of moneys have been raised? What one way was proposed to advance moneys, that was refused by you, though never so prejudiciall to the People, allowing your Committees to force men to pay or lend, or else to sweare that they were not worth so or so: the most destructive course to tradesmen, that could be devised, fifty intire subsidies, to be lent throughout *London*, if not procured, yet authorized by-you; never the like heard of, and the *Excise* that being once setled, all other assessments should cease.

Notwithstanding in few moneths comes forth Ordinance upon Ordinance for more moneys, and for the *Customes*, they were thought an *oppression* in the beginning, and being (so high,) an hinderance to Trade, and extreamly prejudiciall to the Nation, neverthelesse is now confirmed, with many augmentations, in so much as men of inferiour trading finde great trouble to provide moneys for *Customes*, and have so many Officers to please, that it is a very slavery to have any thing to doe with them, and no remedy; the first Commissioners being more harsh and ingenious, then the late *Farmers*, and the last worse then the former.

Truly it is a sad thing, but too true, a plaine quiet-minded man in any place in *England*, is just like a harmelesse sheep in a Thicket, can hardly move or stirre, but hee shall be strech'd, and loose his wooll: such *Committees* have ye made in all Cities and Counties, and none are so ill used as honest Godly men.

Ye have now sate full five yeeres, which is foure yeeres longer then wee intended, for wee could choose you but for (at most) one yeere; and now we wish ye would publish to all the world, the good that you have done for us, the *liberty* ye have brought us unto: if yee could excuse your selves, as ye use to doe; by saying it hath been a time of warre; that will not doe: for when the warre might in the beginning have been prevented, if yee had drawn a little more blood from the right veine, and might often (ere this) have been ended.

Occasion hath been given away, and Treated away, and now, when through the faithfulnesse of the *New Modell*, yee have almost forc'd an end, and have no great part to effect: now againe, at the instigation of those that love their *Kings* more then all this Nation, and their owne, his Sacred or holy Majestie, must againe be treated with, their *Nationall and Solemne League and Covenant with their God,* binding them to be *respecters of Persons in judgement:* and to preserve His Person in the defence of the *true Protestant Religion, and Libertie of the People; that hath constantly against all perswasion and Obligation, done what ever he could to subvert both*: *if this be not the height of the mystery* of iniquitie, what is higher.

But let not these be deceived, nor thus under zealous expressions deceive you; wee wish your soules may no further *enter into their secret: For God will not be mocked, nor suffer such grosse Hypocrisie to passe without exemplary punishment*: And if yee beleeve there is a God; yee must beleeve it; and if yee doe beleeve it, and consider the wayes yee have troad, and truely repent, shew it by walking contrary to what yee have done, or purposed to doe, and let us quickly and speedily partake thereof: For God is a God *that taketh vengeance,* and will not suffer you to goe on to our ruine.

Wee have some hopes ye will; for amongst you, there have been alwayes faithfull and Worthy men, whose aboundant grief it hath been to observe the strange progresse of the Chosen men of the Common-wealth, and have strove exceedingly on all occasions to produce better effects, and some Christians of late produced to their praise.

Others there are, that have been onely misled by the policies, and stratagems of politick men, and these, after this our serious advice, will make you more seriously studdie the common Interrest of this Nation: others there are, and those a great number, that are newly chosen into your house, and wee trust are such as will exceedingly strengthen the good part, that hitherto hath been too weake to steere an even course amidst so many oppositions and crosse waves.

But henceforth joyn'd all in one will be able to doe and carry on whatsoever is just and good for the Common-wealth, the more just and good, the more easily effected, for such things are easily to be made evident to all men, and can never faile of the uttermost assistance of all well-minded People.

And therefore wee would not have you to be discouraged in attempting whatsoever is evidently just, for Wee will therein assist you to the last drop of our bloods: *Feare neither the Anakims, nor the sonnes of the Gyants, For the LORD our God, hee will stand by you in all things that are just, and will blesse and prosper you therein.*

Forsake, and utterly renounce all craftie and subtill intentions; hide not your thoughts from Us, and give us encouragement to be open-breasted unto you: Proclaime afore-hand, what yee determine to doe, in establishing any thing for continuance; and heare all things that can be spoken with or against the same, and to that intent, let the imprisoned Presses at liberty, that all mens understandings may be more conveniently informed, and convinced, as faire as is possible by the *equity* of your Proceedings.

Wee cannot but expect to be delivered from the *Norman* bondage, whereof wee now as well as our Predecessours, have felt the smart by these bloody warres; and from all unreasonable lawes made ever since that unhappy conquest; as wee have encouragement, wee shall informe you further, and guide you, as we observe your doings.

The Worke yee must note is ours, and not your owne, though ye are to be partakers with us in the well or ill doing thereof: and therefore ye must expect to heare more frequently from us then yee have done, nor will it be your wisedome to take these Admonitions and Cautions in evill part.

If yee consider well, yee may wonder Wee are no tarter: Ye may perceive, wee have not yet left our true *English confidence,* but are willing that both you, and all our Neighbour-Nations should know, that wee both see and know all stratagems and Policies that are laid in waite to entrap, and so to enslave us, and that wee bid defyance to their worst our enemies can doe; we know wee have stoore of friends in our Neighbour Countries.

Our head is not yet so intoxicated with this *New mystery of Iniquity,* but that a reasonable *Cordiall* Administered by your hand, will set us fast in our seat.

Yee are not to reckon that yee have any longer time to effect the Great Worke wee have entrusted unto you : for wee must not loose our free choice of a Parliament once every yeer, fresh and fresh for a continuall Parliament.

For so, if a present *Parliament* be mistaken in their understandings, and doe things prejudiciall, We may so long remain under these prejudices, that the *Common-wealth* may be endangered thereby, nor doe wee value a *Trieniall Parliament*: before three yeeres come to an end, Grievances and Mischiefes may be past remedy.

And therefore our advice is, that yee Order a meeting of the chosen of *Parliament-men,* to be expresly upon one certaine day in *November* yeerly throughout the Land in the Places accustomed, and to be by you expressed, there to make choice of whom they think good, according to *Law,* and all men that have a Right to be there, not to faile upon a great penaltie but no summons to be expected.

And if any Person without exception, shall write Letters, or use any endeavours to incline the choosers to choose any man, or use any meanes to disturbe or pervert them from a free Choice, then that all such sinister dealing be made punishable, or a most haynous crime.

And that a Parliament *so chosen in* November, *succeeding yeere by yeere, may come instead of the preceeding* Parliament, *and proceed with the Affaires of the Common-Wealth; nor would wee have it in the* Power *of our* Parliament, *to receive any* Member *from his* Place *or service of the House, without the consent had of those Counties, Cities and Burroughs respectively that choose him; great inconveniences depending thereon, whereof wee have seene and felt too much.*

Now, if yee shall conscionably performe your Trust the yeer ensuing, and order the Parliaments to succeed as aforesaid, then Wee shall not doubt to be made absolute *Free-men* in time, and become a just, plenteous and Powerfull Nation; All that is past will be forgotten, and Wee shall yet have cause to rejoyce in your Wisedome and Fidelity.

POSTSCRIPT.

Moreover, as for me, God forbid that I should sinne against the Lord in ceasing to pray for you: but I will teach you the good and right way. Onely feare the LORD, and serve him in Truth with all your heart: For considder how great things He hath done for you. But if yee still doe wickedly, yee shall be consumed, both yee and your King. 1 Sam. 22, 23, 24, 25.

FINIS.

Document 2

THE PETITION OF MARCH, 1647

Reprinted from a photostat copy of Lilburne's *Rash Oaths*, pp. 29-35 (May 31, 1647) in the McAlpin Collection of Union Theological Seminary. Collated with a photostat copy of another edition, E. 464 (19), Sept. 19, 1648.

The petition of March, 1647, forerunner of democratic manifestoes in Cromwell's army and of *An Agreement of the People,* evolved from Leveller agitation in and around London. This agitation had crystallized the preceding July in *A Remonstrance Of Many Thousand Citizens,* a stirring call to secular reformation. What the Levellers in effect demanded was a constitutional revolution: the annihilation of the veto power and king and Lords and Parliament's recognition of its responsibility to the whole body of citizens.

The March petition presents the concrete measures by which these democratic assumptions were to be translated into reality. The measures are drastic and far-reaching, inimical, as Gardiner has pointed out, to the interests of both the financial and professional classes, and more likely to be achieved in three centuries than in a single Parliament. The abolition of tithes alone would have rooted nine thousand parish ministers out of their state-church positions. The demands for laws in plain English and for exact delineation of lawyers' and judges' duties and fees (Article 7) were antagonistic, of course, to the vested interests of the legal profession. The strong financial power of both the aristocracy and dominant Puritan leaders the Levellers attacked in Article 6. That ancient ally of the creditor class, imprisonment for debt, was still on the statute books, with two centuries yet to live; the Petition (Article 10) attacks its oppressive injustices without declaring, as the Levellers were later to do, for its annihilation. But the most revolutionary proposal was, of course, the abolition of king and Lords as constitutional equals with the Commons.[1]

[1] The Levellers were rebuked (*Old Parliamentary History,* XV, 374) for addressing a petition to the Commons as the "supreme Authority." The petitioners

After five years of victorious civil war against the king and his feudal adherents, the Presbyterian business men and clergy were utterly opposed to such a drastic measure. Forty years later curbing the king's power was to seem logical and safe enough. But now the Presbyterians feared the radical Independents and Levellers more than their old opponents of the feudal order; with the unknowing aid of the Presbyterians the Civil War had set in motion a democratic agitation profoundly disturbing to bankers, lawyers, monopolists, clergy, investors, no less than to kings and nobles.

The tone of the Petition, utterly unlike that of *A Remonstrance*, bears the stamp of Walwyn's conciliatory approach, rather than the belligerent aggressiveness of Overton or Lilburne. Like those of most Leveller manifestoes, however, the ideas of the March petition were undoubtedly arrived at by collaboration, whatever pen phrased the final copy. In his *Just Defence* Walwyn afterward wrote that the Petition was drawn and debated by many persons. The Independents at first favored it, he claimed, but when it was later burnt by the hangman, most of the "uppermost Independents stood aloof, and look'd on." [2] Though Lilburne was always ready to agitate, and undoubtedly contributed from his prison cell to the March petition, he had already voiced his despair of securing justice from the Commons in *The Oppressed Mans Oppressions* (January 28), and was prepared to appeal over their heads to the people. In *The out-cryes of oppressed Commons* (February 28) Lilburne and Overton had been bitingly

show their awareness of this situation by saying (p. 137): "Though it be not now made a crime to mention a *Parliament*, yet is it little lesse to mention the supreme power of this honourable House." In *The Legal Fundamental Liberties* (second edition) Lilburne returned to the topic of the supreme authority and its significance in the origin of the March petition (p. 15): "And besides, when divers honest and well-affected Citizens, it may be out of a sensible apprehension of the mischiefs that acrue to the Kingdom by having *the Supream Authority lodged in three distinct Estates*, which many times so falls out, that when two Estates grant things essentially good for the wellfare of the Kingdom, the third Estate opposeth it, and will not pass it, which many times occasions war, and blood-shed, to the hazard of the beeing of the Kingdom; for the preventing of which, they framed a Petition to your House, *Entitling it, To the Supream Authority of this Nation, the Commons assembled in Parliament;* in which they intreat you to be careful of the mischief of Negative Voyces in any whomsoever; which said Petition your House upon the 20. of *May* 1647. Voted to be burnt at the *Exchange* and *westminster* by the hands of the Common Hangman."

[2] *Walwyns Just Defence*, p. 4.

emphatic on this point: "We for our preservation shall tread in the Parliament steps by *appealing to the People* against them, as they did against the King." [3]

The Petition was printed in March [4] and circulated for subscription in and around London. Through an informer, however, a copy reached the hands of a member of the House, who referred it to Colonel Leigh's committee. On March 19 "divers hundreds" of the supporters of the petition appeared before Colonel Leigh's committee with a certificate to avow their petition as genuine. Thrust out of the committee chamber, the petitioners assembled nearby to hear it read aloud by Nicholas Tue, whereupon the House committed Tue to the custody of the sergeant-at-arms. The next day, March 20, the House committed Major Tulidah to prison "without hearing or examining any witnesses against him." [5] Nothing daunted, the petitioners presented the House with a second petition protesting the treatment of Tue and Tulidah, this also to no avail, "although they followed it extraordinary close, and at the doore presented it to all the Members in print." [6] Still persistent, the petitioners on May 20 presented a third appeal protesting the arbitrary actions of the committee, the prejudging of their original petition, the harsh treatment accorded them by Stapleton, Hollis, and Earle, and the continued restraint of Nicholas Tue. This time the House acted decisively indeed, ordering it to be burned by the common hangman.[7] That the petitioners had some solid support from the Independents, however, is indicated by the closeness of the vote, 94 to 86.[8] At this rebuff Lilburne's ironical advice was to petition the House for a declaration of the subjects' privileges, and what they might be permitted to ask for, so that the people might petition for nothing amiss and *"run upon the pricks of their indignation."* [9] Still im-

---

[3] P. 14.

[4] Thomason did not collect the Petition in March. As a separate pamphlet it did not appear until September 19, 1648. In the Thomason Collection it is number E. 464 (19).

[5] *Rash Oaths*, pp. 35-36.

[6] *Ibid.*, pp. 36-41. On April 23, when a debate on the original petition had been ordered, discussion was postponed. "Many of the Petitioners . . . waited 'till five at Night, but had no Answer." Rushworth, VI, 464. On May 1 the House ordered the petition to be read on May 4. On May 4 the House declared it "did dislike the Petition; and therefore could not approve thereof." Rushworth, VI, 475, 478.

[7] *Ibid.*, p. 44.   [8] *Old Parliamentary History*, XV, 374.

[9] *Rash Oaths*, p. 44.

portunate, however, the petitioners appealed again to the Commons, this time urging a consideration of the desires of officers and soldiers, reception of petitions from the "well affected," and the investigation of persons in authority who had been accused of breach of trust.[10] By a vote of 128 to 112, on June 2 the House decided to give no answer to this petition. Having read the vote of the House, the Levellers replied that they had "discharged themselves from further attendance for the present, and will notwithstanding still seeke just and equitable meanes for to ease the grievances of this poore distracted Kingdome." [11] Thus ended the petitionary thrust and counter-thrust evolving from the large petition of March, 1647. In less than ten weeks the Levellers had appealed to the House *six* times, with four petitions, a certificate of avowal, and a statement virtually acknowledging their defeat through the normal course of appeal.

On May 31 Lilburne inserted the large petition and the ones described above in *Rash Oaths unwarrantable.* On June 14 appeared *Gold tried in the fire,*[12] a preface which the Levellers intended to precede the various petitions in a new effort to circulate them. *Gold tried* traced the history of the March petition much less closely than had Lilburne in *Rash Oaths.*

---

[10] *Rash Oaths,* pp. 44-46.   [11] *Ibid.,* p. 47.   [12] E. 392 (19).

To the right honourable and supreme Authority

of this Nation, the Commons in PARLIAMENT affembled.

The humble Petition of many thoufands, earneftly defiring the glory of God, the freedome of the Common-wealth, and the peace of all men.

Sheweth,

THat as no Civill Government is more just in the constitution, then that of Parliaments, having its foundation in the free choice of the people ; and as the end of all Government is the safetie and freedome of the governed, even so the people of this Nation in all times have manifested most heartie affections unto Parliaments as the most proper remedie of their grievances ; yet such hath been the wicked policies of those who from time to time have endeavoured to bring this Nation into bondage; that they have in all times either by the disuse or abuse of *Parliaments* deprived the people of their hopes: For testimony whereof the late times foregoing this *Parliament* will sadly witnesse, when it was not onely made a crime to mention a *Parliament,* but either the pretended negative voice, (the most destructive to freedome) or a speedie dissolution, blasted the fruit and benefit thereof, whilst the whole Land was overspread with all kinds of oppressions and tyranny, extending both to soule and body, and that in so rooted and setled a way, that the complaints of the people in generall witnessed, that they would have given any thing in the world for one six moneths freedome of *Parliament*. Which hath been since evidenced in their instant & constant readinesse of assistance to this present *Parliament,* exceeding the Records of former ages, and wherein God hath blessed them with their first desires, making this *Parliament* the most absolute and free of any *Parliament* that ever was, and enabling it with power sufficient to deliver the whole Nation from all kinds of oppressions and grievances, though of very long continuance, and to make it the most absolute and free Nation in the world.

And it is most thankfully acknowledged that ye have in order to the freedome of the people suppressed the high Commission, Star-Chamber, and Councell-Table, called home the banished, delivered such as were imprisoned for matters of conscience, and brought some Delinquents to deserved punishment. That ye have suppressed the *Bishops* and Popish *Lords,* abolished *Episcopacy,* and that kind of Prelatick persecuting government. That ye have taken away Ship-money and all the new illegall Patents, whereby the hearts of all the well-affected were enlarged and filled with a confident hope, that they should have seen long ere this a compleat removall of all grievances, and the whole people delivered from all oppressions over soule or body : But such is our miserie that after the expence of so much precious time, of blood and treasure, and the ruine of so many thousands of honest families in recovering our Liberties, we still find this Nation oppressed with grievances of the same destructive nature as formerly, though under other notions ; and which are so much the more grievous unto us, because they are inflicted in the very time of this present *Parliament,* under God the hope of the oppressed. For, as then all the men and women in *England* were made liable to the summons, attachments, sentences, and imprisonments of the Lords of the Councell-boord, so we find by wofull experience and sufferings of many particular persons, that the present Lords doe assume and exercise the same power, then which nothing is, or can be more repugnant and destructive to the Commons just liberties.

As then the unjust power of *Star-Chamber* was exercised in compelling of men and women to answer to Interrogatories tending to accuse themselves and others ; so is the same now frequently practiced upon divers persons, even your cordiall friends that have been, and still are punished for refusing to answer to questions against themselves, and nearest relations. As then the great oppression of the high Commission was most evident in molesting of godly peaceable people, for non-conformity, or different opinion and practice in Religion, judging all who were contrary-minded to themselves, to bee Hereticks, Sectaries, Schismaticks, seditious, factious, enemies to the State, and the like ; and under great penalties forbidding all persons, not licenced by them, to preach or publish the Gospel : Even so now at this day, the very same, if not greater molestations, are set on foot, and violently prosecuted by the instigation of a Clergy no more infallible then the former, to the extreame discouragement and affliction of many thousands of your faithfull adherents, who are not satisfied that controversies in Religion, can be trusted to the compulsive regulation of any : And after the Bishops were suppressed, did hope never to have seen such a power assumed by any in this Nation any more.

And although all new illegall Patents are by you abolished,

yet the oppressive Monopoly of Merchant-adventurers, and others, do still remain to the great abridgement of the liberties of the people, and to the extreme prejudice of all such industrious people as depend on cloathing, or other woollen manufacture, (it being the Staple commodity of this Nation,) and to the great discouragement and disadvantage of all sorts of Tradesmen, Sea-faring-men, and hindrance of Shipping and Navigation. Also the old tedious and chargable way of deciding controversies, or suits in Law, is continued to this day, to the extreame vexation and utter undoing of multiudes of Families ; a grievance as great and as palpable as any in the world. Likewise, that old, but most unequall punishment of malefactors, is still continued, whereby mens lives and liberties are as liable to the law, and corporall pains as much inflicted for small as for great offences, and that most unjustly upon the testimony of one witnesse, contrary both to the law of God, and common equity, a grievance very great, but litle regarded. Also tythes, and other enforced maintenance are still continued, though there be no ground for either under the Gospel ; and though the same have occasioned multitudes of suites, quarrels and debates, both in former and latter times. In like maner, multitudes of poore distressed prisoners for debt, ly still unregarded, in a most miserable and wofull condition throughout the Land, to the great reproach of this Nation. Likewise Prison-Keepers, or Goalers, are as presumptuous as ever they were, both in receiving and detaining of Prisoners illegally committed, as cruell and inhumane to all, especially to such as are well-affected, as oppressive and extorting in their Fees, and are attended with under-officers, of such vile and unchristian demeanour, as is most abominable. Also thousands of men and women are still (as formerly) permitted to live in beggery and wickednesse all their life long, and to breed their children to the same idle and vitious course of life, and no effectual meanes used to reclaim either, or to reduce them to any vertue or industry.

And last, as those who found themselves aggrieved formerly at the burdens & oppressions of those times, that did not conform to the Church-government then established, refused to pay Ship-money, or yeeld obedience to unjust Patents, were reviled and reproached with nicknames of Puritans, Hereticks, Schismaticks, Sectaries, or were tearmed factious or seditious, men of turbulent spirits, despisers of government, and disturbers of the publike peace ; even so is it at this day in all respects, with those who shew any sensibility of the fore-recited grievances, or move in any manner or measure for remedy thereof, all the reproaches, evills, and mischiefs that can be devised, are thought too few or too little to bee laid upon them, as Roundheads, Sectaries, Independents, Hereticks, Schismaticks, factious, seditious, rebellious disturbers of the publike peace, destroyers of all civill relation, and subordinations ; yea, and beyond what was formerly, nonconformity is now judged a sufficient cause to disable any person though of known fidelity, from bearing any Office of trust in the Commonwealth, whilest Neuters, Malignants, and dis-affected are admitted and continued. And though it be not now made a crime to mention a *Parliament,* yet is it little lesse to mention the supreme power of this honourable House. So that in all these respects, this Nation remaineth in a very sad and disconsolate condition; and the more, because it is thus with us after so long a session of so powerfull and so free a *Parliament,* and which hath been so made and maintained, by the aboundant love and liberall effusion of the blood of the people. And therefore knowing no danger nor thraldome like unto our being left in this most sad condition by this *Parliament,* and observing that ye are now drawing the great and weighty affaires of this Nation to some kind of conclusion, and fearing that ye may ere long bee obstructed by somthing equally evill to a negative voice, and that ye may be induced to lay by that strength, which (under God) hath hitherto made you powerfull to all good workes : whilest we have yet time to hope, and yee power to help, and least by our silence we might be guilty of that ruine and slavery, which without your speedy help is like to fall upon us, your selves and the whole Nation; we have presumed to spread our cause thus plainely and largely before you : And do most earnestly entreat, that ye will stir up your affections to a zealous love and tender regard of the people, who have chosen and trusted you, and that ye will seriously consider, that the end of their trust, was freedome and deliverance from all kind of temporall grievances and oppressions.

1. And that therefore in the first place, ye will bee exceeding carefull to preserve your just authority from all prejudices of a negative voice in any person or persons whomsoever, which may disable you from making that happy return unto the people which they justly expect, and that ye will not be induced to lay by your strength, untill ye have satisfied your understandings in the undoubted security of your selves, and of those who have voluntarily and faithfully adhered unto you in all your extremities ; and untill yee have secured and setled the Common-wealth in solid peace

and true freedome, which is the end of the primitive institution of all governments.

2. That ye will take off all Sentences, Fines and Imprisonments imposed on Commoners, by any whomsoever, without due course of Law, or judgement of their equalls : and to give due reparations to all those who have been so injuriously dealt withall, and for preventing the like for the time to come, that yee will enact all such Arbitrary proceedings to bee capitall crimes.

3. That ye will permit no authority whatsoever, to compell any person or persons to answer to questions against themselves, or nearest relations, except in cases of private interest between party and party in a legall way, and to release all such as suffer by imprisonment, or otherwise for refusing to answer to such Interrogatories.

4. That all Statutes, Oathes and Covenants may be repealed so farre as they tend, or may be construed to the molestation and ensnaring of religious, peaceable, well-affected people, for non-conformity, or different opinion or practice in Religion.

5. That no man for preaching or publishing his opinion in Religion in a peaceable way, may be punished or persecuted as hereticall, by Judges that are not infallible, but may be mistaken (as well as other men) in their judgements, least upon pretence of suppressing Errors, Sects or Schisms, the most necessary truths, and sincere professors thereof may be suppressed, as upon the like pretence it hath been in all ages.

6. That ye will, for the encouragement of industrious people, dissolve that old oppressive Company of Merchant-Adventurers, and the like, and prevent all such others by great penalties for ever.

7. That yee will settle a just, speedy, plaine and unburthensome way, for deciding of controversies and suits in Law, and reduce all Lawes to the nearest agreement with Christianity, and publish them in the *English* Tongue, and that all processes and proceedings therein may be true and also in *English,* and in the most usuall Character of writing, without any abreviations, that each one who can read, may the better understand their owne affaires; and that the duty of all Judges, Officers, and practicers in the Law, and of all Magistrates and Officers in the Commonwealth may be prescribed, and their fees limited under strict penalties, and published in print to the view and knowledge of all men : by which just and equitable meanes, this Nation shall be for

ever freed of an oppression more burthensome and troublesome then all the oppressions hitherto by this *Parliament* removed.

8. That the life of no person may be taken away, under the testimony of two witnesses at least, of honest conversation ; and that in an equitable way ye will proportion punishments to offences, that so no mans life may be taken, his body punished, nor his estate forfeited, but upon such weighty and considerable causes as justly deserve such punishments ; and that all prisoners may have a speedy tryall, that they be neither starved, nor their families ruined, by long and lingring imprisonment; and that imprisonment may be used onely for safe custody untill time of triall, and not as a punishment for offences.

9. That tythes and all other enforced maintenance, may be for ever abolished, and nothing in place thereof imposed ; but that all Ministers may be paid onely by those who voluntarily contribute to them, or chuse them, and contract with them for their labours.

10. That ye will take some speedy and effectuall course to relieve all such prisoners for debt, as are altogether unable to pay, that they may not perish in prison through the hard-heartednesse of their Creditors ; and that all such as have any estates, may bee inforced to make paiment accordingly, and not to shelter themselves in prison to defraud their Creditors.

11. That none may be Prison-keepers, but such as are of approved honestie, and that they may be prohibited under great penalties to receive or detaine any person or persons without lawfull warrant : That their usage of prisoners may be with gentlenesse and civility, their fees moderate and certain, and that they may give security for the good behaviour of their under-Officers.

12. That ye will provide some powerfull meanes to keep men, women, and children from begging and wickednesse, that this Nation may be no longer a shame to Christianity therein.

13. That ye will restraine and discountenance the malice and impudency of impious persons, in their reviling and reproaching the well-affected, with the ignominious titles of Round-heads, factious, seditious and the like, whereby your reall friends have been a long time, and still are exceedingly wronged, discouraged, and made obnoxious to rude and prophane people, and that ye wil not exclude any of approved fidelity from bearing office of trust in the Common-wealth for non-conformity ; but rather Neuters and such as manifest dis-affection or opposition to common

freedome, the admission and continuation of such being the chief cause of all these our grievances.

These remedies, or what other shall seem more effectuall to your grave wisdomes, we humbly pray may be speedily applied, and that in doing thereof, ye will be confident of the assistance of your Petitioners, and of all considerate well-minded people, to the uttermost of their best abilities, against all opposition whatsoever, looking upon our selves as more concerned now at last to make a good end, then at the first to have made a good beginning : For what shall it profit us, or what remedy can we expect, if now after so great troubles and miseries this Nation should be left by this Parliament in so great a thraldome, both of body, mind, and estate?

We beseech you therefore, that with all your might whilest he have time, freedome and power, so effectually to fulfill the true end of Parliaments in delivering this Nation from these and all other grievances, that none may presume or dare to introduce the like for ever.

And we trust, the God of your good successe, will manifest the integrity of our intentions herein, and that our humble desires are such, as tend not onely to our owne particular, but to the generall good of the Common-wealth, and proper for this Honourable House to grant, without which this Nation cannot be safe, or happy : And that he will blesse you with true Christian fortitude, suitable to the trust and greatnesse of the worke yee have undertaken, and make the memory of this Parliament blessed to all succeeding Generations.

Shall ever be the fervent desire of your humble Petitioners.

Document 3

A COPIE OF A LETTER

Appeared June 24, 1647. Reprinted from a photostat copy of the original pamphlet, Thomason Collection, E. 393 (33).

A Copie of A Letter, dated at St. Albans June 21, contains the text of *A Solemn Engagement,* the army's manifesto of June 5. *A Solemn Engagement* was the Levellers' response to Parliament's treatment of their March petition. It bound the army not to disband until Parliament had redressed their grievances. What is still more significant, it provided for a representative General Council of the army (the common soldiers to have equal votes with the officers) to frame their grievances and make appropriate representations to Parliament of the army's desires. The General Council, by implication, was a committee of citizens over which the authoritarian discipline of the army was to have no control whatever.[1] In it the soldier laid aside his arms and his deference to officers; he became a citizen legislator. The radical tone of *A Solemn Engagement* reveals the victory of the army Levellers over the fears and moderating admonitions of the officers. The intense democratic propaganda carried on in the army was for the moment triumphant; the organization of the private soldiery described in the *Engagement* (p. 147) had been strikingly effectual. The idea of the army's mutual engagement formed a precedent for *An Agreement* [2] *of the People;* the principle in each was the social contract put into practical operation, with premises and principles first agreed to, then machinery erected to delineate specific patterns of reformation.

A Copie of a Letter opens with a history of the radicals' efforts in the army; it closes with an account of their disappointment

[1] In his *History of the Great Civil War* Gardiner ascribes to Cromwell the idea of the General Council as well as the disavowal of "dangerous principles" at the end of the *Engagement.* Of these ascriptions, the latter I think is sound enough, the former untenable.

[2] The word *agreement* is used to mean *engagement* in this document (p. 150).

with Parliament and an appeal to the seamen for support of their program. These addresses to the seamen show the Levellers' concern for the support of the common sailors, men infinitely more conservative than the New Model soldiery. The pamphlet is indicative of the thorough work of the Leveller organization; they were leaving no avenues unopened by which they might march toward their ideal of social reconstruction.

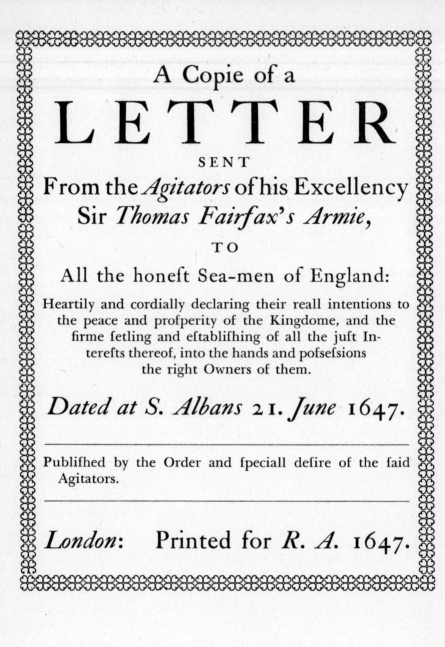

A Copie of a

LETTER

SENT

From the *Agitators* of his Excellency
Sir *Thomas Fairfax's Armie,*

TO

All the honeſt Sea-men of England:

Heartily and cordially declaring their reall intentions to
the peace and proſperity of the Kingdome, and the
firme ſetling and eſtabliſhing of all the juſt In-
tereſts thereof, into the hands and poſſeſsions
the right Owners of them.

Dated at S. Albans 21. *June* 1647.

Publiſhed by the Order and ſpeciall deſire of the ſaid
Agitators.

London: Printed for *R. A.* 1647.

A Letter from the Army to all the honeſt Seamen of England.

Honoured and deare Friends,

THE great designe of our Enemies being to divide, (and so to destroy) we conceive it the maine businesse of friends to unite, and so to spoile that designe: Now the wayes that are at this day, taken to divide, are misrepresentations of persons and actions (especially of us and ours) to the Kingdome, which that we may prevent, we shall endeavour to informe you (our noble and faithfull friends) of the state of things as followeth: Some five yeares since we by Land and you by Sea, upon the apprehension of apparent danger to the Kingdome, were invited to put our selves into a posture of defence, for the preventing and suppressing of that power then rising, which threatned the Kingdomes ruine, for the avoyding of which (at present) and setling an establishment (for the future) of all the free-borne people of England, in the enjoyment of their just Rights and Priviledges, (which was one of the ends of our taking up of Arms) we went with cheerfulnesse to the worke, and after many a sore encounter that you and we have had by Sea and Land, at last (by the blessing of God) came to the end of our worke, hoping now (after such a long and weary journey) to have taken up our rest, and have set down quietly under our vines, and with the rest of the Kingdome to have enjoyed the fruit of our sore travells, but contrary to our expectation and to the amazement and saddening of our spirits, we finde our selves in as bad or worse condition now, then formerly, being denied and deprived of that undoubted right and priviledge which the Subjects of England, in the worst of times, hardly ever were *(viz.)* petitioning, nay, not onely denied of, but declared against as enemies, for making use of those meanes we were directed to in case of grievances, and so we are now made compleatly miserable. When we see this, we knew whose hand was in it, namely, that here was the same persons and principles working our ruine as formerly, onely in another forme, before by power and open hostility, and now by craft, and policy; which caused us to draw up a Vindication of the afore-said intended Petition, yet nothwithstanding our Vindication we still lie under a sentence of condemnation as enemies to the State. Then we drew up a Letter to the Generall, the Lievtenant-Generall, and the Major-Generall, in which was laid open the sad condition how neere ruine and destruction we were, and the causes of it, as we apprehended, and this we did to incite them to improve all the interest they had in or with any, for us, to prevent the ensuing destruction, especially since we could not be heard in our Petition, but this Letter was conceived to be of dangerous consequence, and so presented to the House, where (after some debates) the results were to send downe Commissioners to the Army, to take a view of the distempers reported to bee in it, and to receive their grievances, and present them to the House.

This a little revived us, hoping we should have them heard and redressed, but suddenly after the receiving of them (without the full redressing of any one of them) we were voted to be disbanded piece-meale, apart, one Regiment from another, so as never any faithfull Army was, being marked out for destruction, wanting nothing but disbanding to hasten execution. Hearing of this we drew up a Petition to our Generall to have a Rendezvouz, at which we might advise what was best to be done (for our owne and the Kingdomes safety) in this case, and there entred into a Contract, a copie of which we have here sent you.

A solemne engagement of the Army, under the Command of his Excellency Sir Thomas Fairfax, read, assented unto, and subscribed by all Officers, and Souldiers of the severall Regiments, at the generall Rendezvouz neare Newmarket, on the fift of June, 1647.

WHereas upon the Petition intended and agreed upon in the Army, in *March* last, to have been presented to the Generall, for the obtaining of our due and necessary concernments as Souldiers; the Honorable House of *Commons* being unseason-

ably prepossessed with a Copie thereof, and (as by the sequell
we suppose) with some strange misrepresentations of the carriage
and intentions of the same, was induced to send downe an Order
for surpressing the Petition, and within two or three dayes after,
upon further misinformation, and scandalous suggestions, of the
like or worse nature, and by the indirect practice of some malitious and mischievous persons (as we suppose) surprizing or other
wise abusing the *Parliament*. A Declaration was published in the
name of both Houses, highly censuring the said Petition, and
declaring the Petitioners, if they should proceed thereupon, no
lesse then enemies to the State, and disturbers of the publick
peace. And whereas at the same time and since, divers eminent
Officers of the Army have been brought into question and trouble
about the said Petition, whereby both they and the rest of the
Officers were disabled, or discouraged for the time, from further
acting or appearing therein on the souldiers behalfe, And wheras
by the aforesaid proceedings and the effects thereof, the souldiers
of this Army (finding themselves so stopt in their due, and regular
way of making knowne their just grievances, and desires to, and
by their Officers) were enforced to an unusuall (but in that case
necessary) way of correspondence and agreement amongst themselves, to chuse out of the severall Troops and Companies severall
men, and those out of their whole number, to chuse two or more
for each Regiment, to act in the name and behalfe of the whole
souldiery of the respective Regiments Troops and Companies,
in the prosecution of their rights and desires in the said Petition,
as also of their just vindication and writing in reference to the
aforesaid proceedings upon and against the same, who have accordingly acted and done many things, to those ends, all which
the souldiers did then approve as their owne acts.

And whereas afterwards (upon the sudden sending down of
Field-Marshall *Skippon,* and those other Officers of the Army that
were Members of the House of Commons, to quiet distempers
in the Army, fresh hopes being conceived of having our desires
again admitted to be made known, and considered in a regular
way, and without such misrepresentations as formerly, the Officers
and Souldiers of the Army (except some few dissenting Officers)
did againe joyne in a representation of their common grievances,
and the Officers (except as before) did agree upon a narrative
Accompt of the grounds, rise and growth of the discontents in the

Army, and their proceedings in relation thereunto, with an over-ture of the best expedients, to remove or satisfie the same; both which were presented to the same Members of the House, and by them reported to the House. And wheras the Parliament hav-ing thereupon voted, and ordered some particulars, onely towards satisfaction of our grievances, hath since proceeded to certain resolutions of sudden disbanding the Army by peeces; which reso-lution being taken, and to be executed, before full or equall satisfaction given to the whole Army in any of the grievances, before effectuall performance of that satisfaction in part, which the preceding Votes seem'd to promise, as to some of the griev-ances, and before any consideration at all of some others most materiall, (as by the result of a generall Councell of Warre on Saturday *May* 29. was in generall declared, and is now more fully demonstrated in particular by a representation thereupon, agreed unto by us: we all cannot but look upon the same resolutions of disbanding us in such manner, as proceeding from the same mali-cious and mischievous principles and intentions, and from the like indirect practises of the same persons abusing the Parliament, and is as the former proceedings against us before mentioned did, and not without carnall and bloody purposes (for some of them have not stuck to declare or intimate) after the body of the Army should be disbanded, or the Souldiers divided from their Officers, then to question, proceed against, and execute their malicious intentions upon all such particular Officers and Souldiers in the Army, as had appeared to act in the Premises in the behalfe of the Army: And whereas upon a late Petition to the Generall from the Agitants, in behalfe of the Souldiers (grounded upon the preceding considerations, relating to the same resolutions of disbanding, the same generall Councell of Warre to prevent the danger and inconveniences of those disturbings, or tumultuous actings or confluences which the dis-satisfaction and jealousie thereupon also grounded, were like suddenly to have produced in the Army, to advise the Generall first to con-tract the Quarters of the Army, and then to draw the same to an orderly *Rendezvouz* for the satisfaction of all, and that his Ex-cellency would immediately send up to move and desire the Par-liament to suspend any present proceeding upon the said resolu-tion of disbanding, to resume the consideration of the grievances, and desire, sent up from the Army, and not to disband it in pieces before just and equall satisfaction given to the whole; And whereas some of the Regiments appointed for disbanding, upon notice thereof withdrawing themselves from the Quarters adjacent to the appointed Rendezvouz, and drawing towards the Head-Quarters; and the contracting their Quarters, according to the said advice of the Councel of War.

We the Officers and Souldiers of severall Regiments here after-named, are now met at a generall Rendezvouz, and the Regiments appointed as afore-said to be disbanded, have not appeared, nor can appeare; but are resolved not to appeare at the severall and respective Rendezvouz, appointed as aforesaid for their disband-ing; and divers other things have been done by severall other parties or members of the Army, necessarily relating to the good and concernment of the whole in those affaires. Now for as much as wee know not how far the malice, Injustice, and Tiranicall Principles of our enemies, that have already prevailed so far to abuse the Parliament and the Army (as is afore mentionid) in the past proceedings against the Army may further prevaile to the danger and prejudice of our selves, or any Officers, or Souldiers of the Army, or other persons that have appeared to act any thing in behalfe of the Army, or how far the same may further prevaile to the danger or prejudice of the Kingdome in raising a new warre, or otherwise: Therefore for the better prevention of all such dangers, prejudices, or other inconveniences that may ensue; and withall for better satisfaction to the Parliament and King-dome, concerning our desires of conforming to the authority of the one, and providing the good and quiet of the other, in the present affaires of disbanding, and for a more assured way whereby, that affaires may come to a certaine issue, (to which purpose we herein humbly implore the present and continued assistance of God, the Righteous Iudge of all) wee the Officers and Souldiers of the Army subscribing hereunto; doe hereby declare, agree, and promise, to and with each other, and to, and with the Parliament and Kingdome as followeth.

1. That wee shall chearfully and readily disband when there-unto required by the Parliament, or else shall many of us be willing (if desired) to ingage in further Services either in *England* or *Ireland,* having first such satisfaction to the Army in relation to our grievances and desires heretofore presented, and such se-curity, That we of our selves, when disbanded, and in the condi-tion of private men, or other the free-borne people of *England,*

to whom the consequence of our case doth equally extend, shall not remaine subject to the like oppression, injury, or abuse, as in the premisses hath been attempted and put upon us, while an Army by the same mens continuance, in the same credit and power, especially if as our Judges, who have in these past proceedings against the Army so farre prevailed to abuse the Parliament and us, and to endanger the Kingdome; and also such security that we our selves, or any member of this Army or others, who have appeared to act any thing in behalf of the Army, in relation to the premises before recited, shall not after disbanding be any way questioned, prosecuted, troubled, or prejudiced for any thing so acted, or for the entring into, or necessary prosecution of this necessary agreement: (we say) having first such satisfaction and security in these things as shall be agreed unto by a Councell to consist of those generall Officers of the Army (who have concurred with the Army in the premisses) with two Commission Officers and two Souldiers to be chosen for each Regiment, who have concurred and shall concur with us in the premisses and in this agreement. And by the major part of such of them who shal meet in Councel for that purpose when they shal be thereunto called by the General.

2. That without such satisfaction and security, as aforesaid, we shal not willingly disband, nor divide, nor suffer our selves to be disbanded or divided.

And whereas we find many strange things suggested or suspected to our great prejudice concerning dangerous principles, interests and designs in this Army (as to the overthrow of Magistracy, the suppression or hindering of Presbytery, the establishment of Independent government, or upholding of a general licentiousness in Religion under pretence of Liberty of Conscience, and many such things; we shal very shortly tender to the Parliament a Vindication of the Army from all such scandals to clear our Principles in relation thereunto, and in the mean time we do disavow and disclaim all purposes or designs in our late or present proceedings to advance or insist upon any such interest, neither would we (if we might and could) advance or set up any other particular party or interest in the Kingdom (though imagined never so much our own) but shal much rather (as far as may be within our sphear or power) study to promote such an establishment of common and equal right and freedom to the whole, as all might equally partake of but those that do by denying the same to others, or otherwise render themselves incapable thereof.

FINIS

After this we were commanded to a Rendezvouz by the Parliament and Commissioners sent down with some Votes tending to satisfaction in part, wherein did remain dissatisfaction at present (even to those particular grievances there related) and not security for the future by any thing yet done, especially knowing those were remaining with power in their hands, who could undo all they had done for us, or do as much more against us if disbanded, as may appear in our late Declaration 14. *Iune* 1647. To which we refer you. And therefore the Cry of the whole Army and divers Counties also (by their addresses to his Excellency) was not so much for the taking of the present sad effects from us, as for the removal of that Cause which had (at present) and would (for the future) produce the like (if not worse) mischiefes as appeared by the unanimous voyce of the whole Army, crying out, Justice, Justice; Justice against those persons who have fastly aspersed us, against those who have abused the trust reposed in them; and Justice upon those from whom we can expect no security, but rather destruction; which main desire (once granted) would beget satisfaction, and then, and not till then, can we lay down Arms with safety: Thus we have presented you with our condition for your information. Now we desire you and all rational men to judg, and the God of Heaven and Earth be Judg (between us and those persons who have acted against us) whether ever we have deserved such things at their hands, who have not thought any thing too dear to part with or lay down for their sakes, looking upon them as persons intrusted by and acting for the Weal (not the Woe) of this Kingdom, and though we have suffered much from, and been deprived much by our open Enemies, yet did still expect our professed friends would have dealt better with us, and little thought to have had such a portion from them as to be declared Enemies to the State, even while we were an Army having power in our hands, and they having further occasions to use us: To have this done against us, what will be done if all these considerations were removed? Therefore consider what it is we seek, even that which all creatures of the world do (and Man, the chiefest of all creatures, cannot but do;) *viz.* self-preservation, in avoyding that destruction which is like (if not prevented) to fall on us and the whole Kingdom with us, as it must needs do, if (when lying under many pressures and grievances as we question not but you (as wel as we) and thousands others in the Kingdom do) we may not petition for redress, but must be voted Enemies; judge you what this wants of the protection of slavery, which, we hope, is the real desires of us all to prevent. And we assure you upon the faith of honest Men and Souldiers, that (what ever may be suggested to you by any) we have no other aymes, but that Justice might act in all its parts and to all its ends, as relating to all estates and persons in the Kingdom, that the yokes of Oppression might be taken off the necks of all and Justice equally distributed to all, and the rights of any (though now detained from them) restored, and settled upon them, that so they might not be taken from them, unless they disabled themselves of the enjoyment of them and so doing we trust we shal have the concurrent assistance of (at leastwise not any opposition from any rational Men who love Justice and hate Tyranny, especially from you (deer friends) who together with us, have been imbarqued in the same ship, and have passed through many a desperate encounter by Sea as we have by Land, all to free this poor Kingdom from Tyrannical Oppression, (which notwithstanding, you and we feel too much of at this day) who we trust with us, do hate and scorn to be kept any longer under bondage, having purchased our freedom at so dear a rate, (though free born). We shal say no more, but desire you to take heed of all false suggestions, and vain delusions; and know this is our genuine meaning that is here before you, which [being rightly apprehended by you] we hope wil make all the attempts of men, [to divide you from us either by frownes, Favours, or Gratuities, which assure your selves they wil not be wanting in to accomplish their ends] useless, and all the seeds of malice [by them sown] fruitless, unless to bring them to receive that reward for their worke which may be suitable to it, and so in stead of dividing, we hope may prove such an uniting that maybe as a threefold Cord that shal not easily be broken, which if it shal thus unite us, we shal rejoyce in it, and shal be enabled by it to go on in the prosecution of so good a work til we see Oppression, and Oppressers from us, and the Kingdom removed, a firm and happy peace setled, a poor Kingdom from ruin and destruction delivered, which we hope is and ever shal be your and our joynt desires & endevors of all opposition, and in so doing assure your selvs against we are and wil be yours while you are the

Kingdoms and ours, resoluing to be either happy or miserable together.

Yours and the Kingdoms Servants.

S. ALBANS,
June 21. 1647.

Lewes Audley.	*Edm. Rolphe.*
John Clerke.	*Alex. Brafield.*
John Carter.	*Azariah Husbands.*

Joh. Nufon. *Edm. Vaughan.*	*Gen. Foot Regiment.*
William Allin	*Lieutenant Generals Regiment.*
Nath. Foxgill. *Will. Bridgeman.*	*Collonel Hammons Regiment.*
Henry Anderton *Robert Mason.*	*Collonel Wallers Regiment.*
John Millar. *Richard Colbrand.*	*Collonel Lamberts Regiment.*
Will. Swallow. *Herbert Feild*	*Collonel Lilburns Regiment.*
Barth. Willocke *Richard Clarke*	*Collonel Thomlinsons Regiment.*
Edmund Garne *Daniel Hincksman*	*Collonel Hewsons Regiment.*
Nico. Andrews *Ralph. Reentis*	*Collonel Reads Regiment.*

FINIS.

AN APPEALE

By Richard Overton

Appeared July 17, 1647. Reprinted from a photostatic copy of the
original pamphlet, Thomason Collection, E 398 (28).

On July 6, 1646, had appeared *A Remonstrance Of Many
Thousand Citizens,* written in part or in whole by Overton. It
shows him in the van of the Leveller theorists, who at that time
were just beginning to shift from demands for toleration to demands for secular reform. This pamphlet was the most biting
attack on kingship that had yet appeared and most drastic in its
claims for popular sovereignty. On November 30 Overton sent
forth his *An Vnhappy Game at Scotch And English,* with arguments against kingly prerogative that anticipate the leading ideas
of *Regall Tyrannie discovered* (January 6, 1647), which is easily
the best written anti-monarchical tract of the period, much of it
undoubtedly by Overton. *An Appeale* is a remarkable extension
of Overton's main arguments as they had appeared in these tracts.
It emphasizes again Parliament's responsibility to the people, this
time, however, renouncing Parliament as unfit longer to govern,
and appealing from the "degenerate body" to the citizens themselves. In making his appeal, Overton speaks directly to the army,
assuming that they represent the people and can carry out its will.
In this, of course, he was to be bitterly disappointed.

Overton has worked out a careful theoretical justification for
his stand; he admits that he has no precedents except reason for
his appeal from Parliament to the people; he insists that in betraying its trust, Parliament has relinquished its authority, which then
automatically returns to the "betrusters." In calling upon the
people, then, he is merely following the real power of government to its "fountain." He does not expect to exchange a tyrant
king for a tyrant Parliament. Overton calls attention to Parlia-

ment's crushing and rejection of petitions, "the highest kind of tyranny in the world," like burning the Great Charter.

An Appeale contains many memorable passages; it is a document worth the close attention of the stylist as well as the social thinker. Overton's rejection of all coercion in religious beliefs (pp. 181-182), is one of his many classic statements of toleration. Like Lilburne, he dramatized his own struggles to serve his cause; his wife is in one prison, he in another, his brother in still a third, his children at large, dependent upon the kindness of friends. He exposes dramatically the hardships and injustices of prison life, and it is significant that in his demands for redress of grievances prisons and courts have a prominent place. The "Certain Articles" (p. 189) represent significant deviations from the March petition. Overton's emphasis on schools, hospitals, and the return of inclosed land to communal use is not typical of Leveller propaganda.

AN APPEALE

From the degenerate Reprefentative Body
the Commons of England affembled at
Weftminfter:

To the Body Reprefented

The free people in general of the feveral Counties, Cities,
Townes, Burroughs, and places within this Kingdome
of England, and Dominion of Wales.

And in efpeciall, To his Excellency Sir *Thomas Fairfax*
(Captaine Generall) and to all the Officers and Souldiers under his Command.

---

*By Richard Overton, Prifoner in the infamous Goale of Newgate,
for the Liberties and Freedomes of England.*

---

2. Cor. 10. 16.

*And when all Ifrael faw (as now England feeth doth the Parlia-
ment) that the King would not hearken unto them, the people
anfwered the King, faying, What portion have we in* David?
And we have no inheritance in the fon of Jeffe: *Every man
unto his tents, O Ifrael, and now* David, *fee to thine owne
houfe: [fo all Ifrael went to their tents.]*

† The fame
may now be
applyed to
London.

* The Lord
grant it may
be practical-
ly applyed
by the Citi-
zens of Lon-
don.

Cap. 11.4.

Thus faith the Lord, yee fhall not goe up † *nor fight
againft your brethren, returne every man to his
houfe, for this thing is done of me: [*And they
obeyed the words of the Lord, and returned from
going againft* Jeroboam.]

LONDON,
Printed in the yeare, 1647.

AN APPEALE,

FROM THE DEGENERATE

REPRESENTATIVE BODY OF

the Commons of *England* Affembled
at *Weftminfter*.

To the Body Reprefented,

The free people in Generall of the feverall

Counties, Cities, Townes, Burroughes and
Places within this Kingdom of *England,*
and Dominion of *Wales.*

And in efpeciall,

To His Excellency, Sir *Thomas Fairfax* (Cap-

taine Generall) and to all the Officers and
Soldiers under His Command.

Right Excellent and Illuftrious Generall,	*This Kingdome of*
Honourable and Noble Officers,	*England, and*
Faithfull and honeft Gentlemen Soldiers,	*Dominion*
And all other duly refpected Fellow Sub-	*of*
jects, and free Commoners, of	*Wales.*

IT is confessed, that our *English Histories* and *Records* of the *Actions* and *Transactions* of our *Predecessours,* both of anti-ent and late times, (so far as I can understand) do not afford me any example or president for any A P P E A L E from Parliaments to people, neither is there any such liberty provided in the *Letter* of our law: So that by such as preferre presidents and formalities, formes and figures, before the substance, life and spirit of all just presidents and Lawes, I may probably be censured and condemned for this present enterprize, as an open and desperate

157

enemy to Parliaments and Magistracy, a subverter and destroyer
of all Nationall Lawes and Government, and a reducer (to my
power) of Kingdomes and people into confusion: To such I shall
returne even the late words of (our now degenerate Parliament)
*That Reason hath no president, for Reason is the fountaine of all
just presidents,* I *Book Decl. fol.* 264. 298. 709. 726. therefore
where that is, there is a sufficient and justifiable president.

And if *this Principle* must be granted of, and obeyed by all,
as by no rationall man can bee denyed, then the Act of *Appeale*
in this nature if grounded upon *right Reason* is justifiable and
warranted, even by *That* which gives an equitable Authority,
life and being to all just Lawes, presidents and formes of Government whatsoever, for Reason is their very life and spirit, whereby
they are all made lawfull and warrantable both for *Settlement,
Administration* and *Obedience;* which is the *highest* kind of *Justification* and *Authority* for *humaine Actions* that can be; for
greater is *that,* which *gives Being* and *justifieth,* then *that* which
receiveth and is *justified:* All Formes of Lawes and Governments
may fall and passe away; but *right Reason* (the fountain of all
justice and mercy to the creature) shall and will *endure for ever;*
it is that by which in all our Actions wee must stand or fall, be
justified or condemned; for neither *Morality* nor *Divinity* amongst
Men can or may transgresse the limits of *right reason,* for whatsoever is unreasonable cannot be *justly* tearmed *Morall* or *Divine,*
and *right reason* is only commensurable and discernable by the
rule of merciful *Justice* and just *mercy;* it is graduall in its *Quantity,* but one in its *Quality;* severall are its *Degrees,* but its *perfection* and fulnesse is *only* in *God,* and its several *Branches* and
Degrees are only communicable, and derivated from *Him,* as
severall *Beames* and *Degrees* of *heat* from the *Body* of the *Sunne,*
yet *all heat;* so in *Reason* there are different degrees, as, from
Morality to *Divinity,* and under those two heads, severall *subordinate Degrees,* all derivated and conveyed from the Creator
(the originall Fountaine) to the creature, yet *all one* and the *same*
in *nature,* the difference only lying in the degree of the thing, not
in the thing it selfe; as, a Dwarfe is as much a man as a Gyant,
though not so bigge a man; and so, though the gifts and graces
of God are one *radically,* yet different in their *species,* and all
from one and the same spirit, which can Act nothing contrary
to its owne nature, and God is not a God of irrationality, and
madnesse, or tryranny: Therefore all his communications are
reasonable and just, and what is so, is of God.

And upon *this Principle,* as upon a firme and sure foundation all just Lawes and Governments are founded and erected; and in particular, the fundamentall Lawes and Government of this Kingdome; for, it is a sure and radicall *Maxime* in our *Law, Nihil quod est contrarationem, est licium,* Nothing which is against reason is lawfull, *Reason* being the *very life* of the *Law of our Land:* So that should the Law be taken away from its *Originall reason* and end, it would be made a shell without a kernill, a shadow without substance, a carkasse without life, which presently turnes to putrifaction; and as *Reason* only gives it a *legall Being* and *life,* so it only makes it authoritive and binding; if this be not granted, lust, will, pride, and what the Divell and corruption will, may be a Law; for if *right reason* be not the *only* being and bounder of the Law over the corrupt nature of man, that *what* is *rationall* (the which injustice and tyranny cannot be) may only and at all times be *legall*; and *what* is *legall,* to be simply and purely *rationall,* the which mercy and justice must be whensoever, wheresoever, and by whomsoever it be, for in it selfe it is legall, rationall and just, or else all would fall into confusion, disorder, madnesse and cruelty: and so Magistracie would cease, and be converted into inhumanity and tyranny.

So that it being most evident and cleare to the eye of *Rationall Man,* that this fundamental principle may not (in being to Magistracy it selfe) be expulsed the precincts of Magisteriall Government, but must be preserved (as the apple of its eye) intire and absolute therein, for all present and future supplies, as a sure and safe refuge to fly to in all straites and extremities whatsoever for preservation, safety, removall of oppressions, &c. or else no safety or reliefe from oppression either publique or private, to be lawfully attempted, pursued, or had: So that where that principle is, there legality and authority must be, and is concomitant to, and inseperable there-from, never to be altered while the Sun and the Moone endures; by it Kings and Kingdoms have their essentiall legall Being, without which they cease from being either Kings or Kingdomes. Therefore, that which doth institute, constitute, and authorize the regality of Kings and Kingdomes, certainly must needs be sufficiently authoritive for a particular, as for this expedient of mine, or the like, in case it be found under the protection and authority of the said principle of *right Reason*; as, I shall clearely evidence it to be.[1]

First then, be pleased to consider, that it is a firme Law and

[1] Principle of Reason.

radicall principle in Nature engraven in the tables of the heart
by the finger of God in creation for every living moving thing,
wherein there is the breath of life to defend, preserve, award, and
deliver it selfe from all things hurtfull, destructive and obnoctious
thereto to the utmost of its power: Therefore from hence is conveyed to all men in generall, and to every man in particular, an undoubted principle of reason, by all rationall and iust wayes and
meanes possibly he may, to save, defend and deliver himselfe from
all oppression, violence and cruelty whatsoever, and (in duty to
his own safety and being) to leave no iust expedient unattempted
for his delivery therefrom: and this is rationall and iust; to deny
it, is to overture the law of nature, yea, and of Religion too; for
the contrary lets in nothing but selfe murther, violence and cruelty. Now the unreasonable oppression of my selfe, my wife,
brother and children, under the Arbitrary tyranny of the *Westminster Lords,* and the wayes and means that I have used for
delivery therefrom considered, and weighed in the ballance of this
naturall radicall principle of reason, this mine attempt of Appeale
(though of a desparate nature) will be found the only meane
wherein I may discerne any probability of reliefe for my selfe,
my wife and my brother, to be brought unto iustice, as by and by
I shall make both the one and the other more manifest and
plaine.

    Secondly, *necessity is a law above all lawes,* and this *principle* [2]
conveyeth and issueth forth authority and power, both to generall
and particular cases, even to the taking up of unusuall and un-
exemplary courses for publique and particular deliverances, and
yet such acts warrantable in, and by all sorts and societies of
people whatsoever, and the actor, or actors thereof justified
thereby: And upon this *Principle,* the *Neitherlanders* made an
hostile defence and resistance against the King of *Spaine,* their
then Soveraign Lord, for the recovery of their just rights and freedomes; And upon the same *point* rose the *Scotch* up in Armes,
and entred this Kingdome, without all *formall countenance* or
allowance of King or Parliament, and were justified for that very
act by this present Parliament. Yea, and even this Parliament
upon the same principle, tooke up Armes against the King. And
now (*right worthy patriots of the Army*) you your selves upon the
same principle, for *recovery of common right* and *freedome,* have
entered upon this your present honourable and *Solemne Engagement,* against the oppressing party at *Westminster,* and plead your

    2 Principle of Reason.

selves justfiable thereby, and tell them in the fifth pag. of your Declaration, *That the Parliament hath declared it no resistance of Magistracie to side with the just principles and law of nature and nations, being that law upon which you have assisted them.* So that if I be condemned for a Traytor by all or any of you, whether *Scotch,* Parliament or Army, for proceeding upon the said *iust principles and law of nature,* for *common right and freedom,* I tell you plainly, that out of your *owne mouthes* you shall be judged no less Traytors then my selfe, yea, allowers of that in your selves, which for treason you condemn in others: And if I suffer death by any party of you, all and every such person and persons, deserves to be hang'd, drawn, and quartered for Traytors by the same law, for if it be just against the one, it is also just against the other, for *iustice is no respecter of persons.*

Now concerning my necessity to this course for reliefe, I shall by and by make evident and plaine to every common capacity; which being made evident, *your Excellency, with the Officers and Soldiers under your command,* are bound to endeavour my protection and safety (to your power) with your own in this enterprize of mine, undertaken upon your own principle for common right and freedome, and as well may you deliver one another up to the Gallowes, for this present *Solemne Engagement* of yours, as not visibly appeare in my vindication and justification together with your own, proceeding upon the very same principle with your selves for the same end.

Thirdly, *The equity of the Law is Superiour to the Letter,*[3] the Letter being subordinate and subject thereto, and looke *how much* the *Letter* transgresseth the *equity,* even *so much* it is *unequalle,* of no validity and force: Yea, if the Law should comptroule and overthrow the *equity,* it is to be comptrouled and overthrowne it selfe, and the *equity* to be preserved as the *thing,* only legally, *obligatory and binding.* And by this principle (worthy Officers and Soldiers) you have charged the Parliament from their own *Declarations* to warrant this your present *Expedition* as in the 4 page of your own *Declaration,* is made manifest: To which principle, together with your selves, and with them I lay claime to a title for an equall justification and protection from the *Letter of the Law,* with the edge of that Sword (which both Parliament and Armie by *that principle* award from themselves) may not be sheathed in my bowels for though I am *prisoner* in the *hands of mine enemies,* yet can I not be condemned of them for *this*

3 Principle of Reason.

enterprize, without their *owne condemnation* of themselves in theirs against the King. So that in *this act* I do not *outstrip* the protection of *that,* which themselves have *declared authorative against the letter of the Law,* but am in all iustice and reason as iustifiable as themselves; or as *this present Army* in *either* or *both* their *Engagements.*

Fourthly, *All betrusted powers if forfeit, fall into the hands of the betrusters, as their proper centure:* [4] and where such a forfeit is committed, there is disoblegeth from obedience, and warranteth an *Appeale* to the *Betrusters,* without any contempt or disobedience, to the *powers* in the least; for such an Appeale in that case is not at all from the *power,* but from the *persons,* not forsaking the *power,* but *following* of it in its *retreat* to the *Fountaine.* For as formerly the Parliament averred, and as now this honourable Army assumeth (*Armie Declaration, pag.* 4) *All authority is fundamentally seated in the office, and but ministerially in the persons;* therefore, the persons in their *Ministrations* degenerating from *safety* to *tyranny,* their *Authority* ceaseth and is only to be found in the fundamentall originall, rise and situation thereof, which is the *people* the *body represented*; for though it ceaseth from the hands of the betrusted, yet it doth not, neither can it cease from its being, for Kings, Parliaments, &c. may fall from it, but it indureth for ever, for were not this admitted, there could be no lawfull redresse in extremity, yea, magistracy it selfe should be transitory and fading like, as is corruption, of no certaine duration or moment, but it is unchangeable and certaine, man perisheth but it indureth: it alwayes is either in the hands of the *Betrusted* or of the *Betrusters,* while the *Betrusted* are *dischargers* of their *trust,* it remaineth in their hands, but no sooner the *Betrusted* betray and forfeit their *Trust,* but (as all things else in dissolution) it returneth from whence it came, even to the hands of the *Trusters*: For all iust *humaine powers* are but betrusted, confer'd and conveyed by ioynt and common consent, *for to every individuall in nature, is given an individuall propriety by nature, not to be invaded or usurped by any,* (as in mine *Arrow against tyranny* is proved and discovered more at large) *for every one as he is himselfe hath a selfe propriety, else could not be himselfe,* and on this no second may presume without consent; and by naturall birth, all men *are equall and alike borne to like propriety and freedome, every man by naturall instinct aiming at his owne safety and weale:* And so it is, that there is a

[4] Principle of Reason.

generall communication amongst men from their severall innate properties to their *Elected Deputies* for their better Being, Discipline, Government, Property, and Safety.

Now as no man by nature may abuse, beat, torment or afflict himself, so by nature no man may give that power to another, seeing he may not doe it himselfe, for no more can be communicated to the generall, then is included in the particulars whereof the generall is compounded; for that were to goe beyond it selfe, for *Being* to goe beyond the *power of being,* which is impossible. So that if the betrusted act not for the weal and safety of the betrusters, they depart from their iust power, and act by another, which cannot be tearmed either humaine or divine, but unnaturall and divellish, rendring such usurpers as Monsters amongst men. Now these premises considered, I doe confidently conclude (if confidence may be derived from the iust principles of nature) that the transgression of our weal by our trustees, is an utter forfeiture of their trust, and cessation of their power: Therefore, if I prove a forfeiture of the *peoples trust* in the prevalent party at *Westminster* in Parliament assembled then an *Appeal* from them to the people is not *Anti-parliamentary, Antimagesteriall,* not *from* that *Soveraign power,* but *to* that *Soveraign power.* For the evidence whereof I shall first present a discovery of their dealings with me, relating to the publique, and then their common course to the generall.

First then briefly concerning my selfe, upon the 11. of *August* 1646. the House of Lords sent (without any summons or other due processe for appearance) their Emisaries with a file of Musqueteers who beset mine house and entred the same, one with his drawn sword, and another with a Pistoll ready cock'd in his hand, and surprized me in my bed without any appearance or shew of any warrant eitheir legall or illegall, and in that warlike manner being led, and brought before a Committee of the said house, and afterwards before the house, where being put High Commission like to answer to Interrogatories against my selfe, the which I refusing to answer, & not being willing to yeeld my right as a Cōmoner into their prerogative clutches, I appealed from them being mine improper incompetent Judges, unto the House of Commons, my legall Peers and Equalls, as by the great Charter of England I was bound, which in severall late printed papers I have made evident and clear to the view of all men, I was under pretence of contempt in word and gesture against that house, and for refusing to answer Interrogatories committed to

Newgate, there to be kept till their Lordships pleasure should be further signified. And afterwards the House of Cōmons receiving mine Appeale, I was turned over with mine honoured friend and fellow sufferer in the said cause Lieut. Col. *John Lilburn,* unto the Committee for *consideration of the Commoners Liberties, Mr. Henry Martin* possessing the Chair, before whom in our contest betwixt the Lords about the right and freedome of the Commons of England; upon examination of the Jurisdiction and prerogative of the one, the right and propertie of the other, we were both found illegally imprisoned, and that Act of the Lords desperate invasion and intrusion upon the Commoners freedoms, and our selves as legally free, as if no such arbitrary warrants had been issued forth against us. Whereupon in contempt and defiance of the Arbitrary domination of the Lords over the Commons, scorning to dance attendance any longer after their arbitrary warrants, resolved that as their Lordships found warrants, so should their Lordships find leggs to obey them, for being free from their arbitrary Jurisdiction from the crown of my head, to the sole of my foot, mine should not *dance after their pipe.* Whereupon I was most incivilly and inhumanely dragged to *Newgate* headlong through the streets upon the stones through all the dirt and the mire, and being reviled, otherwise abused and beat, I was thrown into the common Gaole amongst Rogues and Fellons, and laid in double Irons. And since this time which was the 3. of *November* 1646 to this present 8 of *Iuly.* 1647. I could not prevaile with the Chair-man to make my report unto the House thereby to obtaine any reliefe. But as I am informed, that worthy Gentleman hath neither to been necessitated and inforced to forbearance through an absolute indisposition to iustice in the house, by the prevalency of a powerfull faction therein, though for my part I have been ever utterly averse to that lingring prudence, and have earnestly solicited the contrary, let the issue fall with me or against me.

Further, the tyranny of these Lords not ceasing here against me, they send their Catch poules to my house againe, where finding my wife in with her three small Children about her, tooke her and my brother away and brought them before the Lords prerogative Barre, rifled, plundered, and ransacked mine house exposing my 3. helplesse small children to the streets, and all this before any indictment, presentment, or other due processe of law preceeding. And by reason my wife would not be subiect to the arbitrary and diabolicall accustomary proceedings of that house, to

answer to interrogatories, or to make oath against her husband or
her selfe, concerning his or her life, liberty or goods, was, together
with my brother, himselfe also refusing subiection to the said
illegall procedings committed *during pleasure* to the New prison
in *Maiden lane,* where ever since he hath continued in miserable
durance and opression.

And then under the colour of another Order from the said
house, most inhumanely and barbarously they dragged her away
from that prison, with her tender infant of halfe a yeares of age
in her armes headlong upon the stones, through the streets, in the
dirt and mire, reviling and abusing her by the way with the scur-
ielous names of Whore Strumpet, &c. and then not allowing her
so much humane compassion, as might have been justly expected
even from Turks, Infidels and Pagans they denied her the mercy
to be imprisoned with her husband, which either grace or nature
might have taught them in the height of their Arbitrary passion,
had they the least spark either of the one or the other in them,
but as persons voyd of both, without all respect to the Law of
God, or of Nature they violently divided her from mee, and in
the foresaid most contemptible manner threw her into the filthy
Gaole of Bridewell, that common shore, center and receptacle of
Baudes, Whores, Pick-pockets &c. though for her own part shee
never was, nor ever could be so much as taxed of the least in-
civility or immodesty either in countenance, word, action or gesture all the dayes of her life, but alwayes lived in all honest and
godly conversation; in which infamous place shee hath ever since
bin kept in cruel restraint, not permitting her to have the liberty
to visite her husband, or to enjoy the comfort of her children
about her, or to go a little abroad a with Keeper to take the fresh
ayre, though for the want thereof her life hath been visibly and
palpably endangered (a benefit ordinarily allowed to Whores and
Pick-pockets imprisoned there) though unreasonable *Gratuity,*
and extraordinary *Surety* was offered therefore to the *Keepers.*
And in this our unnaturall and cruell division in three severall
prisons, my selfe in one, my wife in another, my brother in the
third, and my three children exposed to the mercy of the wide
world; and our selves deprived of all meanes and wayes by industry to procure any livelihood, and all that we had for our
subsistance and reliefe seised upon without all lawfull Judgement, verdict of our equalls, Indictment, or other due processe
of Law preceeding contrary to the Fundamentall Laws of the
Kingdom, and under this unreasonable oppression & crueltie

without the value of one halfe-peny from the Lords for reliefe, wee are forcibly kept at an extraordinary charge, in those their severall starving, stincking murthering Prison-houses, seven shillings being exacted and extorted weekly for my lodging, three shillings and six pence for my wifes, foure shillings for my brothers, besides the charge of subsistance for us and our children. And being reduced to this miserable condition, I prepared a Petition and Appeale (since published in print) in the behalfe of my wife and brother to the House of Commons, which for the better credence of our miserable condition, was presented by a competent number of women but notwithstanding all the agitation and sollicitation that we could use, an admission thereof into the House (so much as to be read) could not, nor can hitherto be obtained, & all through the prevalent power of a confederate Faction in the House, obstructing all reliefe and redresse of the people; so that, by that deluding over voting party in the House I am deprived and bereft of all meanes and hope of redresse whatsoever: the cause of Lieu. Col. *John Lilb.* and mine betwixt us as *Commoners,* and the Jurisdiction of the Lords, as *Lords* depending upon the Determination of Parliament which so far as in the eye of reason we can judge, will never be till this House either be purged of the factious party therein, or else a new Parliament called. And the case being so with us, that betwixt *Cannot* and *Will not,* no right or justice can be had for us either from King, Parliament, or any Court of Justice in the Kingdome whatsoever, and being not able to see my selfe, my wife brother and children perish under hopelesse & endlesse expectation of mercy from the hands of mine enemies, I am forced to this desperate Attempt for finall destruction or present release, for on deliverance I am resolved by life or death if possibly I may, a sudden death to me being better and rather to be chosen then lingring destruction, the latter being so much the more terrible and cruell, by how much the more tedious then present.

Now therefore being driven thus to this desperate necessity and pinch; and further, the Parliament themselves having declared, that it is the liberty of every subject to enjoy the benefit of the Law and not arbitrarily and illegally be committed to prison, nor to have his or their lives, liberties, goods or estates disseased or taken away, but only by due processe of Law, according to *Magna Charta,* and the *Petition of Right,* which condemnes all High Commission like Interrigatory proceedings in a mans owne cause, enjoyning speedy Trialls for all causes whatsoever, without any intermission or obstruction to the due course or processe of Law. 1 *part. Book Decl. p.* 6 7 38 77 201.277.268 458 459 660 845. But being utterly denyed the Benefit of the Law of the Land, and of the just Declarations of Parliament through an obstructing party in the House: I must therefore, and do hereby in pursuance of my own safety (a principle warranted by the Parliaments owne Declaration to every particular man to provide for, even from the very Law of Nature, 1. *part. Book Decl. p.* 44 and *p* 728.) make mine *Appeale,* and doe by these presents Actually and formally A P P E A L E from and against the Members Representative (as in their present mixture with, and continuance of Traytors and Tyrants) assembled at *Westminster* unto the Body Represented, (the true originall Soveraigne Authority of Parliaments) the free borne Commoners within this Kingdom of *England,* and Dominion of *Wales* for protection and reliefe against those obstructers of Justice and Judgement to wit, *Denzil Hollis,* Sir *Phil. Stapleton,* Sir *Wil. Lewis,* Sir *John Maynard,* Major Generall *Massey,* Mr. *Glyn,* Recorder of *London,* and from & against al other their Accomplices & Confederates members in the House of Commons, and charged, *June* 4. 1647 with High Treason against the Fundamentall Lawes. Rights and Liberties of the Commons of *England,* by His Excellency, Sir *Thomas Fairfax* and the Officers and Soldiers under his Command to be prosecuted in behalfe of themselves and the whole Kingdom. In this my Appeale craving no other benefit for my selfe, my wife and my brother, but a speedy deliverance from our severall respective Imprisonments till such times as the House shall be purged and cleansed from those corrupt and putrified members, (the obstructers and perverters of *common right and freedom* in the House, that I may not be passed upon, or judged in point of publique liberty and freedome, wherein every free commoners right interest and freedome is included by such as are open and declared enemies thereto, for it is most unreasonable and unjust that I should be subjected to the Arbitriment and Determination of mine and the Kingdomes enemies, for in so doing I should not only yeeld up my selfe to destruction, but therein betray the Commoners right and freedom (for which I have thus long contended) now at the last to be delivered up in my condemnation by those men to the Arbitrary Jurisdiction of the Lords: For should my cause be overthrowne by the voyce of the oppressour, and this kind of exorbitant Domination setled and entailed to the Prerogative of the Lords, then the lives, persons and estates of the Com-

moners of *England* would all be laid waste to the wiles and pleasures of those prerogative usurpers; our lives, our wives, our
persons and estates to be deprived, divorsed, imprisoned, & plundered at pleasure, not to be our own any longer, but theirs. And
therefore the case being thus in the House and with mee, and in
mine, with the Commons of *England,* I shall and do from henceforth utterly disclaime and renounce all triall and Judgement
by the degenerate Members Assembled therein, & shall hold all
Orders and Ordinances whatsoever proceeding from them, though
under the name of the two Houses of Parliament assembled at
Westminster, as altogether invallid, and void of all Parliamentory authority and power, not obligatory or binding at all to
the people, but to bee opposed and resisted to the death as counterfeit Orders and Ordinances, abusing the name and authority
of Parliament, for it is no priviledge of Parliament for Traytors and Tyrants to fit and make Orders and Ordinances of Parliament, and then to publish them under the guize and vizor of
that Soveraigne Authority no more then it is for any person to
coyne or counterfeit the Image and superscription of the King,
for Treason and Tyranny are inconsistent with the Being and
priviledge of Parliament; for it is not their sitting upon the
benches, or standing within the wals of that House which makes
them Parliament men, or their Orders or Ordinances Parliamentory, authoritive and binding, but the discharging of their trust
in moving and acting only for the weale and safety of the people
[as] [1] their impowrers and trusters barely for that end. So that in
deed and in truth that cannot bee said, or ought to bee reputed
an Order or Ordinance of Parliament, which is contrary to their
trust and the end of their Election and Session, for being our
Parliament Deputys, doth not invest them with a Priviledge to
destroy or save as at their pleasure, and to do with us as they list,
we cannot do so with our selves, our power over our selves is
but for our safety; therefore how can theirs which are but our
deputies be for our woe.

　　Wherfore, so long as those Traytors to their Trust are not
removed from their Session, but continued therin, over-powring
and over-voting the dischargers of their Trust even so long they
are in the *maine* degenerate from the naturall Essence and Being
of the Parliament of *England,* for if the major part be fallen into
the capacity of Tyrants and Traytors, sure their Parliamentary
Being is therewith defunct and deceased.

[1] Word indecipherable in text. D.M.W.

For how can it in that capacity be tituled the Parliament of *England?* have they not in that degeneration devested and degraded themselves from their betrusted authority of the people, and become no longer their representory Deputies, or Trustees, except tyranny and oppression be the very substance and end of their Trust? certainly tyrants and oppressors cannot be the Representers of the Free-men of *England,* for freedom and tyranny are contraries, that which representeth the one, doth not represent the other; therefore such as are the representers of *Free-men,* must be substantial and reall *Actors* for *freedome* and *liberty,* for such as is the represented, such and no other must the figure or representation be, such as is the proportion, countenance and favour of the man, such and so must be the picture of the man, or else it cannot be the picture of that man, but of some other, or of something else, as the picture of a grim, meager, frowning face is, not the picture of an amiable, friendly smiling countenance; so tyranny neither is nor can possibly be the Representor of Freedome; therfore, though such in the House were once otherwise by their election, yet now they have changed themselves into a contrary capacity, and are so to be reputed and esteemed off; and I for my part do so, and no otherwise esteem of them, and do hereby proclaime and protest against them to all the free-men of *England* and Dominion of *Wales,* as so many traytors to the safety and weale of the people, both the eleven Members that are charged, and all such as are coactours and voters with them in further oppressions and tyrannies, over-swaying and bearing downe the voters for freedome and Justice; imploring and beseeching all lovers of freedome and justice within His Majesties Dominions of *England* and *Wales,* as one man to rise up in the cause of the Army for the removall of those obstructors and traytors, and the bringing of them to a speedy and legall triall, that the wicked may be taken from before the face of the King, that his Throne may be established in righteousnesse and judgement, the liberty and freedom of the people recovered from the hands of oppressors and tyrants, and the Kingdom setled in peace and tranquillity, which only is, and ever shall be the prayers and endevours of your Appellant.

Now for the further clearing and making good of mine Appeal, I shal (as I promised before) briefly touch the accustomary course of their oppressive tyrannous cariage to the generality, whereby their degenerate state and capacity will more clearly appeare. But for brevity sake I shall omit the severall new oppres-

sions, exactions and burthens wherewith the people are loaded
every where, even till their backs are ready to break as every
man by woful experience can witnesse; and shall only relate to the
maine & principall end of their Election and Session, which is for
*bearing the cries and groanes of the people, redressing and easing
their grievances:* And as touching this matter, this is their course,
in stead of Reliefe for oppression, themselves do *oppresse,* and
which is worst, then *stop the* mouthes of the oppressed; crutiate
and torment, and not suffer the tormented to complain, but even
torment them for complaining, sleight, reject and crush their just
and necessary Petitions, which is the highest kind of tyranny in
the world, shut their doores and eares against the cry of the
people, both of Country and City, yea, though the burthens of the
oppressed are so great, that multitudes in a peaceable manner
have attended the House daily with Petitions for no other thing,
then for the *Removall of oppression, and recovery of freedome,*
according to the fundamentall Lawes of this Kingdom, which
they often Declared, covenanted, protested, and sworne with hands
lifted up to the most high God to performe faithfully and truly.

Yet these very men contrary to their many Oathes, Covenants,
Declarations, Vowes and Protestations, call the Petitioners *Rogues,
Villains, seditious, factious fellowes,* and bid *a pox of God on
them,* offer to draw their Swords at them, lift up their *Canes* at
them in a menacing manner, shake them by the shoulders, and
otherwise abuse them, and not only so; but imprison some of
them, as Mr. *Nicholas Tew,* Mr. *Browne,* and Major *Tuliday,*
the two first of them Prisoners to this houre, the third under
Bayle; and they stay not here, but their arogance mounts higher
and higher, even vote their Petitions Seditious, *breach of their
Priviledges,* and cause them to be* burnt by the hand of the
Common hang man, even *such petitions* wherein was *contained*
the *Liberties and freedomes of the Commons of England,* and no
jot of anything either in word or circumstance that was not just,
honest and reasonable, and their sworn duties to performe, and
for which was, and is, the very end of their Election and Session
to, and in the capacitie of Parliament: Yet *these matters,* even
the *Rights and freedomes* of the *people* are *rendred* matters of
Sedition, and to be *set on fire and burnt,* and that in the most
contemptible manner, *by the hands of the Common hangman*:
O most unheard of, unparaleld Treason! heare O Heavens and

---

* See the Relation at large in L. Col. Lil., late book intituled, *Rash Oathes unwarrantable.*

judge Oh ye free Commoners of England, &c. where, and what
is become of your Lawes, & libertyes: thus would they doe with
your persons, even *burne them* by the *hand of the Common hangman,* had they but as much power over them as they have over
your *petitions and papers,* and virtually they have don noe lesse
for essentally and really they have burnt the *Great Charter of
England,* for in those petitions were contained the cheifest heads
of that *Charter,* by virtue whereof you *hold your very lives, liberties, & goods,* so that in that *Act* they did as much as in them lay,
*set all England on fire, burne and destroy all the lawes, Rights
and liberties there of;* and if this bee not High Treason, and an
open and visible forfeiture of their Parliamentory Being and
trust, I would faine know what is: I could adde unto this, their
Declaration against the Army, stiling their petition (which was
honest just and reasonable and their dutys to grant them effectually,) to be *a dangerous petition,* and all such to bee *enemies
to the state and disturbers of the publick Peace as proceeded
therein* making it enmity to the State, and disturbance of the
publicke P E A C E , humbly to Petition for the price of their
Blood, and Sweat of their Brows, so dearly earned in the purchase of their and our safeties and freedome: and to this I could
adde their setling the *Militia* into the hands of men of their
owne faction in the City of London and in other parts of the
Kingdome for the violent setlement of their owne pernitious
tyrannicall ends, with multitude of other impieties, and cruelties,
treacherous and treasonable acts and proceedings against the freedomes of the people, but for brevity sake at this present I shall
commend to your pervsall and weighty consideration a most excellent and worthy treatise, intituled *Plain truth without Feare,
or Flatery,* written (as the Title declares) by A M O N W I L-
B E E. the contents whereof, as concerning the traitorous partie
in the House, I doe hereby actually lay unto their charge, to make
them good against that partie upon the perill of my life, and
concerning the equity and truth of the Charge therein contain'd
against *Denzill Hollis* & the rest of that traiterous Faction I doe
account it and owne it as if writ by my self, though for my part
I do seriously professe unto the world that I was till I read it
as ignorant of the writing composeing printing publishing or
Author thereof as the Child that is unborne, yet such is the equity,
honesty and truth thereof that had, I ten thousand lives, I would
engage them all for the justification and maintenance thereof, and
this will I say concerning that A U T H O R , that He deserves

to *weare the* L A U R E L L from all that have writ (in that ob-
servant natture) since the Parliament began. The matters therein
considered together with their desperate suppression of the petitionary endeavours of the well affected of *London,* besides their
slighting, rejecting and refusing all other Petitions of the oppressed inslaved Countries, as from *Buckingham shire, Hartford-
shire, &c.* Except from Parties which co-operate for the advancement of the Prerogative and priviledge *Faction,* all others being
fob'd off, with a Complementall acknowledgement of the good
affections of the Petitioners, and with a *Verball* returne of
thankes, and that the House would take their businesse into further consideration, or the like; which being all, and the most that
ever could be obtained from them; when their *Aspect* was most
indulgent towards U S , and fairest for our Liberties, I say, those
their Treasonable proceedings, Oppressions, and Tyranies duly
weighed and considered, how can still their P A R L I A M E N-
T A R Y *Being,* and *Station* be granted? If it bee, sure it must bee
pictured with the Heeles upward, for I may as well bee parswaded
out of my *Christen-Name,* as made to beleive, it stands derect
upon its feete; When I see it plainely reversed before mine eyes,
for I shall never while I enjoy my senses, bee so stupid and block-
ish, to esteeme Ruine for Safety; Retrograde motion for direct
Progression: now, this their Trayterous course of stopping and
burning Petitions, abusing and imprisoning Petitioners, of it selfe
is an absolute election, or *putting the people out of the protection
of P A R L J A M E N T* ; no rationall man can gainesay it; for
Oppression is no *Protection,* offence no *Defence.* He that will *not
releife,* is no *Reliever;* and hee that *Oppresseth* for *complainning
of Oppression,* must needs be a *Tyrant* in the highest measure.
Therefore loving Countrey-men and friends, I beseech you, lay
your hands on your hearts & consider, what greater tyrannie and
oppression can be, then *to be oppressed and so to be deprivd of
the means of relief, left hopelesse and helplesse, all passages of
succour and support stopped and blocked up, the waters of your
reliefe utterly dried up?* Oh rub open your eyes for shame, rouse
up your spirits, resume and take up your strength and authority
into your owne hands, disowne and disclaime those desperate
tyrants and traytors, and cast them forth from your trust as dirt
and dung, or salt that hath lost its savour, for wherewith now
shall they be savoured? Halters and Gallowes is more fit for them
then places in Parliament: What, will you be more fearfull of
them to bring them to justice, then they were of you to burne

your Lawes and your Liberties? for shame never let an English spirit be taxed with that dishonour; you have *Othniells, Ehuds, Baraks,* and *Gideons,* before you, even a mighty and puissant ver- tuous Army, which hath most gallantly and honourably engaged for your and their own safety and protection from those unnatural tyrants and usurpers, to remove them from the Seat of your Authority, and to bring them to justice, that you and your chil- dren after you, may be delivered from the feare and prejudice of their cruelties, dwell in peace and safety, enjoy the price of your labour and travell quietly and freely to your selves, be absolute Lords and possessors of your owne, and to be made true and reall *Freemen* indeed; fall therefore into their assistance and protec- tion, and trust no longer your perjured traiterous Trustees dis- sembled at Westminster, but save your selves from that cursed and wicked generation, now is the opportunity, doe not procrasti- nate nor delay, least your destruction be of your selves, I have discharged the *trust of my sufferings unto you,* which hath been simply and purely for your sakes, and have not drawne backe my hand from any thing for your weale, which to others have seemed *too hot or too heavy to lift,* and my conscience beares me witnesse of the honestie and uprightnesse of my heart for your preservation and safety, as its principal aime and intent in this Appellation of mine unto you, I am but one, and can discharge but the *duty of one* unto you, if you will suffer your selves, your Lawes and your Liberties, to be conquered and destroyed, I can- not help it, it is of your selves, and not of me, I have hitherto done my share, doe you but yours, and the worke will be presently done: I may chance be condemned for a mad-man and foole, but if you sit still and yeeld up your selves, as contented slaves, I can- not see, how you can be excused of madnesse or folly: Come, come, now is no time to *sit thrumming of caps,* if they will not give us leave, to use our *tongues and our pens* to present and make knowne our grievances, we must take leave to make use of our *hands and swords* for the *defence* and *redemption* of our lives, our Lawes and our Liberties, from the hand of the *destroyer,* for *our safety* must be maintained.

And can any reasonable man conclude, that *our protection and assistance* of them, and their *protection and assistance* of us are not relatives, and one *dependent* on the other? For what is the reason, that we have engaged our lives and estates thus in their defence, but that they should be as faithfull a *protection* unto us: Now our safety and protection lieth in the full and just enjoy-

ment of our Lawes, our Rights, and Freedomes, and delivery from
bondage and thraldome, the which being utterly denied us, are
wee not quite out of their protection, and left to shift for our
selves, either to destroy or be destroyed? For can they think that
their powerfull Priviledge doth extend not to leave the Commonalty of England *so much,* as even nature hath instincted in
the *very wormes* of the earth, as exanimate and stupid as a blocke,
worse then the bruit beasts of the field, which all to their power
will save and defend themselves from mischiefe and harme? Cer-
tainely, they cannot expect it, for it is no more then their owne
Doctrine hath taught us, and therefore no Blasphemy, Treason
or Heresie, for they tell us, *Dec. 2. Nov. 16. 6 Booke Dec. 1. part
696. & pag. 150. That obedience doth not bind us to cut our
owne throats,* how then can they expect that we should be our
own butchers?

Deare friends, our *destruction* is beyond the *Priviledge of Parliament,* it is out of the compasse of that *Betrusted Authority;*
while they move in the *Sphere of our safety,* their motions are
Parliamentary, legall, and authorative, and to be obeyed, defended, and maintained, but on the contrary, the contrary must
be concluded, for *contraries have contrary consequents.* For there
is a difference betwixt their *Parliamentary,* and their owne *Personall capacity,* and their actions are answerably different; therefore, the rejection, disobedience, and resistance of their *personall
commands,* is no rejection, disobedience, or resistance of their
Parliament Authority: So that he that doth resist their personall
commands, doth not resist the Parliament, neither can they justly
be censured or esteemed as *Traytors, Rebells, Disturbers,* or *Enemies to the State,* but rather as *Preservers, Conservers,* and *De-
fenders* thereof.

And upon this *principle of justice and reason,* they grounded
and justified *their War* against the King, witnesse their owne
words, *Book Dec. part 1. pag. 276.* where they say by the Statute
of *25. Edw. 3. It is a leavying of Warre against the King, when
it is against his Lawes and Authorities, though it be not immediately against his Person, and the levying of force against his
personall commands, though accompanied with his presence, if it
be not against his Lawes and Authority, but in maintenance
thereof, is no levying of Warre against the King, but for him; for
there is a great difference betwixt the King as King, and the King
as* Charles Steward: Therefore *pag. 279.* they say, *That treason
which is against the Kingdome, is more against the King then that*

which is against his person, because hee is King: for that very Treason is not Treason as it is against him as a man, but as a man that is a King, and as he hath relation to the Kingdome, and stands as a Person intrusted with the Kingdome, discharging that trust: Even so, by the equity of the same reason, the represented Commons of England, in the like case, may justly make the same returne unto the Bodie Representative, as thus: *It is a levying of warre against the Parliament of England, when it is against the Lawes, Rights, and Freedomes of the people of England, though it be not immediately against the persons of the Members in Parliament, and a levying of force against their personall arbitrary commands, though accompanied with their presence, if it be not against the Lawes, Rights and Freedomes of the people, but in maintenance thereof, is no levying of war against the Parliament, but for the Parliament, for there is a great difference betwixt Members in Parliament, as Members in Parliament, and Members in Parliament, as they are personally, Philip Stapleton, Denzill Hollis, &c.* And therefore well may the Commonality of England reply, *That Treason which is against the Commonalty, their Lawes, Rights, and Freedomes, is more against the Parliament, then that which is against their persons, because they are Members of Parliament. For that very Treason is not Treason, as it is against* Philip Stapleton, Denzill Hollis, *and the like, considered as they are men, but as men that are Parliament Members, and as they have relation to the people in generall, and stand as persons intrusted with their Lawes, Rights, and Freedomes, discharging their trust.* This is as directly point blank against the Members in Parliament, as ever it was against the King, they must admit of *this principle* against themselves, or else they must grant themselves to be Rebells and Traitors in warring against the King, for they had no way, under heaven, or to this day have any way to justifie their leavying and maintaining of warre against him but that; for it was the very Axeltree upon which the equity of their proceedings were moved, and that by which still they stand justifiable in the eye of reason and justice: therefore the Members in Parliament, either in the particular or in the generall, because they are men intrusted in that capacity, may not therefore turne oppressors and tyrants at pleasure, for it is not their being in Parliament, or being Parliament-men, that will justifie their invasions and incursions upon the freedomes of the people; for as themselves have granted concerning the King, *that the King is for the Kingdome, not the Kingdome for the King, and that the*

Kingdome is no more his owne, then the People are his owne:
If he had a propriety in this Kingdome, what would become of
the Subjects propriety in their Lands throughout the Kingdome,
or of their Liberties? Book Dec. 1. part p. 266. even so may the
Commonality of England reply to their Parliament-Members, that
they are made for the people, not the people for them, and no
otherwise may they deale with the people then for their safety
and weale, for no more then the people are the Kings, no more
are the people the Parliaments, having no such propriety in the
people, as the people have in their goods to doe with them as they
list. As they will not grant it to be the *Prerogative of Kings,*
neither may wee yeeld it to be the *Priviledge of Parliaments,*
for the safety of the people is the reason and end of all Governments and Governours, *Salus populi est suprema Lex,* the safety of
the people is the supreme Law of all Commonwealths; all other
Lawes, Edicts, Ordinances, Orders, &c. (such as most of our late
pretended Parliamentarie *ones* have been) being contradictory
thereto, are all traiterous and Antimagisteriall, to be opposed and
resisted to the death, and the contrivers, promoters, and actors
thereof, to be apprehended, judged and condemned, and executed as traytors to the safety of the people.

And whereas we have engaged our lives and fortunes against
the King, *to free his person from a traiterous and wicked Coune-*
sell about him, and the same they justified for ous by the *rule of*
necessity, and safety, even so and much more, by vertue of the
same principle may the *body represented* doe to the *body repre-*
sentative, there being a more desperate and traytorus Counsell
therein, for *Immedicabile vulnus ense rescidendum est, ne pars*
sincera trahantur, the putrified and incurable members are to be
cut of for the safety of the whole: for it was not the end of our
undertakings to pull downe one kinde of oppressors to set up
others more desperate and dangerous then the old, to remove a
wicked Counsell from the King, and then to set up and tollerate
a Counsell more traiterous and wicked in the Parliament, no, our
ends and intents were simply against obstructions, and obstructers
of justice and judgement, oppressions and oppressors, and to bring
such Delinquents and Traytors to justice, whereby all impedi-
ments and obstacles to our freedomes might be removed; we did
not ingage against them simply because they were concommitant
to the King, but because they were seducers and perverters of
justice, invaders and destroyers of our just Lawes and Freedomes:
Therefore it is in vaine for our Members in Parliament to think

that we will justifie or tollerate the same among them, which we would not indure in the King, to pluck off the *Garments of Royalty* from oppression and tyranny, to dresse up the same in *Parlament Robes*: No, no, that was ever and is farre from our hearts, and wee shall justifie or allow the same no more in the one then in the other, for to allow it in the one is to justifie it in the other, for it is equally unequall in both, and in it selfe resistable wheresoever it is found, for were it not resistable, all defensive war whatsoever were unlawfull: And upon this poynt we moved against the King, the equity thereof arising from an inherent principle of nature, concording with the Commandement of God, for were not tyranny in it selfe resistable, then a man might lawfully murther himselfe or give power to another to be his Butcher, but in regard by the Law of God in nature and in his word both the one and the other is verily unlawfull, therefore such kind of inhumanity and tyranny is to be resisted both in proper person and otherwise, shall we therefore be so inhumane, so unnaturall and diabolicall, to destroy and murther our owne selves, we may as well execute our selves with our own hands, as give leave to others to be our murtherers, for the matter would be all one in the execution, it would only differ in the instrument; therefore if we may not take that leave to our selves, nor give it to another, then wee must resist it in others as well as in our selves, for not *to hinder is to give leave,* and no hindrance can be without resistance, and if resistance must be, as is of necessity to be granted then in all reason and equity we are bound to use the most efectuall manner of resistance, If our destruction be endeavoured by another, faire means is to be used, but if that will not prevaile, we are bound to kill rather then to be killed: And upon this ground, in case we have to deale with a mighty and furious enemy, we are bound to the utmost of our power to arme and fortifie our selves for our just and necessary defence, and by force of Armes to repell and beat back the invading assaulting enemy, whether it be an enemy for the confusion and exterpation of our persons, or for destruction and ruine of our Laws, our freedomes and liberties, for bondage and slavery are not inferiour to death, but rather to be more avoyded, condemned and resisted then present destruction, by how much the more that kind of destruction is more languishing then present, and in pursuance of the just and necessary *defensive Opposition* we may lawfully, and are in Conscience bound to destroy, kill and slay the otherwise irresistable enemy for our own preservation and safety whether in our lives, our Lawes or our liberties: And against the justice of this *defensive principle* no degrees, Orders or titles amongst men can or may prevaile, all degrees Orders and titles, all Lawes, Customs and manners amongst men must be subject to give place and yeeld thereunto, and it unto none, for all degrees and titles Magisteriall, whether emperiall, regall, Parliamentarie, or otherwise are all subservient to *popular safety*, all founded and grounded thereon, all instituted and ordained only for it, for without it can be no humane society, cohabitation or being, which above all earthly things must be maintained, as the earthly soveraigne good of mankind, let what or who will perish, or be confounded, for mankind must be preserved upon the earth, and to this preservation, all the Children of men have an equall title by Birth, none to be deprived thereof, but such as are enemies thereto, and this is the *ground-worke* that God *in nature* hath laid for all common-wealths, for all Governours and Governments amongst men, for all their Lawes, executions and Administrations: therefore all contrary Governments and Governours are ungodly, unnaturall, diabolicall, and trayterous, to be abhorred, condemned and resisted by all possible ways and meanes whatsoever: And from hence ariseth the true *definition* of *Treason,* for indeed Treason is no other then *a destruction to humane society or actions overwhelming or apparently tending to the utter overthrow of publick safety co-habitation and peace, or to the vassalage, bondage and thraledome of a people or Country;* such actions and Actors are only treasonable and trayterous and no other, although it be the custome of tyrants and opressors unhappily intrusted with Imperial Regal or Parliament Authority to proclaim, condemne and execute such cheifly for traytors as are enemies to their opressions and tyrannies, their boundlesse prerogatives, arbitrary *Domination,* or the like, even as our degenerate Members dissembled at Westminster have done in the late Petitioners case of the Armie, making it a matter of Treason to petition for justice and right.

Now in regard, the *Body naturall* for its owne safety may prune, amputate and cut of the corrupt putrified Members from the *Body Representative,* yea utterly renounce, oppose, resist, and dissolve all the Members therein upon *totall forfeiture* of, and *reall Apostacy* from the true *representative capacity* of Parliament, and that this is most evident and cleare; it then inevitably followeth, that this *naturall Body,* by vertue of its instincted, inherent naturall Soveraignity, may *create,* or *depute* any *person* or *persons* for their *Deputy* or *Deputies* for the removall of those dead, corrupt, putrified Members from the *seat* and *name* of their *Formall Authority,* and for the supression of injustice and tyranny, recovery of liberty and freedome; but it may be, it will be objected, that by reason of distraction, confusion and disorder at such an exigency in the *Body naturall,* such a new deputation is not likely, or cannot possibly be formally effected, and therefore those forementioned Members though never so corrupt and destructive, must be continued and subjected unto. I answer, that the *Body naturall* must never be without a mean to save it selfe, and therefore by the foresaid permanent unalterable *rule of Necessity and safety,* any *person* or *persons* (in discharge of their duty to God, themselves and their Countrey) may warrantably rise up in the cause and behalfe of the people, to preserve them from imminent ruine and destruction, such person or persons, doing in that act no more then everie man by nature is bound to performe: For as everie man by the verie bond of nature and neighbourhood, in case his neighbours house be on fire, is bound forthwith without anie formall or verball deputation of the owner, to endeavour the quenching thereof with his utmost power and abilitie; even so and much more may the same bee said and of a whole Countrey or Kingdome, for necessitity in that case of extremity justifies the act of safety and preservation, in anie, though without anie formall election, deputation or condition from the people in generall thereto; for such *Formalities* must give place unto the *maine,* being but circumstances in comparison thereof, and a Kingdome or Commonwealth must not be neglected and lost for a trifle; in the cause of popular safety and freedome, wee must not straine at a gnat and swallow a camell, catch at the shadow and loose the substance, dote on formality while we lose our freedomes; we are bound to lay hold on every thing that comes next to hand, rather then perish; it is not the part of the just and mercifull Freemen of England to behold the Politike Bodie of this Commonwealth fallen amongst a crew of thieves, as *Hollis, Stapleton,* &c. stript of its precious raiment of freedome and safety, wounded and left groveling in its blood, even halfe dead, and passe by on the other side like the mercilesse Priest and the Levite: no, now is the time for the compassionate Samaritane to appeare to binde up its wounds, to powre in wine and oyle to engage in the defence and preservation of a distressed miserable people, for greater love and mercie cannot be amongst men then to take compassion, over the helpelesse and destitute.

Therfore, this Evangelicall principle of mercy (being of the nearest communication to the nature of God) is a warrantable ground for the solemne engagement of the Armie, like the compassionate Samaritan, to bind up the wounds of the almost murthered Lawes and Liberties of England; so that their Christian compassion and pity over the abused, beat, and wounded naturall Body of the land, is as an inpugnable Bulwarke of defence against the violent invective calumnies and reproaches of malitious tongues & Pens, and wil be an undoubted badge of everlasting honor through all generations to come, against which time and envie will never be able to prevaile. And in case they be inforced to a defensive resistance, in so doeing they will be no resisters, despisers, contemners or oppugners of Magistracy, Authority or Government, for tyranny is no *Magistracie,* therefore the resistance of Tyrants is no resistance of Magistrates, except it be of such so nominally; but really and essentially monsters and pests of humanity; for Magistracy hath its proper compasse and confines, and the actors and actions in that compasse are thereby rendered Magisteriall actors and actions to be obeyed by all, and resisted by none; and so such as are resisters thereof, are no Resisters of Magistracy, Authority and Government; but the resistance of the excursions or actions out of that compasse and capacity, is no resistance of Magistracy or Magistrates, for it is not their persons which makes their *Ministrations Magisterial,* but their *Ministerial Magistration* which makes their persons Magisteriall persons: for Magistracy is not inherent or consistent in the person, but in the office; their persons must run a parallell line in their Ministration with their office, or els their formall deputation or Commissions will not inright them into the true definition of Magistrates; for the office is but accidentally consistent in the forme or externall Commission, radically and essentially in the due *Ministration.*

Now *Magistrarcy* in its *nature, institution,* and *administration,* is for such a kinde of *safety* Nationall and generall, as wherein every individuall or particular person, of what sort or society soever, may fully and freely enjoy his liberty, peace and tranquillity, *civill* and *humane*; it is an *Ordinance amongst men* and for *men,* that *all men* may have *an humane* subsistance and safety to live as *men* amongst *men,* none to bee excepted from this humane subsistance, but the unnaturall and the inhumane, it is not for *this opinion,* or that *faction,* this Sect or that *sort,* but equally and alike indifferent for all men that are not degenerated from humanity and humane civility in their *living* and *neighbourhood:* And therfore the destroyers and subverters of humane society, safety, cohabitation and being, are to be corrected, expulsed, or cut off for preservation of safety, and prevention of ruine both *publike* and *private*: and thus is *Magistracy* for the praise of them that doe well, and for the punishment of those that doe evill.

And as for matters of conscience or opinion about *Religion* or Worship, with which humane society, cohabitation, and safety may freely subsist and stand together, that doth not fall under the power of the Magisteriall sword, either for introduction and setlement, or for *extirpation* and subversion; for the limits of Magistracy extend no further then humanity, or humane subsistance, not to spirituallity, or spirituall being; and no further, then its owne nature extends, no further may its compulsive power be stretched: And this is the true distinction for matter of subjection, betwixt God and *Cæsar,* and what is Gods wee must in the first place give unto God, and what is *Cæsars,* in the second place, freely and readily we must give unto *Cæsar*; the inward man is Gods prerogative, the outward man is mans prerogative; God is the immediate Lord over the inward, and mediately over the outward, but man is onely Lord over the outward, and though immediate thereover, yet but by Deputation or Commission from him who is thus both over the one and the other: And God who onely knoweth the heart, and searcheth the reines, hath reserved the governation thereof to himself as his own prerogative, and the onely means which he useth in this kinde of Government, that by his Ministers must be dispensed, is onely by the word, not by the sword; for the sword pierceth but the flesh, it toucheth but the outward man, it cannot touch the inward; therefore *where* by the word (to wit by Doctrine or Argumentation) the proper means to work upon the intellectualls and affections a conversion, is not nor cannot be obtained, there no humane compulsive power or force is to be used, either for *plantation* or *extirpation.*

And therefore it was that Christ refused the *sword* for the *promulgation* and *setlment* of his *doctrine,* for it was *spirituall,* and such were the *weapons* he used for that warfare of his; and therefore in immitation of his patterne (and practice of the Apostles) we must rather *suffer* for matters of *faith,* then be enforced or enforce thereunto: But it does not therefore follow, that by *defensive force* we may not maintaine, our *naturall humane being and subsistance upon earth*; for the contrary doctrine would tend to the utter *confusion of humanity,* the depopulation of Nations,

Kingdomes, and Countries; though for the *spirituall warfare,* we are confined to *spirituall weapons*; yet for this humaine naturall warfare, humaine and naturall weapons may and are to be used, each according to its kinde; so that neither the one nor the other, in their distinctive propriety and administration is distructive or contradictory one to another, but both may properly meet and stand together in one individuall, without the least incroachment or prejudice to each others propriety: And if the Magistrate should so farre extend his *compulsive force* under pretence of *religion* and *conscience,* to the destruction of our humane subsistance or being, we may upon the points of your *humane subsistance and being,* lawfully make our *defensive resistance,* for in it selfe it is defendable against all opposition or destruction from whence or from whomsoever it shall be. And of this *defensive resistance,* none in duty can be excused, but in case of an utter depravation of power, for indeed it is granted of all, that where no power is, there no defence can be expected, and in the case of destruction in that kinde, the patient is innocent, and cleare from the guilt of his owne ruine: where nothing is given, there nothing is required; *but unto whomsoever much is given, of him shall be much required, Luke* 12. 48.

Therefore these premises premised, and deliberately weighed, I appeale to all moderate and rationall commoners to judge impartially about this matter, whether now, without all check or scruple of conscience, in maintainance and presuance of this *Defensive principle of resistance,* we may not every man of us (in duty to our owne natures, and to our native Countrey in generall) to the utmost of our lives and fortunes, be assistant and united to this *faithfull Armie* that now is, or to whomsoever shall rise up, and appeare in the *defensive cause* of this Kingdome, for the recovery of our naturall humane rights and freedomes, that all orders, sorts, and societies of the *Natives* of this Land, may freely and fully enjoy a joynt and mutually *neighbourhood, cohabitation and humane subsistance,* one as well as another, *doing unto all men as we would be done unto*; it being against the radicall Law of nature and reason, that any man should be deprived of an *humane subsistance,* that is not an enemy thereto; hee that is fit for *neighbourhood, cohabitation, humane society and fellowship,* and will freely comply and submit thereunto, ought not to be abridged of the same in the least measure; hee that shall deny, oppose and resist this, the same as an *enemy to mankinde,* and is guilty of the highest kinde of Treason that is, and deservs to be

stoned, as was *Hadoram* by the children of Israel for his execution of the tirannicall commands of King *Rohoboam*, with *stones
that he dye,* and to be cast out as the excrements of mankinde,
unworthy of *humane buriall,* as once the Scots served one of their
tyrannicall Kings, who after they had drag'd him at an Horses
tayle at their pleasure, they threw his body into a Jakes, as Mr.
Prin mentions in his *power of Parliaments.*

And therefore all Decrees, Edicts, Injunctions, Lawes, Ordinances and Orders whatsoever, or from whomsoever, which tend
to the extirpation, suppression, or confusion of such a sort or
party of men which are not onely meet but free and willing to
maintaine, preserve, and uphold humane society, fellowship, tranquillity, and being; doing to all men as they would have all men
doe unto them, are all trayterous, antimagisterall unhumane, and
diabolicall, and the authors thereof no other then traytors and
rebels to the *nature of man.*

Now therefore except such vipers and pests of humanity be
divested from all legislatives and coercive authority, it is not possible that such inhumanities and tyrannies in government can be
prevented or removed, for such Governours, such government,
such Law-givers, such Lawes: If the wicked and unjust be not
removed from the throane of government, it is impossible, that
any *i*such throane should be established in righteousnesse: therefore as all such tyrannies and inhumanities are resistable and of
no man (that is not without *naturall affection*) to be received or
obeyed; so every rationall honest Common-wealths man is in duty
bound even from the just principles of divinity, humanity, and
reason, with all his strength and might, either by pollicy or by
force, or by both, to endeavour the extirpation and removall of
such usurpers and oppressors, from the seat and place of Government, and to be ayding and assisting with life, person, and estate,
to all ingagements and endeavours to bring such inhumane usurpers to exemplary justice: and this our Common-wealth swarming
with such Monsters in nature and humanity, overspreading the
whole Land with these tyrannies and oppressions, must either
speedily be purged and cleansed, especially in the *legislative and
compulsive Authority* thereof from that *unnaturall faction,* or else
nothing but bondage, tyranny, and oppression remaineth for the
inheritance of us, and our children after us.

Now in regard both *King* and *Parliament* are become captives
through the force and pollicy of a powerfull faction at Westminster, that neither the one, nor the other can be any reliefe or protec-

tion to the people from injustice and oppression, both being upon the point dethroaned, the one from his Regall, the other from its Parliamentary Essence and being; So that in effect they are both dead unto the people: And now as the case stands, no publique visible Head, either Regall or Parliamentary, or other appearing on foot in the Kingdome for the people to fly to for succour and reliefe, or protection against the visible destroyers and subverters of their liberties but this renowned and faithfull Army; for it is now the only *formall and visible Head* that is left unto the people for protection and deliverance.

I shall therefore presume (most excellent Generall, honourable Officers, faithfull Adjutators, and Gentlemen Souldiers) and doe hereby presume in pursuance of my *owne safety,* and of *righteous judgement* betwixt the free *Commoners Right,* and the *jurisdiction* of the *Lords,* to make my humble addresse and appeale unto this Army, as to the *naturall Head* of the *Body naturall* of the people at this present, wholly (as much as in me lieth) resigning, submitting, and offring my person and cause unto your defensive protection, that in the behalfe of the people to whom I have appealed, you would, as in duty you are bound, contribute your best assistance for the liberty of the one, and just determination of the other, that neither my person nor yet my cause (which is every Commoners case) may be left to the tryall, censure and sentence of mine, and this Kingdomes enemies; but that both person and cause may be protected (as much as in you lieth) from them, and from all mischiefe and prejudice which their malice and violence may attempt against either or both; for the better facillitation and advancement of their owne arbytrary and tyrannicall ends and designes, appealing thus for my selfe and my cause for no other end, but that impartiall justice may freely proceed upon both without respect of persons or things; which I conceive is not reasonably to be expected from the judgement and determination of mine, and this Kingdomes enemies; this is cordially and freely my desire, that if I have done ought that either by the Law of God, of Nature, Reason, or the just Lawes of the Land, worthy of death, or other punishment whatsoever, that then the due execution thereof may be entailed to your just and solemne engagement, that your selves may cause it, and see it performed upon me accordingly without mercy: But if my person, and my cause in the eye of Religion, reason, and the just knowne Lawes, of this Land be found justefiable thereby and those severall afflictions, imprisonments, and miseries upon my selfe, my wife, brother,

and Family by the Arbitrary Prerogative of the Westminster
Lords be found illegall and tyrannicall, and their proceedings by
vertue of their Lordly Prerogative, as actions apparantly, and
openly tending to the *utter subvertion of the fredomes and rights
of the Commons of England,* that then also, (as you have engaged
your selves for common right to be derived, to every particular)
you would actually & effectually make good that engagement to
me in particular, not only yeur [1] for the formall and legall deliverance of my selfe, my wife, and my brother (imprisoned also by
vertue of their Lordly Prerogative) but also for our just and full
reperations according to the Law of the Land, even as the nature
of our respective abuses, imprisonments, &c. and the demerit of
our Oppressioners shall impartially and justly deserve; and that
justice may be answerably executed upon those Usurpers and
Oppressors. notwithstanding their greatnesse to the future terrefy-
ing of such Prerogative Oppressors and oppressions, preservation
and safety of the due right and freedomes of the people both
to present and succeeding Posterity; and this is but just and
reasonable, for why should not justice touch their Prerogative
Lordships, as well as the meanest Commoners, and why should
such sufferings at their hands passe without due reperation, for
should they, it would be an encouragement to such Arbitrary
spirits to be as exorbitant for the future as these; for where
there is no punishment, there neither is nor will be any feare:
So that if the notorious Act of their Prerogative fury, not only
upon me and mine, but upon divers in the like nature, as Liv.
Col. *John Lilburne,* Mr. *Larners* two servants, &c. be passed by
without exemplary punishment and Mulct, the Commons will not
be righted, nor will their Lordships be curbed in their *exorbitant
ambition;* for should it be so smothered and passed by, the Commoners right would be more abused and invaded then, which then
if wee should never be delivered by you, for by our durance the
cause would be still kept on foot in expectation of future such
determination; but if so delivered, it would be wounded, if not
utterly quashed and destroyed by you, scarce ever to be recovered or reared up againe to this pitch: And this that I require
in point of liberty and reperation is no more, then what your
selves have intituled me justly to claime at your hands; for have
you not told us (as an Article of your engagement to see it performed before you disband) *That all such as are imprisoned may
be put into a speedy way for a just hearing and tryall, and such as
shall appeare to have beene unjustly, and unduely imprisoned,*

[1] Word indecipherable in text. D.M.W.

may with their liberty have reasonable reparations according to their sufferings, and the demerit of their Oppressors (as is expressed in the 11. page your owne Declaration.)

Wherefore (truly honoured and faithfull Armie) thinke it not strange that thus in particular I have presumed to cast my selfe and my cause into the verge of your *solemne engagement* for the publique, for my cause in it selfe is generall, and every free borne Commoners case in the Kingdome, and my person one of that generall for which you have solemnely engaged and declared your selves for safety, deliverance, and protection; now you cannot engage and declare for the generall, but the particulars thereof must be joyntly and severally intituled thereto: Therefore this which I thus claime and expect from your hands, you cannot in justice and honour to your owne undertakings deny me; if you doe, you must deny your selves, and your *solemne engagement,* and so render your selves to the Kingdome as others have done before you, even deluders and deceivers of the people, and thereby instate the people into a just capacity of *Insurrection* against you, as well as your selves are now against others.

But being fully perswaded of the uprightnesse and innocency of your intentions, I shall expect *that your workes will give witnesse to the truth of your words*; for otherwise, they will bee but as *empty shels,* or as a *dead letter* to the people: Be therefore quick and active, and bee not demur'd, protracted and delayed by the old beaten subtile Foxes of Westminster into your owne, and our destruction: Can you imagine that they intend you any good? what have they done I pray you as hitherto, but fob'd, befool'd, and deluded you; say and unsay, backward and forward, hither and thither, no man knowes whither, and all but to circumvent, delude, and delay you, that they might gather time and ground.

For they well know what it is that hath lost thẽ the affections of the people, you must not think, they cã be so insensible, as therof to be ignorant; and now they would run you upon the same rock whereon they have split themselves, to wit, the *distaste of the people,* that your wounds may be their cure; and assure your selves your ruine if you trace in their steps will be swifter then theirs; therefore thinke not to dally with, and beare the people in hand (as they have done before you) with *faire promises, engagements, Declarations, Remonstrances, &c.* and not to put the same into speedy execution; for the affections of the people will not admit of delayes, quick expedition will sharpen, but protraction will turne the edge of their spirits; If you dally with us, and befoole our expectations too long, we shall turne our pens, our hearts, and our hands against you, for our affection and concurrence with you, is but for our safety and protection, expecting more faire and honest dealing from you, then ever we could obtaine from the hands of our false Trustees at Westminster; have a care therefore how you interpose your owne light, and follow their *Ignis fatuis,* into their delusions and delayes, for if you doe not timely beware, your friends will become your enemies, their spirits begin to decline, and their tongues are busied with feares and surmises, therefore from the inch you may judge of the elle; though for a while the Countries may beare the burthen of your Quarters with patience, yet assure your selves, in a small time they will turne impatient, clamour and cry out against you; for the Countries cannot, as indeed there is no reason they should, indure to be oppressed; for such and so great hath beene their oppression, that it is in vaine to suppose, that an additionall oppression will gaine an acceptance or tolleration amongst them; you doe but now the worke of the enemy, for if you will play but a while with their Rattles and Gew-gawes, they will be provided, (what though the redemption of time and the losse of your credits) to give you an encounter, and then be sure the people must suffer, their blood and their treasure must pay for your negligence, therefore expect that the mischiefes of your demurres will be set uppon your account, when all flesh shall appeare, every man to receive according to his deeds.

Therefore right worthy and faithfull Adjutators, be advised to preserve that power and trust reposed in, and conferred upon you by the body of the Army intire and absolute, and trust no man, whether Officer or Souldier, how religious soever appearing, further then hee acts apparantly for the good of the Army and Kingdome: marke them which would and doe bring you into delayes and demurres, let their pretences be what they will be, their counsels are destructive; I am afraid, that your Officers are not too forward to interpose all delayes; therefore as I dare not totally condemne them, but honour them so farre as they have dealt honourably in your engagement, I onely advise you to bee cautious and wary; and keepe up your betrusted power and authority, and let nothing be acted, done, or concluded, without your consent and privity, for by that meanes the cause in a clandestine underhand manner may be given away; and what doe you know, but there is a designe amongst you, to take the power of all Adjutation from the hand of the private Souldier? for why must your late papers bee published, *By the appoyntment of his Excellencie, Sir Thomas Fairfax and the Councell of Warre,* as your Remonstrance and others, and not as formerly, by his *Excellency Sir Thomas Fairfax with the officers and Souldiers of the Armie?* are not the Souldiers as authoritive as formerly, or are they cast out, as if they had nothing to doe with the businesse? Sure I cannot judge that you will altogether bee befooled of your power; if you doe, I am sure we shall all be befooled with you; if that once be accomplished, then farewell our hopes in the Armie; for I am confident, that it must be the poore, the simple and meane things of this earth that must confound the mighty and the strong: therefore your Officers that seeke not themselves, and have no sinister ends nor designes in their brests, will be contented that your betrusted power be preserved intire in your hands till the end of your worke be accomplished; and rather then they will any wayes seeme to infringe it, be continued in their addition to your adjutation onely for advise and consultation, not for controll and conclusion, not desiring a negative voice any more in your Adjutation, then they and you would allow the King in the great councell of Parliament; that so the sence and minde of the Armie may not be prevented or denyed: If I erre in this caution and advice, I am sure that I erre not in my faithfull affections to your *solemne engagement,* and therefore the better to be excused; for my intentions are honest and upright therein, not minding mischiefe or prejudice against any, but solely and simply ayme and intending the good of the Army and Kingdome thereby.

If you wil own me & my cause, I shal take it as a grateful & acceptable service of love & affection, not only to my selfe but to the almost destroyed freedomes of the Commoners of England; if not, I have reckened my cost, and can in this cause for my Countrey upon honest and just priviledges, lay downe my life, as freely and as willingly, as my most malicious enemies can make it a sacrifice to their fury: Doe therefore, as it seemeth good in your owne eyes; I have discharged my conscience, and what I have done, I have done; and commit the issue thereof unto God, And so remaine,

From my Prerogative
Captivity in Newgate
(*the Lords benediction*)
July 10. 1647.

Yours and this Kingdomes faithfull friend and servant for the just Lawes, Rights, and Freedomes of the people, to the death,

Richard Overton.

Certaine Articles for the good of the Common wealth, prefented to the confideration of his Excellencie, Sir *Thomas Fairfax*, and to the Officers and Souldiers under his Command.

By *R. O.*

Concerning Parliaments,

1. THat for the future, the election and expulsion of Parliament Members may be so setled in the Electors, that none may be hindered, debard, or expulsed from serving his Country under any colour or pretence whatsoever, as for refusing the Covenant or other wise without order first, assent or concurrence of their Countrey.

2. That for the better security of the interest and power of the people, all titles, by Prerogative, Priviledge, Pattent, Succession, Peerage, Birth or otherwise to sit and act in the Assembly of Parliament, contrary to, and without the free choice and Election of the People, be utterly abrogated, nuld and made voide, and that all such so sitting, may be removed from sitting therein.

3. That the authority of Parliament may bee preserved and secured for the future from the obstructions and prejudice of a negative voyce in any person or persons whatsoever.

4. That every County may have liberty to choose some certaine number amongst themselves, to inquire and present to the Parliament, what be the just Lawes, Customes, and Priviledges of each County, and that those County Commissioners, be bound to receive all and every impeachment, and impeachments, by any person or persons whatsoever, of the respective Counties, against any of their owne respective Knights or Burgesses in Parliament,

for falsifying and betraying his or their Countries trust, or any wise indeavouring the introduction of an arbitrary power in this Land. And that the said Commissioners have power and be firmly bound to impeach and attach in the name of their respective Counties, their said Member or Members, and to bring him or them to a legall and publique tryall. That in case such be found guilty, justice may be executed, and others in their roome, by the free choyce of the People bee sent. And in case any such Commissioner, or Commissioners shall refuse to prosecute any such complaint or impeachment, that then hee or they be ajudged guilty of Treason.

Articles concerning Courts of Judicature, offices and Officers of the Law.

1. That all Courts which are not established by the just old Law of the Land: and all illegall offices, and Officers, belonging to the same, and all other vexatious and unnecessary Courts, be abolished by act of Parliament. And that provision bee made that for tyme to come, no Courts or Officers whatsoever may be obtruded upon the free Commoners of England, either by Royall grant, Pattent, Act of Parliament, or otherwise contrary to the old Law of the Land.

2. That according to the old Law and custome of the Land, long before, and sometime after the Conquest, There may bee Courts of Judicature for the speedy tryall and determination of all causes, whether Criminall or Civill, erected and established in every Hundred, for the ease and benefit of the Subject, to be holden according to the old custome once or twice every moneth, for the ending of all causes Criminall and Civill whatsoever, which shall happen in the respective Hundreds. That the Freemen of England may have a sudden, quick and easie dispatch of their suits, and be eased also of their vexations and chargable travellings from all parts of the Kingdome, for processe and tryall of their suits unto Westminster Hall.

3. That all such Officers, as by the ancient and common Lawes of this Nation, are illegible, and to be chosen by the free Commons, as Mayors, Sheriffes, Justices of peace, &c. may be left to the free Election of the people, in their respective places, and not otherwise to bee chosen. And that all such publique affaires (now in being) Not so elected and allowed, may be forthwith removed,

and others by the free choice of the people be constituted in their roomes.

Articles concerning Goales, Goalers, and Imprisonment.

1. That the extortions, and oppressive fees of Goalers may bee redressed and eased, and that strict and severe provision be made against all Goalers, and their deputies, to restraine them for the future from the like extortions and cruelties, now frequent in all Goales of the Land. And that there may be a strict and severe Inquisition after the blood of such prisoners as have beene murthered and starved by the cruelties of Goalers, that so the persons guilty thereof may have justice executed upon them.

2. That no Prisoners be put in Irons, or to other paine, before conviction and condemnation.

3. That there may be cleanly and wholesome provision made in all the Goales of England, for the lodging of Prisoners, at the charge and cost of the State, and that no fees for Chamber-rent, for entering or deliverance, or any thing in lieu thereof, be exacted or demanded under a severe penalty.

4. That neither the high Court of Parliament, nor any other inferior Court or Magistrate whatsoever, may commit any free man of England to prison upon any pretended contempts, as is frequent in these dayes, but onely for transgression and breach of the knowne Lawes of the Land. And for the future (to award the free Commons of England from the revenge of arbitrary spirits,) that strong provision be made by Act of Parliament to that end.

5. That there may be a severe penalty provided against all Goalers and their Deputies, which shall receive any prisoner persons whatsaever, without a lawfull charge or commitment drawne up in writing, according to the true forme of the Law, with a lawfull cause therein expressed, and with a lawfull conclusion, him safely to keepe untill hee shall be delivered by due processe or Law, according to *Magna Charta,* and the Petition of Right, and not at the will and pleasure of the Committee.

6. That strong provision be made against all such Goalers as shall detaine any person or persons in prison after a lawfull discharge, as is frequent in all the Goales of the Land, whereby many

poore free Commoners of England have been starved and dyed of hunger.

7. That all criminall persons that are condemned and reprived, may be acquit and set free.

Articles concerning the Lawes, and corruptions thereof, with other publique Grievances.

1. That all Lawes of the Land (lockt up from common capacities in the Latine or French tongues,) may bee translated into the English tongue. And that all records, Orders, Processes, Writs, and other proceedings whatsoever, may be all entered and issued forth in the English tongue, and that in the most plaine and common Character used in the Land, commonly called Roman, or Secretary, and that without all or any Latine or French Phrases or Tearmes, and also without all or any abreviations or abridgements of words, that so the meanest English Commoner that can but read written hand in his owne tongue, may fully understand his owne proceedings in the Law.

2. That no free Commoner of England be inforced to put either by the high Court of Parliament, or by any subordinate Court, Officer or Minister of Iustice, whatsoever in the Land to make Oath, or to answer to any Interrogatories concerning himselfe in any criminall case, concerning his life, liberty, goods or free-hold. And that neither the High Court of Parliament, not any subordinate Court, Officer or Minister whatsoever, before Indictment, presentment, verdict of 12 men, or other due processe of Law, may take away any free Commoners life, liberty, goods, or free-hold, contrary to the State of *Magna Charta*, cap. 29.25. *Edw*. 3. cap. 4.28. *Edw*. 3 cap. 3.41. *Edw*. 3.c.3. 1 *Eliz*. cap. 1 &c.

3. That all Statutes made for the compulsion of persons to heare the Common Prayer Booke, and for the exercise of other Popish Rits, and Ceremonies, may be abrogated and taken away, and that all and singular persons indicted, imprisoned, or otherwise molested upon the aforesaid Statutes may be inlarged and relieved.

4. That neither Membership in Parliament, Office nor function, whatsoever in the Magistracy of the Land, may be any protection or demurre in any wise against the due processe or course of the ancient and common Lawes of this Realme, but that in

all cases of treason, murther, Burglary, and fellonie, in all Actions, Suites, and civill proceedings whatsoever, the greatest Man or men in the Realme, may be made equally lyable at all times and seasons, and in all places in the Land to the tryall, sentence and execution of the Law, with the meanest Commoner.

5. That all wicked persons that shall beare false witnesse against any free man of England concerning his life, liberty, goods or free-hold upon legall discovery, and probation thereof, be adjudged, and condemned of their lives, liberties, and free-holds, according to that which they would have done unto their Neighbours.

6. That the cruell practise of imprisoning Debtors may be provided against, and that due Rights and properties may be recovered upon more mercifull tearmes then by way of imprisonment.

7. That according to the Law of God, and the old Law of the Land, matters of theft may not be punished with death, and that such Malefactors may make satisfaction either by just restitution to the party wronged, or by an answerable servitude, and that such offenders upon the second conviction (lawfully had) be brand markt visibly in the most eminent part of their face, and confind to a singular habit. And upon the third lawfull conviction, to be put to perpetuall servitude, for the benefit of the State, saving to the party wronged, a competent deduction thereon, for restitution according to the theft. that upon all occasions of warre, such Bond-men may be taken for the Military service, and the impressing of free-men on that behalfe in some measure spared.

8. That every English Native, who hath goods, Wares and Merchandize, may have freedome to transport the same to any place beyond the Seas, and there to convert them to his owne profit, it being his true and proper inheritance to doe, according to the Statutes of 14. *Edw.* 3.2.12. *Hen.* 7.6. and therefore to the end the old trade ingrosing Company of Merchants may be dissolved, and the like for the future prevented.

Concerning the Clergy.

1. That the grievous oppressions by Tythes and forced-maintenance for the Ministry be removed, and that the more easie and Evangelicall practice of contribution be granted, and con-

firmed for the benefit of the Subject, and his freedome therein, for prevention of the Lordlinesse, in and the Commotions, oppressions and tyrannies, that might happen by the Clergy.

Concerning Schooles.

That all ancient Donations for the maintenance and continuance of Free-Schooles which are impropriate or converted to any private use, and all such Free-Schooles which are destroyed or purloyned of any freedome for propriety may be restored and erected againe, and that in all parts or Counties of the Realme of England, and Dominion of Wales destitute of Free-Schooles (for the due nurture and education of children) may have a competent number of Such Schooles, founded, erected, and indowed at the publique charges of those respective Counties and places so destitute, that few or none of the free men of England may for the future be ignorant of reading and writing.

Concerning Hofpitalls.

That all ancient charitable Donations towards the constant reliefe of the poor, impropriate, and converted to other use, and all Hospitalls that are either impropriate, corrupted or vitiated from their primitive constitution and end, or be deprived of any of their franchise, profits or emoluments, may be restored, relieved, and rectified, and safely preserved to the reliefe and maintenance of poore Orphants, Widowes, aged and impotent persons, &c. And that there be a convenient number of Hospitalls, founded, erected, and constituted in all the Counties of England and Wales, at the publique charge of the respective Counties, for the good education and nurture of poore fatherlesse or helplesse children, maintenance and reliefe of poore widowes, aged, sick, and lame persons. And to that end, that all the Gleabe-Lands in the Kingdome, may be converted to the maintenance and use of those charitable houses.

Concerning Commons inclofed.

That all grounds which anciently lay in Common for the poore, and are now impropriate, inclosed, and fenced in, may forthwith (in whose hands soever they are) be cast out, and laid open againe to the free and common use and benefit of the poore.

Concerning Petitions.

That strong provision be made that neither the Parliament, nor any inferior Court, Officer, or Minister of the Law whatsoever, may in any wise let, disturb, or molest any person or persons, from contriving, promoting or presenting any Petition or Petitions concerning their grievances, liberties, to the High Court of Parliament.

FINIS.

THE CASE OF THE ARMY TRULY STATED

Appeared October 15, 1647. Reprinted from a photostatic copy of
the original pamphlet in New York Public Library.

The work undoubtedly of several hands,[1] *The Case Of The
Army* is a repetitious and poorly organized document, too long
and complicated to be read and assented to as a social contract
by thousands of soldiers and citizens. Yet it was the necessary
ideological bridge between the agitation of the common soldiers
for a democratic restraint to Parliament's powers and the composition of the first *Agreement Of The People*. It summarizes the
grievances of the soldiers both against Parliament and against
those factions within the army which have thus far prevented a
purging of Parliament's anti-democratic faction. *The Case Of The
Army* authors see no inconsistency, as indeed did none of the
Levellers, in the idea of purging what they considered to be a
thoroughly unrepresentative Parliament. They were setting up
machinery, as they thought, by which a representative Parliament
could be elected, meanwhile assuring themselves that *no* Parliament could abridge or destroy certain fundamental freedoms.
The idea of a "law paramount" (p. 212) to secure successive
elections of Parliament by manhood suffrage had already emerged
in Lilburne's pamphlets; in *The Case,* however, it receives new
emphasis, and is shortly to broaden in *the Agreement* as a concept of permanent protection to unalterable personal rights.
The radicals were really driven to this position by the failure
of all their appeals to the king, the Parliament, and the army

---

[1] Firth suggests that Wildman was the author of *The Case Of The Army*.
Though Wildman was probably the principal author, differences in the style
suggest the work of several hands. The letter of the agents at the end, for example,
is certainly not the work of Wildman. Appearing as the civilian spokesman of
the new agents, Wildman worked in close collaboration with Lilburne, and may
have been directed and paid by him. The platform of reforms near the end of
The Case may actually have been drawn up by Lilburne as his contribution to the
pamphlet.

officers in turn; they "have all been like broken reeds" (p. 210). The *Engagement* of June 5 had been violated; factions within the army had labored to destroy the unity of its demands. In his *Appeale* Overton had stated brilliantly the theoretical justification of an appeal to the populace; in their *Engagement* the common soldiers had tasted the power of a mutual pact. It was now an easy step to apply the same principle to citizens as well as soldiers. How to begin? *The Case Of The Army* contains the germ of their answer; the first *Agreement* is its final form.

The *Case Of The Army* was signed by the agitators on October 9; it appeared in London, according to Thomason's notation, on October 15, and was presented to Fairfax (p. 222) on October 18. On October 28 it was discussed in the General Council, with Sexby, Allen, Lockyer, Wildman, Petty, and two soldiers acting as the radicals' spokesmen. The debate on *The Case* was very brief, however, the issue turning sharply to the conduct of Ireton and Cromwell in representing the wishes of the army to Parliament. On this point Cromwell's reply to Sexby (*Clarke Papers*, I, 229-30) should be very carefully studied, together with the accounts of Cromwell's Parliament speech (p. 229). Cromwell differentiated between his capacity as a representative of the General Council and his capacity as a Parliament member speaking his private opinion. After clashes on this issue, the debate was directed to the new document, the first *Agreement*.

THE CASE
OF THE
ARMIE

Truly ſtated, together with the miſchiefes
and dangers that are imminent, and ſome ſutable remedies.

Humbly propoſed by the Agents of five

Regiments of Horſe, to their reſpective Regiments,
and the whole Army.

As it was preſented by Mr. *Edmond Bear,* and Mr. *William
Ruſſell;* October 15. 1647. unto his Excellency,

Sir Thomas Fairfax.

Encloſed in a Letter from the ſaid Agents: Alſo his Excellencies
Honourable Anſwer thereunto.

Deut. 20.8. *What man is there that is fearfull and faint hearted?
let him go and returne unto his houſe, leaſt his brethrens heart
faint as well as his heart,*
Judg. 7.7. *And the Lord ſaid unto* Gideon, *by the three hundred
men that lapped, will I ſave you and deliver, the* Midianites
*into thine hand, and let all the other people go, every one unto
his place.*

LONDON Printed in the yeare,
1647.

The Case of the Army truly stated, toge-
gether with the mischiefes and dangers that
are imminent, and some sutable remedies, Humbly
propofed by the Agents of five Regiments of Horfe,
to the refpective Regiments and the whole Army.

Whereas the grievances, dissatisfactions, and desires of the Army, both as Commoners and Soldiers, hath been many months since represented to the Parliament; and the Army hath waited with much patience, to see their common grievances redressed and the rights and freedomes of the Nation cleared and secured; yet, upon a most serious and conscientious view of our Narratives, Representations, Ingagement, Declarations, Remonstrances, and compairing with those the present state of the Army and Kingdome, and the present manner of actings of many at the Head Quarters, we not only apprehend nothing to have been done effectually, either for the Army or the poore oppressed people of the nation, but we also conceive, that there is little probabillitie of any good, without some more speedy and vigorous actings.

In respect of the Army,* there hath been hitherto no publique vindication thereof, about their first Petition, answerable to the Ignominie, by declaring them enemies to the State, & disturbers of the peace: No publike clearing nor repairing of the credit of the Officers, sent for about that petition as Delinquents: No provision for Apprentizes, Widowes, Orphans, or maimed Souldiers, answerable to our reasonable addresses propounded in their behalf: No such Indempnitie, as provideth security, for the quiet, ease, or safety of the Soldiers, disbanded or to be disbanded. No securitie for our Arreers, or provision for present pay, to inable the Army to subsist, without burthening the distressed Country. And in respect to the rights and freedomes of our selves and the people, that we declared we would insist upon, we conceive there is no kind or degree of satisfaction given: a there is no determinate

a *Viz.* The copy of the grievances presented to the Parliaments Commissioners at *Saffron Walden.*

period of time set when the *Parliament* shall certainly end: The house is in no measure purged, either from persons unduly elected, or from Delinquents, that appeared to be such at the Armies last insisting upon their rights, or since: the [b] honour of the Parliamentary authoritie not cleared, and vindicated from the most horrid injustice of that Declaration against the Army for petitioning, nor of suppressing and burning Petitions, abusing and imprisoning Petitioners: But those strange presidents remaine upon Record, to the imfamy of Parliamentary authority; and the danger of our own and the peoples freedomes: The people are not righted, nor satisfied in point of accompts, for the vast summes of money disbursed by them. None of the publique burthens, or oppressions, by arbitrary Committees,[c] iniustice in the Law, Tythes, Monopolies, and restraint of free trade, burthensome Oathes, inequalitie of Assessements, Excize, and otherwise are removed or lightned, the rights of the people in their Parliaments concerning the nature and extent of that power, are not cleared and declared.[d] So that we apprehend our own & the peoples case, little (if in any measure) better, since the Army last hazarded themselves for their own and the peoples rights and freedomes. Nay, to the griefe of our hearts, we must declare, that we conceive, the people and the Armies case much impaired, since the first Randezvouz at *New Market,* when that solemne ingagement was entred into: And that from the consideration.

That the Armies Engagement, Representations, Declarations, and Remonstrances, and promises in them contained, are declined, and more and more dayly broken, and not only in some smaller matters, wherein the Armie and the Kingdome are not so neerly concerned, but in divers particulars of dangerous consequence to the Army and the whole Nation. As,

First, In the Engagement, pag. the 5. the Armie promised every Member thereof each to other, and to the Parliament and Kingdome, that they would neither disband nor divide, nor suffer themselves to be disbanded or divided untill satisfaction should be given to the Army in relation to their grievances, and desires; and securitie that neither the Army nor the free borne people of

---

b Viz. the Representation of the Armies dissatisfactions, agreed on upon *Iune* 4. & 5. pag. 17, 18, 19, 20, 21. where these were represented as the ground of the solemn Engagement.

c Viz. the declaration of *Iu.* 14, p. 6, 9.

d Viz. the Remonst, of *Iun.* 23. pag. 6, 7. Its mentioned as one of the disatisfactions, that caused the march to London. See also the disatisfactions of the Armie annexed to the Engagement. pag. 19, 20,

England, should remaine subiect to such injuries, oppression, and abuse, as the corrupt party in the Parliament then had attempted against them.

Secondly, The Traine of Artillery is now to be disbanded, before satisfaction or securitie is given to the whole Army in relation to themselves, or other the free borne people, either in respect to their grievances or desires. And when the strength or sinewes of the Army be broken, what effectuall good can be secured for themselves or the people in case of opposition?

Thirdly, The Army is divided into quarters so farre distant, that one part is in no capabilitie to give timely assistance to another, if any designe should be to disband any part by violence sodainly, although neither our grievances nor desires as Soldiers or Commoners are redressed or answered. And as we conceive this dividing of the Army before satisfaction or securitie as aforesaid, to be contrary to the Armies intention in their Engagement, at the said Randezvouz, so we conceive it hath from that time given all the advantage to the enemies, to band and designe against the Armie, whereby not only pay hath been kept from the Soldiers, and securitie for arreers prevented, but the kingdom was indangered to have been imbroyled in blood, and the settlement of the peace and freedome of the Nation, hath been thus long delayed.

The whole intent of the Engagement, and the equitable sense of it, hath been perverted openly, by affirming, and by sinister meanes making seeming determinations in the Counsell, that the Army was not to insist upon, or demand any securitie, for any of their own or other the free borne peoples freedoms or rights,[e] though they might propound any thing to the Parliaments consideration; and according to that high breach of their Engagement, their actions have been regulated, and nothing that was declared formerly, to be insisted upon, hath been resolvedly adhered to, or claimed as the Armies or the peoples due, and we conceive it hath been by this meanes, that the Soldier hath had no pay constantly provided, nor any security for Arreers given them, & that hitherto they could not obtain so much, as to be paid up equally with those that did desert the Army, it not being possitively insisted upon, although in the Remonstrance of *Iune,* 23. pag. 11. It was declared, that it should be insisted upon re-

[e] *Viz.* His Excellencies letter to the City sent from *Royston, Iune* 16.

solvedly, to be done before the *Thursday* night after the sending that Remonstrance, and its now many moneths since.[f]

Fourthly, In the prosecution of this breach, there hath been many discouragements of the Agitators of the Regiments, in consulting about the most effectuall meanes, for procuring the speedy redresse of the peoples grievances, and clearing and securing the native rights of the Army, and all others the free Commons.

It hath been instilled into them, that they ought not to intermeddle with those matters, thereby to induce them, to betray the trust the Regiments reposed in them; and for that purpose, the endeavours of some hath been to perswade the Soldiery, that their Agitators have medled with more, then concerned them. In the Declaration of *Iune* 14. pag. *I*t was declared that the Army would adheare to their desires of full and equall satisfaction to the whole Soldiery of the Kingdome in Arreers, Indempnity, and all othre things mentioned in the papers, that contained * the grievances, disatisfactions and desires who did then, or should afterward concurre with this Army in these desires.

But many thousands who have concurred with this Army, are now to be sent for *I*reland, or to be disbanded with two moneths pay, before any securitie for Arrears, or sufficient *I*ndempnitie, or any satisfaction to any desires as Soldiers or Commoners, then propounded; so now our Declaration is forgotten, and the faith of the Army, and his Excellency broken, for it may be remembred, that his excellency often promised, that the same care should be taken for those, that concurred, that should be for this Army, therefore if this course be driven on, what better can wee expect for our selves in the end?

Sixtly, In the same Declaration, *June* 14. pag. 6. it is declared that the Army took up Armes, in judgement and conscience, for the peoples just rights and liberties, and not as mercenary Souldiers, hired to serve an arbitrary power of the State, and that in the same manner it continued in armes at that time, and pag. 7. of the same Declaration, it was declared that they proceeded upon the principles of right and freedome, and upon the law of nature and Nations,: But the strength of the endeavours of many hath

[f] The pay since received hath not been so much as since accrued to be due in course, and therefore that answers not the three moneths Arreers that was paid to the deserters of the Armie.

* It was declared to be one of the chiefe grounds of discontent, if any part of the Armie should be disbanded before satisfaction was given to the whole, See the Engagement pag. 3. and the Armies first grievances, and are not all that concurred with the Armie in the same condition?

been, and are now, spent to perswade the Soldiers and Agitators, that they stand as Soldiers only to serve the State, and may not as free Commons claime their right and freedome as due to them, as those ends for which they have hazzarded their lives, and that the ground of their refusing to disband, was only the want of Arrears and *I*ndempnitie.

Seventhly, *I*n the Remonstrance *June* 23. pag. 14. compared with pag. 15. it was declared, that such extraordinary courses should be taken as God should direct & enable them thereunto, to put things to a speedy issue, unles by the *Thursday* then imediately following, assurance and securitie were given to the Army and *K*ingdome, that the things desired in the Declaration, *Iune* the 14 should be speedily granted and setled.

But there hath been ever since, a totall neglect of insisting possitively upon the redresse of those grievances, or granting those desires of the Army as Soldiers. That the Declaration of *June* the 14. pag. the 3. refers unto, as formerly expressed, and not so much as one of those desires, as Commoners of *England* in the behalfe of themselves and others, (propounded in the same Declaration, pag. 6, 9, 10,11.) hath been insisted upon possitively; neither setling a determinate period, wherein the Parliament shall certainly end, nor purging the House, nor clearing the rights of the people, in petitioning, nor the righting of them in accounts, &c. so that by these declinings of the Army, from insisting resolvedly upon the peoples, and the Armies own rights, both are after long expectations, as farre from right and freedome, as though there had been no man to plead [g] their cause. And herein it is to be observed, that the neglect of insisting upon our most just desires, hath given enemies such secret incouragement, that they shufle off any desires,[h] though propounded, as to be insisted upon, as may be mentioned in that our just desire, of recalling publikely the Declaration, inviting al to desert the Army, & professed to be insisted upon, in the same Declaration, *June* 23. pag. 11. which notwithstanding to this day was never publiquely recalled; so likewise the desire of vindicating the Parliaments honour, in relation to a publique disowning the order to suppresse our first Petition, and many others.

Eightly, *I*n the declaration of *Iune* 14. pag. 10. as in all other Remonstrances and Declarations, it was desired, that the rights and liberties of the people might be secured, before the Kings

[g] *Viz.* declaration *I*une 14. pag. 4.
[h] *Viz.* the Armies representation of disatisfaction *I*une 4. 5. page 19.

businesse should be considered.[1] But now the grievances of the people are propounded to be considered after the restoring him to the regall power, and that in such a way according to the proposals *viz,* with a negative voice, that the people that have purchased by blood what was their right, of which the King endeavoured to deprive them, should yet solely depend on his will, for their reliefe in their grievances and oppressions; and in like manner the securitie for the Armies Arrears is proposed, to be considered after the businesse of the King be determined, so that there is a totall declension since the method formerly desired, in the setling the peace of the Nation.

Ninthly, *I*t hath been alwayes professed and declared, that the Army was called forth and conjured by the *P*arliaments Declarations, for defence of the peoples rights, against the forces raised by the King, and for delivering the King from his evill Councell, who seduced him to raise the war, and bringing Delinquents to condigne punishment, But now through the Armies countenance and indulgence, those conquered enemies, that were the Kings forces, abuse, reproach, and againe insult over the people, whose freedome was the grounds of the Armies engagement, yea, the *K*ings evill Councellors, that concurred in designing all the mischiefes in the *K*ings late warre against the people, are againe restored to him, and are admitted free accesse without check into all the Armies quarrets, whereby they are restored to a capacitie of plotting and designing mischiefe against the Armie and kingdome.

Tenthly, When imminent ruine, to the whole nation was apprehended, by meanes of the multitudes of corrupted Members in *P*arliament, diverting and obstructing all good proceedings; then the purging of the House in part, from one kind of Delinquents, was againe insisted upon, and a solemn Protestation was passed in the remonstrance from *Kingstone,* pag. 21. That the Armie would not permit those to sit in the House, that usurped the name and power of Parliamentary authoritie, when the Parliament was by violence suspended, and endeavoured to raise a warre to distroy the Parliament and Army, but that they would take some effectuall course to restraine them from sitting there,

[i] The parliament & *Scots* Commissioners long since resolved that satisfaction and securitie was to be given to the people in relation to those publike ends for which they expended so much treasure and blood, before the King should be provided for this is hinted in the Remonstrance signed *Kingstone,* page 11.

that the people might be concluded only by those Members that are free from such apparant treacherous breaches of their trust.

But hitherto this Engagement for purging the House from those Delinquents, (whose interest ingages them to be designing mischiefe against the people and Army) is declined and broken,. to the black reproach and foulest infamie of the Army; and now these strong cords are cut in sunder and so forgotten, that there are no visible endeavours or intentions, to preserve the honour of the Armie, in its faithfullnesse to its Engagement and Protestation.

Thus all promises of the *Armie* to the people that Petitioned his Excellencie and the Army to stand for the National interest, freedomes and rights, are hitherto wholly declined, and the law of nature and nations now refused by many to be the rule by which their proceedings should be regulated; they now strip themselves of the interest of English men, which was so ill resented when it was attempted by the mallice of the enemies.* And thus the peoples expectations that were much greatned, and their hopes of reliefe in their miseries and oppressions which were so much heightned are like to be frustrate, and while you looke for peace and freedome, the flood-gates of slaverie, oppression and miserie are opened upon the Nation, as may appeare by the present manifold dangers that incompasse about the Army and the whole Nation.

The mischiefes, evills, and dangers, which are and will be the necessary consequence of the Armies declining or delaying the effectuall fulfilling of its first Engagement, Promises and Declarations or of its neglect to insist possitively upon its first principles of common right and freedome.

WHereas its now many moneths since the Army declared (*In* answer to the Petitions of divers Counties, and from the sense of an absolute necessitie thereof,) that they would insist upon the peoples interest; as in the Declaration of *Iune* 14 pag. 13. And yet no reliefe for the people in any of their oppressions, by arbitrary powers, Monopolies, iniustice in the proceeding at Law, Tythes, Excize, &c. is effectually procured; nor any greater probabillitie of future helpe is visible then was before [j]; no foun-

---

* See his Excellencies letter to the City, dated *Iu.* 10. pag. 4.

[j] Then also they professed that they hoped God would cleare it, that they have acted the kingdomes and every honest mans interest. *viz.* the Remonstrance from *Kingstone* pag. 12.

dations of freedome being yet laid; and yet the Soldiery burthening the country with free quarters and occasioning greater taxes.
These five mischiefes and dangers ensue inevitably.

First, The love and affection of the people to the Armie, which
is (an armies greatest strength) is decayed, cooled, and neere lost;
its already the common voice of the people, what good hath our
new Saviours done for us? What grievances have they procured
to be redressed? Wherein is our condition bettered? or how are
we more free then before?

Secondly, Not only so, but the Army is rendred as an heavie
burthen to the people, in regard more pay is exacted dayly for
them, and the people find no good procured by them, thats answerable or equivolent to the charge, so that now the people begin
to cry lowder for disbanding the Army then they did formerly
for keeping us in Armes, because they see no benefit accruing,
they say they are as likely to be oppressed and inslaved both by
King and Parliament, as they were before the Armie engaged
professedly to see their freedomes cleared and secured.

Thirdly, Whilst the peoples old oppressions are continued, and
more taxes also are imposed for pay for the Army, they are disabled dayly more & more for the mantaining of an Army for
their preservation, for they beginne to say, they can but be dis-
troyed by oppression, and its all one to them, whether it be by
pretended friends or professed enemies, it were as good, say they,
that the King should rule againe by prerogative; we were slaves
then to his will and we are now no better; we had rather have one
tyrant then hundreds.

Fourthly, By this meanes, distractions divisions, heart-burnings and jealousies are increased, to the imminent danger of ruine
to the Army and Kingdome; the people are inclined to tumults
crying out, will none procure reliefe for us : shall we alwayes be
deluded with faire words, and be devoured by oppressors? wee
must ere long rise up in armes, and every one catch what he can:
thus confusion is threatned.

Fiftly, The Army is exposed to contempt and scandall, and
the most black reproaches, and infamies are cast upon them, the
people say, that their resolutions not to disband, were because
they would live idly on the peoples labours, and when the Souldiers
are constrained to take free quarters, this (saith the people) is for
freedom, and right, to eat the bread out of our childrens mouths:
so that many Souldiers are ashamed of themselves, and feare that

the people should rise to distroy them : you will doe nothing for us, (say they) we are vexed by malignant Iudges for conscience sake, by arbitrary Committes in the Country, and at Parliament, ordering one thing this day, and recalling it the next, to our intollerable vexation, injustice in the law is the same, and we buy our right at as a dear rate as ever, Tithes are inforced from us double and treble, Excise continues, we can have no accompts of all our moneyes disbursed for the publicke, more is dayly required, and we know not what is become of all we have paid already, the Souldiers have little pay, and the maimed Souldiers Widowes and Orphans are thrust upon us to be parrish charges.

Secondly Whereas the Engagement is broken, and the first principles deserted or neglected, these mischiefes and dangers have ensued.

1. The enemies are incouraged and imboldned to proceed in prejudice to the people & the Army as formerly [k]: they may receive hopes upon the armies own words in their Generall Counsells, that the army will not oppose or disturbe them in their proceedings, to deprive the Armie and people of their native rights, if they can abuse the Parliament, or surprize them as formerly, they may say for themselves, the Army hath declared that they stand only as Souldiers, and will not insist upon any possitive demand of their own and the Nations freedomes: and was it not this that imboldned the enemies formerly to suppresse our first petition, and declare us enemies, for petitioning? they thought we would have stood only as mercenary Souldiers, hired to serve their arbitrary power, and not remembered that we by their invitation took up armes in judgment and conscience, to preserve the nation from tyrannie and opression, and therefore were oblieged to insist upon our rights and freedomes as Commoners, and surely it hath been upon this ground, that they kept us without money so long, thinking we would not or durst not insist upon our demands of that which is due to us, and upon this ground we judge the Parliament hath proceeded of late to increase the peoples oppressions, by an Ordinance for trible dammages, to be paid by all that refuse (though for conscience sake) to Pay Tythes, and an Ordinance to locke up the printing presses against whom they please, which was in the Bishops time complained of, as one of the great oppressions, and have slighted just petitions, and neglected

[k] *They formerly prevailed and proceeded in that way,* viz. *Del. offered to the Commissioners at Saffron Walden.*

to consider, and redresse the prisoners grievances and oppressions
and the sufferings of conscientious persons, by the uniust statutes
against Conventicles so stiled, & statutes for Common prayer Book,
and enforcing all to come to Church, and all other the peoples
grievances.

2. From the Armies declining their first principles, the same
corrupt Members remain in Parliament that caused the *Army* to
be proclaimed enemies for petitioning, and its to be observed that
through the influence of those in the house, there was never any
publike vindication of the Armyes honour, and of the justice of
their petitioning at that time. and can the Army be safe, so long
as its old declared enemies are in power and doe but watch the
fittest opportunity to worke any mischief, but not only those enemies remain in power, and watch to destroy you, but 65. at least
that lately voted and endeavoured to raise a new work to destroy
the Armie, are suffered to vote in the Parliament though the
Army hath * protested solemnly, they would not suffer those
usurpers to sit there, or that they would be concluded by those
that were coactors in such treasonable breaches of their trust.

3. Through the Armies dividing contrary to the Engagement,
and neglecting to insist upon the first Declaration, the enemies
have had power and opportunity, to prevent them of their constant pay, and obstruct all proceedings to security for Arreares,
whereas otherwise the enemies would not have dared to presume
to obstruct good proceedings, and to prosecute their designes
against the Army.

4. *Through the Armies back-sliding from the Remonstrance,
and Protestation from* Kingston, August 18. *those that lately endeavoured to raise a warre against the Parliament and Army, continue in the House, and have passed an Ordinance, wherein those
betrayers of their trust are acknowledged to have been a House of
Parliament, when the Parliament was forced away and suspended,
and the Army having declared them to be no Parliament,*[1] *and
his Excellency slighted their Command, at* Colebrooke, *professing
he knew no Parliament, to which he should send, are by this
made guilty of the highest treason, and so a snare is layd for his
Excellency and the Army, that when the enemies shall have the
advantage, they may be declared traytors, for declaring against the
Parliament, and disowning their authority, so that if some speedy
remedy be not applyed, no man knowes how soon the enemy may*

* *Viz. The Remõstrance from Kingston,* Aug. 18 pag. 21.
[*l*] viz. Dec. shewing the reasons of their last march unto London pag. 9.

prevaile to destroy his Excellency, the Army and Kingdome by this meanes: and the policy of the enemy is to be observed, that they would never suffer that Declaration to be debated in the House, that was published at the Armies marching towards London; *wherein those that usurped the power of a Parliament, when the Parliament was suspended, were declared to be no legall Parliament : but the Declaration and Remonstrance of August* 18. *wherein the Army protested against the sitting of those usurpers in the House, may together be made the ground of their declaring us Traytors upon any advantage, for disowning, and declaring against the supreame authority of the Nation, in case those usurpers shall continue to be acknowledged an house of Parliament, as it remaines at present by the late Ordinance of August* 20. *procured to be passed by those Vsurpers themselves sitting iudges of their own case.*

5. *By this neglect and declining of the Army, The Parliament is returned to their old delatory way of proceeding, neither insisting upon the relieving the people speedily and effectually in any of their grievances, nor providing constant pay for the Army, nor security for Arreares; so that the delayes that are occasioned through the Armies declining their first principles are as distinctive to the Army and Kingdome, as if there were direct actings by the Army against the Kingdomes peace.*

6. *Through the same declension of the Armies first principles, and the good and necessary method propounded for setling the nation in peace and freedome before the Kings businesse be considered, the King is likely to recover his old capacity, before the peoples freedoms (which they have redeemed out of the hands of him and his forces by blood) be cleared and established securely, and likewise before any security be given for Arreares; and then what probability there is, that then there should be any good security of pay obtained for the Army that conquered him, and for the freedoms of those that assisted them, let any rationall man judge? It may more certainly be expected, that he will provide for the pay and Arreares of his own Souldiery rather then of ours. And likewise by the same meanes, the Armies and their assistants indempnity, is propounded to receive its strength from the Kings consent; whereas not onely his sign of, or consent to any act is wholly null and void in Law, because he is under restraint, and so our indempnity, will be insufficient, if it shall depend in the least, on his confirmation. But also its the highest disparagement to the supream authority of this Nation, the Parliament, that*

when they have commanded an Army upon service against the
King, they should not have sufficient power to save them harm-
lesse for obedience to their commands, and also its the highest
dishonour to the Army, that they should seeke to the conquered
enemy to save them harmlesse for fighting against them, which is
to aske him pardon, and so will remaine as a perpetuall reproach
upon them, & render them traytors to psterity.

7. *Through the Armies declining its first principles, to insist*
upon satisfaction and security as Souldiers and Commoners before
disbanding or dividing the Army, is it now likely to be so far
scattered into severall quarters, that it shall be in no capacity, to
insist upon security for arreares, sufficient indempnity, or upon
any its own or the nations rights, in case they shall be still denyed
them.

8. It is to be considered that the enemies on the one hand,
and the other increase dayly in their boldnesse, confidence, and
strength, whilest securitie for the armies arreers, and constant
future pay (so long as it shall be continued) are not provided, and
and the rights and freedomes of the people are not cleared and
secured, & the armie may divide, in case one part should insist
upon the first just principles, and be faithfull thereunto, and another part should by flatteries, preferments, feare or negligence
decline or desert them, and let it be considered what strength that
would adds to the enemies, and how far it will indanger the ruine
of the armie and kingdome.

Now we cannot but declare, that these sad apprehensions of
mischiefes, dangers and confusion gaping to devoure the armie
hath filled our hearts with troubles, that we never did, nor doe
regard the worst of evills or mischiefes that can befall our selves
in comparison to the consequence of them to the poore Nation,
or to the security of common right and freedom, we could not
but in (reall not formall fained) trouble of heart for the poore
Nation and oppressed people, breake forth and cry, O our bowels!
our bowels! we are troubled at the very heart to heare the peoples
dolfull groanes, and yet their expected deliverers will not heare
or consider, they have run to and fro, and sighed & even wept
forth their sorrowes and miseries, in petitions, first to the King
then to the Parliament, and then to the armie, yet they have
all been like broken reeds, even the armie it selfe upon whom
they leaned have pierced their hands, their eyes even faile with
looking for peace and freedome, but behold nothing but distraction, oppression and trouble, and could we hope that helpe

is intended, yet the people perish by delayes, we wish therefore that the bowells of compassion in the whole armie might yearne towards their distressed brethren, and that they might with one consent say each to other, come let us joyne together speedily to demand present redresse for the peoples grievances, and securitie for all their and our own rights and freedomes as Soldiers and Commoners. Let us never divide each from other till those just demands be answered really and effectually, that so for the peoples case as many forces as are not absolutely necessary may be speedily disbanded and our honour may be preserved unspotted, when they shall see, that we minded not our own interest, but the good, freedome, and welfare of the whole Nation. Now to all that shall thus appeare we propound.

That whatsoever was proposed to be insisted on either, in the Declaration of *June* the 14. or the Remonstrance Iune 23 and in the Remon. from *Kingstone, August* 18. be adhered to resolvedly, so as not to reced from those desires, untill they be throughly and effectually answered: more particularly, that whereas it appeares by possitive lawes and antient iust customes, that the people have right to new successive elections for Parliaments, at certain periods of time, and that it ought not to be denyed them, being so essentiall to their freedome, that without it they are no better then slaves, the nature of that legislative power, being arbitrary: and that therefore it be insisted on so possitively, and resolvedly, as not to recede from it.

1. That a determined period of time, be forthwith set, wherein this Parliament shall certainly be desolved, provided also that the said period be within 9. or 10. moneths, next ensuing, that so there may be sufficient time for setling of peace and freedome.

2. Whereas all good is obstructed and diverted by the power & influence of Delinquents, the late usurpers, & undu elected ones in the Parliament, that therefore it be possitively & resolvedly insisted on; that the house be forthwith purged, from al that have forfited their trust, or were unduly elected, but especially that an order be passed forthwith, for the expelling all those from the house, who sate in the late pretended Parliament, & that likewise a severe penalty be ordered to be imposed on every of those usurpers that shall presume to sit in the House, for the passing of such an order, before they shall have given sufficient evidence, that they neither voted for a new warre, or for the Kings comming to London upon his own tearmes.

3. Wheras his Excellencie & the whole armie, were guilty of

the highest treason if the pretended Parliament had been a legall
Parliament, and its apparent that they were no legall Parliament,
that therefore it be possitively and resolvedly insisted upon, that
the Declaration of the army upon their last march up to London
be forthwith publikely owned, and approved of by the Parliament,
and that the same publique approbation be Passed upon the Remonstrance, & protest sent from *Kingstone August* 18.

4.Whereas Parliaments rightly constituted are the foundation
of the hopes of right and freedome to this people, and whereas
the people have been prevented of Parliaments, though many
possitive lawes have been made for a constant succession of Parliaments, that therefore it be possitively and resolvedly insisted
upon, that a law paramount be made, enacting it, to be unalterable by *P*arliaments that the people shall of course meet without
any warrants or writs once in every two yeares upon an appointed
day in their respective Countyes, for the election of their representors in Parliament, & that all the freeborn at the age of 21.
yeares and upwards, be the electors, excepting those that have
or shall deprive themselves of that their freedome, either for
some yeares, or wholly by delinquency, and that the Parliament
so elected and called, may have a certaine period of time set,
wherein they shall of course determine, and that before the same
period they may not be adjurnable and disolvable by the King,
or any other except themselves.

Whereas all power is originally and essentially in the whole
body of the people of this Nation, and whereas their free choice
or consent by their Representors is the only originall or foundation of all just government; and the reason and end of the choice
of all just Governors whatsoever is their apprehension of safety
and good by them, that it be insisted upon possitively. That the
supreame power of the peoples representors or Commons assembled in Parliament, be forthwith clearly declared as their power
to make lawes, or repeale lawes, (which are not, or ought not to
be unalterable) as also their power to call to an account all officers
in this Nation whatsoever, for their neglect or treacheries in their
trust for the peoples good, and to continue or displace and remove
them from their offices, dignities or trust, according to their demerits by their faithfulnesse or treacherie in the businesse or
matters where with they are intrusted. *A*nd further, that this
power to constitute any kind of governors or officers, that they
shall judge to be for the peoples good, be declared, and that upon
the aforesaid considerations it be insisted upon, that all obstruc-

tions to the freedome and equallitie of the peoples choice of their Representors, either by *Pattents,* Charters or usurpations, by pretended customes, be removed by these present Commons in Parliament, and that such a freedome of choice be provided for, as the people may be equally represented. This power of Commons in Parliament, is the thing against which the King hath contended, and the people have defended with their lives, and therefore ought now to be demanded as the price of their blood.

That all the oppressions of the poore by Excize upon Beare, Cloath, Stuffes, and all manufactures, and English commodities; be forthwith taken off, and that all Excize be better regulated, and imposed upon forraign commodities, and a time set wherein it shall certainly end, if there be a necessity of its present continuance on such commodities.

5. Whereas the people have disbursed such vast sums of money, by Pole-money, Subsidies, proposition money, Contribution, the five and twentieth part, viewes and reviewes of the same monethly assessements, Excize, and other wayes, and such vast sums have been collected and enforced by Sequestrations, Compositions, sale of Bishops lands, and other wayes, that the whole charge of the forces by sea and land might have been defrayed to the utmost farthing, and yet many millions of money remained if all that hav been disbursed freely or enforced, had been faithfully brought into the publike treasury, and improved for the publique use only : therefore, in respect to the peoples right, and for their ease, and for better and more easie provision of money for the Soldiery, that it be insisted upon possitively, that faithfull persons be chosen to receive accounts in every part of the kingdome, especially considering that former Committees for accounts were constituted in a time when corrupt men over powred the Parliament, and that they have done no service in discovering moneys since their constitution; and herein its to be insisted on that all without distinction, as well parliament men as others, may be equally accountable to persons chosen for that purpose.

Now herein its further to be insisted on, that whereas the time was wholly corrupt when persons were appointed to make sale of Bishops lands, and whereas Parliament men, Committee men, and their kinsfolkes were the only buyers, and much is sold, and yet its pretended, that little or no money is received, and whereas Lords, Parliament-men, and some other rich men, have vast sums of arreers allowed them in their purchase, and all their moneys lent to the state paid them, while others are left in necessitie, to

whom the state is much indebted, and so present money that
might be for the equall advantage of all, is not brought into the
publique Treasury by those sales *I*ts therefore to be insisted on
that the sale of Bishops lands be reviewed, and that they may be
sold to their worth, and for present moneys, for the publike use,
& that the sale of all such be recalled, as have not been sold to
their worth, or for present moneys.

And it is further offered, in consideration that the Court have
occasioned the late warre, and reduced the state to such necessity,
by causing such vast expence of treasure, that therefore whereas
the many oppressions of the people, and the danger of absolute
tyrany, were the occasion of the expence of so much blood, and
whereas the people have bought their rights and freedomes, by
the price of blood, and have in vaine waited long since, the common enemie, hath been subdued for the redresse of their grievances and oppressions, that therefore it be demanded as the peoples due, which ought not to denyed to the Army or to them, that
before the King hath his Court and lives in honour, yet before
his businesse be further considered, because the people are under
much oppression and misery, it be forthwith the whole worke of
the Parliament, to heare or consider of, & study effectually redresse for all common grievances and oppressions, and for the
securing all other the peoples rights and freedomes, besides all
these afore mentioned, and in particuler.

First, that all the orders, votes, ordinances or declarations, that
have passed either to discountenance petitions, suppresse, prevent
or burne petitions, imprison or declare against petitioners, being
dangerous presidents against the freedom of the people, may be
forthwith expunged the Journall books, and the injustice of them
clearly declared to all the people, and that in such a declaration
the soldiery be vindicated, as to the right and equity of their first
petition.

That all those large sums of money that were alowed to
needlesse pretended Officers of the Court which did but increase
wickednesse and prophanenesse, may be reserved for a publiqve
treasure to be expended in paying those forces that must be
maintained for the peoples safety, that so through a good and
faithfull improvement of al the Lands pertaining to the Court,
there might be much reserved for leaving publique charges, and
easing the people.

And its further offered, that whereas millions of money have
been kept in dead stocks in the City of *Lonndon* the Hals and
Companies, and the free men of the City could never obtaine

any account thereof, according to their right; That therefore a just and strict account may be forthwith given to all the freemen of all those dead stocks, & whereas there hath been nothing paid out of those, nor for the lands pertaining to the City, whiles the estates of others have been much wasted, by continuall payments, that therefore proportionable summs to what other estates have payd, may be taken out of those dead stocks, and lands which would amount to such vast sums, as would pay much of the soldiers arreares, without burthening the oppressed people.

And its further offered, that forrest lands, and Deanes and Chapters lands be immediately set appart for the arrears of the Army, and that the revenue of these and the resedue of Bishops lands unsold till the time of sale may be forthwith appoynted to be paid unto our Treasury, to be reserved for the soldiers constant pay. And its to be wished that only such part of the aforesaid lands be sold as necessity requires, to satisfie the soldiery for arreares, and that the resedue be reserved and improved for a constant revenue for the State that the people may not be burthened, and that out of the revenues publique debts may be paid, and not first taken out of their own purses to be repayed to them.

And its further offered for the peoples ease, that the arreers of all former assessements be duly collected from those who have sufficient estates, and have not been impoverished by the warre.

And whereas its conceived that the fees of receivers of customes and Excize if they were justly computed, would amount to neere as much as the Armies pay, its therefore offered that speedy consideration be had of the multitude of those officers and their excessive fees, & profits, as 500. 600. 1000. 1200. l *per annum*. And wheras that many Excize men appoint whom they please as their substitute, and alow what they please for their pay, that the officers may be few, and constant stipends allowed them, none exceeding 200. l. *per annum,* that so more moneys may be brought into the publike treasury.

And for the ease and satisfaction of the people, its further to be insisted on, that the charge of all the forces to be kept up in the kingdome by sea or land, be particularly computed and published, and that all taxes that shall be necessary, may be wholly proportioned, according to that charge; and that there be an equall rate propounded throughout the kingdome in all assessements, that so one town may not beare double the proportion of another of the same value.

4. That all Monopolyes be forthwith removed, and no persons whatsoever may be permitted to restraine others from free trade.

5. That the most sad oppressions of prisoners be forthwith eased and removed, and that no person that hath no estate reall or personall, nor any person that shall willingly yeeld up his estate to satisfie his creditors may be detained in prison to the ruine of their persons and families, and likewise, that no person imprisoned in a criminall cause, may be detained from his legall tryall any longer then the next tearme.

6. That all Statutes, for the Common prayer book, and for enforcing all to come to Church, whereby many religious and conscientious people are dayly vexed and oppressed, be forthwith repealed and nulled. As also that all Statutes against Convinticles, under the pretence of which, religious people are vexed for private meetings about the worship of God, may be likewise repealed and nulled.

7. That all the oppressive statutes, enforcing all persons though against their consciences to pay Tythes, whereby the husbandman cannot eate the fruit of his labours, may be forthwith repealed and nulled.

8. That all statutes enforcing the taking of oaths, as in townes corporate, the oath of Supreamacy, &c. Wherein either the whole oaths, or some clauses in them, are burthens, and snares to conscientious people may be repealed and nulled.

9. That it be declared that no person or Court shall have power or be permitted to enforce any person to make oath, or answer to any Interrogatories concerning himself, in any criminall case.

10. That a Committee of conscientious persons be forthwith selected to consider of the most intollerable oppressions by unjust proceedings in the law, that with all the lawes might be reduced to a smaller number, to be comprized in one volume in the the English tongue, that every free Commoner might understand his own proceedings, that Courts might be in the respective Counties or Hundreds, that proceedings might become short and speedy, and that the numberlesse grievances in the law and Lawyers, might be redressed as soone as possible.

11. That all priviledges and protections above the law, whereby some persons are exempted from the force and power thereof, to the insufferable vexation and ruine of multitudes of distressed people, may be forthwith abbrogated.

12. That all the antient rights and donations belonging to the poore, now imbezled and converted to other uses, as inclosed Commons, Alms houses, &c. throughout all parts of the land, may be forthwith restored to the antient publique use and service of the poore, in whose hands soever they be detained.

Many other grievances are and ought to be redressed, but these as they are propounded, we conceive might be in a very short time redressed to the reliefe of many distressed ones, and to a generall ease; or at least, put into a way, wherein there might be visible hopes of remedie, and therefore these might be demanded as due to the people, though we desire the Counties might be encouraged to represent all their other grievances also for speedy redresse.

7. Generall head. That it be insisted on, that such Indempnitie be forthwith given both for the Soldiery and all that gave them assistance, and shall provide securely for their quiet, ease and safety, and prevent all chargeable journeys to London, to seek after and waite upon Committees.

8. That in some of the fore mentioned wayes, security be given for arreers forthwith, that as soone as the rights and freedomes of the people be secured according as its hereupon propounded, and the other desires of the Army in relation to their particular freedome from pressing, and provision to be made in a certaine and no dishonourable way for maimed soldiers, Widowes, and Orphans, that shall continue during their lives, that then the Armes may be disposed into the hands of the faithfull well affected of the Nation, which may be so formed into a military posture, as to be ready on all occasions of service, and as many of the forces that are kept in constant pay, as shall not be absolutely necessary for the preservation and safety of the people, may be as speedily as possible disbanded, that they may not be a burthen to the Nation.

9. Whereas mercy and justice are the foundations of a lasting peace, its necessary to be insisted on (for the healing differences as far as possible,) That all those whose estates have been sequestered, and yet were not in armes for the King, or gave any actuall assistance to him in men, money, or armes, plate, horse, &c. in the late warre, that all such be discharged forthwith from their sequestrations; and that all such as have compounded, may not be enforced, to pay the five or twenteth part, seeing their whole estates were so long under sequestration : and that all those that have not compounded, who were in Armes for the King, may be compelled forthwith to compound, provided, that their Compositions be so moderate, as none may exceed two yeares revenue, that their families be not ruined, and they put upon desperate attempts against the peace of the Nation to preserve themselves.

These things propounded are no more then what we conceived, should have been thoroughly done long since, being as to the principall of them but the substance and equitable sense of our former declarations, Remonstrances, and representations, And therefore though our restlesse desires of the peoples good, and of the welfare of the Army, have constrained us, thus publiquely to state our case, and the remedie according to the best improvement of the small Tallent of understanding that God hath given freely to us? yet let not the matter be prejudged because of the unworthy Authors, neither let it be thought presumption. It may be remembred that the *Fathers* danger made a dumb child to speake, and the Armys yea all the peoples dangers and miseryes have wrested open our mouthes, who had otherwise been silent in this kinde to the grave, and let it not be thought that we intend the division of the Army, we professe we are deeply sensible and desire all our fellow soldiers to consider it.

*I*n case the union of the Army should be broken, (which the enemie waite for,) ruine and destruction will breake in upon us like a roaring sea, but we are much confident that the adhearing to those desires and to that speedy way of attaining our just ends for which we first ingaged, cannot be interpreted to be a desire of division, but the strongest vigorous endeavours after union, and though many whom we did betrust have been guilty of most supine negligence, yet we expect that the same impultion of judgement and conscience that we have all professed, did command us forth at first for the peoples Freedome, will be againe so effectuall, that all will unannimusly concurre with us, so that a demand of the peoples and Armyes rights shall be made by the whole Army as by one man, that then all the enemies to, or obstructors of the happy settlement of common right, peace and freedome, may heare of our union and resolution, and their hands may be weake, and their hearts may fayle them, and so this Army that *God* hath cloathed with honour in subduing the common enemie, may yet be more honourable in the peoples eyes, when they shall be called the Repayrers of their breaches, and the restorers of their peace, right, and freedome.

And this is the prayer, and shall alwayes be the earnest endeavours of.

The Armies and all the peoples most faithfull servants,

Lievt. Gen.	{ Robert Everard. { George Sadler.	Com. Gen.	{ George Garret. { Thomas Beverly.	Col. Fleetwood.
{ William Priar. { William Bryan.		Col. Whalyes.	{ Matthew Wealy. { William Russell. { Richard Seale.	C. Riches. { Iohn Dober. { William Hudson. { Agitators.

Gilford, October 9. 1647.

FINIS.

A Copy of a Letter from the Agents of the a-
forefaid five Regiments of Horfe, unto his Excellency
Sir *Thomas Fairfax.*

May it please your Excellency,

*F*Rom *the deep sense of our duty to God, to our native Country, to your Excellency, to this Army, and to our selves, and
to posterities to come, we find such obligations upon our consciences, written naturally by the finger of God in our hearts,
that we cannot behold the honour of God to be impaired, the
workes of his hands the land of our nativity, your Excellency, this
Army, our selves, or posterities, ready to be swallowed and devoured up in confusion, thraldome and ruine, and to sit still, and
not arise in the strength of his might, to contribute our best endeavours for the prevention thereof: for, God hath given no man
a talent to be wrapt up in a Napkin & not improved, but the
meanest vassall in the eye of the Lord is equally oblieged and
accomptable to God with the greatest Prince or Commander under the Sun, in & for the use of that talent betrusted unto him:
and therefore we presume that your Excellency (who does acknowledge your selfe a creature of, & servant to the same God)
will not think it strange, or judge us disobedient or refractory,
that we should, as we have presumed. State the case of the Army,
how declined from its first principles of safety, what mischiefes
are threatned thereby, and what remedies are sutable for prevention, which herewith we do humbly present & offer unto your
Excellencie : for, Sir should you, yea, should the whole Parliament
or Kingdome exempt us from this service, or should command our
silence & forbearance, yet could not they nor you discharge us of
our duties to God, or to our own natures, for we must be accomptable, & judgment will come for the deeds done in our flesh,
whether good or evill : and hee that hath not improved and put
forth his talent to use, shall be bound hand and foot, & cast into
the lake of eternall vengeance : Therefore, whether God or Man
in this case must be obeyed, judge you So that we are bold from
our sense of your Excel. piety, honesty and uprightnesse to God
and to your Countrie, that in this our discharge of our duties to
both, we shall not incur your displeasure or discountenance, but*

*that you will freely commit us and the issue of our endeavours to
God, & if it be of him it will stand; & from our consciences we
attest, and protest in the presence of this all seeing diety, as we
desire safety in this life, or in that which is to come, we have no
other then cordiall & faithfull intents and resolutions to the undoubted safety and weale of our native Countrie, to Parliaments,
your Excellencie, and this Armie, in this businesse represented
in these inclosed Papers, & we do utterly abhorre and renounce
all secret or private designes, or interest under the same, together
with all that is contrary to the plaine and vulgar sense expressed
in the premises thereof. And if by any one your Excellencie shall
be suborned, that we are transgressors of all order and forme, and
in that sense only to look upon us We desire to mind your Excellencie; that the law of nature & nations attested in our own
publike Declarations & Papers may be an answer to such for the
justification of our present expedient, for all formes are but as
shadowes & subject to the end, & the safety of the people is above
all formes, customes, &c. and the equitie of popular safettie is the
thing which justifieth all formes, or the change of formes for the
accomplishment thereof; and no formes are lawfull longer then
they preserve or accomplish the same. If our dutie bind us when
we see our neighbours house on fire, to wave all formes, ceremonies or complements, and forthwith (not waiting for order or
leave) to attempt the quenching thereof without further scruple,
as thereunto called of God, we say if we be so oblieged & called in
the case of a particular, then much more are we oblieged and
called, when we behold the great Mansion House of this Common
wealth, and of this Army (wherein all the families of the Nation
are contained) on fire, all ready to be devoured with slaverie, confusion and ruine, & their nationall native freedome (the price of
their treasure & bloud) wrested out of their hands, as at this present appeareth to our best understandings: And therefore in this
exigencie & straight of extremity, we from the very dictates of
Divinity, Nature & Reason ingraven in our hearts could not otherwise chuse, with quiet and peace to our consciences [which no
mortall man can take from us or suppresse the over powring motives thereof] but consider with our selves what we should do to
award those threatning mischiefes from this Nation and Army,
and to that end we find nothing more effectuall then to knit our
selves together with this fixed resolution, to part with our lives
and all that is neare and deare unto us, before we part with our
freedomes; and in relation thereunto we the Agents to five Regi-*

ments of your Horse, have after our weak manner in this our
Representation directed to our respective Regiments and to the
whole Army, discharged our duties; And we presume we have
not erred from the equitable sense of our solemn Engagement, or
from the just maximes and matters contained in our Declarations,
Remonstrances, &c. from the which we are resolved not to receed.
Thus humbly craving your Excellencies favourable construction
on our innocent intentions and endeavours, we (as we alwayes
have been) cordially remaine,

Your Excellencies and this Nations
faithfull Servants and Soldiers to
ftand or fall with you and it, for
common Right and Freedome.

Edward Trevers.
Edmon Bear. } Lieut. Gen.

George Garret.
Jeremiah Cole. } Com. Gen.

William Prior.
William Bryan. } Col. Fleetwod.
John Fletcher.

John Dober.
William Hudfon. } Col. Riches.

Matth. Wealey.
William Ruffel. } Col. whaleys.

Hemftead, *October,* 15.
1647.

We appoint *Edmond Bear* and *William Ruffell* abovefaid,
in our names to prefent this Letter, together with our
Reprefentation, entituled *The cafe of the Army, &c. to
his Excellency Sir* Thomas Fairfax.

Upon the prefentation to, and ferious per-
ufall thereof by his Excellency, the fum of his
anfwer was to this effect. That he judged their
intentions were honeft, and defired that every
one of a publique fpirit would be acting for
the Publique, and that for his part hee had
freely ventured his life for common right and
freedome, and fhould freely engage it againe,
adding further, that he thought it meet it
fhould be prefented to the Generall-Councel.

Octob. 18. 1647.

AN AGREEMENT OF THE PEOPLE

Appeared November 3, 1647. Reprinted from a photostat of the original pamphlet, Thomason Collection, E 412 (21).

Anticipating the fundamentals of the American constitution, *An Agreement Of The People* is a landmark in the history of constitutional theory. The primary purpose of the *Agreement,* which was to be subscribed to by both soldiers and citizens, was to "have Parliaments certainly cal'd and have the time of their sitting & ending certain, & their power or trust cleare and unquestionable." So that Parliaments may be called and dissolved regularly, the time of their election is fixed by the *Agreement* itself. Parliament's power is to be limited, however, by the people's wishes as expressed in the *Agreement.* No Parliament is to abridge the right of each person to worship as he chooses in the church of his choice; it is not to conscript men into the army; nor is it to exempt any from the court action by virtue of rank, birth, property, position, tenure, or any rights previously secured by law.

The authors of the *Agreement* intended to submit it to thousands of citizens; they also wanted to make it as acceptable as possible to the officers who had hitherto hindered their efforts. Hence, unlike *The Case Of The Army,* the *Agreement* has a temperate, constructive tone; it avoids recriminations, speaks of grievances with restraint and dignity, assumes a unity of army sentiment that did not in fact exist. By specifically exempting all from punishment who had fought in the Civil War, it attempts to conciliate even the royalist supporters. The authors take pains to trace the genesis of their document. In the Declaration of June 14, they had "promised to the people, that we would with our lives vindicate and cleare their right and power in their Parliaments." This was done in *The Case Of The Army,* from which they have taken several of the main planks of the *Agreement.*

Now they are presenting the *Agreement, "whereby the founda-tions of your freedomes provided in the Case, &c. shall be settled unalterably."* The authors show that they have gained little re-dress of their grievances, notwithstanding all their declarations and representations; now they will act for decisive action through a mutual pact.

As is shown by Cromwell's statement (*Clarke Papers,* I, 229), a reply to *The Case Of The Army* had been prepared and presented to the agitators. The agitators brought back an answer to this criticism that has been interpreted by Professor Firth (*Clarke Papers,* I, 234) as being the *Agreement* itself. If this is true, it seems likely that the *Agreement* was written with the officers' ob-jections to *The Case* in mind; the authors still thought it possible to secure Cromwell's support. The Levellers considered the time factor of pre-eminent importance; the *Agreement* meant imme-diate action: the securing of signatures. Meanwhile the highest officers might still be won over. The *Agreement,* which is un-dated, was written before October 28, when it was mentioned in the General Council for the first time. I think it was not written earlier than October 20. *Two Letters From the Agents of the Five Regiments,* which restates many of the arguments of *The Case,* and reviews the types of attacks levelled against it, does not men-tion the *Agreement.* It appeared in London October 28, and could hardly have been printed earlier than October 23.

The *Agreement* was read and opened to discussion in a meet-ing of officers and agitators on October 29. One of the most re-markable debates in constitutional history followed, with Ireton's objections to manhood suffrage as the focal point of disagreement. The debate fortunately was preserved in shorthand and may be read in *Clarke Papers,* I, 299ff. Critical discussion of the debates on the *Agreement* may be found in Gardiner, *History of the Great Civil War,* Pease, *The Leveller Movement,* and my *Milton in the Puritan Revolution.* Gardiner has reprinted the *Agree-ment* in *Great Civil War,* III, 392-94. Unfortunately, however, he omitted the last seven pages of the pamphlet (E 412, 21), which are of the utmost importance in explaining the genesis and justifi-cation of the Leveller position.

AN
AGREEMENT
OF THE
PEOPLE
FOR

A firme and prefent Peace, upon
grounds of common-right and freedome;

As it was propofed by the Agents of the five
Regiments of Horfe; and fince by the generall approbation of the Army, offered to the joynt concurrence of all the free COMMONS of
ENGLAND.

The Names of the Regiments which have already appeared for the
Cafe, of *The Cafe of the Army truly ftated*, and for this
prefent Agreement, *VIZ*.

1. *Gen. Regiment.*	1. *Gen. Regiment.*
2. *Life-Guard.*	2. *Col. Sir Hardreffe*
3. *Lieut. Gen. Regiment.*	*Wallers Reg.*
4. *Com. Gen. Regiment.*	3. *Col. Lamberts Reg.*
5. *Col. Whaleyes Reg.* — Of Horfe	4. *Col. Rainfboroughs* — Of Foot.
6. *Col. Riches Reg.*	*Regiment.*
7. *Col. Fleetwoods Reg.*	5. *Col. Overtons Reg.*
8. *Col. Harrifons Reg.*	6. *Col. Lilburns Reg.*
9. *Col. Twifldens Reg.*	7. *Col. Backfters Reg.*

Printed *Anno. Dom.* 1647.

An Agreement of the People, for a firme and present Peace, upon grounds of Common-Right.

Having by our late labours and hazards made it appeare to the world at how high a rate wee value our just freedome, and God having so far owned our cause, as to deliver the Enemies thereof into our hands: We do now hold our selves bound in mutual duty to each other, to take the best care we can for the future, to avoid both the danger of returning into a slavish condition, and the chargable remedy of another war: for as it cannot be imagined that so many of our Country-men would have opposed us in this quarrel, if they had understood their owne good; so may we safely promise to our selves, that when our Common Rights and liberties shall be cleared, their endeavours will be disappointed, that seek to make themselves our Masters: since therefore our former oppressions, and scarce yet ended troubles have beene occasioned, either by want of frequent Nationall meetings in Councell, or by rendring those meetings ineffectuall; We are fully agreed and resolved, to provide that hereafter our Representatives be neither left to an uncertainty for the time, nor made uselesse to the ends for which they are intended: In order whereunto we declare,

I.

That the People of England being at this day very unequally distributed by Counties, Cities, & Burroughs, for the election of their Deputies in Parliament, ought to be more indifferently proportioned, according to the number of the Inhabitants: the circumstances whereof, for number, place, and manner, are to be set down before the end of this present Parliament.

II.

That to prevent the many inconveniences apparently arising from the long continuance of the same persons in authority, this present Parliament be dissolved upon the last day of September, which shall be in the year of our Lord, 1648.

III.

That the People do of course chuse themselves a Parliament once in two yeares, viz. upon the first Thursday in every 2d. March, after the manner as shall be prescribed before the end of this Parliament, to begin to sit upon the first Thursday in Aprill following at Westminster, or such other place as shall bee appointed from time to time by the preceding Representatives; and to continue till the last day of September, then next ensuing, and no longer.

IV.

That the power of this, and all future Representatives of this Nation, is inferiour only to theirs who chuse them, and doth extend, without the consent or concurrence of any other person or persons; to the enacting, altering, and repealing of Lawes; to the erecting and abolishing of Offices and Courts; to the appointing, removing, and calling to account Magistrates, and Officers of all degrees; to the making War and peace, to the treating with forraign States: And generally, to whatsoever is not expresly, or implyedly reserved by the represented to themselves.

Which are as followeth,

1. THat matters of Religion, and the wayes of Gods Worship, are not at all intrusted by us to any humane power, because therein wee cannot remit or exceed a tittle of what our Consciences dictate to be the mind of God, without wilfull sinne: neverthelesse the publike way of instructing the Nation (so it be not compulsive) is referred to their discretion.

2. That the matter of impresting and constraining any of us to serve in the warres, is against our freedome; and therefore we do not allow it in our Representatives; the rather, because money (the sinews of war) being alwayes at their disposall, they can never want numbers of men, apt enough to engage in any just cause.

3. That after the dissolution of this present Parliament, no person be at any time questioned for anything said or done, in reference to the late publike differences, otherwise then in execution of the Judgments of the present Representatives, or House of Commons.

4. That in all Laws made, or to be made, every person may

be bound alike, and that no Tenure, Estate, Charter, Degree, Birth, or place, do confer any exemption from the ordinary Course of Legall proceedings, whereunto others are subjected.

5. That as the Laws ought to be equall, so they must be good, and not evidently destructive to the safety and well-being of the people.

THese things we declare to be our native Rights, and therefore are agreed and resolved to maintain them with our utmost possibilities, against all opposition whatsoever, being compelled thereunto, not only by the examples of our Ancestors, whose bloud was often spent in vain for the recovery of their Freedomes, suffering themselves, through fradulent accommodations, to be still deluded of the fruit of their Victories, but also by our own wofull experience, who having long expected, & dearly earned the establishment of these certain rules of Government are yet made to depend for the settlement of our Peace and Freedome, upon him that intended our bondage, and brought a cruell Warre upon us.

For the noble and highly honoured the Free-born People of ENGLAND, in their refpective Counties and Divifions, thefe.

Deare Country-men, and fellow-Commoners,

FOr your sakes, our friends, estates and lives, have not been deare to us; for your safety and freedom we have cheerfully indured hard Labours and run most desperate hazards, and in comparison to your peace and freedome we neither doe nor ever shall value our dearest bloud and wee professe, our bowells are and have been troubled, and our hearts pained within us, in seeing & considering that you have been so long bereaved of these fruites and ends of all our labours and hazards, wee cannot but sympathize with you in your miseries and oppressions. It's greife and vexation of heart to us; to receive your meate or moneyes, whilest you have no advantage, nor yet the foundations of your peace and freedom surely layed: and therefore upon most serious considerations, that your principall right most essentiall to your well-being is the clearnes, certaintie, sufficiencie and freedom of your power in your representatives in Parliament, and considering that the original of most of your oppressions & miseries hath been either from the obscuritie and doubtfulnes of the power you have committed to your representatives in your elections, or from the want of courage in those whom you have betrusted to claime and exercise their power, which might probably proceed from their uncertaintie of your assistance and maintenance of their power, and minding that for this right of yours and ours wee engaged our lives; for the King raised the warre against you and your Parliament, upon this ground, that hee would not suffer your representatives to provide for your peace safetie and freedom that were then in danger, by disposing of the *Militia* and otherwise, according to their trust; and for the maintenance and defense of that power and right of yours, wee hazarded all that was deare to us, and God hath borne witnesse to the justice of our Cause. And further minding that the only effectual meanes to settle a just and lasting peace, to obtaine remedie for all your greivances, & to prevent future oppressions, is the making clear & secure the power that you betrust to your representatives in Parliament, that they may know their trust, in the faithfull execution whereof you wil assist them. Vpon all these grounds, we propound your joyning with us in the agreement herewith sent unto you; that by vertue thereof, we may have Parliaments certainly cal'd and have the time of their sitting & ending certain & their power or trust cleare and unquestionable, that hereafter they may remove your burdens, & secure your rights, without oppositions or obstructions, & that the foundations of your peace may be so free from uncertainty, that there may be no grounds for future quarrels, or contentions to occasion warre and bloud-shed; & wee desire you would consider, that as these things wherein we offer to agree with you, are the fruites & ends of the Victories which God hath given us: so the settlement of these are the most absolute meanes to preserve you & your Posterity, from slavery, oppression, distraction, & trouble; by this, those whom your selves shall chuse, shall have power to restore you to, and secur you in, all your rights; & they shall be in a capacity to tast of subjection, as well as rule, & so shall be equally concerned with your selves, in all they do. For they must equally suffer with you under any common burdens, & partake with you in any freedoms; & by this they shal be disinabled to defraud or wrong you, when the lawes shall bind all alike, without priviledge or exemption; & by this your Consciences shall be free from tyrannie & oppression, & those occasions of endlesse strifes, & bloudy warres, shall be perfectly removed: without controversie by your joyning with us in this Agreement, all your particular & common grievances will be redressed forthwith without delay; the Parliament must then make your reliefe and common good their only study.

Now because we are earnestly desirous of the peace and good of all our Country-men, even of those that have opposed us, and would to our utmost possibility provide for perfect peace and freedome, & prevent all suites, debates, & contentions that may happen amongst you, in relation to the late war: we have therefore inserted it into this Agreement, that no person shall be questionable for any thing done, in relation to the late publike differences, after the dissolution of this present Parliament, further then in execution of their judgment; that thereby all may be secure from all sufferings for what they have done, & not liable hereafter to be troubled or punished by the judgment of another Parliament, which may be to their ruine, unlesse this Agreement be joyned in, whereby any acts of indempnity or oblivion shalbe made unalterable, and you and your posterities be secure.

But if any shall enquire why we should desire to joyn in an Agreement with the people, to declare these to be our native Rights, & not rather petition to the Parliament for them; the reason is evident: No Act of Parliament is or can be unalterable, and so cannot be sufficient security to save you or us harmlesse, from what another Parliament may determine, if it should be corrupted; and besides Parliaments are to receive the extent of their power, and trust from those that betrust them; and therefore the people are to declare what their power and trust is, which is the intent of this Agreement; and its to be observed, that though there hath formerly been many Acts of Parliament, for the calling of Parliaments every yeare, yet you have been deprived of them, and inslaved through want of them; and therefore both necessity for your security in these freedomes, that are essentiall to your well-being, and wofull experience of the manifold miseries and distractions that have been lengthened out since the war ended, through want of such a settlement, requires this Agreement and when you and we shall be joyned together therein, we shall readily joyn with you, to petition the Parliament, as they are our fellow Commoners equally concerned, to joyn with us.

And if any shall inquire, Why we undertake to offer this Agreement, we must professe, we are sensible that you have been so often deceived with Declarations and Remonstrances, and fed with vain hopes that you have sufficient reason to abandon all confidence in any persons whatsoever, from whom you have no other security of their intending your freedome, then bare Declaration: And therefore, as our consciences witnesse, that in simplicity and integrity of heart, we have proposed lately in the Case of the Army stated, your freedome and deliverance from slavery, oppression, and all burdens: so we desire to give you satisfying assurance thereof by this Agreement wherby the foundations of your freedomes provided in the Case, &c. shall be setled unalterably, & we shall as faithfully proceed to, and all other most vigorus actings for your good that God shall direct and enable us unto; And though the malice of our enemies, and such as they delude, would blast us by scandalls, aspersing us with designes of Anarchy, and community; yet we hope the righteous God will not onely by this our present desire of setling an equall just Government, but also by directing us unto all righteous undertakings, simply for publike good, make our uprightnesse and faithfulnesse to the interest of all our Countreymen, shine forth so clearly, that malice it selfe shall be silenced, and confounded. We question not, but the longing expectation of a firme peace, will incite you to the most speedy joyning in this Agreement: in the prosecution whereof, or of any thing that you shall desire for publike good; you may be confident, you shall never want the assistance of

Your most faithfull fellow-Commoners, now in Armes for your service.

Edmond Bear Robert Everard	Lieut. Gen. Regiment.
George Garret Thomas beverley	Com. Gen. Regiment.
William Pryor William Bryan	Col. Fleetwoods Regiment.
Matthew Weale William Russell	Col. Whalies Regiment.
Iohn Dover William Hudson.	Col. Riches Regiment.

Agents coming from other Regiments unto us, have subscribed the Agreement to be proposed to their respective Regiments, and you.

For Our much honoured, and truly worthy Fellow-Commoners, and Souldiers, the Officers and Souldiers under Command of His Excellencie Sir THOMAS FAIRFAX.

Gentlemen and Fellow Souldiers;

THe deepe sense of many dangers and mischiefes that may befall you in relation to the late War, whensoever this Parliament shall end, unlesse sufficient prevention be now provided, hath constrained Us to study the most absolute & certain means for your security; and upon most serious considerations, we judge that no Act of Indempnity can sufficiently provide for your quiet, ease, and safety; because, as it hath formerly been, a corrupt Party (chosen into the next Parliament by your Enemies meanes) may possibly surprize the house, and make any Act of Indemnity null, seeing they cannot faile of the Kings Assistance and concurrence, in any such actings against you, that conquered him.

And by the same meanes, your freedome from impressing also, may in a short time be taken from you, though for the present, it should be granted; wee apprehend no other security, by which you shall be saved harmlesse, for what you have done in the late warre, then a mutuall Agreement between the people & you, that no person shall be questioned by any Authority whatsoever, for any thing done in relation to the late publike differences, after the dissolution of the present house of Commons, further then in execution of their judgment; and that your native freedome from constraint to serve in warre, whether domestick or forraign, shall never be subject to the power of *Parliaments,* or any other; and for this end, we propound the Agreement that we herewith send to you, to be forthwith subscribed.

And because we are confident, that in judgment and Conscience, ye hazarded your lives for the settlement of such a just and equall Government, that you and your posterities, and all the free borne people of this Nation might enjoy justice & freedome, and that you are really sensible that the distractions, oppressions, and miseries of the Nation, and your want of your Arreares, do proceed from the want of the establishment, both of such certain rules of just Government, and foundations of peace, as are the price of bloud, and the expected fruites of all the peoples cost: Therefore in this Agreement wee have inserted the certaine Rules of equall Government, under which the Nation may enjoy all its Rights and Freedomes securely; And as we doubt not but your love to the freedome and lasting peace of the yet distracted Country will cause you to joyn together in this Agreement.

So we question not: but every true English man that loves the peace and freedome of England will concurre with us; and then your Arrears and constant pay (while you continue in Armes) will certainly be brought in out of the abundant love of the people to you, and then shall the mouthes of those be stopped, that scandalize you and us, as endeavouring Anarchy, or to rule by the sword; & then will so firm an union be made between the people and you, that neither any homebred or forraigne Enemies will dare to disturbe our happy peace. We shall adde no more but this; that the knowledge of your union in laying this foundation of peace, this Agreement, is much longed for, by

Yours, and the Peoples most faithfull Servants.

Postscript.

GENTLEMEN.

WE desire you may understand the reason of our extracting some principles of common freedome out of those many things proposed to you in the Case truly stated, and drawing them up into the forme of an Agreement. Its chiefly because for these things wee first ingaged gainst the King, He would not permit the peoples Representatives to provide for the Nations safety, by disposing of the Militia, and otherwayes, according to their Trust, but raised a Warre against them, and we ingaged for the defence of that power, and right of the people, in their Representatives. Therefore these things in the Agreement, the people are to claime as their native right, and price of their bloud, which you are obliged absolutely to procure for them.

And these being the foundations of freedom, its necessary, that they should be setled unalterably, which can be by no meanes, but this Agreement with the people.

And we cannot but mind you, that the ease of the people in all their Grievances, depends upon the setling those principles or rules of equal Government for a free people, & were but this Agreement established, doubtlesse all the Grievances of the Army and people would be redressed immediately, and all things propounded in your Case truly stated to be insisted on, would be forthwith granted.

Then should the House of Commons have power to helpe the

oppressed people, which they are now bereaved of by the chiefe Oppressors, and then they shall be equally concerned with you and all the people, in the settlement of the most perfect freedome: for they shall equally suffer with you under any Burdens, or partake in any Freedome. We shall onely adde, that the summe of all the Agreement which we herewith offer to you, is but in order to the fulfilling of our Declaration of Iune the 14. wherein we promised to the people, that we would with our lives vindicate and cleare their right and power in their Parliaments.

Edmond Bear Robert Everard	Lieut. Gen. Reg.
George Garret Thomas Beverley	Com. Gen. Reg.
William Pryor William Bryan	Col. Fleetwood Reg.
Matthew Wealey William Russell	Col. Whaley Reg.
Iohn Dober William Hudson	Col. Rich Reg.

Agents coming from other Regiments unto us, have subscribed the Agreement, to be proposed to their respective Regiments and you.

Document 7

THE PETITION OF NOVEMBER 23, 1647

Reprinted from a photostat of the original, Thomason Collection
669 f. 11 (98).

In the weeks that had passed since the first discussion of the
Agreement in the General Council of the Army, events had forced
Cromwell and his chief officers into a break with the Leveller faction of soldiers. Cromwell could accept conscientiously neither
the revolutionary principle of the *Agreement,* which he said must
first have the approval of Parliament, or its most striking innovation, manhood suffrage. On November 8, after declaring bluntly
against this article of the *Agreement,* he succeeded in getting a
motion passed returning officers and agitators to their regiments.[1]
The next day the Commons took adverse notice of the *Agreement,*
declaring it subversive to the fundamental constitution of the
kingdom.[2] The soldiers generally were bitterly disappointed in
not securing arrears. The radicals were now convinced that Cromwell and Ireton were bent on breaking the power of the agitators;
they spoke their fears in *A Copy of a Letter Sent by the Agents
of severall Regiments,* and on November 11 scattered it up and
down the streets of London.[3] Cromwell understandably was disposed to subordinate the General Council, representing a democratic organization of the army as civilians, to the Council of
War, a purely military executive body. The discipline of the
army was disintegrating daily. Cromwell and Fairfax yielded to
the Leveller demand for a general rendezvous on November 15,
but on the day of the rendezvous reasserted military discipline
with the court-martialling and execution of a Leveller mutineer.[4]
Thus did the army chiefs break the power of the agitators and
dash the hopes of the Levellers for an *Agreement* constitution
through army pressure.

[1] *Clarke Papers,* I, 411. *Introduction,* p. 60 of this volume.
[2] *Commons Journals,* V, 353.   [3] Thomason's note.
[4] Gardiner, *Civil War,* IV, 23. Cf. *Introduction,* p. 64 of this volume.

Within a week the Levellers of London had resorted undaunt-edly to their traditional method of appeal: the petition. They appealed on November 23 for a ratification of the *Agreement* by Parliament, a measure which, if taken, would have severely lim-ited the powers of that body. The men who presented the petition are named in the document; they were immediately arrested and thrust into prison. On November 25 appeared the document as it is here reprinted, with the Commons' disposal of the original peti-tion, and the Levellers propaganda appeal at the end. No docu-ment better illustrates the Leveller method of prompt and per-sistent action, whatever the odds against them; they were ever ready with a new dramatization of their principles, whether to the army, to Parliament, or to "the people."

To the Supream Authority of *England*, the *Com-mons* in *Parliament* affembled. The humble
Petition of many free-born people. Together
with a Copy of the Order of the Commitment
of five of the Petitioners, *viz.* Mr. *Thomas Prince,*
and Mr. *Samuel Chidley* in the Gate-Houfe.
Capt. *Taylor,* Mr. *William Larner,* and
Mr. *Jves* in Newgate. As alfo fome
Obfervations upon the faid
Order.

Sheweth,

THat as the ground of the late war between the King and
you, was a contention whether he or you should exercise
the supreame power over us, so its vain to expect a settlement, of peace amongst us, untill that point be clearely and justly
determined, that there can be no liberty in any Nation where the
Law giving power is not solely in the people or their Representatives.

That upon your Invitation, the people have hazarded their
lives, consumed their estates, lost their trades, and weltered in
blood to preserve that your just authority, and therein their own
freedoms.

That notwithstanding, for attributing the supream authority
of this Nation to this Honourable House, which alone represents
the people, we have been accounted the off-scouring of the land,
we have had our Petitions burned, our persons imprisoned, and
many other wayes abused.

That when the ears of the chosen deliverers were stopped, the
Law of Nature enjoyned us to addresse our selves to the Army,
from whom we had reason to expect relief, according to their
many promises and engagements.

That those promises seeming to be wholly forgotten by the
ruling part of the Army; it pleased God to raise up the spirits of
some Agents therein, to consider of an agreement of the people
upon grounds of common right; & to offer it to the Generall
Councell of the army for their concurrence; the matter whereof

(seriously debate being had thereupon) was so far from being dis-
allowed, that a necessity of ending this Parliament at the day
prefixed therein, was concluded; the providing for a constant
succession of Parliaments thought necessary, that the people
should be more equally represented was confessed; and a certain
rule to be set between the people and their representative was
judged fit, and the supream authority of this nation acknowledged
by that Councell to be where the Agreement placeth it: And particularly Lievtenant General *Cromwell,* and Commissary General
Jreton declared, that in case they did not Act for the settlement
of those freedoms, yet they would never oppose.

That those Agents in further discharge of their duty to their
Country; did not long since present unto this Honourable House
the said Agreement, with a petition relating thereunto.

That the same Agreement, with another Petition, was lately
offered to the Generall, by a worthy Commander, and divers Officers of the Army, at the first generall Rendezvouz neare Ware:
and all that was done in a further prosecution, was a peaceable
proposing of the same Petition, to the Souldiery, for their concurrence: and we wonder that we should now be reputed mutinous, to offer a Petition to the Souldiery when it was esteemed
formerly good service to draw them to an ingagement.

That notwithstanding all this clear open and legal dealing,
in those our friends, for the performance of their solemne engagements, both they and we, who adhered to them, are reproached
and slandered with imputations of plottings and designing not
only the Kings death, in a base murderous way; and of imbrueing
the nation in blood, but of strange endeavours to levell all mens
estates, and subvert all Government and although the scandals
are but the same which the open enemies formerly cast upon your
selves, yet our just endeavours for freedom, are so ill resented by
this meanes, that some of us are imprisoned, and others threatned
to be proceeded against as persons disaffected to this Honourable
House, whereas the true object of our enemies mallice is, that
authoritie of yours, which we labour to preserve. Yet such is our
sad condition, as our actions and intentions are in like manner
mis-apprehended by you, though we doubt not but the Agreement
duly weighed, will demonstrate all such reproaches to be only the
invention of wicked men to exasperate you against us.

And therefore we beseech you in your bowells of compassion
to an oppressed people, to review and debate impartially the particulars of that Agreement of the people, wherein many thousands

have already concurred: And to suffer us by your countenance, to use our Native Liberty, in moving the people for an happie union amongst themselves, in setling those foundations of Common freedome; that thereby this honourable house, may with more assurance of the peoples alliance, proceed forthwith (without attending for the assent and concurrence of any other) to deliver them from all kind of tyranny and oppression.

And that you would be pleased to account of the sufferings of our dear fellow Commoners Co. *Ayers,* Ca. *Bray,* and others at the severall Rendezvouz of the Army, only for their just and peaceable persuance of *Freedome.*

And especially that you will make inquisition for the blood of that Soldier, *viz. Richard Arnall* of Col. *Lilburns* Regiment, which was shot to death neere Ware.

And we further desire, that without prejudice against our persons, it might be laid to heart, that the large effusion of blood, and the many spoyles made in the late War, cannot be justified upon any other ground, then the settlement of those freedoms contained in the Agreement, and in your just indeavours to clear and secure those you may expect the blessing of peace and prosperity,   *And your petitioners shall pray.*

Die Martis. November, 1 6 4 7 .

Resolved, that Thomas Prince, *Cheesemonger, and* Samuel Chidley *be forthwith committed prisoners to the prison of the Gate-house, there to remain prisoners during the pleasure of this House, for seditious and contemptuous avowing and prosecuting of a former Petition and paper annexed, stiled an agreement of the people, formerly adiudged by this house, to be destructive to the being of Parliaments, and fundamentall government of this kingdom.*   Hen. El. Cl. Par. Dom. Com.

By vertue of an Order of the House of Commons, these are to require you to receive from the Sergeant at armes his deputie or deputies, the bodies of Thomas Prince, *Cheese monger, and* Samuel Chidley *into the prison of the Gate house Westminster, and them safely to detain as your prisoners, untill the pleasure of the house be signified to you to the contrary, and for so doing this shall be your Warrant.*   William Lenthall, Speaker.
Dated 23. *Novemb.* 1647.   To the Keeper of the prison of the
                    Gate house of Westminster.

O men of England that love your freedom I beseech you observe the injustice, arbitrarynesse, and tyranny of this your Parliament, who have invited you, and caused your deare friends to expend their blood upon pretences to deliver you from injustice and arbitrary powers. *See their Rmon. of May* 26. 1642.

1. Observe their palpable iniustice in stiling an humble, rationall and iust petition (presented in a peaceble manner) a seditous and contemptuous, avowing a former petition, these men declared formerly, that they ought to receive petitions, though against things established by law, and now when a petition striks at their corrupt interest, its seditious because its against a vote of theirs, and what damnable endeavours here are to deceive you Commons, they represent these mens petition as a contempt of them when they rendred them the highest honour in their petition.

2 Observe their iniustice in committing these your brethren without laying any crime to their charge, by the law, sedition nor faction is no crime, for no man knows what is sedition or faction, but they put unknown reproachfull tearms upon their just petition to deceive you, and let me informe you, that these treacherous dissemblers that put these infamous tearms upon the petition, durst not suffer this petition to be printed with their votes concerning it, for when they ordered the votes should be printed, an honest member moved that the petition it selfe might be printed with them, that the people might see the reason of such votes, and these Hypocrites opposed it with rage and fury, will ye be alwayes thus abused O yee Commons.

3. Observe the falshood and lyes in their vote. First, these petitioners did not avow any former petition or paper annexed, as this vote say they did. 2ly. The House did never adiudge the Agreement to be distructive to the being of Parliments, &c. but only the petition of the Agents of the Army, they never durst debate the Agreement, lest they should be forced by the strength of reason to consent to it, they shut their eyes and will not see, for many of the greatest opposers have confessed its iust, *but they love not the light because their deeds are evill.* But seeing it was never debated in one particular, could a iudgement be passed upon it, and have you not a wise, faithfull Parliament, that would not debate the particulars of such great concernment to settle a peace.

4. Observe how these men exercise an absolute tyranny over you, ruling by their crooked wills, and damnable lusts, they com-

mit your fellow Commoners to prisons amongst Theeves and Murtherers, only for begging for their fredoms, and this during their pleasure, that is, till their base malicious humors be satisfied. According to law and iustice, imprisonment is only for safe custody of persons, untill the appointed day of tryall in the ordinary Courts of iustice, and it was the Councell table and High Commission that ruled by their lusts, which imprisoned men during their pleasure, and yet these Apostates dare in the face of the sun proclaime their wickednesse and arbitrarinesse, by committing men during their lust. Certainly their consciences tell them that these faithfull, honest petitioner did not offend, for if they had known any offence, they would have been ready to have proceeded against them, or reserved them for tryall which they intend not. O yee Commons of England ! can you still beare it? to see your freedomes undermined, and your brethren abused, and presidents made daily for inslaving you to the wills and lusts of tyrants, when will you shew your selves English men? O now! now is the opportunity. O! that you might see even in this your dayes the things that belong to your peace and freedom, before they be hid from your eyes.   *Vale.*

Document 8

ENGLANDS FREEDOME, SOULDIERS RIGHTS

Appeared December 14, 1647. Reprinted from a photostat of the original, Thomason Collection, E 419 (23).

The pamphlet that follows, which was probably written by Lilburne himself, brings to a focus one of the crucial issues that beset Cromwell's unique army in 1647 and 1648, an issue still starkly controversial three centuries later. The Levellers took a position incompatible with military discipline; they maintained, as is revealed in this pamphlet (p. 253), that after the *Engagement* of June 5 the army remained undissolved by mutual agreement alone; that now it was a body of citizens joining democratically in an effort to redress grievances and settle a constitution; that therefore no officer had a right to use military discipline to frustrate agitation for civil reform; that least of all did the Army Council have a right to judge a man in court-martial and impose military penalties. Not only, according to the Levellers, were martial law and courts-martial inconsistent with the *Engagement;* they were nullified by the very fact that now the nation was at peace. After seven years of successful war under military discipline, however, it was impossible for either officers or men to act wholeheartedly on such a concept; in a crisis, as at Corkbush Field on November 15, the tenacious habit of army obedience and command easily overwhelmed the theories and resolutions of manifestoes. The Levellers wished to use the threat of army might to impose their *Agreement* on the land; yet they rejected the assumption that the army could impose military sanctions upon its members. The truth was, of course, that in Cromwell's army civil and military action had become inextricably intertwined; not even a body of men so resolute in action, so accustomed to paradoxes and contradictions, so politically alert and zealous for reformation as the New Model army, could combine the functions of the citizen and the soldier. The attempted democratic organization of the army was essentially hostile to traditionally autocratic army discipline. Nowhere does one find this conflict so brilliantly explained as in *The Hunting of the Foxes* (March 21, 1649).

The following passage from *The peoples Prerogative* is a succinct statement of Lilburne's position on this fundamental issue. In itself it is an important document. According to Lilburne it appeared separately as the *Plea for the Agents*.[1] He and Ireton engaged in an altercation about its charges on the steps of the House of Commons, Ireton maintaining that it was *"full of falsehoods and mistakes."* [2]

A Defence for the honeſt Nownſubſtantive Soldiers of the Army, againſt the proceedings of the Gen. Officers to puniſh them by Martiall Law.

First. THe arbtirary Government of the Army by Law Martiall (which is only necessary when an Army is marching against its enemy, or when no other Courts of Iustice in a Land are open and free) was wholly dissolved at the Rendezvouz at *New-market,* upon the 4. and 5. of *Iune* last, and this I prove by these following reasons.

1. They associated themselves only as a company of free Commons of *England,* to stand together upon the just principles, and law of nature and nations, to recover their own and all the peoples just rights and liberties, *See the solemn Engagement upon Iune 4.* The words are these *We the Officers and Soldiers of the Army subscribing hereunto, doe hereby declare, agree, and promise to and with each other, that we shal not willingly disband, nor divide, nor suffer our selves to be disbanded nor divided, untill we have security, that we as private men or other the free-born people of England shall not remaine subject to the like oppression, iniury, or abuse as have been attempted.* Compare the latter end of page the 4. with page 5. And upon their march towards *London,* in prosecution of this design, whereupon they associated,

---

[1] I have been unable to find a copy of this document as a separate publication. It is not mentioned in Thomason. I have reprinted it here from pp. 42-44 of *The peoples Prerogative.*

[2] *The peoples Prerogative,* p. 56. This defense of the General Council is further proof that the idea of such a body did not come from Cromwell, as Gardiner assumes.

the General declared in his letter to the City, *that they as English men insisted upon the settlement of the peace of the Kingdome, and the liberty of the Subject, which they had right to demand.* See the letter from the Generall, and the Generall Officers at *Royston* upon *Iune* 10. page 2. 3. And in their further opening of their meaning and intentions in their agreeing together, or associating as before, they declared upon *Iune* 14. *That they were not a mercenary Army, hired to serve the arbitrary power of a State, but continued in armes in judgement and conscience for the defence of their own and the peoples iust rights and liberties.* Now the Army thus refusing to serve the Arbitrary power of the State and agreeing together as English men, to stand upon Principles of Right and Freedome. From hence.

1. Its cleare, that the Officers and Soldiers kept in a body, and so were an Army not by the wil of the State, but by their own mutuall Agreement.

2. From thence its as cleare, that they not being an Army by the States will, they were not under those rules of Martiall Government, which were given by the will of the State to rule those which were a Military body or Army by their will and power.

3. From thence its also as cleare, as they continuing an Army at that time, not by the States will, power or Command, but their mutuall Agreement, they could be under no other government as an Army but such as they did constitute or appoint for themselves by mutuall agreement, and this leades to a 2. Reason, proving the dissolution of the Armies government by Martiall Law.

2. The Soldiers with some Officers of the Army, having by mutual agreement gathered themselves into, or at least continued themselves a Military body or Army, to stand upon principles of right and freedom, did by the same mutual agreement with or engagement to each other frame, constitute or appoint, a forme of government for themselves in their prosecuting that iust design of common right and freedome to themselves and the nation.

The wordes of the Engagement, pag. 4. 5. are these. *Wee doe hereby declare, agree, and promise to and with each other, that wee shall not willingly disband, nor divide, nor suffer our selves to be disbanded or divided without satisfaction in relation to our grievances and desires heretofore presented, and security that we as private men or other the free born people of England, shall not remaine subject to the like oppression and iniury, as have been attempted, and this satisfaction and security to be such as shall be agreed unto by a Councell to consist of those generall Officers of*

the Army (who have concurred with the Army in the premises)
with two Commission Officers, and two Soldiers to be chosen for
each Regiment, who have concurred and shall concurre with us
in the premises and in this agreement. Hereby a new Councell
was constituted contrary to all Martiall Law, and Discipline, by
whom only they ingaged to be ordeered in their prosecution of
the ends for which they associated, and by consequence seeing
they continued an Army by their own wils, and only to prosecute
those ends of common right and freedome, this Engagement to be
ordered only by that new Councell in their prosecution of those
ends, extends to a whole rule of them as an Army.

Now that this Councell was wholly new, and in a way diverse
or different from all Martiall Courts or Councels of Warre, that
ever the Sun beheld in a mercenary Army, and as different from
the Councell by which this Army was formerly governed appeares
thus.

1. The Members of this Councell by which they ingaged to be
ordered, are different wholly from the Members of all former
Councells in the Army.

1. The quality of them is different, none but such as concurred in disobeying the Parliament, and in the Principles of common right and freedome, upon which they stood, were to be Members of this Councell, neither the Generall, nor the Lievtenant
Generall themselves were to be Members of this Councell unlesse
they had concurred in owning the Regiments refusall to disband,
and in their ingagement or association, and by consequence they
had been no Officers, as will appeare hereafter.

In this all the Orders of Warre and Martiall Lawes were
broken, for if the Generall, Lievtenant Generall, and Commissary
Gen. *Ireton,* had not concurred, they could not all have cashiered
one Officer that did concurre, all the Soldiers had beene Engaged
to oppose them, nay they could not have cashiered one Soldier
that joyned in the Engagement, for they promised each to other,
not to suffer themselves to be divided before the ends of their
Engagements was accomplished.

2. The station of the Members of this new councel in this
Army was different from the station of al Members of former
Councels, by the Engagement there was to be two Soldiers in no
office out of every Regiment to have voices equall to the Generall
himself in all votes, a thing never practised nor heard of in an
Army serving the will of a State.

3. The number of the Members of this Councel is different from al customes and rules of Martiall Discipline.

In this Councel, there was to be but foure of every Regiment with the General Officers which concurred, thus this Councel differed from all Customes in any Army in respect of the Members whereof it was constituted.

2. This new Councell differed from the rules of Warre in the manner of its constitution, this was not to be constituted by the Gens. wil or according to the degrees or offices of men in the Army, but in a *Parliamentary* way by the Soldiers free election, the Gen. is bound from calling an Officer to the Councell unlesse he be chosen by his *Regiment*.

3. Reason, proving the dissolution of Martiall Government in the Army.

The Gen. in associating with the Soldiers did in the very Engagement, give away all his power of exercising Martial Disciplin, *he engaged to them & they to him, that they would not suffer themselves to be disbanded or devided, till the ends of their uniting were obtained.* Hereby he divested himselfe of his arbitrary power of cashiering Officers and Soldiers at his pleasure, the cashiering one Officer, or Soldier which associated with the body of the *A*rmy in the engagement, is a disbanding, & deviding one part of the Army from another, which he & the Army mutually reciprocally engaged, neither to attempt nor suffer; likewise by this engagement he divested himself of power to command the Soldiers to march to what 'distance he pleaseth one from an other, this is an other kinde of dividing the Army which he enaged neither to effect, nor suffer.

4. Reason, proving the dissolution of the Government of the Army. by Law Martiall.

The whole Army by agreement or joynt consent cashiered all Officers at *New maket Heath,* that would not associate with them, and engage to stand for common right and freedom, though against the *P*arliament, and so they houted divers Officers out of the field, unhorsed some and rent their cloathes, and beat them: & this in the face of the Gen. al which acts weare death by Martiall Law; but this was an actuall declaration that the Army did admit of Officers by mutuall agreement onely, and therefore Government by law Martiall was dissolved unlesse it had been established by mutuall consent throughout the Army, for Officers at that time being only admitted by mutuall consent they could have no power, but what was betrusted to them by the Soldiers.

2. Plea, But in case the Government of the Army by Law Martiall had not been dissolved by a mutuall ingagement, yet the very being of peace did dissolve it, for in the Petition of * Right its declared *that no person ought to be adjudged by Law Martiall except in time of Warre and that all Commissions given to execute Martiall Law, in time of peace are contrary to the Lawes and Statutes of the Kingdome, and it was the Parliaments complaint that Martiall Law, was then commanded to be executed upon Soldiers for robbery, mutiny, or murther.*

And it was setled as the undoubted right of every English man, that he should be punishable only in the Ordinary Courts of justice, according to the Lawes and Statutes of the Kingdome. By all this it appeares that it is illegall and uniust for the Officers of the Army to try or punish any Agent, or other by Law Martial, upon pretence of Muteny or any other offence: the whole Army stand as Englishmen, and if they offend are not exempted from the proceedings against them, and punishments to be inflicted upon them, by the lawes, and statutes of the Kingdome, and therfore cannot in *I*ustice be subject also to law martiall, so that all Agents and Soldiers now accused for mutiny, for their late prosecution of publick freedome, according to the agreement of the people, without their Officers consent shall unworthily betray their owne and their Countryes *L*iberty, if they shall submit to be tryed in any other way then by the knowne *L*awes and statutes of the *L*and.

* See *Poultons'* collection of statutes p. 1431. 1432.

Englands Freedome, Souldiers Rights:

Vindicated againft all arbitrary unjuft Invaders of them, and in particular againft thofe new Tyrants at *Windfore,* which would deftroy both under the pretence of Marfhall Law.

O R ,

The juft Declaration, Plea and Proteftation of *William Thompfon,* a free Commoner of *England,* unjuftly imprifoned at *Windfore.*

Delivered to his Excellency Sir Thomas Fairfax, *and that which is called his* Councell of Warre, *the* 14. *of December,* 1 6 4 7.

Unto which is annexed his Letter to the Generall, wherein the faid Plea was inclofed. Alfo a Petition of the reft of his Fellow-Prifoners to his Excellency.

May it please your Excellency,

I Am by birth a free Commoner of England, and am thereby *intailed or intituled unto an equall priviledge with your selfe, or the greatest men in England, unto the freedome and liberty of the Lawes of England,* as the Parliament declares in their Declaration of the 23. of October, 1642. 1 part Book Decl. pag. 660. And the 29. Chap. of *Magna Charta* expresly saith, *That no man shall be taken or imprisoned, or be disseised of his Freehold or Liberties, or free customes, or be outlawed or exiled, or any other wayes destroyed, nor past upon nor condemned, but by the lawfull Iudgement of his Peers* (or equalls) *and that by due course,* or processe of the Law of the Land,[1] which expresly saith, *that no man shall be taken or restrained of his liberty, by petition or suggestion* (made unto whomsoever in authority) *unlesse it be by indictment or presentment of good and lawfull men where such deeds be done: and that no man whatsoever be put to answer* (any crime whatsoever) *without presentment before Iustices or matter of record, or by due processe and Writ originall, according to the old Law of the Land: and if anything from henceforth be done to the contrary, it shall be void in law, and holden for* [2] *error.*

[1] *See Sir* Ed. Cooks *Exposition hereof in his* 2. *part Institut. fol.* 46, 47, 50, 51. [Lilburne's marginal notes were indicated by asterisks and crosses, for which I have substituted numerals. D. M. W.]

[2] *See the* 5. Ed. 3. 9. & 25. Ed. 3. 4. & 28. Ed. 3. 3. & 37. Ed. 3. 18. & 42. Ed. 3. 3. *and the* Petition of Right in the third of the King *and the Statutes that*

Therefore Sir, for you who are a *Generall* of an Army, and other of your *Marshall Officers,* who are no Civill Court of Justice, nor authorized with the least legall power in the world to administer Justice, and execute the Law of the Land, upon, or unto any of the Commoners of England, to dare or presume to restraine, imprison, trie or meddle with me, as you have done, who am in no other capacitie in the world, but barely and altogether as a Commoner of England, is the height of arbitrarie tyrannie, injustice and [3] oppression, and an absolute destruction of the very fundamentall Lawes of England, the bare endeavouring of which cost the Earl of *Strafford* his head. And what the doome of him is that destroyes the fundamentall Lawes of the Land, I shall give you out of the words of your own friend Mr. *St. John,* in his Argument of law concerning the Bill of Attainder of high Treason of *Thomas Earl of Strafford,* at a Conference in a Committee of both Houses of Parliament, printed by *G.M.* for *John Bartlet* at the signe of the gilt Cup neere *S. Austins* Gate in *Pauls* Church-Yard 1641. who in the 70. page thereof saith, *That the destruction of the Lawes dissolves the arteries & ligaments that hold the Body together: he that takes away the Lawes, takes not away the allegiance of one Subject alone, but of the whole Kingdome: it was* (saith he) *made treason by the Statute of the* 13. Eliz. *for her time, to affirme, that the Lawes of the Realme do not bind the descent of the Crowne; no Law, no descent at all: No Lawes,* saith he, *no Peerage, no ranks or degrees of men* [4]; *the same condition to all. It's treason to kill a Judge upon the Bench, this kills not the Judge, but the Judgement.* And in pag. 71. he saith, *It's Felonie to imbezell any of the Judiciall Records of the Kingdome; this,* viz. the destruction of the Law, *sweeps all away, and from all.*

abolished the Starre-Chamber and Ship-money, made this present Parliament; *and* Lievtenant-Colonell Lilburnes *Booke called* The Resolved Mans Resolution, p. 2,3,8,9. *and his* Grand Plea against the Lords, p. 7,8,9.

[3] *VVell saith Sir* Edward Cooke *in the* 2. *part of his Institutes fol.* 48. that every oppression against Law, by colour of any usurped authority, is a kind of destruction: for when any thing is forbidden, all that tends to it is also forbidden: and it is *(saith he)* the worst oppression that is done by colour of justice. *See also Lib.* 10. *fol.* 14. *in the case of the Marshalsea.*

[4] And therfore you, with your dealings with me, that am meerly a free Commoner of *England,* and so not in the least under your Marshall Discipline (but solelie and onelie under the discipline of the knowne, declared and established Lawes of *England*) by your arbitrarie tirannicall actings upon me, have absolutelie as much as in you lies, destroied the fundamentall Lawes of *England,* and therfore are as absolute Hedge-breakers and Levellers as ever were in this Kingdome.

It's treason to counterfeit a twenty shilling piece, here is a counterfeiting of the Law, we can call neither the counterfeit, nor the true coyne our owne.

It's Treason to counterfeit the great Seale for an Acre of Land, no property hereby (viz. the destruction of the Law) *is left to any Land at all: nothing Treason now, either against King or Kingdome, no Law to punish it.*

And therefore I advise you as a friend to take heed that you go no further on in your illegall, arbitrary, tyrannicall and Law-destroying practises with and towards me, least when for your owne lives you claime the benefit of the Law, you be answered in the words of your foresaid friend in pag. 72. "That he in vaine "calls for the help of the Law that walks contrary unto Law, and "from the Law of like for like; hee that would not have others to "have Law, why should he have any himselfe? why should not that "be done to him, that himselfe would have done to another? It is "true, (saith he *Ibid.*) we give Law to Hares and Deers, because "they be beasts of chase, but it was never accounted either cruelty "or foule play to knock Foxes and Wolves on the head as they can "be found, because these be beasts of prey : the Warrener sets "traps for Poulcats and other vermine, for preservation of the "Warren.

And in *pag.* 76. hee saith, in the 11.*R*.2. *Tresilian, And some others attainted of Treason for delivering opinions in the subversion of the Law, and some others for plotting the like.*[5]

But if you shall object, that you deale with me as you are a Generall and Officers of an Army by Marshall Law, for endeavouring to make mutinies or tumults in your Army, or by blasting and defaming your reputations, and so drawing your Souldiers from their affection and obedience unto you.

I answer in the first place, there can in this Kingdome be no pretence for Marshall Law, but when the Kingdome is in a generall hurly-burly and uproare, and an Army or Armies of declared enemies in the Field, prosecuting with the sword the destruction of the whole, and thereby stopping the regular and legall proceedings of the Courts of Justice from punishing offenders and transgressors.

But now there being neither Army nor Armies of declared enemies in the field, nor no Garrisons in the possessions of any such men, nor no generall hurly-burlies and uproares by any such

---

[5] *Read also to this purpose Mr.* John Pyms *Speech against the Earl of* Strafford, *the* 12. *of April* 1641. *printed by* John Bartlet, *but especially p.* 5.6.8.9.13.18.23.24.

men in the Kingdome, but all such are visibly subdued and
quieted, and all Courts of Justice open and free to punish offenders and transgressors; and therefore even to the Army it selfe and
the Officers and Souldiers therein, there is no reason or ground
for exercising of Marshall Law, much lesse over Commoners that
are not under the obedience of the Army, which is my cause.

And that in time of peace, there neither is, nor can be any
ground of exercising and executing of Marshall Law; I prove out
of the Petition of Right, which was made in the third yeare of the
present King, and is printed in *Pultons* Collection of Statutes at
large, *fol.* 1431.1432. which expresly saith, that by Authoritie of
Parliament, in the 25. yeare of the Reign of King *Edward* the
third, it is declared and enacted, "That no man should be fore-
"judged of life or limb against the forme of the great Charter
"and the Law of the Land, and by the said great Charter, and
"other the Lawes and Statutes of this Realme, no man ought to
"be adjudged to death, but by the Law established in this
"Realme.[6]

"And whereas no offendor of what kind soever is exempted
"from the proceedings to be used, and punishments to be inflicted
"by the Lawes and Statutes of this your Realme: Neverthelesse
"of late divers Commissions under your Majesties great Seale have
"issued forth, by which certaine persons have been assigned and
"appointed Commissioners, with power and authority to proceed
"within the land, according to the justice of Martiall Law, against
"such Souldiers and Mariners, or other dissolute persons joyning
"with them, as should commit any murder, robberie, felonie, mu-
"tinie, or other outrage or misdemeanor whatsoever, and by such
"summarie course and order, as is agreeable to Martiall Law, and
"as is used in Armies in time of Warre, to proceed to the triall
"and condemnation of such offendors, and them to cause to be
"executed and put to death according to the Law Martiall. By
"pretext whereof your Majesties Subjects have been by some of
"the said Commissioners put to death, when & where, if by the
"Lawes and Statutes of the land they had deserved death, by the
"same Lawes and Statutes also they might, and by no other ought
"to have been judged & executed.[7]   And also sundry grievous

6 *See the* 9.H.3.29.5.Ed.3.9. & 25.Ed.3.4 & 28.Ed.3.3.
7 *Yet it is very observable, that at the very time when this Martiall Law
complained of was executed, the King had warres with France, a forraigne enemy,
but there is no such thing now; and therefore the Army, or the grand Officers
thereof have not the least shadow or pretence to execute it in the least, or to
deale with me a free Commoner, as they have done.*

"offendors, by colour thereof claiming an exemption, have escaped
"the punishment due to them by the Lawes and Statutes of this
"your Realme, by reason that divers of your Officers and Ministers
"of Justice have unjustly refused, or forborne to proceed against
"such offendors according to the same Lawes and Statutes, upon
"pretence that the said offendors were punishable onely by Mar-
"tiall Law, and by authoritie of such Commissioners as aforesaid.
"Which Commissions, and all other of like nature, are wholly
"and directly contrarie to the said Lawes and Statutes of this your
"Realme.

Therefore Sirs, if you have any care of your own heads & lives,
(though you have none of the Liberties and Freedoms of *England*) I again as a friend advise you, to take heed what you doe
unto me anie further in your illegall, arbitrarie and tirannicall
way that hitherto you have proceeded with me; for largely understand that *Canterbury* and *Strafford* were this Parliament questioned for their arbitrarie and tirannicall actions that they did
and acted manie years before, and the Lord Keeper *Finch* was by
this Parliament questioned for actions that he did when he was
Speaker of the House of Commons in the third of the present
King *An.* 1628. and forced to flie to save his head.

In the second place I answer, that if since the warres ended,
it was or could be judged lawfull for your Excellency and your
Councell of Warre to execute Marshall Law: yet you have divested your selfe of that power upon the 4. and 5. of June last at
Newmarket Heath, you owned the souldiers and joyned with
them, when they were put out of the States protection and declared enemies and further associated with them by a *mutuall
solemne ingagement, as they were a Company of free Commoners
of England to stand with them according to the Law of Nature
and Nations*,[8] to recover your owne and all the peoples Rights and
Liberties; the words are these: *We the Officers and Souldiers of the
Army subscribing hereunto, do hereby declare, agree and promise
to and with each other, that we shall not willingly disband nor
divide, nor suffer our selves to be disbanded nor divided, untill
we have security; that we as private men, or other the free-borne
people of England, shall not remaine subject to the like oppression, injury, or abuse, as have been attempted*.[9]

Hereby it appears, that from this time you and the souldiery
kept in a body and so were an Army, not by the States or Parlia-

8 *See the late Plea for the Agents.*
9 *See the ingagement in the Armies* Book of Declarations, pag. 25.26,27,28

ments will, but by a mutuall agreement amongst all the Souldiers, and consequently not being an Army by the Parliaments wills; they were not under those rules of martiall Government which were given by the will of the Parliament: and your Excellencie could no longer exercise any such power over them, as was allowed you by those Martiall Laws; nay, the Souldiers keeping in a body, and continuing an Army only by mutuall consent, did by their mutuall Agreement or Ingagement, constitute a new kind of Councell, wherby they would be Governed in their prosecution of those ends for which they associated, and made every Officer incapable of being in that Councell, which did not associate with them in that Ingagement. The words of the Agreement or Ingagement are these: "we do hereby declare, agree, and promise, to and "with each other, that we shall not willingly disband, nor divide, "nor suffer our selves to be disbanded or divided without satisfac-"tion in relation to our grievances and desires heretofore pre-"sented, and security that we as private men or other the free-born "people of England, shall not remain subject to the like oppres-"sion and injury as hath been attempted, and this satisfaction and "security to be such as shall be agreed unto by a Councell to con-"sist of those generall Officers of the Army, who have concurred "with the Army in the premises, with two Commission-Officers, "and two Souldiers to be chosen for each Regiment, who have "concurred and shall concurre with us in the premises and in this "Agreement.

.So that your Excellency is so far from having a power to exercise the old Martiall Discipline, that you would have been no Officer nor Member of the Councell appointed to govern them, unlesse you had associated with them, and by that Association or mutual Ingagement, the Souldiers were so far from allowing to their Generall, who ever it should have been (for at that time it was uncertain) the power of exercising the old Martiall Discipline, that according to the Ingagement, no Officer or Souldier can be rightly Cashiered unlesse it be by the Councell constituted by that Ingagement: so that your Excellencie by your own Ingagement have put a period to your power of exercising your old Martiall Discipline, and whatsoever Discipline shall appear to the Army to be necessary, must be constituted by the mutuall consent of the Army or their representatives, unlesse you and they will disclaim the Ingagement at Newmarket, and those principles upon which you then stood, and yeeld up your selves to the Parliaments pleasure, as their hirelings, to serve their arbitrarie power, like Turkish Janisaries.

In the third place I answer, that it is against reason, law, conscience, justice and equitie, to subject me at one and the same time, or any other free Commoner of England, under the sting and power of two *distinct Lawes,* and such a bondage as is insupportable, and such a snare of intanglement, that no mans life whatsoever can be safe or secure under it, that I shall be liable to be questioned and destroyed by the *common Law of the Kingdome,* and then be at the wills of *mercenarie Turkish Iansaries,* (in case the common Law will not reach me) to be questioned and destroyed by an unjust arbitrarie Marshall law; and if it can be justly proved against me that I have made any tumults, the Law and the ordinary Courts of Justice are open, by which and by no other rules and proceedings I ought to be tried, and if it be said or can be proved, that I have belied or scandalized the Generall, to the taking away of his good name, &c. yet *scandalum Magnatum* is not to be tried by Martial Law, nor yet either *by the House of Commons, or the House of Lords,* but only & alone (now the Star-Chamber is down) by an Action at Common Law,[10] by a Jurie of my equalls, and no where else, it being a Maxime in Law, *That where remedy may be had by an ordinary course in Law, the party grieved shall never have his recourse to extraordinaries:* [11] And besides, for you to proceed with me, and to be both Parties, Jurie and Judges, is a thing that the Law abhorres.[12]

In the fourth and last place I answer, that the Parliament it selfe, neither by Act nor Ordinance can justly or warrantably destroy the fundamentall liberties and principles of the common Law of *England,* it being a Maxime in law and reason both, *That all such Acts and Ordinances are* ipso facto *null and void in Law, and bind not at all, but ought to be resisted and stood against to the death.*

But for them to give you a power by Marshall Law, or under any other name or title whatever, by your arbitrary tyrannicall wills without due course and processe of Law, to take away the

---

10 *As is cleare by the Statutes of* 3. Ed. 1. 33.& 37.Ed.3.18.& 38.Ed. 3.9. & 42.Ed. 3.3.& 2.R.2.5.& 12.R.2.11. 5.*part Cooks Reports,* pag. 125.& 13.H.7.Kelway.& 11.Eliz. Dier 285.&30. Assize pla. 19.& Liev. Col. *Lilburnes* Grand Plea of 20. Octob. 1647. pag.7.8.

11 *See* Vox Plebis *pag.* 38.& *Lievt. Col.* Jo. Lilburnes Anatomie of the Lords Tirannie, pag.10.

12 *See* 8.H.6.fol.21. & 5.Eliz.Dier 220. & Dr. Bonhams Case, 8. *part of* Cooks Reports, & *Lieut. Col.* Jo. Lilburnes grand Plea, pag.10.

life or Liberty of me, or any free Commoner of England whatsoever, yea, or anie of your owne souldiers in time of peace, when
the Courts of Justice are all open and no visible declared enemy
in Armes in the Kingdome readie to destroy it, is an absolute
destroying of our fundamentall Liberties, and a rasing of the
foundation of the Common-Law of England.[13]

Ergo, such a power of arbitrary Marshall Law, cannot justly
by the Parliament in time of peace, &c. be given unto you, nor
(if it were) be justly or warrantably executed by you.

And besides, both Houses themselves by an Ordinance (unlesse they alter the whole Constitution of this Kingdome) can take
away the life of no free Commoner of England whatsoever, especially in time of peace.

And therefore that which is not within their own power to do,
they cannot by an Order or Ordinance grant power to Sir *Thomas
Fairfax* &c. to do, it being a Maxime in nature, *That beyond the
power of being there is nor can be no being.* But it is not in the
power of the Parliament, or the two Houses, or the House of Commons themselves, as the present Constitutions of this Kingdome
stands, either by Order or Ordinance to take away the life of any
free Commoner of England.[14]

Ergo, they cannot by an Ordinance or Order, especially in
times of peace, give power to Sir *Thomas Fairfax* by Marshall
Law, (unlesse they totally alter the Constitutions of the Kingdome) to take away the life or lives of any free Commoners of
England, *(which all Souldiers are as well as others,[15])* and therefore it is absolute murder in the Generall and the Councell of
Warre, now to shoot to death, hang or destroy any Souldier or
other Commoner whatever by Marshall Law.

And therefore I doe the third time as a friend advise you, to

[13] *But besides all this I doe confidently believe, that the Parliamement never
gave power unto the Generall since the Wars ended, to execute Marshall Law;
neither doe I believe that some chiefe Executors of Marshall Law have any legall
Commission from the Parliament, who never that I could heare of, ever gave power
unto the Generall of himselfe to make generall Officers: and besides, all the Parliament-men that are Officers in the Army were (as I have been groundedly told
formerly) taken off by an Ordinance of both Houses, which was never repleaded
since.*

[14] *See Sir* Ed. Cooks 2. *part Institut. fol.* 47, 48. & 3. *part, fol.* 22. & 4. *part, fol.*
23.25. 48. 291. *all of which Bookes are published for good Law to the Kingdome
by two speciall Orders of the present House of Commons, as you may read in the
last page of the* 2. *part Institut. see also the Petition of Right.*

[15] *See the Armies Declaration of the* 14. *June,* 1647. *Book of their Declarations,
pag.* 39. *and their Letter from Roiston to the Lord Mayor of London of the* 10.
June, 1647. *which the Printer hath neglected to print in their Book of Declarations.*

cease your illegall, arbitrarie, tirannicall Martiall Law-proceedings with me that am no Souldier, and so not under the least pretence of your Martiall Jurisdiction, least in time to come you pay as deare for your arbitrarie illegall proceedings with me, as Sir *Richard Empson* and Mr. *Edward Dudley* Justices did, who as Sir *Edward Cooke* declares in his 2. & 4. part of his Institutes, were very officious and ready "to execute that illegall Act of Parliament "made in the 11.*H*.7. chap. 3. which gave power unto Justices of "Assize, as well as Justices of the Peace (without anie finding or "presentment by the verdict of twelve men, being the ancient "birth-right of the Subject) upon a bare information for the King "before them made, to have full power and authoritie by their "discretions to hear & determine al Offences or contempts com-"mitted or done by anie person, or persons against the form, ordi-"nance, effect of anie Statute made and not repealed, &c. by colour "of which act of Parliament, shaking (saith he) this fundamentall "Law (viz. the 29. Chapter of *Magna Charta*) it is not credible what "horrible oppressions and exactions, to the undoing of infinite "numbers of people, were committed by them, for which (though I cannot read they shot anie man to death, and though they had an expresse Act of Parliament to beare them out, abundantly lesse questionable then an Ordinance for exercising Martial Law) "they were both indicted of high treason both by the common "Law and Act of Parliament, and in the 2. yeare of *Henry* 8. they "both lost their heads.[16]

Therefore, from all the premises by way of conclusion. I draw up this protestation against you, that by the Laws and constitutions of this Kingdome, you have not the least Indicative power in the world over me; therefore, I cannot in the least give you any Honour, Reverence or Respect, either in word, action, or gesture: and if you by force and compulsion compell me again to come before you, I must and will by Gods assistance keep on my Hat, and look upon you as a company of murderers, Robbers and Theives, and doe the best I can to raise the Hue and Crie of the Kingdome against you, as a company of such lawlesse persons, and therefore if there be any Honor, Honesty and Conscience in you, I require you as a free-born English man, to doe me Justice and right, by a formall dismissing of me, and give me just reparation for my monethes unjust imprisonment by you, and for that losse of credit I have sustained thereby, that so things may goe no

---

[16] *See* 2. part Instit. fol. 51. & 4. part, fol. 41. 196, 197. *but especially read their* Jndictment *verbatim set downe* ibid.fol.198,199.

further; or els you will compell and necessitate me to study all waies and meanes in the world to procure satisfaction from you, and if you have any thing to lay to my charge, I am as an Englishman ready to answer you at the common Law of England, and in the mean time I shall subscribe my selfe

From my arbitrary and most illegall imprisonment in Windsore, this 14. Decemb. 1647.

Your servant in your faithfull discharge of your dutie to your Masters (the Commons of England) that pay you your wages,

William Thompson.

The forementioned Letter thus followeth.

To his Excellency Sir Thomas Fairfax *Knight, Captain-Generall of the Forces in the Nation for Imperiall Justice and Libertie, these present.*

May it please your Excellency,

I Here present unto you a Declaration and Protestation against the illegall and unjust proceedings of your Counsell of Warre against me, I being a free Commoner of England, as in the presence of the just God, before whose Tribunall both you and I shall stand to give an Account of all ungodly deeds committed against him. And so I rest,

Decemb. 14 1647.

Your Excellencies servant, if you are a true servant to the most excellent God for justice and righteousnes in the earth, without respect of persons.

William Thompson.

The Petition thus followeth.

To the right Honourable his Excellency Sir Thomas Fairfax *Knight, Captain Generall of all the forces raised in the Kingdome of England.*

The humble Petition of some of your Excellencies Officers and *Souldiers, being under the custody of the* Marshall Generall.

Sheweth,

THat whereas there are mis-presentations of the intentions of the late *Agents* of the Army and their adherents. by men of corrupt minds, who would make all the end of your own and your Armies *noble* and *valiant Atchievements* (under the power of God) fruitlesse; and would destroy Justice and righteousnesse from amongst men; and instead of common good, and equall distribution of justice, would advance a particular selfish interest: and to accomplish their unworthy selfish ends, amongst many other scandals cast upon the late *Agents,* they have blazed abroad that they intended to murther the King, and that one of them should affirm it was lawfull: And wheras this was reported by one L. C. *Henry Lilburne;* it being altogether most abominable in our eyes, and detracts from the purity and righteousnesse of our Principles; tending only to make us odious to the *People,* for whose good alone we have run not only all former, but also these late hazards.

Wee therefore desire that the said L. C. Hen. Lilburne may be speedily sent for to testifie upon Oath (as in the presence of God) who used those words, where those words were used, and when: and what in particular the words were; That so, such a person may come under a publique cognizance, and your Excellencies faithfull servants and souldiers may free themselves and others from such aspersions.

And your Petitioners shall ever pray, &c.

Will. Eyers,	John Wood.	John Crosseman.
Will. Bray,	George Hassall.	Tho. Beverly.
Will. Prior.	Will. Everrard.	Will. Thomson Commoner.

FINIS.

Document 9

PETITION OF JANUARY, 1648

Appeared in London on or about January 18, 1648. In *An Impeachment* Lilburne calls it the "Petition of the 19 *of January*."
The petition was not collected by Thomason. It is reprinted here
from *A Declaration of Some Proceedings*, February 14, 1648, pp.
26-34. Lilburne later (July 17, 1649) reprinted it in his *An Impeachment of High Treason Against Oliver Cromwell*, pp. 45-53.

When the organization of agitators failed to secure the united
support of the army for the promulgation of *An Agreement Of The
People,* the Levellers, believing that either chaos or a Cromwellian
dictatorship lay in the offing, turned again to the device of petitioning to secure mass support for their scheme of government.
Apparently the petition was never formally presented to Parliament. According to one of his enemies, Lilburne declared on
the evening of January 17 that thirty thousand copies were
printed and would be ready for distribution the next day.[1] Lilburne himself directed the organization of the campaign; he promoted mass meetings in London; he caused a committee to be
selected to plan and co-ordinate a nation-wide effort to secure
signatures to the petition; he appointed Chidley and Prince to
collect contributions ranging from two pence to a half crown a
week for sending messengers with the petition into all the counties. "Trustees" were to serve in every parish.[2] Lilburne told the
Commons that he had had "a finger" in the framing of the document, that he and his comrades had brought it forth "as a salve
to cure all our sores and diseases, and to knit the hearts together

[1] *A Declaration of Some Proceedings*, p. 17. In a later edition of Masterson's
information, this figure was changed to three thousand. *The Triumph stain'd*,
February 10, 1648, p. 14.

[2] *An Impeachment Of High Treason*, pp. 21 and 22. In *The Triumph stain'd*
Masterson reproduces an interesting letter signed by Lilburne, Wildman, John
Davis, and Richard Woodward, addressed to the people of Kent, and dated January
9, 1648. The letter urges meetings in every division of the county and appointment
of active men in every town to rouse the citizens to support of the petition. On
January 23 the supporters of the petition were to confer with the signers at Dart-
ford. The letter is certainly authentic, but so far as I know it does not appear
elsewhere.

of all ingenuous men, in every faction or interest, that had but the least spark of a desire to do unto their neighbours as they would be done unto." [3] He thought the petition "of transcendent concernment to all honest and just men in my native Country," [4] and claimed that had it not been for Cromwell's agents a hundred thousand people would have signed it.

Sounding the tone of Lilburne and Overton rather than the conciliatory accents of Walwyn, the petition is much more peremptory in tone and specific in demands than its predecessor of March, 1647. Every sentence speaks the bitterness and despair of the Leveller faction. They still fear, as is apparent in the introduction, that king and Lords will be restored to their pre-war power. Hence the emphasis in the first three articles on the constitutional responsibility of the Commons to the people only, and its complete supremacy as the governing body. Article 4 reveals a widely shared dissatisfaction with Parliament's powerful committees, reflected also in Milton's bitter condemnations; this article has no counterpart in the March petition. Another new Leveller plank is the sharp demand for accounting of national expenditures (Article 10); still others appear in Article 14, for the levying of taxes according to ability to pay; in Article 13, for provisioning the poor and raising wages; and in Article 16, against Parliament members appearing for private clients in courts of law. Strangely enough, no demand appears for the annihilation of tithes; the Levellers for the first time announce themselves content with toleration of all sects, without accompanying abolition of the state church.[5] Their constitutional demands show a sharp shift to redress of economic grievances, now intensified by the scanty harvests of 1647, and a new awareness of the insistent pressure of economic power.

When the January petition was printed, over two months had passed since the presentation of *An Agreement Of The People*. Yet in the petition appears no specific limitation of Parliament's power, no suggestion of "a law paramount." The only reflection of *Agreement* influence is the threat of appeal to the people and the demand for manhood suffrage in Article 11. This is highly

[3] *An Impeachment*, p. 21.   [4] *Ibid.*
[5] Wildman says the plank on tithes was omitted in order not to "disingage any considerable partie, and so continue our distractions." *Truths triumph*, p. 3.

significant, of course, representing, as it does, a constitutional pattern not realized until two centuries later, and then not in England. There were several advantages, from the Leveller point of view, of foregoing for the moment the principle of a written constitution. The first was that the petitionary principle was well established, acceptable in theory even to their enemies, and therefore not subject to attack as a revolutionary proposal; it therefore could be used as a propaganda instrument to rally mass support. A second was that legal precedents favorable to democratic ideas, in the use of which Lilburne was by this time more expert than any other English leader, could be advanced as justification for specific demands. Its enemies remonstrated against the long marginal notes,[6] which gave the impression that every article had its roots deep in English history. Then, too, according to his own statements, Lilburne was seeking relief from the injustices and imprisonment heaped upon him by the Lords, the Commons, judges, Parliamentary committees, and jailors. The petition was at once the most effective means of seeking redress and of dramatizing the wrongs suffered, as he thought, by thousands of workers and tradesmen. From each new arraignment, each new imprisonment, he emerged with a new application of an ancient freedom, demanding recognition of this freedom for every commoner. The *Agreement*, on the other hand, admittedly had no forerunner in English practice. Moreover, it embodied an abstract principle, difficult to comprehend for the average mind; whereas the abolition of monopolies, the reduction of the sales tax, the right to vote, the righting of Lilburne's wrongs,—all these struck instant response in the thoughts and feelings of thousands of Londoners.

The enemies of the Levellers recognized a new danger in the January petition. The radicals had proved themselves too formidable in raising up rebellious spirits and forcing their sentiments into army covenants to be taken lightly. On February 14, therefore, an Independent pamphleteer sent forth *A Declaration Of some Proceedings*, a tract of skillful and penetrating propaganda analysis. Invaluable to a comprehension of both Leveller doctrine and its impact upon conservative mentality, *A Declaration* deftly probes the weak points in the ideological armor of the Levellers. The author claims that they have distorted the very

[6] *A Declaration Of some Proceedings*, p. 36.

purpose of the petitioning act: "A Petition is to *set forth* your grievances, and not to *give a rule* to the Legislative Power." [7] The Levellers complain of hard times. But would the execution of all their particulars turn famine into plenty? They speak of the right of all men to vote. But who are they to determine the qualifications of electors? Constantly they speak of themselves as representing the English people, whereas no one in his senses can assume that they represent more than a small minority. Every one agrees that improvements can be made, and has not Parliament abolished the Star Chamber, curbed the bishops and defeated the King's forces? It is not for Parliament to create a utopia; no nation can leap from confusion to perfection in a single bound. "He that out of a desire to repair his house, shall move all the foundations, will sooner be *buried* in the ruines of the *old*, then *live* to see the erection of a *new* structure." [8] The writer is evidently what John Harris in *The royall Quarrel* calls a "royal Independent," more aristocratic than Milton or Vane, for instance, leaning to the Independents on religious issues and to the Presbyterians on economic and political assumptions. He defends Parliament members effectively against Lilburne's accusations, defends the excise as a means of winning the war. Though in places the author falls into absurd platitudes, and though his arguments fell on deaf ears among the lower middle class, his arguments have the tenaciousness of countless repetitions in seventeenth-century pamphleteering.

[7] *A Declaration*, p. 40.
[8] *A Declaration*, p. 43.

To the Supream Authority of *England*, the Commons Affembled in Parliament.

The earneft Petition of many Free-born People of this Nation.

SHEWETH,

THAT *the devouring fire of the Lords wrath, hath burnt in the bowels of this miserable Nation, until its almost consumed.*

That upon a due search into the causes of Gods heavy Judgments, we find [a] *that injustice and oppression, have been the common National sins, for which the Lord hath threatened woes, confusions and desolations, unto any People or Nation;* Woe *(saith God) to the oppressing City. Zeph.* 3. 1.

That when the King had opened the Flood-gates of injustice and oppression [b] *upon the people, and yet peremptorily declared that the people, who trusted him for their good, could not in, or by their Parliament* require any account of the discharge of his trust; *and when by a pretended* negative voyce [c] *to Laws, he would not suffer the strength of the Kingdom,* the [d] Militia, *to be so disposed of, that oppressions might be safely remedied, & oppressors brought to condign punishment, but raised a War* [e] *to protect the* subvertors *of our Laws and Liberties, and maintain* Himself *to be subject to no* accompt, *even for such oppressions, and pursuing after an oppressive power, the Judg of the Earth,*

a *Amos* 5, 9.10.11.12. *Micah* 2, 2.3. *Micah* 3, 3.4.9.10.11.12. *Habba* 2, 8.17. *Joel* 3, 3.

b See the Remonstrance of the State of the Kingdom, *Decem.* 1641, p. 5, 6, 7, 8, 9, 10, 11, 14, 15.

c See the Kings Answer to the Parliaments Remonst. of May 19, 1642. 1 part book Decla. page 254, 284, 285. See the Kings Answer to the *Parl.* Decla of May 26, 1642, page 298.

d See the Ordinance for the *Militia, Feb.* 1641. 1 book Decla. page 89 & pa. 96. 105, 106, 114, 126, 175, 176, 182, 243, 289, 292.

e See the Parliaments Votes May 20, 1642 1 part Book Decla, 259, see also page 509, 576, 577, 580, 584, 617.

with whom the Throne of iniquity can have no fellowship, hath brought him low, and executed fierce wrath upon many of his adherents.

That God expects Justice from those before whose eyes he hath destroyed an unjust generation. *Zeph.* 3. 6. 7. *and without* doing justly, and releeving the oppressed, *God abhors* fastings and prayers, *and accounts himself mocked.* Esa. 58.4 5,6,7. Mic. 6.6,7,8.

That our eyes fail with looking to see the Foundations of our Freedoms and Peace secured by this Honorable House, and yet we are made to depend upon the Will *of the* King, *and the* Lords, *which were never chosen or betrusted by the People, to redress their grievances. And this Honorable House, which formerly declared, that they were the representative of al England, & betrusted with our Estates, Liberties and Lives,* 1 *part Book of* Decla. 264. 382. *do now declare by their practise, that they will not redress our grievances, or settle our Freedoms, unless the King and the Lords will.*

That in case you should thus proceed, Parliaments wil be rendered wholly useless to the People, and their happiness left to depend solely upon the Will *of the King, and such as he by his Patents creates Lords; and so the invaluable price of all the precious* English blood; spilt in the defence of our freedoms *against the* King, *shal be imbezelled or lost; and certainly,* God the avenger of blood, *wil require it of the* obstructors of justice and freedom. *Iudges* 9.24.

That though our Petitions have been burned, and our persons imprisoned, reviled, and abused only for petitioning, *yet we cannot despair absolutely of all bowels of compassion in this Honorable House, to an* inslaved perishing people. *We still nourish some hopes, that you wil at last consider that our* estates *are* expended, *the whole trade of the* Nation decayed, *thousands of families impoverished, and merciless* Famine *is entered into our* Gates, *and therefore we cannot but once more assay to pierce your eares with our dolefull cries for Iustice and Freedom, before your delays wholly consume the Nation. In particular we earnestly intreat:*

First, That seeing we conceive this Honorable House is intrusted by the People, with all power to redress our grievances, and to provide security for our Freedoms, by making or repealing Laws, errecting or abolishing Courts, displacing or placing Officers, and the like: And seeing upon this consideration, we have often made our addresses to you, and yet we are made to depend for all our expected good, upon the wils of others who have brought all our misery [f] upon us: That therefore in case this Honorable House, wil not, or cannot, according to their trust, relieve and help us; that it be clearly declared; That we may know to whom, as the Supream power, *we may make our present addresses before we perish, or be inforced to flie to the prime Laws of nature [g] or refuge.*

2. *That as we conceive all Governors and Magistrates, being the ordinance [h] of man, before they be the ordinance of God, and no Authority being of God, but what is erected by the mutuall consent of a People: and seeing this Honorable House alone represents the People of this Nation, that therefore no person whatsoever, be permitted to exercise any power or Authority in this Nation, who shal not clearly and confessedly, receive his power from this House, and be always accountable for the discharge of his trust, to the People in their Representers in Parliament: If otherwise, that it be declared who they are which assume to themselves a power according to their own* Wills, *and not received as a trust from the People, that we may know to whose* Wils *we must be subiect, and under whom we must suffer such oppressions, as they please, without a possibility of having Iustice against them.*

3. *That considering, that all iust Power and Authority in this Nation, which is not immediatly derived from the People, can be derived only from this Honorable House, and that the People are perpetually subiect to Tyranny, when the Iurisdiction of Courts, and the Power and Authority of Officers are not clearly described, and their bounds and limits [i] prefixed; that therefore the Iurisdiction of every Court or Iudicature, and the Power of every Officer or Minister of Iustice, with their bounds and limits, be forthwith declared by this honorable House; and that it be enacted, that the Iudges of every Court, which shal exceed its Iurisdiction, and every other Officer or Minister of Iustice, which shal intermedle with matters not coming under his Cognizance, shall incurr the forfeiture of his, and their whole estates. And*

f See the Kings Decla. of the 12 *Aug.* 1642. 1 part book Decla. page 522, 526, 528, 548, & pa. 617.

g See 1 part book decla. pa. 44, 150, 382, 466, 637, 690.

h See Col. *Nath. Fines* his Speech against the Bishops Canons, made in 1640, in a book called Speeches and Passages of Parliament, from 3 *Nove.* 1640 to *June* 1641, page 50, 51, 52.

i See your Remonstrance of the state of the kingdom, book decla. pag, 6, 8. See also the Acts made this Parliament, that abolished the *Starchamber* and *High Commission.*

likewise, that all unnecessary Courts may be forthwith abolished; and that the publike Treasury, out of which the Officers solely ought to be maintained, [k] may be put to the lesse Charge.

4. *That whereas there are multitudes of Complaints of oppression, by Committees of this House, determining particular matters. which properly appertains to the Cognizance of the ordinary Courts [l] of Iustice; and whereas many persons, of faithful and publike spirits, have bin, and are dayly molested, vexed, Imprisoned by such Committes, sometimes for not answering Interrogatories, and sometimes for other matters, which are not in Law Criminall; and also without any legal warrants expressing the cause, and commanding the Jaylor safely to keep their bodies, untill they be delivered by due course [m] of Law; And by these oppressions, the persons and estates of many are wasted, and destroyed: That therefore henceforth, No particular cause, whether Criminal or other, which comes under the Cognizance of the ordinary Courts of Iustice, may be determined by this House, or any Committee thereof; or any other, then by those Courts, whose duty it is to execute such Laws as this honorable House shal make; and who are to be censured by this House in case of injustice: Always excepted, matters relating to the late War, for Indempnity for your Assisters; and the exact Observation of al articles granted to the adverse [n] Party: And that henceforth, no Person be molested or Imprisoned by the wil or arbitrary powers of any, or for such Matters as are not Crimes, [o] according to Law: And that all persons Imprisoned at present for any such matters, or without such legall warrants as abovesaid, upon what pretence, or by what Authority soever, may be forthwith releast, with due reparations.*

5. *That considering its a Badg of our Slavery to a* Norman Conqueror, *to have our Laws in the French Tongue, and it is little lesse then brutish vassalage to be bound to walk by Laws which the People [p] cannot know, that therefore all the Laws and Customs of this Realm, be immediatly written in our Mothers*

---

k See the Statute of Westmin. 1, made 3 E*dw*. 1 *chap*. 26, & 20 E*dw*. 3, 1, and the Judges oath made in the 18 E*dw*. 3, *Anno* 1344, recorded in P*ultons* collections of statutes, *fol.* 144.

l See the 29, chap of M*agna Charta*, and Sir E*d* C*ooKs* ezposition upit, in his **2**, part *instit*. fol. 187, and the Petition of R*ight*.

m See the P*etition of right* made in the 3 of the King, & Sir E*dward* C*OOKS* 2 par., *insti.* fol. 52, 53, 589, 590, 591.

n See P*sal* 15, 4.   o See R*om* 4, 15.

p See the 36 E*dw*. 3, 15, & 1 C*or*. 147, 11, 16, 19, 23.

See also the English Chronicles, in the Raign of W*il.* the *Conqueror*.

Tongue [q] *without any abreviations of words, and the most known vulgar hand,* viz. *Roman or Secretary, and that Writs, Processes, and Enroulments, be issued forth, entered or inrouled in English, and such manner of writing as aforesaid.*

6. *That seeing in* Magna Charta, *which is our Native right, it's pronounced in the name of all Courts,* That we wil sel to no man, we will not deny, or defer to any man either Justice or Right, *notwithstanding we can obtain no Justice or Right, neither from the common ordinary Courts or Judges, nor yet from your own Committees, though it be in case of indempnity for serving you, without paying a dear price for it; that therefore our native* [r] *Right be restored to us, which is now also the price of our blood; that in any Court whatsoever, no moneys be extorted from us, under pretence of Fees to the Officers of the Court, or otherwise: And that for this end, sufficient sallaries or pensions be allowed to the Iudges, and Officers of Courts, as* was of old, out of the common Treasury, *that they may maintain their Clerks and servants, and keep their Oaths uprightly; wherein* they swear to take no money or Cloaths, or other rewards except meat and drink, in a smal quantity, besides what is allowed them by the King; *and this we may with the more confidence claim as our Right, seeing this honorable House hath declared, in case of Shipmoney, and in the case of the Bishops Canons that not one peny, by any power whatsoever, could be leavied upon the people, without common consent in Parliament, and sure we are that the Fees exacted by Iudges, and Clerks, and Iaylors, and all kind of Ministers of Iustice, are not setled upon them by Act of Parliament, and therefore by your own declared principles, destructive to our property;* [s] *therefore we desire it may be enacted to be death for any Iudg, Officer, or Minister of Iustice, from the highest to the lowest, to exact the least moneys, or the worth of moneys, from any person whatsoever, more then his pension or sallary allowed from the Common Treasury. That no Iudg of any Court may continue above three yeares.*

q See *Deut* 30, 12.13.14.

r See Sir Ed. *Cook* in his 1 part *insti.* lib, 3 chap 13, Sect, 701, fol. 3, 8, where he possitively declares it was the native & ancient Rights of all Englishmen, both by the Statute & Common Law of England, to pay no Fees at all to any Administrators of justice whatsoever. See also 2 part *insti.* fol, 74, 209, 210, and 176, and he there gives this Reason, why Judges should take no fees of any man for doing his office, because he should be free, and at liberty to do justice, and not to be fettered with golden fees, as fetters to the subvertion or suppression of truth and justice.

s See the Articles of high treason in our Chronicles against Iudg *Tresilian,* in R*ich,* the seconds time.

7. *That whereas according to your own complaint in your first Remonstranee of the* [t] *State of the Kingdom, occasion is given to bribery, extortion and partiallity, by reason, that judicial places, and other Offices of power and trust, are sold and bought: That therefore for prevention of all iniustice, it be forthwith enacted, to be death for any person or persons whatsoever, directly or indirectly, to buy, or sell, or offer, or receive moneys, or rewards, to procure for themselves or others, any Office of power or trust whatsoever.*

8. *Whereas according to Iustice, and the equitable sense of the Law, Goals and Prisons ought to be only used as places of safe custody, until the constant appointed time of tryall, and now they are made places of* [u] *torment, and the punishment of supposed offenders, they being detained many years without any Legal tryalls: That therefore it be enacted that henceforth no supposed offender whatsoever, may be denyed his Legal tryall, at the first Sessions, Assizes, or Goal delivery, after his Commitment* [w] *and that at such tryal, every such supposed offender, be either condemned or acquitted.*

9. *Whereas Monopolies of all kinds have been declared by this honorable House, to be against the Fundamentall Laws of the Land, and all such restrictions of Trade, do in the consequence destrey not only Liberty but property: That therefore all Monopolies whatsoever, and in particular that oppressive Company of Merchant Adventurers be forthwith abolished, and a free trade restored, and that all Monopolizers may give good reparation to the Common-wealth, the particular parties who have been damnified by them, and to be made incapable of bearing any Office of power, or trust, in the Nation, and that the Votes of this House* Novemb. 19. 1640. *against their siting therein, may be forthwith put in due execution.*

10. *Whereas this House hath declared in the first Remonstrance of the* (x) *State of the Kingdom, that Ship-money, and Monopolies, which were imposed upon the people before the late War, did at least amount to* 1400000 *l.* per annum, *and whereas since then, the Taxes have been double and treble, and the Army*

t See 1 part book decla. p. 9.

u See Sir *Edward Cook* 1 part *Insti.* lib. 3, Cha. 7. sect. 438 fol. 260. who expresly saith, that imprisment must be a safe custody, not a punishment; and that a prison ought to be for keeping men safe, not to punish them. See also 2 par. instit. fol 589, 590, 591.

w See the Statute of the 4. *E.* 3.2. 12 R. 2. 10.

x See 1 part book decl. pa. 14.

(y) *hath declared that* 1300000 *l.* per annum, *would compleatly pay all Forces and Garisons in the Kingdom, and the Customs could not but amount to much more then would pay the Navy; so that considering the vast sums of moneys, raised by imposition of money, the fifth and twentieth part, Sequestrations, and Compositions, Excise, and otherwise, it's conceived much Treasure is concealed: that therefore an Order issue forth immediatly from this Honorable House, to every Parish in the Kingdom, to deliver in without delay to some faithful persons, as perfect an accompt as possible, of all moneys Leavied in such Town, City, or Parish; for what end or use soever, since the begining of the late War, and to return the several receivers names, and that those who shal be imployed by the several Parishes in every Shire or County, to carry in those accompts to some appointed place in the County, may have liberty to choose the receiver of them, and that those selected persons by the several Parishes in every County or Shire, may have liberty to invest some one faithful person in every of their respective Counties or places, with power to sit in a Committee at* London *or elsewhere, to be the General Accomptants of the Kingdom, who shal publish their Accompts every moneth to the publick view, and that henceforth there be only one Common Treasury where the books of Accompts may be kept by several persons, open to the view of all men.*

11. *Whereas it hath been the Ancient Liberty of this Nation, that all the Free-born people have freely elected their Representers in Parliament, and their Sheriffs and* (z) *Iustices of the Peace, &c. and that they were abridged of that their native Liberty, by a Statute of the* 8. H. 6. 7. *That therefore, that Birth-right of all English men, be forthwith restored to all which are not, or shal not be legally disfranchised for some criminal cause, or are not under* 21 *years of age, or servants, or beggers; and we humbly offer, That every County may have its equal proportion of Representers; and that every County may have its several divisions, in which one Representer may be chosen, and that some chosen Representatives of every Parish proportionably may be the Electors of the Sheriffs, Iustices of the Peace, Committee-men, Grandjury men, and all ministers of Iustice whatsoever, in the respective*

y See the Armies last Representation to the House.

z 28. E*dw.* 1 Chap. 1,8. and 13. See a part instit. fo. 174. 175 where Sir E*d. Cook* positively declares that in ancient times by the common law of England the Coroner, the high Sheriff, Iustices of Peace, Verderors of Forests yea, and in times of war, the leader of the Counties soldiers, were chosen in ful county by the freeholders.

Counties, and that no such minister of justice may continue in his Office above one whole year, without a new (a) Election.

12. *That all Statutes for all kind of Oaths, whether in Corporations, Cities, or other, which insnare conscientious people, as also other Statutes, injoyning all to hear the Book of Common Prayer, beforthwith repealed and nulled, and that nothing be imposed upon the consciences of any to compel them to sin against their own consciences.*

13. *That the too long continued shame of this Nation, viz. permission of any to suffer such poverty as to beg their bread, may be forthwith effectually remedied: and to that purpose that the Poor be enabled to choose their Trustees, to discover all Stocks, Houses, Lands, &c. which of right belong to them, and their use, that they may speedily receive the benefit thereof; and that some good improvement may be made of waste Grounds for their use; and that according to the promise of this honorable House, in your first Remonstrance, care be taken forthwith to advance the native commodities of this Nation, that the poor may have better wages for their labor; and that Manufactures may be increased, and the* Herring-fishing *upon our own Coasts may be improved for the best advantage of our own Mariners, and the whole Nation.*

14. *Whereas that burthensom Tax of the Excise lies heavy only upon the Poorer, and most ingenious industrious People, to their intolerable oppression; and that all persons of large Revenues in Lands, and vast estates at usury, bear not the least proportionable weight of that burthen, whereby Trade decays, and all ingenuity and industry is discouraged: That therefore that oppressive way of raising money may forthwith cease, and all moneys be raised by equal Rates, according to the proportion of mens estates.*

15. *That M.* Peter Smart, *Doctor* Leighton, *M.* Ralph Grafton, *M.* Hen. Burton, *Doctor* Bastwick, *M.* William Prinne, *Lievt.* Conell *Iohn* Lilburne, *the heires and executors of M.* Brewer, *M.* Iohn Turner, *and all others that suffered any cruelty, or false illegall imprisonment, by the* Star-Chamber, *the high Commission, or* Councell-Board, *as M.* Aederman Chambers, *and all others that suffered oppression before the* Parliament, *for refusing to pay*

ᵃ It hath been a maxime amongst the wisest Legislators, that whosoever means to settle good Laws, must proceed in them with a sinister, or evil opinion of all mankind; and suppose that whosoever is not wicked, it is for want of oportunity, & that no State can be wisely confident of any publick minister continuing good longer then the Rod is over him.

illegall imposts, customes, or Shipmoney, or yeeld conformity to Monopolizing Patentees, may (after 7. years attendance for justice and right) forthwith by this House receive legall and just reparations out of the estates of all those without exception, who occasioned, acted in, or procured their heavy sufferings, that so in future Ages men may not be totally discouraged to stand for their Liberties and Freedomes, against Oppressors and Tyrants.

16. Whereas we can fix our eyes upon no other but this honourable House for reliefe in all these our pressing grievances, untill we shall be forced to despaire, we therefore desire, that the most exact care be had of the right constitutions thereof: And therefore we desire that all Members of this House chosen in their Nonage, may be forthwith ejected, and that all Votes for suspension of Members from this House may be forthwith put in execution; provided, that the House proceed either finally to expell them, that others may be elected in their stead, or they be restored to serve their Countrey: And likewise that all Lawyers who are Members of this House (by reason of their over-awing power over Judges of their owne making) may wholly attend the peoples service therein, and that every of them may be expelled the House who shall hereafter plead any cause before any Court or Committee whatsoever, during his Membership in this House: And we further desire, that every Member of this House may be enjoyned under some great penalty, not to be absent above three dayes, without the expresse license of this House, and not above one month without the licence of the place by which they are betrusted: And likewise that no Law may be passed, unlesse two third parts of all the Members of this House be present, and that the most speedy care be had to distribute Elections equally throughout the Nation.

Now whereas the particular requests in our Petitions, are for the most part never debated in this House, but when we are at any time rightly interpreted in our meanings and intentions, we onely receive thankes for our good affections, or promises that in due time our desires shall be taken into consideration, and by such delayes our distractions are daily increased, and our burdens made more heavy; therefore we desire, that a Committee be forthwith appointed by this honourable House, who may be enjoyned under some penalty, to sit from day to day, untill they have debated every particular of our requests, and reported their sense of the justnesse and necessity of them to this House, that we may attend for an answer accordingly; and that a time be fixed when such a Committee shall make their report. And we further desire the same Committee may be invested with power to heare all our other complaints, and offer sutable remedies to this honourable House, and to bring in the Appeales of any persons from the Iudges at Westminster, to this honourable House, against their injustice, bribery, or illegall delay and oppression.

Now O ye worthy Trustees! let not your eares bee any longer deafe to our importunate cries, let not our destruction be worse then that of Sodome, who was overthrown in a moment. Let us not pine away with famine and bee worse then those who die by the sword. Oh dissolve not all Government into the prime Lawes of nature, and compell us to take the naturall remedy to preserve our selves, which you have declared no people can bee deprived of (*b*.) Oh remember that the righteous God *standeth in the congregation of the mighty, and judgeth among the gods, and saith, How* (c) *long will ye judge unjustly, and accept the persons of the wicked, defend the poor and fatherless, do justice to the afflicted and needy, deliver the poor and needy, and rid them out of the hands of the wicked,*

And your Petitioners shall ever pray, &c.

b *See* your Declaration of *May* 19. 1642. 1 book dec. pag. 207. And your Declaration *Nov.* 1642. pa. 728. as also pa. 150.
    c *Psal.* 82, 1.2.3.4.

THE MOURNFULL CRIES OF MANY THOUSAND POORE TRADESMEN

Appeared January 22, 1648. Reprinted from a photostat of the original, Thomason Collection broadside 669 f. 11 (116).

The mournfull Cries is an illustration of the intensified class appeal of Leveller propaganda, now based to a greater extent than ever before on economic factors. Essentially a city phenomenon, the Leveller movement was born of the dissatisfaction of thousands of tradesmen, apprentices, and business men of the growing middle class; they demanded a limited political democracy, but no thoroughgoing economic reformation. Their economic demands were limited to free trade, abolition of feudal-owned monopolies that hampered their business efforts, higher wages, reduction of the excise tax, increased assistance to the poor. Their leaders comparatively prosperous Londoners, the Levellers had adapted themselves well to the accelerated economic patterns of merchandising, shipping, manufacturing. It is significant that only in Richard Overton's *An Appeale* did the Levellers emphasize redress from the oppressive enclosures that had transferred the ownership of untold acres of common land from the community to the wealthy few. The demand for rural economic reform came from a man disillusioned with buying and selling as an institution: Gerrard Winstanley; only he called for a thorough economic reconstruction of the England of his day.[1] *The mournfull Cries,* then, is important as a statement of the Levellers' extreme economic position. The language is effectively inflammatory. It is evident from a careful reading of the broadside that the Level-

[1] Cf. *The Works of Gerrard Winstanley,* by Dr. G. H. Sabine (Cornell University Press, 1941); my *Milton in the Puritan Revolution,* Chapter XII, and Appendix IV, a reprint of Winstanley's *A Watch-Word;* and *Left-Wing Democracy of the English Civil War* (Gollancz, 1940), by David Petegorsky.

lers are taking advantage of the prevailing economic distress to crystallize sentiment for their petition.[2]

[2] In *A Declaration*, which contains a reprint of *The mournfull Cries*, the author calls it *"a Whelp* of the same *litter"* as the petition. He attacks the broadside thus (p. 56):

It seemes to be written by some of the *Professors of Rhetorick* in *Newgate*, or *Ludgate*, whose long practice of *that kind* of *Oratory* had made him as great a stranger to *truth*, as to *blushing*. The whole matter of it composed of so *grosse* an hypocrisie, that it scarce deserves *that name;* mixed with *impudency*, and *lyes*, of the same *Genius* with the Petition, boldly affirming in *generals*, and brings not forth *one particular* with proofe. Where are those *famishing babes?* and where are those *pining carkasses?* Why are they not brought forth to the view of *some* pitifull eye? You cry for *pitie*, why shew you not the *object?* Where are those faces *black with sorrow and famine?*

The mournfull Cryes of many thousand poor Tradesmen, who are ready to famish through decay of Trade.

Or, The warning Tears of the Oppreſſed.

OH that the cravings of our Stomacks could be heard by the Parliament and City ! Oh that the Tears of our poor famishing Babes were botled ! Oh that their tender Mothers Cryes for bread to feed them were ingraven in Brasse ! Oh that our pined Carkasses were open to every pitifull Eye ! Oh that it were known that we sell our Beds and Cloaths for Bread ! Oh our Hearts faint, and we are ready to swoon in the top of every Street !

O you Members of Parliament, and rich men in the City, that are at ease, and drink Wine in Bowls, and stretch your selves upon Beds of Down, you that grind our faces, and flay off our skins, Will no man amonst you regard, will no man behold our faces black with Sorrow and Famine ? Is there none to pity ? The Sea Monster drawes out the brest, and gives suck to their young ones, and are our Rulers become cruell *like* the Ostrich in the Wildernesse? *Lament.* 4.3.

OH ye great men of *England,* will not (think you) the righteous God behold our Affliction, doth not he take notice that you devour us as if our Flesh were Bread? are not most of you either Parliament-men, Committee-men, Customers, Excise-men, Treasurers, Governors of Towns and Castles, or Commanders in the Army, Officers in those Dens of Robbery, the Courts of Law ? and are not your Kinsmen and Allies, Colectors of the Kings Revenue, or the Bishops Rents, or Sequestratours? What then are your russling Silks and Velvets, and your glittering Gold and Silver Laces ? are they not the sweat of our brows, & the wants of our backs & bellies ?

Its your Taxes, Customs, and Excize, that compells the Countrey to raise the price of food, and to buy nothing from us but

meer absolute necessaries ; and then you of the City that buy our
Work, must have your Tables furnished, and your Cups overflow ;
and therefore will give us little or nothing for our Work, even
what you * please, because you know we must sell for moneys to
set our Families on work, or else we famish : Thus our Flesh is
that whereupon you Rich men live, and wherewith you deck and
adorn your selves. Ye great men, Is it not your plenty and abundance which begets you Pride and Riot? And doth not your Pride
beget Ambition, and your Ambition Faction, and your Faction
these Civil broyles? What else but your Ambition and Faction
continue our Distractions and Oppressions? Is not all the Controversie whose *Slaves* the poor shall be? Whether they shall be
the Kings Vassals, or the Presbyterians, or the Independent Factions? And is not the Contention nourished, that you whose
Houses are full of the spoils of your Contrey, might be secure
from Accounts, while there is nothing but Distraction? and that
by the tumultuousnesse of the people under prodigious oppression, you might have fair pretences to keep up an Army, and
garrisons? and that under pretence of necessity, you may uphold
your arbitrary Government by Committees, &c.

Have you not upon such pretences brought an Army into the
bowels of the City? and now Exchange doth rise already beyond
Sea, and no Merchants beyond Sea will trust their Goods hither,
and our own Merchants conveigh their * Estates from hence, so
there is likely to be no importing of Goods, and then there will
be no Exporting, and then our Trade will be utterly lost, and
our Families perish as it were in a moment.

O ye Parliament-men hear our dying cry, *Settle a Peace, settle
a Peace ! strive not who shall be greatest untill you be all confounded.* You may if you will presently determine where the supream Power resides, and settle the just common Freedomes of
the Nation, so that all Parties may equally receive Iustice, and
injoy their Right, and every one may be as much concerned as
other to defend those common Freedoms ; you may presently put
down your Arbitrary Committees, and let us be Governed by

* And since the late Lord Mayor *Adams,* you have put in execution an illegall
wicked decree of the Common Councel, whereby you have taken our goods from
us if we have gone to the Inns to sell them to country men; and you have mur-
dered some of our poor wives that have gone to Innes to finde country men to
buy them.

* The Merchants have already kept back from the Tower, many hundred thousand pounds, and no bullion is brought into the Tower, so that mony will be
more scarce daily.

plain written Lawes, in our own Tongue, and pay your Ministers of Justice out of a common Treasury, that every one may have Justice freely and impartially.

You have in your hands the Kings, Queens, and Princes Revenue, and Papists Lands, and Bishops, and Deans, and Chapters Lands, and Sequestered Lands, at least to the value of eighteen hundred thousand pounds by the year, Which is at least five hundred thousand pounds a year more then will pay the Navy, and all the Army, and the Forces which need to be kept up in *England* and *Ireland* ; and out of that the Kingdoms debts would be paid yearly ; whereas now you run further into Debt daily, and pay one thousand pounds by the day at least for use Money. Besides you may if you will Proclaim Liberty, for all to come and discover to a Committee of disingaged men, chosen out of every County, one for a County, to discover to them what Monies and Treasure, your own Members, and your Sequestrators, &c. have in their hands, and you may by that means find many Millions of Money to pay the publique Debts. You may find 30000. li. in Mr. *Richard Darley's* hand, 25000. li. in Mr. *Thorpes* hand,* a Member of Yours, who first Proclaimed Sir *Iohn Hotham* Traytor. And thus you may take off all Taxes presently, and so secure Peace, that Trading may revive, and our pining, hungry, famishing Families be saved.

And O ye Souldiers who refused to disband, because you would have Iustice and Freedom, who cryed till the Earth ecchoed, Iustice, Iustice ; forget not that cry, but cry speedily for Peace and Iustice, louder then ever. There is a large Petition of some pittifull men, that is now abroad, which contains all our desires, and were that granted in all things, we should have Trading again, and should not need to beg our Bread, though those men have so much mercy, as they would have none to cry in the Streets for Bread.

Oh though you be Souldiers, shew bowels of Mercy and Pity to a hunger-starved People; Go down to the Parliament, desire them to consume and trifle away no more time, but offer your desires for Us in that large Petition, and cry Justice, Justice ;

---

* M. *William Lenthall*, Speaker of the House, to cover his cozenage, gave 22000 li. to his servant Mr. *Cole*, to purchase land in his own name, though for his use; which he did, and then died suddenly, and the land fell to his son, and the widdow having married a Lawyer, keeps the land for the childes use, and saith he knows not that his predecessor received any mony from the Speaker, and now Mr. Speaker sueth in Chancery for the land. A hundred such discoveries might be made.

Save, save, save the perishing People ; O cry thus till your importunity make them hear you.

O Parliament men, and Souldiers ! *Necessity dissolves all Laws
and Government,* and *Hunger will break through stone Walls* ;
Tender Mothers will sooner devour You, then the Fruit of their
own womb, and Hunger regards no Swords nor Canons. It may
be so great oppressours intend tumults, that they may escape in a
croud, but your food may then be wanting as well as ours, and
your Arms will be hard dyet. O heark, heark at our doors, how
our children cry Bread, Bread, Bread ; and we now with bleed-
ing hearts, cry, once more to you, pity, pity an oppressed, inslaved
People : carry our cries in the large Petition to the Parliament,
and tell them, if they be still deaf, the Teares of the oppressed
will wash away the foundations of their houses. Amen, Amen,
so be it.

THE PETITION OF SEPTEMBER 11, 1648

Reprinted from a photostat of the original petition, Thomason Collection, E. 464 (19). Collated with the broadside edition, 669 f. 13 (16).

In the summer of 1648 Leveller hopes for a realization of their aims had dimmed almost to darkness. In Cromwell and Ireton they were reluctant to place any confidence.[1] Whether from choice or necessity, the organization of army agitators had fallen to pieces.[2] In the midst of Cromwell's successes against the king's forces, moreover, the Presbyterians in Parliament were rapidly moving from one royalist victory to another.[3] Hollis and his faction had returned in triumph to their places in the Commons. In reaffirming its determination to settle the traditional government of king, Lords, and Commons, the Presbyterians felt rightly that the overwhelming sentiment of the country was the justification of their position, a position supported by large numbers of the Independents themselves.

The Levellers were accustomed, however, to the psychology of fighting hardest when the political dice seemed most heavily weighted against them. Some months before, in his remarkable speech before the Commons, Lilburne had laid bare his motives for agitation in the face of apparent failure. "To sit stil in such a universall perishing case as this is," he said, "was so far below a Christian, that it was beneath . . . the very light of nature and selfe-preservation. . . I am a part of the whole Nation, and if it perish in the eye of reason, I and mine must perish with it." [4] He would act, he said, though the very people he sought to save might obstruct their own rescue: "In case my neighbor were a drowning of himself, and I see it, I were bound by the Law of God and Nature, whether he would or no, to save him." [5] Whatever his

---

[1] See *Introduction*, p. 76. [2] *Ibid.*, p. 77. [3] *Ibid.*, p. 84.
[4] *An Impeachment Of High Treason*, p. 24. [5] *Ibid.*

weaknesses, Lilburne was an incorruptible idealist; even his enemies made no attempt to show that he agitated for gain of office
or money. He possessed, moreover, two qualities rare in the ro-
manticist: a fierce courage and realistic tactical resourcefulness in
the shadow of defeat.

For over two years the Levellers had clamored for the abolition of the king's negative voice. They had achieved, they knew,
partial success. In 1647 thousands of private soldiers and powerful officers had been won over to their position. Now, a year later,
they knew that Ireton himself, and other officers who had hitherto
opposed them, were leaning toward the Leveller premises of the
Putney debates. Yet Parliament remained obdurate. The Levellers looked with dismay at a Parliament so blind, they thought,
to the very issues for which the Civil War had been fought. The
significance, then, of the first pages of the Petition is the contradiction so ably set forth by Wildman in *Putney Projects:* Having
defeated the king on the battlefield, Parliament now begs that he
return invested with the same prerogatives that justified his leading an army against them in 1642. The writer of the Petition
traces deftly the Commons' defiance of the right of either king or
Lords to veto its decisions; thus he tries to achieve a unanimity
between the Leveller theoretical position and the inexorable implications of the Commons' own actions. Is the Commons now to
reject the power it has assumed during six years of civil war? Is it
to settle the government by king, Lords, and Commons, without
declaring which of these three had the final voice in the nation's
destiny? Can there be two or three "supreams"? Thus did the
Levellers focus not only the constitutional issue finally resolved
in 1688, when the king's negative voice was, in effect, repealed;
they also anticipated the momentous decision of 1908, when the
Lords assented to the nullification of their restriction on the
power of the Commons.

The Petition repeats many of the demands of January, 1648,
and that of March, 1647. One finds, however, significant changes
and additions. In Article 12 appears for the first time a demand
for the abolition of enclosures, with emphasis on the opening of
fens; this demand was certainly incidental to the Leveller program. Articles 4, 16, and 23 reflect the sharp concern of the Levellers for religious freedom and the abolition of tithes, a concern

more insistent than had appeared in the January petition. Article 25 shows Leveller support for the trial of Charles, a procedure now resolved upon by Ireton and Cromwell, and urged long before by radical spirits like Harrison and Rainsborough. In Article 26 the Levellers take their stand with the army and speak between the lines their hopes for the army's approval of their program. In Article 18 the Levellers for the first time take cognizance of the charge of communism levelled against them; this declaration, which was to appear often in future manifestoes, reflects the fundamental economic position of the Levellers, a position scored as ineffectual reformism by Gerrard Winstanley and his Diggers. A new demand for reform of London elections appears in Article 20. Like its January predecessor, the September petition ignores the creation of a "law paramount," the mainspring of the *Agreement Of The People;* and although it insists upon annual Parliamentary elections, it ignores the issue of manhood suffrage. Two new planks reminiscent of the *Agreement* appear in Articles 19 and 24, requiring strict definition of the powers of both king and Lords. On the whole the September petition is more comprehensive than the one of January, giving less emphasis to redress of prisoners' grievances (now that Lilburne and Overton are at large again), less attention to national finance and economic oppressions,[6] and more to the immediate problem of the constitutional position of king and Lords.

In style and tone the September petition is less conciliatory than the March manifesto, but pale and weak indeed beside the ringing phrases of the preceding January. Though Lilburne said that he was bound by conscience to have a hand in the September petition,[7] its opening pages, which attempt to strike a note of

[6] The plank on imprisonment for debt, however (Article 13), which had been passed over in the January petition, is much more inclusive and emphatic than the demand of March, 1647.

[7] *Legal Fundamental Liberties* (second edition), p. 33: "And being at liberty, not liking in the least the several juglings I observed in divers great ones in reference to the personal Treaty, and that there was nothing worth praising or likeing thought of or presented by the Parliament in reference to the Peoples Liberties or Freedoms, (especially considering their late large expences and hazards for the procurement of the settlement of them) I was compelled in conscience to have a hand in that most excellent of Petitions of the 11 of *Septemb.* 1648, *which (I am sure) was no small piece of service to* Cromwel *and his great Associates:* though his Church-men now my chiefest Adversaries, durst not joyn with it, nor own it for very fear."

harmony with the Commons' actions, is typical of Walwyn's appeal to reason. One phrase, "in so fruitful a Nation as through Gods blessing this is," is almost identical with Walwyn's words in his *Just Defence*.[8] Overton's biting tones, so dominant in the January petition, do not echo here; the writing appears to be mainly that of Walwyn, stiffened and sharpened in tone at the suggestion of less conciliatory minds.

At the end of the September petition appears the response of the Commons. This insertion, however, apparently misrepresents the Commons' treatment of the Leveller demands. On September 13 officers and citizens brought a new petition to the House, demanding immediate consideration of the petition of September 11; they "became so bold as to clamour at the very Door against such Members as they conceived cross to their Designs; and said they resolved to have their large petition taken into Consideration before a Treaty; that they knew no Use of a King or Lords any longer; and that such Distinctions were the Devices of Men, God having made all alike." [9] The new petitioners asserted that forty thousand men had signed the petition, in which claim they were supported by several radical members of the House itself.[10]

---

[8] *Walwyns Just Defence*, p. 24: "I think it a sad thing, in so fruitfull a land, as, through Gods blessing, this is; and I do think it one main end of Government, to provide, those who refuse not labour, shall eat comfortably."

[9] *Old Parliamentary History*, XVII, 462.

[10] *Ibid.*

TO THE
RIGHT HONORABLE,
THE
Commons of England
In Parliament Aſſembled.

The humble Petition of divers wel affected Perſons inhabiting the City of London, *Westminſter, the Borough of Southwark, Hamblets, and places adjacent.*

With the Parliaments Anſwer thereunto.

SHEWETH,

THat although we are as earnestly desirous of a safe and wel-grounded Peace, and that a finall end were put to all the troubles and miseries of the Common-wealth, as any sort of men whatsoever: Yet considering upon what grounds we engaged on your part in the late and present Wars, and how far (by our so doing) we apprehend ourselves concerned, Give us leave (before you conclude as by the Treaty in hand) to acquaint you first with the ground and reason which induced us to aid you against the King and his Adherents. Secondly, What our Apprehensions are of this Treaty. Thirdly, What we expected from you, and do still most earnestly desire.

Be pleased therefore to understand, that we had not engaged on your part, but that we judged this honourable House to be the supream Authority of *England,* as chosen by, and representing the People; and entrusted with absolute power for redresse of Grievances, and provision for Safety: and that the King was but at the most the chief publike Officer of this Kingdom, and accomptable to this House (the Representative of the People, from whom all just Authority is, or ought to be derived) for discharge of his

283

Office: And if we had not bin confident hereof, we had bin desperately mad to have taken up Armes or to have bin aiding and assisting in maintaining a *War against Him;* The Lawes of the Land making it expresly a crime no lesse than Treason for any to raise War against the King.

But when we considered the manifold oppressions brought upon the Nation, by the King, His Lords, and Bishops; and that this Honourable House declared their deep sence thereof; and that (for continuance of that power which had so opprest us) it was evident the King intended to raise Forces, and to make War; and that if he did set up his Standard, it tended to the dissolution of the Government: upon this, knowing the safety of the People to be above Law, and that to judge thereof appertained to the Supream Authority, and not to the Supream Magistrate, and being satisfyed in our Consciences, that the publike safety and freedom was in imminent danger, we concluded we had not only a just cause to maintain; but the supream Authority of the Nation, to justifie, defend, and indempnifie us in time to come, in what we should perform by direction thereof; though against the known Law of the Land, or any inferiour Authority, though the highest.

And as this our understanding was begotten in us by principles of right reason, so were we confirmed therein by your own proceedings, as by your condemning those Judges who in the case of Ship-money had declared the King to be Judge of safety; and by your denying Him to have a Negative voice in the making of Laws; where you wholly exclude the King from having any share in the supream Authority: Then by your casting the Bishops out of the House of Lords, who by tradition also, had bin accounted an essential part of the supream Authority; And by your declaring to the Lords, That if they would not joyn with you in selling the Militia, (which they long refused) you would settle it without them, which you could not justly have done, and they had any real share in the supream *Authority.*

These things we took for real Demonstrations, that you undoubtedly knew your selves to be the supream Authority; ever weighing down in us all other your indulgent *expressions concerning the King or Lords.* It being indeed impossible for us to believe that it can consist either with the safety or freedom of the Nation, to be governed either by 3. or 2. Supreams, especially where experience hath proved them so apt to differ in their Judgements concerning Freedom or Safety, that the one hath been known to punish what the other hath judged worthy of reward; when not only the freedom of the people is directly opposite to the Prerogatives of the King and Lords, but the open enemies of the one, have been declared friends by the other, as the Scots were by the House of Lords.

And when as most of the oppressions of the Common-wealth have in all times bin brought upon the people by the King and Lords, who nevertheless would be so equal in the supream Authority, as that there should be no redress of Grievances, no provision for safety, but at their pleasure. For our parts, we profess our selves so far from judging this to be consistent with Freedom or Safety, that we know no great cause Wherefore we assisted you in the late Wars, but in hope to be delivered by you from so intollerable, so destructive a bondage, so soon as you should (through Gods blessing upon the Armies raised by you) be enabled.

But to our exceeding grief, we have observed that no sooner God vouchsafeth you victory, and blesseth you with success, and thereby enablet you to put us and the whole Nation, into an absolute condition of freedom and safety: but according as ye have bin accustomed, passing by the ruine of a Nation, and all the bloud that hath bin spilt by the King and his Party, ye betake your selvs to a Treaty with him, thereby puting him that is but one single person, and a publike Officer of the Common-wealth, in competition with the whole body of the people, whom ye represent; not considering that it is impossible for you to erect any authority equall to your selves; and declared to all the world that you will not alter the ancient Government, from that of King, Lords, and Commons : not once mentioning (in case of difference) which of them is supream, but leaving that point (which was the chiefest cause of all our publike differences, disturbances Wars and miseries) as uncertain as ever.

In so much as we who upon these grounds have laid out our selves every way to the uttermost of our abilities : and all others throughout the land, Souldiers and others who have done the like in defence of our supream authority, and in opposition to the King, cannot but deem our selves in the most dangerous condition of all others, left without all plea of indemnity, for what we have done; as already many have found by losse of their lives & liberties, either for things done or said against the King; the law of the land frequently taking place, and precedency against and before your authority, which we esteemed supreame, and against which no law ought to be pleaded. Nor can we possibly conceive how any that have any waies assisted you, can be exempt from the guilt of murders and robbers, by the present laws in force, if you persist to disclaime the Supreame Authority, though their owne conscience do acquit them, as having opposed none but manifest Tyrants, Oppressors and their adherents.

And whereas a Personall Treaty, or any Treaty with the King, hath been long time held forth as the only means of a safe & wel-grounded peace; it is well known to have been cryed up princi-pally by such as have been dis-affected unto you; and though you have contradicted it : yet it is believed that you much fear the issue ; as you have cause sufficient, except you see greater altera-tion in the King and his party then is generally observed, there having never yet been any Treaty with him, but was accompanied with some underhand dealing; and whilst the present force upon him (though seeming liberty) will in time to come be certainly pleaded, against all that shall or can be agreed upon: nay, what can you confide in if you consider how he hath been provoaked; and what former Kings upon lesse provocations have done, after Oaths, Laws, Charters, Bonds, Excommunications, and all ties of Reconsilliations, to the destruction of all those that had provoked and opposed them : yea, when your selves so soone as he had signed those bils in the beginning of this Parliament, saw cause to tell him, *That even about the time of passing those bils, some design or other was one fact which if it had taken effect would not only have rendred those bills fruitlesse, but have reduced you a worse condition of confusion than that wherein the Parliament found you.*

And if you consider what new wars, risings, revolting inva-sions, and plottings have been since this last cry for a Personall Treaty, you will not blame us if we wonder at your hasty proceed-ings thereunto: especially considering the wonderfull victories which God hath blessed the Army withall.

We professe we cannot chuse but stand amazed to consider the inevitable danger we shall be in, though all things in the Propositions were agreed unto, the Resolutions of the King and his party have been perpetually violently and implacably prose-cuted & manifested against us; and that with such scorn and in-dignation, that it must be more than such ordinary bonds that must hold them.

And it is no lesse a wonder to us, that you can place your own security therein, or that you can ever imagine to see a free Parlia-ment any more in England.

were authors, actors or promoters of so intollerable mischiefs, and that without much attendance.

22. That you would have abolished all Committees, and have conveyed all businesses into the true method of the usuall Tryalls of the Commonwealth.

23. That you would not have followed the example of former tyrannous and superstitious Parliaments, in making Orders, Ordinances or lawes, or in appointing punishments concerning opinions or things super-naturall stiling some blasphemies others heresies; when as you know your selves easily mistaken and that divine truths need no human helps to support them: such proceedings having bin generally invented to divide the people amongst themselves, and to affright men from that liberty of discourse by which Corruption & tyranny would be soon discovered.

24. That you would have declared what the businesse of the Lords as, and ascertain their condition, not derogating them the Liberties of oither men, that so there might be an end of striving about the same.

25. That you would have done Justice upon the Capitall Authors and Promoters of the former or late Wars, many of them being under your power: Considering that mercy to the wicked, is cruelty to the innocent: and that all your lenity doth but make them the more insolent and presumptuous.

26. That you would have provided constant pay for the Army, now under the Command of the Lord Gen. *Fairfax,* and given rules to all Judges, and all other publike Officers throughout the Land for their indempnity, and for the saving harmlesse all that have any wayes assisted you, or that have said or done any thing against the King, Queen, or any of his party since the begining of this Parl. without which any of his party are in a better condition then those who have served you ; nothing being more frequent with them, then their reviling of you and your friends.

The things and worthy Acts which have bin done and atchived by this Army and their Adherents (how ever ingratefully suffered to be scandalized as Sectaries and men of corrupt Judgements) in defence of the just authority of this honourable House, and of the common liberties of the Nation, and in opposition to all kind of Tyranny and oppression, being so far from meriting an odious Act of Oblivion, that they rather deserve a most honourable Act of perpetual remembrance, to be as a patern of publike vertue, fidelity, and resolution to all posterity.

27. That you would have laid to heart all the abundance of

innocent bloud that hath bin spilt, and the infinite spoil and havock that hath been made of peaceable harmlesse people, by express Commissions from the King; and seriously to have considered whether the justice of God be likely to be satisfyed, or his yet continuing wrath appeased, by an Act of Oblivion.

These and the like we have long time hoped you would have minded, and have made such an establishment for the Generall peace and contentfull satisfaction of all sorts of people, as should have bin to the happines of all future generations, and which we most earnestly desire you would set your selves speedily to effect; whereby the almost dying honour of this most honourable House, would be again revived, and the hearts of your Petitioners and all other well affected people, be a fresh renewed unto you, the Freedom of the Nation (now in perpetuall hazard) would be firmly established, for which you would once more be so strengthened with the love of the people, that you should not need to cast your eyes any other wayes [under God] for your security: but if all this availeth noteing, God be our Guide, for men sheweth us not a way for our preservation.

The houſe received this Petition, and returned anſwer thereunto which was to this effect viz. That the houſe gave them thanks for their great paines, and care to the publike good of the Kingdom, and would ſpeedily take their humble deſires into their ſerious conſideration

FINIS.

Document 12

FOUNDATIONS OF FREEDOM: OR AN AGREEMENT OF THE PEOPLE

Appeared December 15, 1648. Reprinted from a photostat of the original in the McAlpin Collection. Collated with Thomason E. 476 (26) and British Museum 103. A. 12, P 512. These three editions are of different typography but almost identical in wording. E. 476 (26) was dated by *AN* Friday, December 10, 1648. This must have been an error, however, since December 10 fell on Sunday. The other editions are dated by *AN* December 15.

The second *Agreement* is much more comprehensive and specific than its predecessor of November, 1647. The Levellers in the intervening year have gained new confidence in their proposed constitutional medium; and now they have incorporated into its provisions most of the demands that had appeared in their petitions of January and September, 1648. Of the three hundred members of the Commons, each town and county is to elect its share, the number varying with the population. The manner of proceeding to elections the *Agreement* describes in detail, though curiously enough it does not specify whether they shall be annual or biennial. The qualifications of the electors, not outlined in the first *Agreement,* are now exactly limited, showing the willingness of the Levellers to exclude not only servants and beggars and all not classified as householders, but also all men who have aided the king and are unwilling to sign the *Agreement.* For the ensuing fourteen years no one is to be elected to the Commons who is not already an elector in good standing; thus do the Levellers intend to retain their power, if necessary, through approval of the "well-affected" voters only, though leaving the door open to royalist converts to their cause. The essential constitutional innovation of limiting Parliament's power is retained in the second *Agreement:* the Commons are not to have power to remove or abridge liberty of conscience (though a continuance of the state church is permitted); nor is Parliament to conscript citizens into the armed services, interfere with executive or judicial processes, vote money to its own members, exempt any citizen from legal responsibilities, question men for their part in the Civil War. At the end of the *Agreement* Lilburne and his followers, with the concurrence of Independent members of the committee, have inserted a number of articles from their petitions, these to be satisfied by the new Representative, as the House of Commons is henceforth to be named; the fulfilment of these aims require specific Parliamentary action. Like the first, the second *Agreement* passes by the whole burning question of the status of kingship and Lords; in view of the long Leveller antagonism to both institutions, this is a curious omission, though the Levellers had not proposed a republic, apparently more concerned with the thorough going subordination of king and Lords than with their abolition. Writing in the shadow of an impending revolution, the Levellers and Independents knew that the second *Agreement* was no mere manifesto to be brushed impatiently aside by a skeptical Parliament; they tried realistically to anticipate specific problems, particularly the civil power of army officers and the unrepresentative actions of the council of state (Articles VII and IX). The historical significance of the second *Agreement,* aside from its astonishing anticipation of modern constitutional ideology, lies in the active support it commanded from large sections of the army and London Independents, men now possessing the power to strike for either a representative republic or a military dictatorship. What had been only a year before the effusion of a nameless Leveller had now, through the tireless propaganda of the radicals, captured the enthusiasm of thousands and won even the reluctant support of the mighty Ireton himself.

Foundations of *Freedom;*

OR AN

AGREEMENT

OF THE

PEOPLE:

Propofed as a Rule for future
Government in the Eftablifhment of
a firm and lafting PEACE.

Drawn up by feverall wel-affected Perfons, and
tendered to the confideration of the

Generall Councell of the ARMY.

And now offered to the Confideration of all Perfons who are at
liberty by Printing or otherwife, to give their Reafons,
for, or againft it.

Unto which is annexed feverall Grievances by
fome Perfons, offered to be inferted in the faid Agreement, but
adjudged only neceffary to be infifted on, as fit to be
removed by the next

REPRESENTATIVES.

Publifh'd for fatisfaction of all honest Interefts.

London, Printed for *R. Smithurft,* 1648.

The Publiſher to the Judicious Reader.

Dear Countryman,

THis agreement having had its conception for a common good,
as being that which containes those Foundations of freedom,
and Rules of Government, adjudged necessary to be established
in this Nation for the future, by which all sorts of men are to be
bound, I adjudged it a just and resonable thing to publish it to
the vew of the Nation, to the end that all men might have an
opportunity to consider the Equity thereof, and offer their Rea-
sons against any thing therein contained, before it be concluded;
That being agreeable to that Principle which we professe, viz. to
do unto you, as we would all men should do unto us ; not doubt-
ing but that the Justice of it will be maintained and cleared,
mauger the opposition of the stoutest Calumniator, especially in
those clear points in the Reserve so much already controverted,
viz. touching the Magistrats power to compel or restrain in matters
of Religion, and the exercise of an arbitrary power in the Repre-
sentative, to punish men for state offences, against which no law
hath provided; which two things especially are so clear to my
understanding, that I dare with confidence aver, That no man can
demand the exercise of such a power, but he that intends to be a
Tyrant, nor no man part with them, but he that resolves to be a
slave, And so at present I rest,

Friday. *Decemb.*
15. 1648.

Thy true hearted
Countryman.

AN

An Agreement of the People of England, and the places there-with Incorporated, for a firm and prefent Peace, *upon* Grounds *of* Common-Right *and* Freedom.

Aving by our late labors and hazards made it appear to the world, at how high a rate we value our just Freedoms, and God having so farr owned our cause, as to deliver the enemies thereof into our hands; we do now hold our selves bound, in mutuall duty to each other, to take the best care we can for the future to avoid both the danger of returning into a slavish condition, and the chargeable remedy of another War: For as it cannot be imagined that so many of our Countrymen would have opposed us in this quarrel, if they had understood their own good, so may we safely promise to our selves, that when our common Rights and Liberties shall be cleared, their endevors will be disappointed, that seek to make themselves our Masters: Since therefore our former oppressions, and not yet ended troubles have been occasioned, either by want of freqnent National meetings in Councel, or by the undue or unequal constitution thereof, or by rendring those meetings ineffectual ; we are fully agreed and resolved to provide, that hereafter our Representatives be neither left for uncertainty for time, nor be unequally constituted, nor made useless to the end for which they are intended.

In order whereunto we declare and agree,

I. That to prevent the many inconveniences apparently arising from the long continuance of the same persons in authority, this present Parliament be dissolved upon or before the last day of April, in the year of our Lord, 1649.

II. That the people of England being at this day very unequally distributed, by Counties, Cities, or Boroughs for the election of their Representatives, be more indifferently proportioned, and to this end, That the Representative of the whole Nation, shall consist of 300 persons; and in each County, and the places thereto subjoyned, there shall be chosen to make up the said Representative at all times, the severall numbers hereunder mentioned.

V I Z.

The County of Kent, with the city of Rochester, and the Boroughs, Towns, and Parishes therein 11

The city of Canterbury 1
The county of Sussex, with the city, boroughs, towns and parishes therein 7

The Countytown of Southampton   1
The county of Southampton, with the boroughs, towns, and parishes therein   6
The county of Dorset, with the town of Pool, and all other boroughs, towns, and parishes therein   6
The city of Exeter   2
The county of Devon, with the boroughs, towns and parishes therein, except Plymouth   11
The town of Plymouth   1
The county of Cornwall, with the boroughs, towns and parishes therein   6
The city of Bristoll   2
The county of Somerset, with the cities of Bath and Wels, and the boroughs, towns and parishes therein, except Taunton   8
The town of Taunton   1
The city of Salisbury   1
The county of Wilts, with the boroughs towns and parishes therein   7
The county of Berks, with the boroughs, towns and parishes therein, except Reading   6
The town of Reading   1
The county of Surrey, with all the boroughs, towns, and parishes, therein, except Southwark   5
The Burrough of Southwark   2
The county of Hertford, with the Burroughs, towns, and parishes therein   8
The city of London   8
The city of Westminster   1
The county of Middlesex, with the towns and parishes therein   7
The county of Buckingham with the boroughs, towns, and parishes therein   8
The city of Oxon   1
The University of Oxon   1
The county of Oxford, with the boroughs, towns and Parishes therein   4
The city of Glocester   1
The county of Glocester, with the boroughs, towns and Parishes therein   7
The city of Hereford   1
The county of Hereford, with the boroughs, towns and parishes therein   4
The city of Worcester   1
The county of Worcester, with the towns, boroughs and parishes therein   5
The city of Coventry   1
The county of Warwick, with the boroughs, towns and parishes therein   5
The town of Northampton   1
The county of Northampton, with the boroughs, towns & parishes therein   5
The county of Bedford, with the boroughs, towns and parishes therein   5
The University of Cambridg   1

The town of Cambridg   1
The county of Cambridg, with the boroughs, towns and parishes therein   4
The county of Essex, with the boroughs, towns, and parishes therein, except Colchester   10
The town of Colchester   1
The county of Suffolk, with the boroughs, towns, and parishes therein, except Ipswich   10
The town of Ipswich   1
The city of Norwich   2
The county of Norfolk, with the boroughs, towns, and parishes therein   9
The county of Lincoln, with the city, boroughs, towns, & parishes therein   11
The county of Rutland, with the boroughs, towns and parishes therein   2
The county of Huntington with the boroughs, towns, and parishes therein   3
The borough of Leicester   1
The county of Leicester, with other boroughs, towns & parishes therin   5
The county of Nottingham, with boroughs, towns & parishes therin   5
The county of Derby, with the boroughs, towns, and parishes therein   6
The county of Stafford, with the city of Lichfield, and the boroughs, towns, and parishes therein   5
The county of Salop, with the boroughs, towns, and parishes therein   5
The town of Shrewsbury   1
The city of Chester   2
The county of Chester, with the boroughs, towns, and parishes therein   4
The county of Lancaster, with the boroughs, towns, and parishes therein   7
The city of York   2
The town of Kingston upon Hull   1
The county of York, with the boroughs, towns, and parishes therein   13
The county of Durham, with the city of Durham, and the boroughs, towns, and parishes therein   3
The town of Newcastle   1
The town of Berwick   1
The county of Northumberland, with the other boroughs, towns, and parishes therein   2
The county of Cumberland, with the boroughs, towns, & parishes therin   2
The county of Westmerland, with the boroughs, towns & parishes therin   2
The county of Anglesey, with the boroughs, towns and parishes therein   1
The county of Brecknock, with the boroughs, towns and parishes therein   2
The county of Cardigan, with the boroughs, towns and parishes therein   2
The county of Carmarthen, with the

boroughs, towns and parishes therein   1
The county of Carnarvan, with the boroughs, towns and parishes therein   1
The county of Denbigh, with the boroughs and parishes therein   1
The county of Flint, with the borough and parishes therein   1
The county of Monmouth, with the boroughs and parishes therein   3

The county of Glamorgan, with the Burroughs, and Parishes therein   2
The county of Merioneth, with the Burroughs, and Parishes therein   1
The county of Montgomery, with the Burroughs, and Parishes therein   2
The county of Radnal, with the Burroughs, and Parishes therein   1
The county of Pembroke   1

In all 300

The maner of Elections.

1. THat the Electors in every Division, shall be Natives or Denizons of *England,* such as have subscribed this Agreement ; not persons receiving Alms, but such as are assessed ordinarily towards the relief of the poor ; not servants to, or receiving wages from any particular person. And in all Elections (except for the Universities) they shall be men of one and twenty yeers old, or upwards, and Housekeepers, dwelling within the Division, for which the Election is: Provided, That until the end of seven yeers next ensuing the time herein limited ; for the end of this present Parliament, no person shall be admitted to, or have any hand or voyce in such Elections, who have adhered to, or assisted the King against the Parliament in any of these Wars or Insurrections; or who shall make or joyn in, or abet any forcible opposition against this Agreement ; and that such as shall not subscribe it before the time limited, for the end of this Parliament, shall not have Vote in the next Election ; neither, if they subscribe afterwards, shall they have any voyce in the Election next succeeding their subscription, unless their subscription were six moneths before the same.

2. That until the end of fourteen yeers, such persons, such onely, may be elected for any Division, who by the rule aforesaid, are to have voyce in Elections in one place or other: Provided, That of those, more shall be eligible for the first or second Representatives, who have not voluntarily assisted the Parliament against the King, either in person before the fourteenth of *June,* 1645. or else in Money, Plate, Horse, or Arms, lent upon the Propositions before the end of *May,* 1643. or who have joyned in, or abbetted the Treasonable Engagement in *London,* in the yeer 1647. or who declared or engaged themselves for a Cessation of Arms with the *Scots,* who invaded the Nation the last Summer, or for complyance with the Actors in any the Insurrections of the same Summer, or with the Prince of *Wales,* or his accomplices in the revolted Fleet.

3. That whoever, being by the Rules in the two next preceding Articles incapable of Electiod, or to be elected, shall assume to Vote in, or be present at such Elections for the first or second Representative, or being elected, shall presume to sit or Vote in either of the said Representatives, shall encur the pain of confiscation of the moyety of his estate visible, to the value of fifty pounds. And if he have not such an estate, then he shall encur the pain of imprisonment for three moneths. And if any person shall forcibly oppose, molest, or hinder the people (capable of electing as aforesaid) in their quiet and free Election of their Representatives ; then each person so offending, shall encur the pain of confiscation of his whole estate, both real and personal ; and if he have not an estate, to the value of fifty pound, shall suffer imprisonment, during one whole yeer, without bayl, or mainprise: Provided, That the offender in each such case, be convicted within three months, nextafter the committing of his offence.

4. That for the more convenient Election of *Representatives*, each County, with the severall places thereto conjoyned, wherein more then three R*epresentatives* are to be chosen, shall be divided by a due proportion in so many parts, as each part may elect two, and no part above three *Representatives*. And for the making of these Divisions, two persons be chosen in every Hundred, Lath, or Wapentake, by the people therein (capable of election, as aforesaid) which people shall on the last Tuesday in February next, between eleven and three of the clock, be assembled together for that end at the cheif Town, or usual meeting place in the same Hundred, Lath or Wapentake: And that the persons in every Hundred, Lath or Wapentake so chosen, or the major part of them, shall on the 14 day after their election, meet at the common Hall of the County-Town, and divide the County into parts, as aforesaid, and also appoint a certain place in each respective part or Division, wherein the people shall always meet for the choice of their *Representatives,* and the Parliament Records in writing under the hands and seals of the major part of them present ; and also cause the same to be published in every Parish in the County before the end of March now next ensuing : And for the more equall division of the City of *London* for the choice of its Representatives, there shall one person be chosen by the people in every Parish in the said City (capable of Election, as aforesaid) upon the last Tuesday in February aforesaid, on which day they shall assemble in each Parish for the same purpose, between 2 and 4 of the clock ; and that the persons so chosen, or the major

part of them, shall upon the fourteenth day after their election, meet in the Guild-Hall of the said city, and divide the same city into eight equall Parts or Divisions, and appoint a certain place in every Division respectively, wherein the people of that Division shall always meet for the choice of their Representatives ; and shall make Return thereof, and cause the same to be published in the manner prescribed to the severall counties ; as in this Article.

5. That for the better provision for true and certain Returns of persons elected, the chief publick Officer in every Division aforesaid, who shall be present at the beginning of the Election, and in absence of every such Officer, then any person eligible as aforesaid, whom the people at that time assembled shall choose for that end, shall regulate the Elections, and by poll or otherwise cleerly distinguish and judge thereof, and make true Return thereof in writing indented under the hands and seals of himself, and of six or more of the Electors, into the Parliaments Records, within 21 days after the Election ; and for default thereof, or for making any false Return, shall forfeit 100 *l.* to the Publick use.

III. That 153 Members at least be always present in each sitting of the Representatives at the passing of any Law, or doing of any Act whereby the people are to be bound.

IV. That every Representative shall within 20 days after their first meeting, appoint a Councel of State for the mannaging of publick Affairs, untill the first day of the next Representative, and the same councel to act and proceed therein according to such Instructions and Limitations as the Representatives shall give, and not otherwise.

V. That to the end all Officers of State may be certainly accomptable, and no factions made to maintain corrupt interests, no Member of a councel of State, nor any Officer of any salary Forces in Army or Garison, nor any Treasurer or Receiver of any Publick moneys, shall (while such) be elected to be a Representative : And in case any such Election shal be, the same to be void ; and in case any Lawyer shall be chosen of any Representative or councell of State, then he shall be uncapable of practice as a Lawyer, during that trust.

VI. That the power of the peoples Representatives extend (without the consent or concurrence of any other person or persons) to the enacting, altering, repealing and declaring of Laws; to the erecting and abolishing Officers of courts of Justice, and to whatsoever is not in this Agreement excepted or reserved from them.

As particularly,

1. We do not empower our Representatives to continue in force or make any Laws, Oaths, and covenants, whereby to compel by penalties or otherwise, any person to any thing in or about matters of Faith, Religion or Gods Worship, or to restrain any person from the professing his Faith, or exercise of Religion according to his conscience, in any house or place (except such as are or shall be set apart for the publick Worship): Nevertheless, the instruction or directing of the Nation in a publick way, for the matters of Faith, Worship or Discipline (so it be not compulsive, or expresse Popery) is referred to their discretion.

2. We do not empower them to impresse or constrain any person to serve in War either by Sea or Land ; every mans conscience being to be satisfied in the justnesse of that cause wherein he hazards his life.

3. That after the dissolution of this present Parliament, none of the people be at any time questioned for any thing said or done in reference to the late Wars or publick differences, otherwise then in execution or pursuance of the determination of the present House of commons, against such as have adhered to the king, or his interest against the People : And saving that Accomptants for publick moneys received, shall remain accomptable for the same.

4. That in all Laws hereafter to be made, no person by vertue of any Tenure, Grant, Charter, Patent, Degree or Birth, shall be priviledged from subjection thereto, or being bound thereby as well as others.

5. That all Priviledges or Exemptions of any persons from the Laws, or from the ordinary course of legall proceedings, by vertue of any Tenure, Grant, Charter, Patent, Degree or Birth, or of any place of residence or refuge, shall be henceforth void and null, and the like not to be made nor revived again.

6. That the Representatives intermeddle not with the execution of Laws, nor give judgement upon any mans person or estate, where no Law hath been before provided ; save onely in calling to an account, and punishing publick Officers for abusing or failing their trust.

7. That no Member of any future Representative be made either Receiver, Treasurer or other officer during that imployment, saving to be a member of the councel of State.

8. That no Representative shal in any wise render up, or give

or take away any the foundations of Common Right, Liberty or Safety contained in this Agreement, nor shall levell mens Estates, destroy Propriety, or make all things common.

VII. That the councel of State, in case of imminent danger or extream necessity, may in each Interval summon a Representative to be forthwith chosen, and to meet, so as the Sessions thereof, continue not above forty dayes and so it dissolve two months before the appointed time for the meeting of the next Representative.

VIII. That all securities given by the Publick Faith of the Nation, shalbe made good by the next and all future Representatives save that the next Representative may continue or make nul in part or in whole, all gifts of moneys made by the present House of commons to their own Members, or to any of the Lords, or to any of the Attendants of either of them.

IX. That every Officer or Leader of any Forces in any present or future Army or Garison that, shall resist the Orders of the next, or any future Representative (except such Representatives shall expresly violate this Agreement) shall forthwith after his or their resistance, by vertue of this Agreement, lose the benefit and protection of all the Laws of the Land, and die without mercy.

These things we declare to be essentiall to our just Freedoms, and to a through composure of our long and woful distractions. And therefore we are agreed and resolved to maintain these certain Rules of Government, and all that joyn therein, with our utmost possibilities, against all opposition whatsoever.

These following Particulars were offered to be inserted in the Agreement, but judged fit, as the most eminent grievances, to be redressed by the next Representative.

1 IT shall not be in their power to punish, or cause to be punished, any person or persons, for refusing to answer to Questions against themselves in Criminal cases.

2 That it shall not be in their power to continue or constitute any proceedings in Law, that shall be longer then three or four months, in finally determining of any Cause past all Appeal, or to continue the Laws (or proceedings therein) in any other Language then in the English Tongue,

3 It shall not be in their power to continue or make any Laws, to abridge any person from trading unto any parts beyond the Seas, unto which any are allowed to trade, or to restrain trade at home.

4 It shall not be in their power to continue Excise longer then 20 days after the begining or the next Representative, nor to raise moneys by any other way, except by an equal rate proportionably to mens real or personal estates, wherein all persons not worth above thirty pounds, shall be exempted from bearing any part of publike charge, except to the poor, and other accustomary charge of the place where they dwell.

5 It shall not be in their power to make or continue any Law, whereby mens estates, or any part thereof, shall be exempted from the payment of their debts ; or to continue or make any Law to imprison any mans person for debts of any nature.

6 It shall not be in their power to make or continue any Law for taking away any mans life, except for Murther, or for endeavouring by force to destroy this Agreement ; but shall use their uttermost endeavour to propound punishments equal to offences ; that so mens lives, limbs, liberties and estates may not, as hitherto, be liable to be taken away upon trivial or slight occasion ; and shall have special care to keep all sorts of people from Misery and Beggery.

7 They shall not continue or make a Law to deprive any person, in Case or Trial, from the benefit of Witnesses, as well for as against him.

8 They shall not continue the burthen and oppression of Tythes longer then to the end of the first Representative ; in which time they shall provide for and satisfie all Impropriators: Neither shall they force any persons to pay toward the maintenance of the publike Ministers, who out of conscience cannot submit thereunto ; but shall provide for them in some other unoppressive way.

9 They shall not continue or make a Law for any other ways of Judgement or Conviction of life, liberty or estate, but onely by twelve sworn men of the Neighbourhood.

10 They shall not continue or make a Law to allow any person to take above six pounds *per cent.* for loan of money for a yeer.

11 They shall not disable any person from bearing any Office in the Common-wealth for any opinion or practice in Religion, though contrary to the publike way.

Unto these I shall adde,

1 That the next Representative be most earnestly pressed for the ridding of this kingdom of those vermine and caterpillars, the Lawyers, the chief bane of this poor Nation ; to erect a Court of Justice in every Hundred in the Nation, for the ending of all Differences arising in that Hundred, by twelve men of the same Hundred, annually chosen by Free-men in that Hundred, with express and plain Rules in English, made by the Representative, or supreme Authority of the Nation, for them to guide their Judgements by.

II That for the preventing of Fraud, Thefts and Deceits, there be forthwith in every County or Shire in England and the Dominion of Wales, erected a County-Record for the perfect registering of all Conveyances, Bills, Bonds, &c. upon a severe and strict penalty.

III. That in case there be any need, after the erection of Hundred-Courts, of Maiors Sheriffs Justices of the Peace Deputy Lieutenants &c. that the people capable of Parliament-men, in the foregoing Agreement, be restored by the Representative, unto their native just and undoubted Right, by common consent, from amongst themselves annually to chuse all the foresaid Officers in such manner as shall be plainly and clearly described, and laid down by the supreme Authority of the Nation : And that when any Subsidies or publike Taxes be laid upon the Nation, the Freemen of every Division or Hundred, capable of Election as aforesaid, chuse out persons by common consent from amongst themselves, for the equal division of their Assesments.

IV. That the next Representative be earnestly desired to abolish all base Tenures.

FINIS.

NO PAPIST NOR PRESBYTERIAN

Appeared December 21, 1648. Reprinted from a photostat of the original in Thomason Collection, pamphlet E. 477 (17).

Appearing just after the Levellers had clashed with Ireton on the issue of unrestricted freedom of conscience, *No Papist nor Presbyterian* demands full toleration even for the hated Papists, a position that Milton and Cromwell, though ardent lovers of religious freedom, could not abide. Among the Independents only Roger Williams would have extended to Catholics that liberty of conscience so persistently denied to Protestants of the left. "Why," asked Williams, "should their *Consciences* more then others be oppressed?" [1] Now that the critical moment was at hand, when the victorious Independent army could transform into reality its campfire dreams of toleration, the great leaders hesitated. Cromwell was absent. His London adherents, who four years before had marched in the van of tolerationists, now cautiously retreated. Ireton championed familiar patterns of Presbyterian intolerance. Only the Levellers, to whom secular freedoms had risen uppermost in the scale of cherished aims, now defended an extreme tolerationist view. Of the radicals Overton and Walwyn had wielded the most skilful pamphlet rapiers against the Presbyterian hatred of "the great Diana," toleration. "Why should we [Protestants and Catholics] hate and destroy one another?" Overton had exclaimed. "Are we not all creatures of one God?" [2] Less manifestly religious than the Independents, certainly more rational and worldly in their outlook, the Levellers nevertheless found themselves in the curious position of defending religious freedom more ardently than their pious allies.

"We hope," say the authors, "this successe of the sword will not cause any of the chiefe Officers of the Army or others to recede from their former principles, or forget their so often declared *Liberty of Conscience* without exception." This passage shows

[1] *The Bloudy Tenent of Persecution, Narragansett Club Publications,* IV, 312.
[2] *The Araignement Of Mr. Persecution,* 1645, p. 11.

the aim of the pamphlet: To press the officers now debating the issue to accept the extreme tolerationist stand of the second *Agreement*. The timely appearance of the pamphlet bears the imprint of Leveller propaganda methods. The fact that the officers modified their own *Agreement* to prohibit the practice of Catholicism shows that there was discussion of this point, though the debate is not recorded in *Clarke Papers* and no mention of it is made in later Leveller tracts. Though in my opinion *No Papist* was written by a Leveller or Leveller sympathizer, the style cannot be identified as that of Walwyn or Overton, the men most likely to have made the contribution. The emphasis on toleration for Catholics, moreover, though commanding the full sympathy of the Levellers, finds no such complete expression in any other Leveller tract. The demand for smaller doctors' fees and the plea for the return of Catholic property are not typical of Leveller aims. It is barely possible, therefore, that *No Papist* was written by a Catholic apologist such as John Austin, whose *The Christian Moderator* (1651 and 1652) speaks in much the same tolerationist vein as *No Papist;* it assumes, moreover, as does the author of *No Papist,* the position of a liberal Protestant.

Whatever its authorship, *No Papist* is one of the most significant manifestoes of 1648. One of the few tracts of the Puritan Revolution to speak forthrightly for toleration of the Papists, it represents a social awareness two centuries remote from public acceptance. Its pleas are remarkable for that appeal to charity and reason typical of the extreme leftward sweep of Puritan dynamics, represented in the rare spirits of John Saltmarsh, William Walwyn, and Gerrard Winstanley. Moreover, *No Papist* faces realistically the insuperable psychological difficulties of persecution methods; it clarifies, too, the fundamental implications of restricted freedom of conscience, affirming, as Walwyn and Williams and Overton had done, the essential unity of all persecution for religious belief, whatever its direction or attempted discrimination. Finally, *No Papist* outlines the concrete measures Parliament must take to destroy legalized persecution according to the spirit of the *Agreement:* penal statutes revoked, religious oaths repealed, the National Covenant formally abolished, tithes discontinued, prisoners for religious offenses released, office-holders not to be questioned for their religious opinions.

No Papist nor Presbyterian:

But the modest

Desires and Proposalls

OF

Some well-affected and Free-born People:

Offered to

The Generall Councell of the ARMIE, *for Redresse of Grievances,*

In order to the late Representative, and Agreement of the People.

Quod tibi non vis, alteri nè feceris.

Published for generall satisfaction, 1649.

Propoſalls from ſome well-affected free-born People, for Redreſſe of Grievances.

Having long and sadly expected the settlement of this King-dome in a firme and lasting Peace, freed from all Tyranny and oppression, and that the Free-borne People of this Land may enjoy such Immunities and Priviledges as of right belong unto us, which we being in some present and apparent hope (by the goodnesse of God) to enjoy; and having alwaies professed and owned that Principle of *doing to others as we would be done unto,* have thought fit to propound to those, who are at present impowered and intrusted by us the People, as our *Representatives,* some additionall grievances to be inserted into the *Peoples Agreement,* and these as well in behalfe and out of a fellow-feeling of others interests, as of our owne, being clearly in order to that so often repeated and promised *Liberty of Conscience;* which promise we are confident hath caused some interests to acquiesce, which otherwise might in all probability have assisted or adhered unto our professed enemies, even in the time of ours and the Armies greatest Exigence; But now since God has been pleas'd to subjugate our enemies, and thus far to advance and owne this cause, we hope this successe of the sword will not cause any of the chiefe Officers of the Army or others to recede from their former principles, or forget their so often declared *Liberty of Conscience* without exception ; In confidence whereof, and in order whereunto, we propound as followeth.

1. That all penall Statutes against non-conformists in Religion may be forthwith repealed, and made null, since for the most part all the well-affected and conscientious men of this Kingdome are as well concerned therein, and lyable thereunto, as the Papists. And that all Justices of Peace, Pursuivants, or other Persecutors, that shall any waies proceed upon any of those Statutes, may be severely punished.

2. That the Oathes of Supremacy and Allegiance, with the Nationall Covenant, and all other compulsory Oathes may be effectually declared against, and taken away.

3. That there may be a free and unmolested exercise of Religion, at least in private houses, for all sorts of People that professe *Christ,* none excepted.

4. That no person be forced to pay or contribute towards the maintenance of the publique Ministers, who out of Conscience cannot submit thereunto, but that they may be provided for in some other unoppressive way.

5. That (as it hath been well propounded by others against Lawyers, and the expence and protraction of Law Suites,) so likewise, that the excessive Fees of Physitians may be regulated and reduced, whereby the poore for a small and reasonable Fee may have the benefit of their skill; As in *France,* a Physitians common Fee for coming to a patient is a *Quard' escu,* or 1.sh.6.d.

6. That the Lands and Goods of all Papists, who cannot be lawfully charged or convicted by two sufficient witnesses either to have been in Arms against the Parliament, or to have aided or assisted the King, be immediately discharged of all sequestrations, and unjust seizures; since that delinquency being cleared, it will follow, that they suffer meerly for Conscience sake, if still sequestred.

7. That Papists in Armes may be no worse dealt with in their Compositions then others in Armes ; since to lay a Fine or mulct upon their Religion, is no waies in order to *Liberty of Conscience.*

8. That no person be disabled from bearing any Office in the Common-Wealth, for any opinion or practice in Religion, though contrary to the publique way.

9. That all persons whatsoever now in durance, who cannot be charged with any crime against the State, or are not imprisoned for debt, but that suffer only for *Conscience sake,* may be forthwith discharged.

Some perhaps may here object, that to grant thus much, would be too much in favour of the Papists; Whereunto we answer, That as we beare them no more love then what one Christian is bound to shew unto another, and their tenets much lesse ; so we are clear of opinion, that it cannot perfectly be said to be *Liberty of Conscience,* nor can it be warranted by Scripture, that they or any others that weare the Title of Christians, should be excluded; besides, if any restrictions or penalties shall be continued on the

Papists, though for the present we and other well-affected persons may be secure and unmolested , yet we know not how soon the same Lawes or penalties by any change of times, may be laid upon us ; As hath been too evident of late yeares, when as the penall Statutes which we know were primarily intended against Papists and their Adherents, were made a foundation for the Bishops to exercise their Lordly and tyrannicall wills over many peaceable and conscientious men, for non-conformity in matters of Religion.

Here we may add the consistency of *Liberty of Conscience,* with many, nay most Governments, whether Monarchicall, Popular, or mixt, As in *France, Holland, Germany, Switzerland,* &c. where diversity of Faith exiles no confidence, but persons of all Religions are indifferently employed and found faithfull in Offices and places of greatest trust.

Againe if there be such penalties and restrictions put upon mens Consciences, they cannot be termed Free-borne People, and English Natives, but rather aliens, outlawes or men bar'd of all propriety of persons and goods, and without the protection of the Lawes, which are every mans birth-right ; and what is the case of others to day, may be ours to morrow, according to the ebb or flow of fortune.

Here perhaps some others will object and say, that though all other Religions ought to be tolerated, yet Papists ought not, because they are Idolaters; whereto if you will take the answer, which we have heard some of them deliver (for we think it just to hear all parties, and hold it a work of Charity to convert any, by arguments from the *Written Word*) their answer is this, that they give not Pictures or such representations (as they call them) any Soveraigne honor, which is that that properly belongs to God, but an inferiour or relative kind of reverence or honor.

And if we take Papists in our or the common received sence, yet we cannot say they are such Idolaters, as those mentioned in the old Testament, who absolutely adored, even with Soveraigne honor, the Images of false Gods, which these Papists (for ought we can learne) doe not doe, but doe adore the Image of the true God ; and therefore cannot properly be called Idolaters, at least in Scripture sence, but rather superstitious and Popish persons.

But supposing it to be lawfull or warranted by the Word of God, to persecute the Papists or any other sort of people professing *Christ,* yet we have observed in these last 7. years of their

persecution, (which we confesse has been very severe, and we beleeve that their persecutors, if they ever get the power, will be as
rigid and unchristian towards us) when many of them have been
hang'd, drawn and quartered, others 7. or 8. yeares imprisoned
onely for refusing such oathes as we, or perhaps the persecutors
themselves cannot in conscience take, and many of their Estates
sequestred onely for non-conformity in matters of Religion, yet
we doe not see that this persecution hath any thing at all abated
or lessened the number of them, but that they are rather in-
creas'd by suffering; so that whether we respect our own principle,
of *doing to others as we would be done unto,* or be steered by
reasons of Religion or of common policy, we humbly offer and
think fit, that no *Agreement* of the People be concluded (or
offered to publike test) by any *Representative,* but that as a principal & materiall part which belongs to God, Liberty of Conscience to all that professe Christ without exception may be inserted, and the foresaid grievances redressed ; so shall we with
all true and Free-borne English men joyne hands and hearts
against all Enemies to Peace and Godlinesse.

FINIS.

SEVERAL PROPOSALS FOR PEACE AND FREEDOM

Dated December 22, 1648. Reprinted from a photostat of the
original pamphlet, Thomason Collection E. 477 (18). The *Proposals*
appeared again in Jubbes' *Apology*, May 4, 1649.

Though not a Leveller pamphlet, *Several Proposals* is important as an offshoot of Leveller agitation, stating *Agreement* principles with a persuasion unmatched either by *Foundations of
Freedom* or the officers' own *Agreement* of January 20. John
Jubbes, the author of *Several Proposals,* apparently represented
no organized group; he wrote only for himself and a few liberal
members of the London Common Council. As an Independent
with Leveller leanings, he sought with his *Proposals* to resolve the
differences, not only between Leveller and Independent, but also
between the Independent and the liberal Presbyterian. Jubbes'
accent in the introduction and the first article on the guilt of the
king was of course highly acceptable to the leading Independents.
In Articles II and IV, however, Jubbes shows that he expected
kingship to be continued, and was willing to have Charles himself
reinstated, provided that the king would recognize the Commons
as the supreme authority, foregoing forever his negative voice.
Such an arrangement might have placated less reactionary Presbyterian sentiment without sacrificing the main aims of the *Agreement,* and undoubtedly would have satisfied the Levellers, despite
their fulminations against kingship. On other points the *Proposals* are very similar to the officers' platform. The Parliaments
are to be biennial, with dates of election and meeting certainly
fixed. Extending Cromwell's suggestion, Jubbes would grant the
suffrage to all copyholders as well as freeholders possessing property valued at forty shillings a year (Article IX). Though he
would allow some form of tithing (and hence a state church) to
be continued, he would eliminate all requirements of church attendance, allowing each person full freedom of conscience, Catholics and Anglicans specifically included (XIV).[1] To guide the

[1] Neither Leveller nor Independent proposed a toleration plank more inclusive
than Article XIV. It places Jubbes in the van of tolerationists; on this issue in the
December debates he certainly would have sided with the Levellers against Ireton.

Commonwealth until a new Parliament can be selected, Jubbes proposes (Article 17) that a committee with dictatorial powers be set up by the *Agreement* itself. In his attempt to compose differences, Jubbes names Independents, Presbyterians, and Levellers on the interim committee, giving places to Wildman, Lilburne, and their republican sympathizer, Ludlow.

In *An Apology Unto The honorable and worthy Officers* (May 4, 1649),[2] Jubbes recounted the origin and history of his constitutional document. In April, 1648, unsympathetic with the plan to reduce Ireland, convinced, indeed, that war could not bring the liberty they had all hoped for, somewhat disillusioned in Cromwell ("how easie is it for such a Leader by his false light to put out the true candle of sincerity in most of the godly people it shines upon"), he had laid down his sword and turned his energies to shaping a peaceful solution. He was determined to avoid the elevation of a single person, "whether under the name of Commoner, King, Emperor or Captain-General." He had labored for the union of all factions, being particularly hopeful of reconciling the army with the City, barring only the royalists from the government, and them for the next two Parliaments only. At Colchester he had presented his *Several Proposals* to the general officers, to Rainsborough, and all the other colonels. At Yarmouth he had proffered it to Ireton, though "with him it stuck, and went no further." Both Fairfax and Harrison had encouraged prosecution of his scheme. When the army entered London (December 2), Jubbes and his friends tried again to secure Ireton's approval; but Ireton "was pleased to cause answer to be returned, that it was then too late." After the death of the king, continues Jubbes, the righteousness that he hoped for did not prevail. Now, therefore, he is again presenting his document to the officers, hoping for their approbation, hoping, too, that they will resolve all questions "by balls and a ballading box for that purpose," in order to allay suspicions of their procedures. Though not a Leveller, or of their councils, concludes Jubbes, "I must witness it on the behalf of God, you have and do give cause of just exception against much of what you have done and said."[3]

[2] E. 552 (28). The *Proposals* themselves are reprinted on pp. 9-16 of the pamphlet.

[3] *Ibid.*, pp. 2-8.

SEVERAL

PROPOSALS

FOR

Peace & Freedom,

BY AN

AGREEMENT

OF THE

PEOPLE,

Offered unto Commiſſary General *IRETON* for the
Concurrence of the Army, by the Approbation and
Conſent of many worthy Perſons of the

Common Councel

And others of the City of *LONDON*, on the
Eleventh of this inſtant *December,*

To be Agreed unto, and Subſcribed by all the
Inhabitants

OF

England & Wales.

LONDON:
Printed for *J: Hanes,* Decemb. 22. 1648.

SEVERAL
PROPOSALS
FOR
Peace & Freedom,
BY AN
AGREEMENT
OF THE
PEOPLE.

Hereas those His Majesties failings published to us and the World by the several Declarations and Remonstrances of Parliament cannot be denyed, whereby, through the violation of his Oath and Covenant made unto the People at his Coronation, all our late and present Woe and Miseries of War both in *England* and *Ireland* have come; as also the great Divisions amongst our most worthy and eminent persons of the Commonwealth, with the great distempered and unconstant actings and high failings even in the Parliament it self: And for that it is the due Right and Priviledge of the folk or People of this Nation, to make and choose our and their Laws by an equal Representative in Parliament, as by the aforesaid Coronation Oath and Covenant fully appeareth; Therefore the Right Honorable the Lord Major, Aldermen and

Common-Councel, of the City of *London,* do in the Name of the City, First, Humbly offer unto the Right Honorable, The High Court of Parliament assembled at *Westminster,* this present intituled Paper, called, *A Great Agreement of all the People of* England *and* Wales, for their Approbation and Subscription; and that it may thence be dismissed, and forthwith sent into every part of the Land, to be Agreed on, Consented to, and Subscribed by all the Free-born People of the same (above the age of Sixteen) on pain for the Refusers to be excluded and debarred the protection of the Law of the Land; and that all the Subscriptions may be brought in to the present particular Representatives of Parliament, to be Returned and Recorded there for a grand Law forever.

First, We Agree,

I. THat the King, by the Advice of his evil Councel, through usurping and incroaching upon our Freedoms, and by leaving the Parliament, and leavying a War against it, is guilty of all the Blood, vast expence of Treasure, and Ruine that hath been occasioned by these Wars within the Kingdoms of *England* and *Ireland.*

II. That if any King of *England* shall hereafter challenge to himself a Negative Voyce, to the Determinations of the Representative in Parliament ; and shall not according to the Duty of his Kingly Office, Consent and Sign all such Laws as the People by their Representative, The Commons of *England,* from time to time assembling in Parliament, after Consultation had with the Lords therein (when sitting) shall make and choose, may be deposed by the same Parliament : And that what Subject of the Nation that shall assist, or side with him therein, may upon good proof thereof, not onely from thenceforth be deemed and taken for Enemies to the State, and therefore not onely void of the protection of the Laws, but dealt with as in a case of high Treason. And that the particular Representatives do from time to time wholly prosecute and pursue in Parliament all such Instructions as the People for whom they are chosen and serve, shall at the day of their Elections and afterwards be required unto. And that no Officer of War, or Member of the Committee of State, shall be chosen into any first next following Parliament, after their discharge thereof.

III. That in all Laws made or to be made, every person may be bound alike ; and that no Degree of Lords, Peers of Parliament (now or hereafter assembled) or others, No Tenure, Estate, Charter or Office soever, shall confer any exemption from the ordinary Course of Justice, and Legal Proceedings, whereunto others are subjected.

IV. That our meanings and intentions are, Not to leave our selves lyable to the least of mercy, touching our Freedoms, either of the most Righteous, or evil and unrighteous Princes, (disclaiming confidence in vain man) But knowing that Justice of punishment ought never to be inflicted, but where in Reason it will convert into mercy ; and seeing that it hath pleased God, That a Covenant is passed between this Nation and our Brethren of *Scotland,* whereby mercy is claimed by that Nation on his Majesties behalf : Therefore if the King shall Assent unto this Agreement, that then He may be Proclaimed and Crowned King again. And who (after the first four years in which the Kingdoms Debts may be paid) may in a Parliamentary way have as great an Annual Revenue conferred upon him, as (one year with another of his Reign) was yet ever brought into the Exchequer, notwithstanding those vast illegal sums thereof, raised by the multitude of Monopolies, and destroying usurping Projects, Except what shall be defalked for such Charges as henceforth shall be thought fit to be defrayed by the Parliament, which formerly was done by the King.

V. That all or any person or persons that shall approve, or any way allow of any thing which the King, or any person by or under him have done in this late miserable and destructive War, may be dealt with as in a case of high Treason : And that neither any such who have assisted the King in person or otherwise, and such as have approved of any thing done against the State in the said War, may not sit, or have place in the next Parliament, or Voyces in the Elections thereof.

VI. That if any person or persons whatsoever, that shall any way wilfully endeavor to disgrace (by approbrious speeches) any person or persons for assisting the King in his War against the Parliament, may be bound to the good Behavior, with great Surety for the same ; And that no man whatsoever be hereafter questioned for any thing done in reference to the late publique Differences since the year, 1641. further then in execution of the Judgement of this present Parliament.

VII. That a general Revisement may be had of all the Laws and Statutes now in force ; and that those intending and relating to the maintenance of Popery, Prelacy, Episcopacy, Superstition, and all Ecclesiastical Jurisdiction or Government, and whatsoever else that will not best stand with the good of the nation according to this present age, may be Repealed: And that all those that shall be continued unto us, may be put in execution, according to the purity and truth thereof, that the tediousness and long delays formerly exercised therein, as also all undue practice thereof, may be wholly taken away, so as that intended chiefest good for the peaceable well-being of the Commonwealth, may not henceforth be exercised to the great disquieting and wasting of the people, as formerly (even hitherto) it hath done. And that such sure provisions be speedily made, not onely for the hinderance and avoiding of all Vagabonds and Beggars, but for a conscientious and sufficient Relief for all the poor and indigent people, that none may perish with want ; as also for the extirpating of Drunkenness and Swearing, upon such high penalties, and ways of incouragement for the prosecutors thereof, as, through God, may wholly take away all those Evils.

VIII. That the Excize may continue but until the present Engagement thereupon be discharged ; And that what moneys soever the Parliament shall be necessitated to use, may be raised by Subsidies and Taxes, and such other open and known ways as may be most visible and apparently equal to the whole Commonwealth.

IX. That the people being at this time very unequally distributed for Electing their Representatives, may be more indifferently proportioned ; And that not onely every Freeholder, but Copyholder also, that is worth 40 s. *per Annum,* and every other person that is worth 50 l. personal Estate, may have Voyces in the Election thereof.

X. That the people do of course choose themselves a Parliament once every two years, after the most free and uncontrollable maner, upon pain of high Treason to the Disturbers, over-bearer or over-bearers of any person or persons of the Elections for ever, and to continue by the space of five Moneths, to begin on every first Thursday in every second March ; and to begin to sit upon the first Thursday in April then next ensuing, after the dissolution of this ; and to continue till the last day of August then next following also, and no longer ; and that this may terminate and end before May 1649.

XI. That the Irish may not be still proceeded against, as to execute cruelty for cruelty, but that both they and those other Offendors of our Brethren of *England* that have not Compounded, may yet Compound, and have such Fines set upon them, and so to be payed, as that with respect unto their conditions, may not ruine and undo them and their posterities, except the Beginners and Fomenters of the War.

XII. That out of every Parliament there may be a Committee of State appointed, consisting of Forty of the Members thereof, six whereof to be out of the City of *London, Westminster,* and the Borough of *Southwark* ; and the next to be equally proportioned for the several other Counties, Cities and Towns Corporate of *England* and *Wales,* to Negotiate in the Intervals of Parliament, of all things given them in charge by the said Parliament.

XIII. That annually there may be an equal Tax in every Parish within the Kingdom of *England* and *Wales,* as well of Lands as Goods, proportionable to that of the accustomed Tythes (Impropriations excepted) to be raised, leavied and paid into the hands of one or more Treasurers in every County for that purpose, to be paid and issued forth again to the Teachers in the Word, as cause shall require : And that all Tythes of Impropriations may be bought in at such conscientious Rates as the Committee of State (as hereafter followeth) or Commissioners from them appointed for that purpose shall think most reasonable and meet.

XIV. That whereas God the Creator and Father of Spirits is Omnipotent and unlimited by man, giving to every one a various and different Spirit, of which no man is certainly Master, no, not for a minute, therefore ought Liberty of Conscience to be granted to all godly Conscientious walkers (protesting against the State-destroying Tenents, as to Peace and Freedom) not onely of the Church of *Rome,* but of Episcopal and all Ecclesiastical Jurisdiction by Courts and Offices for that purpose also ; yet the way of instructing the people is referred to the Ministery.

15. That all inslaving Tenures upon Record by Oaths of Fealty, Villanage, Homage, and Fines at will of the Lords, may

all be bought in at such rates as shall not exceed twenty years purchase to the Lord, upon a conscientious computation of profits made according to the Reign of King *James*.

16. That all the Marish Lands, Fens and Common Pastures, within the Kingdom of *England* and *Wales,* may be enclosed and divided, one fourth part to be equally proportioned to the several Tenants of the several Parishes, where such Land lieth ; and another fourth part to the Poor of the same ; and the other two parts to be divided for, and towards the payment of all the Officers and Souldiers Arrears; To be holden and taken up by Copy of Court-Roll of the proper Lord or Lords of the Soyls, giving and paying the sum of five shillings, *per Acre,* Fine, for Admittance at every Alienation, Charge, and Taking up, by death or otherwise, if the Annual Rent of every Acre be worth so much, or else not to exceed the value thereof ; and twelve pence *per Acre* at the most, or the sixt part of the yearly value for the Annual Rent of all that fourth part divided among the Poor, and six pence *per Acre* at the most for the other three parts of the yearly Revenue to be proportioned certainly for ever.

17. That his Excellency the *Lord General,* Lieutenant General *Cromwel,* the Lord Mayor of our City, the Earl of *Northumberland,* the Lord *Grey* of *Grooby,* the Lord *Wharton,* Major General *Skippon,* Commissary General *Ireton,* Sir *John Potts,* Sir *William Waller,* Sir *William Brereton,* Sir *John Maynard,* Colonel *Harlo,* Mr Alderman *Fouke,* Mr Alderman *Gibbs,* Mr *Fran. Allen,* Major General *Massey,* Col. *Wilson,* Col. *Fleetwood,* Col. *Harrison,* Col. *Russel,* Sir *Arthur Haslerig,* Sir *Gilbert Pickering,* Sir *Henry Vane* junior, Mr *Perpoint,* Col. *Marten,* Col. *Rigby,* Mr *Holland,* Sir *John Palgrave,* Major *Wildeman,* Lieutenant Colonel *Lilburn,* Col. *Ludlow,* may be a Committee to continue until the first day of the next Parliament to regulate, place, displace, confirm, commissionate or non-commission all Justices belonging to the Courts of *Westminster,* with the Officers and Offices thereunto belonging, all Sheriffs of Counties and Justices of Peace, and all other the Officers and Offices whatsoever, formerly occasioned to be granted by his Majesty, whether by usurpation or otherwise : And after the expiration and end of the aforesaid Committee, to be desposed of by succeeding Parliaments or Committees of State : And that his Majesty may degrade all such persons, either in part or in whole, as were the Cause and Beginners of the Wars, or the Continuance thereof ; as also to confirm such honors on such worthy Members as have most self-denyingly en-

deavored our Freedoms, according to the judgment and wisdom of this most excellent and honorable Committee, or the major part thereof. And after the expiration of this Committee, that then all such persons as his Majesty shall for the future dignifie with titles of Honor, as aforesaid, may first have certificate of their Demerits for Services done unto the State, either from the Parliament, or Committee of State, as aforesaid, to signifie the same.

18. That the Earl of *Pembrook,* the Earl of *Denby,* the Earl of *Kent,* Mr Serjeant *St. John,* Lord chief Justice of the Common Pleas, Mr Serjeant *Wylde,* Sir *Thomas Wydrington,* the Lord *Lisle,* Sir *John Danvers,* Sir *Henry Myldmay,* together with his Excellency the Lord General, Lieutenant General *Cromwel,* the Lord Mayor, with the rest of the Members of the excellent and honorable Committee for the regulating of Offices and Officers, may be the Committee of State for the next ensuing Intervals of Parliament.

19. That all Debts, upon the first Propositions, due upon the Publique Faith, and all other Moneys and Values, lent upon the fifth and twentieth parts, may be satisfied and payd by the Inhabitants in every County within it self, by an equal rate as well of Lands, as Goods, by Commissioners to be chosen within themselves also for that purpose.

20. That henceforth no Free-born person of this Nation be hereafter pressed to serve in the War.

21. That a strict Accompt may be taken of all those persons that have been Treasurers, Receivers, or otherwise any way intrusted with the Treasure of the State.

22. That all the Dean and Chapters Lands may be sold for payment of the Publique Debts, or for what other uses the Parliament shall think fit ; and that all the Soldiers of the new Model now in Arms may either be payd by proportions out of the Marish Lands, Fens and Common Pastures ; For every Trooper that is behind, and in Arrear for every year (or proportionable according to that time) the sum of four pounds *per annum,* during his life, without allowance for Free Quarter, and every Footman the sum of fifty shillings *per annum,* with proportion to time as aforesaid ; and if it shall happen that the said Marish Lands, Fens, and Common Pastures will not be sufficient to perform the same, that then it may be made up out of the aforesaid Deans and Chapters Lands : Conditionally provided, That all such, as shall be assigned by the General Council of the Army for the Service of *Ireland,* do not refuse the same ; but that all such, as shall be

dismissed thither, shall have the Fee-simple of the said proportions of Land to them and their heirs for ever : And all others, that
shall desire to leave the Wars, and shall be dismissed the Army by
the Councel of War also, may forthwith be satisfied their Arrears
upon his Excellency's discharge.

23. That the great Weight and Charge of *Ireland* may be intrusted in a faithful Committee, consisting of nine at the least,
for ordering that high Affair, whereof two to be Members of the
City of *London*.

24. That for the frustrating of the several perilous designs of
the many parties, which are now so strongly working to carry on
their particular Interests for Ruine and Destruction to us ; and
for the setling of a firm Peace in this distracted Nation ; That
after all have subscribed this present Agreement for the maintaining of all our just Right, by the Power and Authority of Parliament, that then all the Parliaments Forces now in the Kingdom
may be paid, or else effectually satisfied all their Arrears due unto
them ; be acquitted of all or any past failings, and forthwith dismissed for *Ireland*, with all convenient speed, under their present
Conduct and Command, except what Forces shall be thought
meet for the Garrisons of *England* and *Wales* ; as also that the
Lord General may still be continued with us in his Renowned
Command (General of *England* and *Wales*) aforesaid ; and that
Lieutenant General *Cromwel* may be sent General into *Ireland*
aforesaid, and have the Command of all the Forces for the re-
ducement thereof ; and that the Scots there, being put under the
Command aforesaid, may then be there equally capable with our
own in all benefits, priviledges and profits whatsoever, that our
mercy and moderation may be known unto all, and that the Lord
is our Councell.

FINIS

TO THE . . . COMMONS OF ENGLAND

Appeared January 19, 1649. Reprinted from a photostat of the original broadside in Thomason Collection, 669 f. 13 (73).

In his *A Defiance Against All Arbitrary Usurpations* (1646), Richard Overton had written that "this persecuted means of unlicenced Printing hath done more good to the people, then all the bloodie wars; the one tending to rid us quite of all slavery; but the other onely to rid us of one, and involve us into another." Through hidden presses the Levellers year after year had carried on their able, insistent propaganda, first on behalf of toleration, then against king and Lords, finally for their *Agreement.* No minds in England had struck off bolder manifestoes, more skilful appeals to action. Always in the van of the surging impetus of revolutionary dynamics, they had roused the army to mutinous enthusiasm for their cause, persuaded or forced the high officers to a partial acceptance of their constitutional solution, all through timely, irrepressible, unlicensed pamphleteering. Wrath and fire against oppressors, ringing words, phrases that leaped and burned, sufferings of their imprisoned leaders, letters to Cromwell, Marten, Fairfax, speeches before the Lords and Commons, citations of ancient rights and liberties—these were the weapons of the Leveller word-masters, the Tom Paines of their day, unequalled among their contemporaries, even by Milton himself, in the art of propaganda.

Though the Levellers had scattered through their pamphlets many pertinent passages on liberty of the press, they had not found it necessary until 1649 to make press freedom a main concern. The classic pamphlet on this topic, the *Areopagitica,* anticipating all the arguments that the Levellers made then, or three centuries have accumulated since, had appeared in 1644. But now, in January, 1649, with a constitutional overturn in the offing, the Levellers saw in the new press restrictions an unexpectedly dire threat to their propaganda. On January 5 the Rump had voted "to enable the Marshal to go on with the said Service, concerning scandalous Pamphlets, and Prisoners."[1] According to Rushworth: "The House this day spent some time in debate of scandalous and unlicensed Pamphlets, and how far they are prejudicial and dishonourable to this Nation, and destructive to present Affairs: and for the suppression of the same for the future, the House ordered that his Excellency the Lord General should be desired to command his Marshal General of the Army by himself and Deputies to put the Ordinance of the *28th* of *September,* 1647 . . . into speedy execution."[2] The ordinance of September 30, 1647 (not September 28) one of the most drastic of the Civil War period, had been passed at the request of Fairfax himself. In the midst of seething Leveller agitation in the army, Fairfax had written from Putney on September 20 to ask for the suppression of "the poisonous writings of evil Men sent abroad daily." He had enclosed some pamphlets "scandalous and abusive to this Army in particular."[3] Within a few days the House acted. Mabbott was appointed licenser, as Fairfax had asked, and severe penalties were again imposed on unlicensed pamphleteering. The writer was to be fined forty shillings or suffer a forty-day imprisonment; the printer was to be fined twenty shillings and have his printing press and equipment seized and broken to pieces; the bookseller was to forfeit ten shillings; the hawker or peddler was to lose his stock of pamphlets and suffer whipping as a common rogue. The ordinance further directed all mayors, constables, and justices to act vigorously to enforce the ordinance, giving them authority to enter all houses that they suspected might harbor either hidden presses or unlicensed pamphlets.[4] It was inevitable that such an ordinance, directed mainly against the Leveller manifestoes, should have been enacted unhesitatingly by the predominantly Presbyterian Commons of 1647; but its full approval by the Rump Independents in 1649 was, as the petition itself reveals, an unexpected jolt to the Levellers, a rough hint of what they could now expect from their former allies. The degree of enforcement counted more heavily, of course, than the mere statute; but by January 18, 1649, only two weeks after the ordinance had been

[1] Commons' *Journals*, VI, 111.   [2] *Collections* (1721), VII, 1384.
[3] *Old Parliamentary History*, XVI, 301.   [4] *Ibid.*, XVI, 310.

passed, the Levellers evidently had cause to believe that the officers would engage in a determined, painstaking elimination of their medium of propaganda. No longer could they count on the half-hearted, inefficient searches of the Commons' agent.

In the petition the Levellers object to the harsh penalties of the new ordinance, "fit only for slaves or bondsmen"; they protest strenuously against the Rump's committing the enforcement of a civil statute to a military power; they object, as Milton has, to the very concept of a censorship, of any group of men acting as tutors and controllers of the country's intellectuals. A censorship "hath ever ushered in a tyrannie," shut men's mouths "whilst they are robd of their liberties." Moreover, if a censorship of the printed word is to be imposed, all private and public teachers must be watched over; censorship must extend to speech as vigorously as to writing. Like Milton before them, the Levellers ask for an open battleground for the clashing of truth and error. No government should fear to "hear all voices and judgements, which they can never do, but by giving freedom to the Press." If accusations against the government are false and malicious, the just answer is not jails and broken presses, but the truth itself, protagonists for which no Parliament will ever lack.

The Leveller authors show in this petition an historical awareness not only of the place of unlicensed printing in the sharp ideological clashes of the Civil War, but also its shaping of the events themselves. One of the first acts of the Rump had been to declare a Leveller truism, a truism never before proclaimed by a House of Commons: "The People under God are the Original of all just Powers." [5] The House had gone further: It had declared its acts to have the force of law without the assent of king or Lords. Why is it possible, ask the Levellers, in effect, that the House can proceed with such revolutionary votes? Is it not because unlicensed printing has "prepared and smoothed your way for them"? What now is received by the people with "great content and satisfaction" might otherwise have made the House many enemies. Likewise unlicensed printing has prepared the army to strike for fundamental freedoms. In the beginning of the war, it was unlicensed printing that pointed the way to liberty, struck off the shackles of tyranny; whereas licensed pamphlets were filled

5 Rushworth, VII, 1383.

with lies and destructive principles. Always, when licensers have had the upper hand, freedom has suffocated; and unlicensed printing has been synonymous with the enlargement of freedom and progress. The authors reveal in the Petition that Larner, Lilburne, and Overton, Levellers all, were the first to be persecuted for printing pamphlets; they hint that the Levellers have been the most energetic users of secret presses.

In a sober evaluation of the authors' estimate of Leveller propaganda pressure in the Puritan Revolution, we may assert that their influence was more apparent than actual, not the explosive but the smoke of dynamic social restlessness, of the clash between an expiring feudal order and inevitable expansion of the trading classes. Among many thousands, however, who were freshly aware of the magic of the printed word, peculiarly susceptible to the power of ideas, as in the New Model army, the decisive effect of Leveller propaganda can hardly be disputed; action followed step by step the insistent hammering of petitions, committees, agitators. To the modern critic Leveller ideas loom more significant than Leveller political action: In a few short years they compassed the sharp transitions of political thinking that society was gradually to achieve in twenty decades. But in January, 1649, the Levellers seemed on the verge of realizing a democratic constitutional solution, the embodiment of their ripest hopes, now in part accepted by the army and presented to the Commons of Independents. All this had come to England, they thought, through the pressure of their tireless, unlicensed propaganda.[6]

[6] Though Walwyn may have had a hand in this petition, I do not think now, as I formerly did (*Milton in the Puritan Revolution*, p. 133) that he was the principal author. The styptic style, uncompromising demands, and philosophical overtones appear to be those of Overton.

TO THE RIGHT HONOURABLE,
THE SUPREME AUTHORITY OF THIS NATION,
THE COMMONS OF ENGLAND
in Parliament aſsembled.

The humble Petition of firm and conſtant Friends to the Parlia-
ment and Common-wealth, Preſenters and Promoters of the
late Large Petition of September 11. MDCXLVIII.

Sheweth,

THat having seriously considered how many large and fair
opportunities this honourable House hath had within these
eight yeers last past to have made this Nation absolute free
and happy ; and yet that until this time, every of those oppor-
tunies have (after some short space of hope) faded, and but altered,
if not increased our bondage.

When we call to mind what extraordinary things the Army
undertook (and this honourable House approved) in behalf of
the liberties of the people, in the yeer 1647. and that nevertheless,
the first fruits of their great and unexpected success, was a more
oppressive Ordinance for enforcing of Tyths, than ever had bin before, and which hath bin severely executed, and is still continued,
to the extreme vexation of Friends, and encouragement of Pulpit
Incendiaries; And how that great and wonderful opportunities
wasted it self away in contending with, and imprisoning of cordial
Friends, or in tampering with known enemies, and at length
ended in a most dangerous and bloudy war; whereas rightly applied, it might have given peace and security to the Nation for
many Generations.

These things considered, although we exceedingly rejoyced in
your just and excellent Votes of the 4 of this instant *Ianuary*, as a
people who had long suffered the reproches of Sectaries & Levellers, for maintaining the supreme original of all just power to
be in the people, & the supreme Authority of this Nation to be
in this honourable House, (which our burnt Petitions, and that
of *Sept.* 11. do fully witness. Yet since we understand, that within

few daies after you admitted a message from the House of Lords, and gave an accustomed respect thereunto. We have bin very much troubled, how already the same doth essentially derogate from your foresaid Votes.

And since also, we have seen a printed Warrant of his Excellency the Lord General *Fairfax,* directed to his Marshal General, for suppressing of unlicensed Books and Pamphlets, authorising him (upon the oath of one witness) to take all persons offending into custody, and inflict upon them such corporal punishments, and levie such fines upon them, as your Ordinances impose ; and not to discharge them, until after payment and punishment : And further, to make diligent search in all places where the said Marshal shall think meet, for unlicensed printing presses, employed in printing scandalous, unlicensed pamphlets, Books, &c. and to seise and carry away such printing presses, &c. And likewise to make diligent search in all suspected printing houses, ware-houses, and other shops and places whatsoever, for such unlicensed books, &c. And in case of opposition, to break open (according to your Ordinances) all dores and locks, and to apprehend all persons so opposing and take them into custody, till they have given satisfaction therein. And all this by vertue of an order of yours of the fift of this instant *Ianuary.* Since we have seen this, we profess, we cannot but already fear the issue and consequence of those excellent Votes, nothing more dangerous to a people, than the mis-application of their supreme entrusted Authority; and therefore we entreat herein to be excused, though we appear herein, as in a cause of very great Importance.

For what-ever specious pretences of good to the Common-wealth have bin devised to over-aw the Press, yet all times fore-gone will manifest, it hath ever ushered in a tyrannie; mens mouth being to be kept from making noise, whilst they are robd of their liberties ; So was it in the late Prerogative times before this Parliament, whilst upon pretence of care of the publike, Licensers were set over the Press, Truth was suppressed, the people thereby kept ignorant, and fitted only to serve the unjust ends of Tyrants and Oppressers, whereby the Nation was enslaved : Nor did any thing beget those oppressions so much opposition, as unlicensed Books and Pamphlets.

A short time after the begining of this Parliament, upon pretense of publike good, and at the solicitation of the Company of Stationers (who in all times have bin officiously instrumental unto Tyrannie) the Press again (notwithstanding the good service it

immediately before had done) was most ungratefully committed
to the custody of Licensers, when though scandalous Books from
or in behalf of the Enemy then at *Oxford* was the pretended occasion; yet the first that suffered was M. *Lawrence Sanders,* for
Printing without license, a book intituled, *Gods Love to Mankind;* and not long after, M. *Iohn Lilburn,* M. *William Larnar,*
and M. *Richard Overton,* and others, about books discovering the
then approching Tyrannie ; whilst scandalous Pamphlets nevertheless abounded, and did the greater mischief, in that Licensers
have never bin so free to pass, as good men have bin forward to
compile proper and effectual answers to such books and pamphlets: And whether Tyrannie did soon follow thereupon, the
courses you were forced unto in opposition, and the necessities
you were put upon for your preservation, will most cleerly demonstrate. And if you, and your Army shall be pleased to look a little
back upon affairs, you will find you have bin very much strengthened all along by unlicensed Printing; yea, that it hath done (with
greatest danger to the doers) what it could to preserve you, when
licensed did its utmost to destroy you; and we are very confident,
those very excellent and necessary Votes of yours fore-mentioned,
had made you a multitude of enemies, if unlicensed printing had
not prepared and smoothed your way for them, whereas now they
are received with great content and satisfaction.

And generally, as to the whole course of printing, as justly in
our apprehensions, may Licensers be put over all publike or private Teachings, and Discourses, in Divine, Moral, Natural, Civil,
or Political things, as over the Press; the liberty whereof appears
so essential unto Freedom, as that without it, its impossible to
preserve any Nation from being liable to the worst of bondage ;
for what may not be done to that people who may not speak or
write, but at the pleasure of Licensers?

As for any prejudice to Government thereby, if Government
be just in its Constitution, and equal in its distributions, it will
be good, if not absolutely necessary for them, to hear all voices
and judgements, which they can never do, but by giving freedom
to the Press ; and in case any abuse their authority by scandalous
Pamphlets, they will never want able Advocates to vindicate their
innocency. And therefore all things being duely weighed. to refer
all Books and Pamphlets to the judgement, discretion, or affection of Licensers, or to put the least restraint upon the Press,
seems altogether inconsistent with the good of the Common-
wealth, and expresly opposite and dangerous to the liberties of

the people, and to be carefully avoided, as any other exorbitancy or prejudice in Government.

And being so, we beseech you to consider how unreasonable it is for every man or woman to be liable to punishment, penal or corporal, upon one witness in matters of this Nature, for compiling, printing, selling or dispersing of Books and Pamphlets, nay to deserve even whipping (as the last yeers Ordinance, an Engine fited to a Personal Treaty) doth provide a punishment, as we humbly conceive, fit only for slaves or bondmen. But that this honourable House, that is now by an extraordinary means freed from that major part, (which degenerating from the true Interest of the people, were the unhappy authors of that Ordinance) and reduced to that minor part, which we alwaies hoped did really oppose the same, should now approve thereof, and of all other Ordinances of like nature ; and not onely so, but in cases so meerly Civil, to refer the execution thereof to a Military power : This is that which in the present sense and consequence thereof, afflicts us above measure; because according to this rule, we may we know not how soon, be reduced under a military jurisdiction, which we humbly conceive, we ought not to be, and which above any thing in this world, we shall desire in this and all other cases for ever to avoid.

And therefore we most earnestly entreat, First, That as you have voted your selves the supreme Authority, so you will exactly preserve the same entire in it self, without intermixing again with any other whatsoever.

Secondly, That you will precisely hold your selves to the supreme end, the Freedom of the People; as in other things, so in that necessary and essential part, of speaking, writing, printing, and publishing their minds freely; without seting of Masters, Tutors, and Controulers over them ; and for that end, to revoke all Ordinances and Orders to the contrary.

Thirdly, That you will fix us onely in a Civil Jurisdiction, refering the Military to Act distinct, and within it self, except in cases of warlike opposition to Civil Authority.

Fourthly, That you will recal that oppressive Ordinance for Tyths, upon treble damages; that so, as we have rejoyced in the notion, we may not have cause to grieve, but to rejoyce also in the exercise of your supreme Authority; and that the whole Nation in this blessed opportunity may receive a full reward of true Freedom for its large expense of bloud and treasure, and by your Wisdom and Fidelity, be made happy to all Future Generations.

Die Jovis, January 18. 1648.

*T*HE *House being informed that divers Inhabitants within the
Citie* of London *and Borough of* Southwark, *were at the Dore;
they were called in, and then presented a Petition to this House;
which after the Petitioners were withdrawn, was read, and was
entituled,* The humble Petition of firm and constant friends to
Parliament and Common-wealth, the Presenters and Promoters of
the late large Petition of *Sept.* 11. 1648.

*Ordered by the Commons assembled in Parliament, that the
said Petition be referred to the Committee appointed yesterday
to consider of Petitions of this nature.*

Hen. Scobell *cler. Parl. Dom. Com,*

The Petitioners being again called in, M. Speaker by command
of this House gave them this answer. Gentlemen, *The House have
read your Petition, and have referred it to a Committee to consider of the matters of consequence therein; and have taken notice
of your continued good affections to this House, and they have
commanded me to give you thanks for your good affections, and
I do accordingly give you thanks for your good affections.*

Hen. Scobell *Cleric. Parl. Dom. Com.*

A PETITION . . . CONCERNING . . . AN AGREEMENT OF THE PEOPLE

Presented to the Commons, January 20, 1649. Reprinted from a photostat of the original pamphlet in the McAlpin Collection of Union Theological Seminary. The officers' *Agreement* was reprinted July 23, 1649, in broadside 669 f. 14 (59).

Reading the officers' *Agreement* in the light of subsequent constitutional theory, the historian is struck by its remarkable anticipation of democratic safeguards and procedures, all an outgrowth of Leveller agitation and the crystallization of their main concepts in the first *Agreement*. The Levellers were not unaware of the progress they had made in securing acceptance of their leading principles. "That an Agreement between those that trust," wrote Lilburne later, "and those who are trusted, hath appeared a thing acceptable to this honorable House, his Excellency, and the Officers of the Army, is . . . much to our rejoycing." [1] Like its original, the officers' *Agreement* provides for election of Parliament by householder suffrage, disregarding the traditional power of kings and Lords. Furthermore the power of the Commons, as in the original, is limited; the Commons cannot conscript men, question men for their differences in the war, "give judgement upon any mans person or estate, where no Law hath before provided," [2] establish communism, or compel men to attend the state church.

Nevertheless the Levellers were dissatisfied with the officers' document. They distrusted first the army's gesture in presenting it for approbation and possible modification to the unrepresentative Rump. The *Agreement,* they maintained, needed no Parliamentary ratification to become effective; it was a mutual contract among the people creating a supreme law and its own representative body. In this demand, of course, the Levellers nevertheless were willing to use the threat of army might, as in

[1] *Englands New Chains Discovered,* no pagination.   [2] P. 348.

331

1647, to secure the people's signatures; they needed official army support to secure the subscriptions of even the well-affected citizens. Unwilling to face this ugly reality, the Levellers nevertheless attacked the officers' procedure in petitioning the Rump. They saw, moreover, in certain provisions of the *Agreement* the tentacles of a new tyranny. The Rump, according to the officers' document, was to dissolve on or before April 1, 1649; a new Commons would not be elected until June. For two or three months the country would then be in control of a Council of State, which "may design to perpetuate their power, and to keep off Parliaments forever." [3] Furthermore the new Commons would continue in session only six months, or until December, 1649; after which its successor would not be elected until June, 1651, the Council of State meanwhile remaining at the helm of state. The Levellers wanted annual Parliaments (though this had not been explicit in their own *Agreement*),[4] with power to sit a full year, and Councils of State appointed for one year only; whereas the officers' *Agreement* permitted each Council of State to sit eighteen months.[5] The officers, moreover, had not inserted any demands for economic reforms or particular grievances to be redressed such as those added to the original *Agreement*. The Levellers were highly critical of the ambiguity of the sections on liberty of conscience; of the right, under the officers' *Agreement*, of Parliament's power to erect special courts of justice, this being contrary to traditional jury trial; of the officers' failure to abolish tithes, excise, and monopolies.[5] All these sharp discrepancies Lilburne and his followers discerned immediately in the new *Agreement;* but they waited until February 26 before publishing them to the world in *Englands New Chains Discovered.*

[3] *Englands New Chains.*

[4] Professor Pease (*The Leveller Movement*, p. 267) states that the committee *Agreement* provides for biennial Parliaments. This is an error, but a minor and understandable one. The document leaves this point undecided, mentioning neither annual or biennial elections.

[5] Though the Levellers had omitted all mention of Lords and king in their own *Agreement*, they criticized the officers for not prohibiting, in their document, the restoration of these two institutions.

A
PETITION

FROM

His Excellency Thomas Lord Fairfax

And the

General Councel of Officers of the Army,

To the Honorable the

COMMONS of ENGLAND

in Parliament affembled,

Concerning the Draught of An

AGREEMENT of the PEOPLE

For a fecure and prefent Peace,

by them framed and prepared.

Together with the faid Agreement

prefented *Saturday, Jan.* 20.

And a Declaration of his Excellency and the faid
General Councel, concerning the fame.

Tendred to the Confideration of the PEOPLE.

B Y *the Appointment of the Generall Councel of Officers
of the Army.*   Signed,

John Rushworth, Sec'

LONDON,

Printed for *John Partridge, R. Harford, G. Calvert,* and
G. Whittington.   MDCXLIX.

To the honorable the Commons of
ENGLAND in Parliament affembled;

The humble Petition of his Excellency Thomas *Lord* Fairfax, *and the General Councel of Officers of the Army under his Command, concerning the Draught of* An Agreement of the People, *by them framed and prepared.*

IN our late Remonstrance of the 18 of November last, we propounded (next after the matters of publike Justice) some Foundations for a general settlement of Peace in the Nation, which we therein desired might be formed and Established in the nature of a generall Contract or Agreement of the People ; and since then, the matters so propounded be wholly rejected, or no consideration of them admitted in Parliament (though visibly of highest Moment to the Publique) and all ordinary Remedies being denyed , we were necessitated to an extraordinary way of Remedy ; whereby to avoyd the mischiefs then at hand, and set you in a condition (without such obstructions or diversions by corrupt Members) to proceed to matters of publique Justice and general Settlement. Now as nothing did in our own hearts more justifie our late undertakings towards many Members in this Parliament, then the necessity thereof in order to a sound Settlement in the Kingdom, and the integrity of our intentions to make use of it only to that end : so we hold our selves obliged to give the People all assurance possible , That our opposing the corrupt closure endeavoured with the King, was not in designe to hinder Peace or Settlement, (thereby to render our employments , as Souldiers , necessary to be continued,) and that neither that extraordinary course we have taken, nor any other proceedings of ours, have been intended for the setting up of any particular Party or Interest, by or with which to uphold ourselves in Power and Dominion over the Nation, but that it was and is the desire of our hearts, in all we have done, (with the hindering of that imminent evil, and destructive conjunction with the King) to make way for the settlement of a Peace and Government of the Kingdom upon Grounds of common Freedom and Safety : And therefore because our former Overtures for that purpose (being only in general terms, and not reduced to a certainty of particulars fit for practise) might possibly be understood but as plausible pretences, not intended really to be put into effect, We have thought it our duty to draw out these generals into an intire frame of particulars, ascertained with such circumstances as may make it effectively practicable. And for that end, while your time hath been taken up in other matters of high and present Importance, we have spent much of ours in preparing and perfecting such a draught of Agreement, and in all things so circumstantiated, as to render it ripe for your speedier consideration, and the Kingdoms acceptance and practise (if approved,) and so we do herewith humbly present it to you. Now to prevent misunderstanding of our intentions therein, We have but this to say, That we are far from such a Spirit, as positively to impose our private apprehensions upon the judgments of any in the Kingdom, that have not forfeited their Freedom, and much lesse upon your selves : Neither are we apt in any wise to insist upon circumstantial things, or ought that is not evidently fundamental to that publique Interest for which You and We have declared and engaged; But in this Tender of it we humbly desire,

1. *That whether it shall be fully approved by You and received by the People (as it now stands) or not, it may yet remain upon Record, before you, a perpetual witness of our real intentions and utmost endeavors for a sound and equal Settlement; and as a testimony whereby all men may be assured, what we are willing and ready to* acquiesce *in; and their jealousies satisfied or mouths stopt, who are apt to think or say, We have no bottom.*

2. *That (with all expedition which the immediate and pressing great affairs will admit) it may receive your most mature Consideration and Resolutions upon it, not that we desire either the whole, or what you shall like in it, should be by your Authority imposed as a Law upon the Kingdom, (for so it would lose the intended nature of* An Agreement of the People,) *but that (so far as it concurs with your own judgments) it may receive Your Seal of Approbation only.*

3. *That (according to the method propounded therein) it may be tendred to the People in all parts, to be subscribed by those that are willing, (as Petitions, and other things of a*

voluntary nature, are ;) and that meanwhile, the ascertaining of those circumstances, which it refers to Commissioners in the several Counties, may be proceeded upon in a way preparatory to the practise of it : And if upon the Account of subscriptions (to be returned by those Commissioners in April *next) there appear to be a general or common Reception of it amongst the People, or by the well-affected of them, and such as are not obnoxious for Delinquency ; it may then take place, and effect according to the Tenor and Substance of it.*

And Your Petitioners shall pray, &c.

WHITEHALL

Jan. 15. 1649.

By the Appointment of his Excellency, and the general Councel of Officers of the Army.

JO: RUSHVVORTH *Secr'.*

AN
AGREEMENT
OF THE
PEOPLE
OF
ENGLAND,

And the places therewith
INCORPORATED,

For a ſecure and preſent Peace, upon Grounds
of Common Right, Freedom and Safety.

HAving by our late labors and hazards made it appear to the
world at how high a rate we value our Juſt Freedom, And
God having so far owned our cause as to deliver the Enemies
thereof into our hands, We do now hold our selves bound in mutuall duty to each other to take the best care we can for the future,
to avoyd both the danger of returning into a slavish condition ,
and the chargeable remedy of another War : For as it cannot be
imagined , That so many of our Country men would have opposed us in this Quarrell, if they had understood their own good,
so may we hopefully promise to our selves , That when our Common Right and Liberties shall be cleared, their endeavors will be

disappointed, that seek to make themselves our Masters, since therefore our former oppressions, and not yet ended troubles, have been occasioned, either by want of frequent National Meetings in Councel, or by the undue or unequal Constitution thereof, or by rendering those meetings uneffectual. We are fully agreed and resolved (God willing) to provide, That hereafter our Representatives be neither left to an uncertainty for time, nor be unequally constituted, nor made useless to the ends for which they are intended.

In Order whereunto We Declare and Agree;

1. That to prevent the many inconveniencies, apparently arising from the long continuance of the same persons in supream Authority, this Present Parliament end and dissolve upon, or before the last day of *April,* in the year of our Lord. 1649.

2. That the People of *England* (being at this day very unequally distributed, by Counties, Cities and Burroughs, for the Election of their Representatives) be indifferently proportioned : And to this end, That the Representative of the whole Nation shall consist of four hundred persons, or not above ; and in each County, and the places thereto subjoyned, there shall be chosen, to make up the said Representative at all times, the several numbers here mentioned ; *VIZ.*

In the County of *Kent,* with the Burrough, Towns, and Parishes therein (except such as are hereunder particularly named)　　ten.　10

The City of *Canterbury,* with the Suburbs adjoyning, and Liberties thereof,　　two.　2

The City of *Rochester,* with the Parishes of *Chatham* and *Strowd,* one.　1

The Cinque Ports in *Kent* and *Sussex, viz. Dover, Rumney, Hyde, Sandwich, Hastings,* with the townes of *Rye* and *Winchelsey,* three.　3

The County of *Sussex,* with the Burroughs, Towns and Parishes (therein except *Chichester* and the Cinque Ports)　　eight.　8

The City of *Chichester,* with the Suburbs and Liberties thereof,　one.　1

The County of *Southampton,* with the Burroughs, Towns and Parishes therein, except such as are hereunder named,　　eight.　8

The City of *Winchester,* with the Suburbs and Liberties thereof, one.　1

The County of the town of *Southampton,*　　one.　1

The County of *Dorset,* with the Burroughs, Townes and Parishes therein (except *Dorchester*)　　seven.　7

The Town of *Dorchester,*　　one.　1

The County of *Devon,* with the Burroughs, Towns and Parishes therein, except such as are hereunder particularly named,   twelve.   **12**

The City of *Excester,*   two.   2

The Town of *Plymouth,*   two.   2

The Town of *Barnstaple,*   one.   1

The County of *Cornwall,* with the Burroughs, Towns, and Parishes therein,   eight.   8

The County of *Somerset* with the Burroughs, Townes and Parishes therein, except such as are hereunder named,   eight.   8

The City of *Bristoll,*   three.   3

The Towne of *Taunton-Deane,*   one.   1

The County of *Wilts,* with the Burroughs, Towns and Parishes therein (except *Salisbury*),   seven.   7

The City of *Salisbury,*   one.   1

The County of *Berks,* with the Burroughs, Towns and Parishes therein, except *Reading,*   five.   5

The Town of *Reading,*   one.   1

The County of *Surrey,* with the Burroughs, Towns, and Parishes therein, except *Southwarke,*   five.   5

The Burrough of *Southwarke,*   two.   2

The County of *Middlesex,* with the Burroughs, Towns, and Parishes therein, except such as are hereunder named,   four.   4

The City of *London,*   eight.   8

The City of *VVestminster,* and the *Dutchy,*   two.   2

The County of *Hartford,* with the Burroughs, Towns, and Parishes therein,   six.   6

The County of *Buckingham* with the Burroughs, Towns and Parishes therein,   six.   6

The County of *Oxon,* with the Burroughs, Towns, and Parishes therein (except such as are here under-named)   four.   4

The City of *Oxon,*   two.   2

The University of *Oxon,*   two.   2

The County of *Glocester,* with the Burroughs, towns and Parishes therein (except Glocester)   seven.   7

The City of *Glocester,*   two.   2

The County of *Hereford,* with the Burroughs, towns, and Parishes therin (except *Hereford*)   four.   4

The Citie of *Hereford,*   one.   1

The County of *Worcester,* with the Burroughs, towns, and Parishes therein (except *Worcester*)   foure.   4

The City of *Worcester,*   two.   2

The County of *Warwicke,* with the Burroughs, townes, and Parishes therein (except *Coventrey*)   five.   5

The City of *Coventrey,*   two.   2

The County of *Northampton,* with the Burroughs, towns and Parishes therein (except *Northampton*)   five.   5

The Town of *Northampton,*   one.   1

The County of *Bedford,* with the Burroughs, townes, and Parishes therein,   foure.   4

The County of *Cambridge,* with the Burroughs, towns, and Parishes therein (except such as are here under particularly named)   foure. } 4

The University of *Cambridge,*   two.] 2

The Town of *Cambridge,*   two.] 2

The County of *Essex,* with the Burroughs, towns, and Parishes therein (except *Colchester*)   eleven. } 11

The Town of *Colchester,*   two.] 2

The County of *Suffolk,* with the Burroughs, Towns, and Parishes therein (except such as are hereunder named)   ten. } 10

The Town of *Ipswich,*   two.] 2

The Town of *S. Edmonds Bury,*   one.] 1

The County of *Norfolk,* with the Burroughs, Towns, and Parishes therein (except such as are hereunder named)   nine. } 9

The City of *Norwich,*   three.] 3

The Town of *Lynne,*   one.] 1

The Town of *Yarmouth,*   one.] 1

The County of *Lincoln,* with the Burroughs, Towns, and Parishes therein (except the City of *Lincoln,* and the town of *Boston*)   eleven. } 11

The City of *Lincoln,*   one.] 1

The Town of *Boston,*   one.] 1

The County of *Rutland,* with the Burroughs, Townes, and Parishes therein,   one. } 1

The County of *Huntington,* with the Burroughs, Towns and Parishes therein,   three. } 3

The County of *Leicester,* with the Burroughs, Townes and Parishes therein (except *Leicester*)   five. } 5

The Town of *Leicester,*   one.] 1

The County of *Nottingham,* with the Burroughs, Towns and Parishes therein (except *Nottingham*)   foure. } 4

The Town of *Nottingham,*   one.] 1

The County of *Derby,* with the Burroughs, Townes, and Parishes therein (except *Derby*)   five. } 5

The Town of *Derby,*   one.] 1

The County of *Stafford,* with the City of *Lichfield,* the Burroughs, towne and Parishes therein,   six. } 6

The County of *Salop,* with the Burroughs, towns, and Parishes therein (except *Shrewsbury*)   six. } 6

The Town of *Shrewsbury,*   one.] 1

The County of *Chester,* with the Burroughs, townes, and Parishes therein (except *Chester*)   five. } 5

The City of *Chester,*   two.] 2

The County of *Lancaster,* with the Burroughs, townes, and Parishes therein (except *Manchester*)   six. } 6

The town of *Manchester,* and the Parish,   one.] 1

The County of *Yorke,* with the Burroughs, towns, and Parishes, therein, except such as are here under named,   fifteen. } 15

The City and County of the City of *Yorke,*   three.] 3

The Town and County of *Kingston* upon *Hull,*   one.] 1

The town and Parish of *Leeds*,	one.]	1
The County *Palatine* of *Duresme*, with the Burroughs, towns, and Parishes therein, except *Duresme* and *Gateside*,	three. }	3
The City of *Duresme*,	one.]	1
The County of *Northumberland*, with the Burroughs, towns and Parishes therein, except such as are here under named,	three. }	3
The Town and County of *Newcastle* upon *Tyne*, with *Gateside*,	two.]	2
The Town of *Berwicke*,	one.]	1
The County of *Cumberland*, with the Burroughs, towns, and Parishes therein,	three. }	3
The County of *Westmerland*, with the Burroughs, towns and Parishes therein,	two. }	2
The Isle of *Anglesey* (with the Parishes therein)	two.]	2
The County of *Brecknock*, with the Burroughs, towns, and Parishes therein,	three. }	3
The County of *Cardigan*, with the Burroughs and Parishes therein,	three. }	3
The County of *Caermarthen*, with the Burroughs and Parishes therein,	three. }	3
The County of *Carnarvon*, with the Burroughs and Parishes therein,	two.]	2
The County of *Denbigh*, with the Burroughs and Parishes therein	two.]	2
The County of *Flint*, with the Burroughs and Parishes therein,	one.]	1
The County of *Monmouth*, with the Burroughs and Parishes therein,	foure. }	4
The County of *Glamorgan*, with the Burroughs and Parishes therein,	foure. }	4
The County of *Merioneth*, with the Burroughs and Parishes therein,	two. }	2
The County of *Mountgomery*, with the Burroughs and Parishes therein,	three. }	3
The County of *Radnor*, with the Burroughs and Parishes therein,	two.]	2
The County of *Pembroke*, with the Burroughs, Towns and Parishes therein,	foure. }	4

Provided, That the first or second Representative may (if they see cause) assigne the remainder of the foure hundred Representors, (not hereby assigned) or so many of them as they shall see cause for, unto such Counties as shall appear in this present distribution to have lesse then their due proportion. Provided also, That where any Citie or Burrough to which one Representor or more is assign'd shall be found in a due proportion, not competent alone to elect a Representor, or the number of Representors assign'd thereto, it is left to future Representatives to assigne such a number of Parishes or Villages neare adjoyning to such City, or Burrough, to be joyned therewith in the Elections, as may make the same proportionable.

3. That the people do of course choose themselves a Repre-

sentative once in two yeares, and shall meet for that purpose upon
the first Thursday in every second May by eleven of Clock in
the morning, and the Representatives so chosen to meet upon the
second Thursday in June following at the usuall place in Westminster, or such other place as by the foregoing Representative,
or the Councell of State in the intervall, shall be from time to
time appointed and published to the People, at the least twenty
daies before the time of Election. And to continue their Session
there or elsewhere untill the second Thursday in December following, unlesse they shall adjourne, or dissolve themselves sooner,
but not to continue longer. The Election of the first Representative to be on the first Thursday in May, 1649. And that, and
all future Elections to be according to the rules prescribed for
the same purpose in this Agreement, viz.

1.   That the Electors in every Division, shall be Natives, or
Denizons of England, not persons receiving Almes, but such
as are assessed ordinarily, towards the reliefe of the poore; not
servants to, and receiving wages from any particular person.
And in all Elections, (except for the Universities,) they shall be
men of one and twenty yeares old, or upwards, and housekeepers, dwelling within the Devision for which the Election
is provided, That untill the end of seven yeares next ensuing
the time herein limited for the end of this present Parliament,
no person shall be admitted to, or have any hand or voice in
such Elections, who hath adhered unto, or assisted the *King*
against the *Parliament,* in any the late Warres, or Insurrections, or who shall make, or joyne in, or abet any forcible
opposition against this Agreement.

2.   That such persons and such only, may be elected to be of
the Representative, who by the rule aforesaid are to have voice
in Elections in one place or other; provided, That of those,
none shall be eligible for the first or second Representatives,
who have not voluntarily assisted the *Parliament* against the
King, either in person before the 14th. of *June* 1645. or else in
Money, Plate, Horse, or Armes, lent upon the Propositions before the end of *May* 1 6 4 3. or who have joyned in, or abetted
the treasonable Engagement in *London,* in the year 1 6 4 7.
or who declared or engaged themselves for a Cessation of
Armes with the *Scots,* that invaded this Nation, the last Summer, or for complyance with the Actors in any the insurrections, of the same Summer, or with the Prince of *Wales,* or his

accomplices in the Revolted Fleete. And also provided, That such persons as by the rules in the preceding Article are not capable of electing untill the end of seven years, shall not be capable to be elected untill the end of fourteen years, next ensuing. And we do desire and recommend it to all men, that in all times the persons to be chosen for this great trust, may be men of courage, fearing God, and hating covetousnesse, and that our Representatives would make the best Provisions for that end.

3.   That who ever, by the two rules in the next preceding Articles, are incapable of Election, or to be elected, shall assume to vote in, or be present at such Elections for the first or second Representative, or being elected shall presume to sit or vote in either of the said Representatives, shall incur the pain of confiscation of the moyety of his Estate, to the use of the publike, in case he have any Estate visible, to the value of fifty pounds. And if he have not such an Estate, then shall incur the pain of imprisonment, for three months; And if any person shall forcibly oppose, molest, or hinder the people, (capable of electing as aforesaid) in their quiet and free Election of Representors, for the first Representative, then each person so offending shall incur the penalty of confiscation of his whole Estate, both reall and personall; and (if he have not an Estate to the value of fifty pounds,) shall suffer imprisonment during one whole year without Bayle, or mainprize. Provided, That the Offender in each such case, be convicted within three Months next after the committing of his offence, And the first Representative is to make further provision for the avoyding of these evills in after Elections.

4.   That to the end, all Officers of State may be certainly accomptable, and no factions made to maintain corrupt interests, no Member of a Councel of State, nor any Officer of any salary forces in Army, or Garison, nor any Treasurer or Receiver of publique monies, shall (while such) be elected to be of a Representative. And in case any such Election shall be, the same to be void. And in case any Lawyer shall be chosen of any Representative, or Councel of State, then he shall be uncapable of practice as a Lawyer, during that trust.

5.   For the more convenient Election of Representatives, each County wherein more then three Representors are to be chosen, with the Townes Corporate and Cities, (if there be any) lying within the compasse thereof, to which no Representors are

herein assigned, shall be divided by a due proportion into so many, and such parts, as each part may elect two, and no part above three Representors; For the setting forth of which Divisions, and the ascertaining of other circumstances hereafter exprest, so as to make the Elections lesse subject to confusion, or mistake, in order to the next Representative, *Thomas* Lord *Grey* of *Grooby,* Sir *John Danvers,* Sir *Henry Holcraft,* Knights; *Moses Wall* Gentleman, *Samuel Moyer, John Langley, William Hawkins, Abraham Babington, Daniel Taylor, Mark Hilsley, Richard Price,* and Col. *John White,* Citizens of *London,* or any five, or more of them are intrusted to nominate and appoint under their Hands and Seales, three or more fit persons in each County, and in each Citie, and Borough, to which one Representor or more is assigned to be as Commissioners for the ends aforesaid, in the respective Counties, Cities, and Burroughs, and by like writing under their Hands and Seales shall certifie into the Parliament Records, before the fourteenth day of *February* next, the names of the Commissioners so appointed for the respective Counties, Cities, and Burroughs, which Comissioners or any three, or more of them, for the respective Counties, Cities, and Burroughs, shall before the end of *February* next, by writing under their Hands and Seales, appoint two fit and faithfull persons, or more in each Hundred, Lath, or Wapentake, within the respective Counties, and in each Ward, within the City of *London,* to take care for the orderly taking of all voluntary subscriptions to this Agreement by fit persons to be imploy'd for that purpose in every Perish who are to returne the subscriptions so taken to the persons that imployed them, (keeping a transcript thereof to themselves,) and those persons keeping like Transcripts to return the Originall subscriptions to the respective Commissioners, by whom they were appointed, at, or before the fourteenth of *Aprill* next, to be registred and kept in the County Records, for the said Counties respectively, and the subscriptions in the City of *London,* to be kept in the chief Court of Record for the said City. And the Commissioners for the other Cities and Borroughs respectively, are to appoint two or more fit persons in every Parish within their Precincts to take such subscriptions, and (keeping transcripts thereof) to return the Originalls to the respective Commissioners by the said fourteenth of *Aprill* next, to be registred and kept in the chief Court within the respective Cities and Burroughs. And the same Commis-

sioners, or any three, or more of them, for the severall Counties, Cities, and Boroughs, respectively, shall, where more then
three Representors are to be chosen, divide such Counties (as
also the City of *London*) into so many, and such parts as are
aforementioned, and shall set forth the bounds of such divisions, and shall in every County, City, and Borough (where any
Representors are to be chosen) and in every such division as
aforesaid within the City of *London,* and within the severall
Counties so divided, respectively, appoint one certaine place
wherein the people shall meet for the choise of their Representors, and some one fit Person or more inhabiting within
each Borough, City, County, or Division, respectively, to be
present at the time and place of Election, in the nature of
Sheriffes to regulate the Elections, and by Pole, or otherwise,
clearly to distinguish and judge thereof, and to make returne
of the Person or Persons Elected as is hereafter exprest, and
shall likewise in writing under their hands and Seales, make
Certificates of the severall Divisions (with the bounds thereof)
by them set forth, and of the certaine places of meeting, and
Persons, in the nature of Sheriffes appointed in them respectively as aforesaid,[1] and cause such Certificates to be returned
into the Parliament Records before the end of *April* next, and
before that time shall also cause the same to be published in
every Parish within the Counties, Cities, and Boroughs respectively, and shall in every such Parish likewise nominate and
appoint (by Warrant under their hands and Seals) one Trusty
person, or more, inhabiting therein, to make a true list of al
the Persons within their respective Parishes, who according to
the rules aforegoing are to have voyce in the Elections, and
expressing, who amongst them are by the same rules capable
of being Elected, and such List (with the said Warrant) to bring
in, and returne at the time and place of Election, unto the
Person appointed in the nature of Sheriffe, as aforesaid, for that
Borough, City, County, or Division respectively; which Person
so appointed as Sheriffe being present at the time and place of
Election; or in case of his absence by the space of one houre
after the time limited for the peoples meeting, then any Person
present that is eligible, as aforesaid, whom the people then and

[1] Memorandum, *That the Commissioners for the respective Counties, Cities,
and Boroughs, are to returne a Computation of the number of Subscribers in the
severall Parishes unto the Trustees herein named before the end of* April *next, at
such place, and in such forme as the said Trustees, or any five or more of them
shall direct.*

there assembled shall chuse for that end, shall receive and keep the said Lists, and admit the Persons therein contained, or so many of them as are present unto a free Vote in the said Election, and having first caused this Agreement to be publiquely read in the audience of the people, shall proceed unto, and regulate and keep peace and order in the Elections, and by Pole, or otherwise, openly distinguish and judge of the same: And thereof by Certificate, or writing under the hands and Seales of himself, and six or more of the Electors (nominating the Person or Persons duly Elected) shall make a true returne into the Parliament Records, within one and twenty dayes after the Election (under paine for default thereof, or for making any false Returne to forfeit one hundred pounds to the Publique use.) And shall also cause Indentures to be made, and interchangeably sealed and delivered betwixt himselfe, and six or more of the said Electors on the one part, and the Persons, or each Person Elected severally on the other part, expressing their Election of him as a Representor of them, according to this Agreement, and his acceptance of that trust, and his promise accordingly to performe the same with faithfulnesse, to the best of his understanding and ability, for the glory of God, and good of the people.

This course is to hold for the first Representative, which is to provide for the ascertaining of these Circumstances in order to future Representatives.

4. That one hundred and fifty Members at least be alwaies present in each sitting of the Representative, at the passing of any Law, or doing of any Act, whereby the people are to be bound; saving, That the number of sixty may make an House for Debates, or Resolutions that are preparatory thereunto.

5. That each Representative shall within twenty dayes after their first meeting appoint a Councell of State for the managing of Publique Affaires, untill the tenth day after the meeting of the next Representative, unlesse that next Representative thinke fit to put an end to that trust sooner. And the same Councell to Act, and proceed therein, according to such Instructions and limitations as the Representative shall give, and not otherwise.

6. That in each intervall betwixt Bienniall Representatives, the Councell of State (in case of imminent danger, or extreame necessity) may summon a Representative to be forthwith chosen, and to meet; so as the Session thereof continue not above fourescore dayes, and so as it dissolve, at least, fifty dayes before the

appointed time for the next Bienniall Representative, and upon the fiftyeth day so preceeding it shall dissolve of course, if not otherwise dissolved sooner.

7. That no Member of any Representative be made either Receiver, Treasurer, or other Officer, during that imployment, saving to be a Member of the Councell of State.

8. That the Representatives have, and shall be understood, to have, the Supreame trust in order to the preservation and Government of the whole, and that their power extend, without the consent or concurrence of any other Person or Persons, to the erecting and abolishing of Courts of Justice, and publique Offices, and to the enacting, altering, repealing, and declaring of Lawes, and the highest and finall Judgement, concerning all Naturall or Civill things, but not concerning things Spirituall or Evangelicall; Provided, that even in things Naturall and Civill these six particulars next following are, and shall be understood to be excepted, and reserved from our Representatives, *viz.*

1. We doe not impower them to imprest or constraine any Person to serve in Forraigne Warre either by Sea or Land, nor for any Millitary Service within the K I N G D O M E, save that they may take order for the the forming, training and exercising of the people in a Military way to be in readinesse for resisting of Forrain Invasions, suppressing of suddain Insurrections, or for assisting in execution of Law; and may take order for the imploying and conducting of them for those ends; provided, That even in such cases none be compellable to goe out of the County he lives in, if he procure another to serve in his roome.

2. That after the time herein limited for the commencement of the first Representative, none of the people may be at any time questioned for any thing said or done in relation to the late Warres, or publique differences, otherwise then in execution or pursuance of the determinations of the present House of Commons against such as have adhered to the King, or his interest against the people: And saving that Accomptants for publique monies received, shall remaine accomptable for the same.

3. That no securities given, or to be given by the Publique Faith of the Nation, nor any engagements of the Publique Faith for satisfaction of debts and dammages, shal be made void or invalid by the next, or any future Representatives; except to such Creditors, as have, or shall have justly forfeited

the same; and saving, That the next Representative may confirme or make null, in part, or in whole, all gifts of Lands, Monies, Offices, or otherwise, made by the present Parliament to any Member or Attendant of either House.

4.   That in any Lawes hereafter to be made, no person, by vertue of any tenure, grant, Charter, patent, degree or birth, shall be priviledged from subjection thereto, or from being bound thereby, as well as others.

5.   That the Representative may not give judgement upon any mans person or estate, where no Law hath before provided; save onely in calling to Account, and punishing publique Officers for abusing or failing their trust.

6.   That no Representative may in any wise render up, or give, or take away any the Foundations of common Right, Liberty and Safety contained in this Agreement; nor levell mens Estates, destroy Propriety, or make all things common : And that in all matters of such fundamentall concernment, there shall be a liberty to particular Members of the said Representatives to enter their dissents from the *major* vote.

   9. *Concerning Religion, we agree as followeth:*

1.   It is intended, That Christian Religion be held forth and recommended, as the publike Profession in this Nation (which wee desire may by the grace of God be reformed to the greatest purity in Doctrine, Worship and Discipline, according to the Word of God.) The instructing of the People whereunto in a publike way (so it be not compulsive) as also the maintaining of able Teachers for that end, and for the confutation or discovery of Heresie, Errour, and whatsoever is contrary to sound Doctrine, is alowed to be provided for by our Representatives; the maintenance of which Teachers may be out of a publike Treasury, and wee desire not by tithes. Provided, That Popery or Prelacy be not held forth as the publike way or profession in this Nation.

2.   That to the publique Profession so held forth none be compelled by penalties or otherwise, but onely may be endeavoured to be wonne by sound Doctrine, and the Example of a good Conversation.

3.   That such as professe Faith in God by Jesus Christ (however differing in judgement from the Doctrine, Worship or Discipline publikely held forth, as aforesaid) shall not be restrained from, but shall be protected in the profession of their Faith and exercise of Religion according to their Consciences in any

place (except such as shall be set apart for the publick Worship, where wee provide not for them, unlesse they have leave) so as they abuse not this liberty to the civil injury of others, or to actuall disturbance of the publique peace on their parts; neverthelesse it is not intended to bee hereby provided, That this liberty shall necessarily extend to Popery or Prelacy.

4.   That all Lawes, Ordinances, Statutes, and clauses in any Law, Statute, or Ordinance to the contrary of the liberty provided for in the two particulars next preceding concerning Religion be and are hereby repealed and made void.

10. It is agreed, That whosoever shall by Force of Armes, resist the Orders of the next or any future Representative (except in case where such Representative shall evidently render up, or give, or take away the Foundations of common Right, Liberty and Safety contain'd in this Agreement) shall forthwith after his or their such Resistance lose the benefit and protection of the Laws, and shall be punishable with Death, as an Enemy and Traitour to the Nation.

The form of subscription for the Officers of the Army.

Of the things exprest in this Agreement, The certain ending of this Parliament (as in the first Article) The equall or proportionable distribution of the number of the Representators to be elected (as in the second.) The certainty of the peoples meeting to elect for Representatives Bienniall, and their freedome in Elections with the certainty of meeting, sitting and ending of Representatives so elected (which are provided for in the third Article) as also the Qualifications of Persons to elect or be elected (as in the first and second particulars under the third Article) Also the certainty of a number for passing a Law or preparatory debates (provided for in the fourth Article) The matter of the fifth Article, concerning the Councel of State, and the sixth concerning the calling, sitting and ending of Representatives extraordinary; Also the power of Representatives, to be, as in the eighth Article, and limitted, as in the six reserves next foling the same; Likewise the second and third particulars under the ninth Article concerning Religion, and the whole matter of the tenth Article; (All these) we doe account and declare to be Fundamentall to our common Right, Liberty, and Safety; And therefore doe both agree thereunto, and re-

solve to maintain the same, as God shall enable us. The rest of the matters in this Agreement, wee account to be usefull and good for the Publike, and the particular circumstances of Numbers, Times and Places expressed in the severall Articles, we account not Fundamentall, but we finde them necessary to be here determined for the making the Agreement certain and practicable, and do hold those most convenient that are here set down, and therefore do positively agree thereunto.

A Declaration of the Generall Councell of Officers of the Army:

Concerning the Agreement by them framed in order to peace, and from them tendred to the People of England.

HAVING ever since the end of the first War longingly waited for some such settlement of the Peace and Government of this Nation, whereby the Common Rights, Liberties and safety thereof, might in future be more hopefully provided for, and therein something gained, which might be accounted to the present age and posterity (through the mercy of God) as a fruit of their labours, hazards and sufferings, that have engaged in the common cause, as some price of the bloud spilt, and ballance to the publique expence and damage sustained in the War, and as some due improvement of that successe, and blessing God hath pleased to give therein: And having not found any such Establishment assayed or endeavoured by those whose proper worke it was, but the many addresses and desires of ourselves, and others, in that behalfe, rejected, discountenanced and opposed, and onely a corrupt closure endeavoured with the King, on tearmes, serving onely to his interest, and theirs that promoted the same; And being thereupon (for the avoidance of the evil thereof, and to make way for some better settlement) necessitated to take extraordinary wayes of remedy (when the ordinary were denied;) Now to exhibit our utmost endeavors for such a settlement, whereupon we, and other Forces, (with which the Kingdome hath so long beene burthened above measure, and whose continuance shall not be necessary for the immediate safety and quiet thereof) may with comfort to our selves, and honesty towards the publique, disband, and returne to our homes and callings; and to the end mens jealousies and fears may be removed concerning any intentions in us to hold up our selves in power, to oppresse or domineer over the people by the sword; And that all men may fully understand those grounds of Peace and Government wherupon (they may rest assured) We shall for our parts acquiesce; We have spent much time to prepare, and have at last (through the blessing of

God) finished a Draught of such a settlement, in the nature of an Agreement of the People for Peace amongst themselves; Which we have lately presented to the Honourable the Commons now assembled in Parliament, and doe herewith tender to the people of this Nation.

We shal not otherwise commend it, then to say, It contains the best and most hopefull Foundations for the Peace, & future wel Government of this Nation, that we can devise or think on, within the line of humane power, and such, wherin all the people interested in this Land (that have not particular interests of advantage & power over others, divided from that which is common and publique) are indifferently and equally provided for, save where any have justly forfeited their share in that common interest by opposing it, and so rendred themselves incapable thereof (at least) for some time: And we call the Consciences of all that reade or hear it, to witnesse, whether wee have therein provided or propounded any thing of advantage to our selves in any capacity above others, or ought, but what is as good for one as for another: And therefore as we doubt not but that (the Parliament being now freed from the obstructing and perverting Councels of such Members, by many of whom a corrupt compliance with the Kings Interest hath beene driven on, and all settlement otherwise hath hitherto beene hindred) Those remaining worthy Patriots to whom we have presented the Agreement, will for the maine allow thereof, and give their seale of Approbation thereby; So we desire and hope, That all good People of *England* whose heart God shall make sensible of their, and our common concernment therein, and of the usefulnesse and sutablenesse thereof to the publique ends it holds forth, will cordially embrace it, and by subscription declare their concurrence, and accord thereto, when it shall be tendred to them, as is directed therein; wherein, if it please God wee shall finde a good Reception of it with the people of the Nation, or the Well-affected therein, We shall rejoyce at the hoped good to the Common-wealth, which (through Gods mercy) may redound therefrom, and that God hath vouchsafed thereby to make us instrumentall for any good settlement to this poor distracted Country, as he hath formerly made us for the avoiding of evill. But if God shall (in his Righteous Judgement towards this Land) suffer the people to be so blinded as not to see their own common good and freedome, endeavoured to be provided for therein, or any to be so deluded (to their own and the publique prejudice) as to make opposition thereto, whereby the effect of it be hindred, we have, yet, by the preparation and tender of it discharged our Consciences to God, and duty to our native Country in our utmost endeavours for a settlement, (to the best of our understandings) unto a just publique interest; And hope we shall be acquitted before God and good men, from the blame of any further troubles, distractions, or miseries to the Kingdom, which may arise through the neglect or rejection thereof, or opposition thereto.

Now whereas there are many good things in particular ters which our own Reasons & observations or the Petitions of others have suggested, and which we hold requisite to be provided for in their proper time and way (as the setting of moderate Fines upon such of the Kings party, as shal not be excepted for life, with a certain day for their coming in and submitting, and an Act of pardon to such as shall come in and submit accordingly, or have already compounded, The setling of a Revenue for all necessary publique uses, in such a way as the people may be most eased, The assigning and ascertayning of securities for Souldiers Arrears; and for publique Debts and Damages. The taking away of Tithes, and putting that maintenance which shall be thought competent for able Teachers to instruct the people, into some other way, lesse subject to scruple or contention, the clearing and perfecting of Accompts for all publique Monies, the relieving of prisoners for Debt; the removing or reforming of other evills or inconveniencies in the present Lawes, and Administrations thereof, the redresse of abuses, and supplying of Defects therein, the putting of all the Lawes and proceedings thereof into the English tongue, the reducing of the course of Law to more brevity and lesse charge, the setling of Courts of Justice and Record in each County or lesse Divisions of the Kingdome, and the erecting of Courts of Merchants for controversies in trading, and the like.) These and many other things of like sort being of a particular nature, and requiring very particular and mature consideration, with larger experience in the particular matters then we have, and much Caution, that by taking away of present Evills greater inconveniences may not ensue for want of other provisions in the room thereof, where it is necessary; and we (for our parts) being far from any Desire or thought to assume or exercise a Law-giving, or Judiciall power over the Kingdome, or to meddle in any thing save the fundamentall setling of that power in the most equall and hopefull way for Common Right, Freedom, and Safety (as in this Agreement) and having not meanes nor time for, nor the necessitie of some present generall settlement admitting the delay of, such a consideration, as seems requisite in relation to such numerous particulars, we have purposely declined the inserting of such things into this Agreement. But (as we have formerly expressed our desires that way, so) when the matters of publique Justice, and generall settlement are over, we shall not be wanting (if needfull) humbly to recommend such particulars to the Parliament, by whom they may more properly, safely, and satisfactorily be provided for, and we doubt not but they will be so, such of them, at least, as are of more neare and present concernment, by this Parliament, and the rest by future Representatives in due time.

And thus we recommend for present the businesse of this Agreement without further addition to the best consideration of all indifferent and equall minded men, and commit the issue thereof (as of all our wayes and concernments) to the good pleasure of the Lord, whose will is better to us then our own, or any inventions of ours, who hath decreed and promised better things then we can wish or imagine, and who is most faithfull to accomplish them in the best way and season.

By the appointment of the Generall Councell of Officers.
Iohn Rushworth Secretary.

FINIS.

THE HUNTING OF THE FOXES

[Richard Overton]

Appeared March 21, 1649. Reprinted from a photostat of one of the original pamphlets in New York Public Library.

Of the pamphlets describing Leveller disillusionment with Independent revolutionary aims, none is so sharply focussed, so brilliantly phrased, or so comprehensive as *The Hunting of the Foxes*. Though oversimplifying through his acute bias the crucial class antagonisms of the Civil War, and their resolution in the internal struggles of the New Model army, the author has traced an unforgettable outline of the historic conflict, voicing democratic implications still wrathfully championed and damned in the twentieth century.

In the army, according to *The Hunting,* the soldiers were the heroes of reformation, the officers, especially Cromwell and Ireton, the hypocritical villains, with the words *God* and *Christ* often on their lips, deceit and wile in their hearts. The private soldiers, not the officers, wrote the *Engagement* of June 5, organizing the army by mutual consent but against Cromwell's wishes, electing two officers and two soldiers from each regiment to represent them. But this concept of the General Council the officers resisted: "The title of *free Election* (the original of all just authorities) must give place to *prerogative patent* (the root of all exorbitant powers)." The soldiers wanted political grievances redressed, and a new constitutional settlement, whereas the officers were content to have arrears and indemnity. The officers were the lords of the army, "deriving their title from the will of their General, as the other [the Lords in Parliament] did theirs, from the will of the King." Gradually they rendered "the Agitatours but as ciphers amongst them, corrupting some with places, overruling and overawing others," later breaking their power with martial discipline, and disbanding twenty men from each troop to eliminate their sympathizers and supporters. All the time the chief officers, "Foxes in the habit of Saints," pretended great anxiety for the people's freedoms, and in 1648 won the Levellers' "acquiescence in them for a season" by their seeming strong support of the *Agreement*. Now, says the author, the chief officers are lords of the whole country, combining in their tyrannies the sins of the High Commission, the Star Chamber, and the negative voices of king and Lords. Forbidden even to petition, all soldiers must now "bow to the Lordships," and forget their rights as free Commoners of England. As Christ to Belial, and light to darkness, so are the soldiers to the officers.

In such violent, intemperate phrasing did Overton set forth his analysis, unmindful of the stern authoritarian necessities of war, incapable of visualizing Cromwell's attempt to reconcile conflicting interests. To Overton the issue was simple: Possessing the power to impose on the land a constitutional settlement on Leveller terms, the army had failed to do this only because the officers had been hostile to the political aspirations of the rank and file. None of the Levellers attempted, however, to compute the proportion of their followers even among the common soldiers. It is highly doubtful that they were more than a large vocal minority, capturing the leadership of the men by their zeal, conviction, and indefatigable energy. The Levellers often assured Cromwell that if he were to carry through their program, they could gain for him large mass support. In this assertion they were not overestimating their persuasiveness, but even support from large masses of the lower middle class would not have compensated for the defection of the propertied interests, both Independent and Presbyterian. Even under Leveller auspices, the revolution would have been maintained, for years, at least, only by the power of the sword. This was a fact that Cromwell knew well enough, but the Levellers were unwilling to face.

The suspicion of the General Council that the letter to Fairfax (pp. 372-73), which brought about the degradation of the five men (*Introduction*, p. 98), was not written by them was well founded. None of the men claimed, indeed, that he had written the letter. In my opinion both the letter and *The Hunting* itself were written by Richard Overton. The satirical thrusts, the bold comparisons, the mature and sophisticated democratic theorizing, the

sharp, clear phrasing, the large proportion of biting, stinging epi-
thets, the paragraph arrangement—all are typical of Overton and
of no other Leveller leader in the same degree or combination.
The only other possible Leveller author was John Wildman, who
by this time was an apostate to the cause. Wildman's style, however, differs in marked degree from Overton's. His sentences are
less flexible, his comparisons less imaginative and less frequent,
his satire less brilliant and forceful.

The Hunting of the Foxes

FROM

NEW-MARKET and TRIPLOE-Heaths

TO

WHITE·HALL,

By five fmall Beagles (late of the Armie.)

OR THE

GRANDIE-DECEIVERS Unmasked

(that you may know them.)

Directed to all the Free-Commons of *England*, but in efpeciall, to all that have, and are ftill engaged in the Military Service of the COMMON-WEALTH.

By *Robert Ward*, *Thomas Watfon*, *Simon Graunt*, *George Jellis*, and *William Sawyer*, late Members of the Army.

Printed in a Corner of Freedome, right oppofite to the Councel of Warre, *Anno Domini*, 1649.

The Hunting of the Foxes, &c.

WHen we remember our *solemn Engagement* at New-market and Triploe-Heaths, and but therewith consider and compare the strange actings that have been, and still are carried on in the name of the Army (as if upon the ac-compt of that Engagement) we are even startled at the palpable contrariety and disparity that appeareth betwixt them; for the difference is as great and as wide, as betwixt bondage and free-dom: So that it hath put us upon consideration to finde out and discover, where the fault lurketh; and upon serious thoughts, wee cannot impute the declinings of the first Principles of the Army, to the Army it self, but rather to some Persons of private and dan-gerous interests, usurping and surprising the name of the Army; like as it was said of the 11 impeached Members, concerning the Name and Authority of Parliament, imprinting the face and stampe of that Authority upon their prodigious designs, to the great abuse of the Parliament, as this must needs be of the Army. These, as too many such there be, are *Foxes of the deepest kinde,* more deceitfull and pernitious than their predecessours; and that such there are, wofull experience puts it out of question : and who they are the print of their footsteps is so evident, that you may trace them from step to step, from hole to hole to their *Master Den,* where you may finde the whole *litter* of *Foxes* in *conspiracy,* and you may know them by their shapes. Thus then to their footsteps.

When in the times of *Stapleton* & *Hollis,* the then faction was aspired to that height of tyranny and insolency, as to overtop the authority and native freedom of the People, threatning generall vassalage to the whole Nation, then the private souldiery (to inter-pose betwixt the people and their destroiers) drew themselves into that solemn *Engagement* of *June* 5. 1647. in the attempting and transaction of which they found no small opposition (as may well be remembred) amongst the Officers; and at that time *Crom-well* highly dissented, notwithstanding the earnest solicitation and importunity of many friends, til he was forced for fear of impris-onment, to fly to the then engaging souldiery (the day after the first *Rendezvous*) for refuge, and then *Cromwell* and *Ireton,* when they saw no other way to preserve themselves and their interest, engaged in the subversion of that domineering, tyrannical faction, and assuming high offices to themselves, acting as generall Officers, without the election of the soldiery, or Commission from the Parliament, being out by the self-denying Ordinance, and the General having no power to make generall Officers.

And being thus seated, even before they were well warmed in their places, they begin to stomack the sitting of the private souldiers in Councel with them; although it is wel known, that the actions of the Army, moving *as an Army,* in relation to that Engagement, was, first to be concluded of by a Councell, to consist of those generall Officers (who concurred with the Army in their then just undertakings) with two Commission Officers and two soldiers to be chosen for each Regiment; but a Councell thus modelled, was not sutable to their wonted greatnes and ambition, it was somewhat of scorn to them, that a private soldier (though the Representour of a Regiment) should sit cheek by joll with them, and have with an Officer an equall vote in that Councel: This was a thing savoured too much of the peoples authority and power, and therefore inconsistent with the transaction of their lordly Interest; the title of *free Election* (the original of all just authorities) must give place to *prerogative patent* (the root of all exorbitant powers) that Councel must change the derivation of its session, and being from Agreement and election of the souldiery to the patent of the Officers, and none to sit there but commission Officers, like so many patentee Lords in the high Court of Parliament, deriving their title from the will of their General, as the other did theirs, from the will of the King: so that the difference was no other, but in the chang of *names:* Here was (when at this perfection) as absolute a *Monarchy,* and as absolute a *Prerogative Court* over the Army, as *Commoners,* as ever there was over the Common-wealth, and accordingly this Councel was overswarmed with Colonels, Lieut. Colonels, Majors, Captains, &c. contrary to and beyond the tenour of the Engagement.

Hence followed secret murmurings & *whisperings* amongst the *Prerogative Officers* against the session and power of the *Agitators,* and at length palpable endeavors broke forth to suppress them:& so soon as the *Officers* had *wound up* themselvs to a *faction,* sufficient to overtop them, and finding the *privity* of the *Agitators* in their *Councels* was an *impediment* to their *evil interest* and *ambition,* then it was openly given out, *That they stood as souldiers,*

only to serve the State, and might not as free Commons insist upon
their liberty; and that the ground of their refusing to disband,
was, only the want of Arrears and Indempnity; which, how contrary to their *Engagement, Declarations, Representations,* &c.
Hear, O heavens, and judge, O earth! for doth not their *Declara-*
tion of *Jun.* 14. 1647. in *their persons* thus speak.[1]

"We shall before disbanding proceed in our own and the
"*Kingdoms* behalf, *&c.* especially considering, that we were not a
"*Mercinary Army,* hired to serve any *Arbitrary power* of *a state,*
"but *called forth* and *conjured* by the *several Declarations of Par-*
"*liament* to the defence of our own,& the peoples *just Rights* &
"*Liberties.* And if of our own, then not to destroy our *right of*
Petitioning, for that is in the *number* of our own, and so formerly owned by themselves. And further some few lines after
they thus proceed.

"The said Declaration stil directing us to the equitable sense
"of all Laws and Constitutions, as dispensing with the very letter
"of the same, and being supream to it, when the safety and preser-
"vation of all is concerned, and assured us, That all Authority is
"fundamentally seated in the Office, and but ministerially in the
"Persons: And then to confirm and justifie their motion, as Commoners in behalf of the People, they cite the Presidents of *Scotland,*
Netherlands, Portugall, and others; adding this, "That accord-
"ingly the Parliament hath declared it no resisting of Magistracy,
"to side with the just principles and law of Nature and Nations,
"being that Law, upon which we have assisted you; and that
"the souldiers may lawfully hold the hands of the Generall (and
if of the Generall then of *Cromwell, Ireton* and *Harrison*) who
"will turn his Cannon against the Army, on purpose to destroy
"them; the Sea-man the hands of that Pilot who wilfully runs the
"ship upon a rock, as our brethren of *Scotland* argued, and such
"were the proceedings of our Ancestours of famous memory, *&c.*

Here out of their owne mouths it is confest, That the souldiery
are not, nor ought to be mercinary; and that the General (and so
consequently all the Officers) may be opposed by the souldiery in
case of an immanent destruction to them; and how absolutely destructive it is to them, to be deprived of their right as Commoners,
and not suffered upon pain of death or cashierment to petition the
Parliament, but to be rendred meerly mercinary to the lusts and
ambitions of two or three persons, to serve their pernicious ends,
let the world judge: This is a case so plain, so obvious and evi-

[1] *Book Decl.* f. 39.

dent, as none can deny, but that it is a palpable subversion of the Right of the Souldiery; and therfore in such a case they are bound to oppose their Officers, and it is no resisting of the General, nor of the Officers, no more than it is a resisting Magistracy, to side with the just Principles and law of Nature and Nations, as themselves have owned and confest, and if they will not stand to it, they must be kept to it.

And besides, if the equity of the Law be superiour (as they say) to the letter, and if the letter should controll and overthrow the equity, it is to be control'd and overthrown it self, and the equity to be preserved, then the rule of the same reason doth tell them, that the Officer is but the form or letter of the Army; and therefore inferiour to the equitable or essentiall part, *the Souldiery*, and to be controlled and overthrown themselves, when they controll and overthrow the Souldiery in the essentials of their being, life, liberty and freedom, as the souldiery are, when by the Officers rendred meerly mercinary, and denied their right of addresse by way of Petition to the Parliament, for to be tortur'd, enslav'd and opprest, and not suffer'd to complain, but tormented and abused for complaining (although to the Parliament, the undoubted right of an *English-man*) is the highest cruelty, villany and slavery can be imagined, even *Tyranny at the height*, and therfore to be opposed by the Souldiery.

And thus, and upon these fundamentals of Nature and Reason the *Netherlands* made their resistance against the King of *Spain*. Thus rose the *Scots* up in arms, and entered this Kingdom, immediately before this Parliament, without all formal countenance or allowance of King or Parliament, since owned and justified by this Parliament. Thus this Parliament took up arms against the King: and thus the Parliament of *France* now taketh up armes: yea thus this Army enter'd upon their *solemn Engagement against the oppressing party at Westminster*. And thus may the souldiery renue and revive the same, and even oppose, contradict, dispute and overrule the *commands* of their Officers themselvs to the contrary, and be equally justifiable with the foregoing presidents. But to return to the matter in hand.

When *Cromwell* and *Ireton*, and their faction of self interested Officers thought they had got the souldiery fast by the brain, as to dote sufficiently upon their transaction and conduct of busines, they then decline the Agitators, decline the *Engagement*, sleight their *Declarations* and *Promises* to the people and Army, rendring the Agitatours but as ciphers amongst them, corrupting some with places, overruling and overawing others, and so bringing the transactions of the Army in order to their *solemn Engagement,* only to themselves, under the impression and name of his *Excellency, and his Councel of War,* & so by degrees, step after step they cast out the interest of the souldiery from amongst them, destroied the *Engagement,* and *broke the faith of the Army.*

So that the honest souldiery not seeing any redresse, the rights and freedoms of the Nation not cleared or secured, no indempnity or security for arrears, or provision for present pay, no determinate period of time set, when the Parliament should certainly end, no publike vindication of the Army from that most horrid Declaration against the souldiery for petitioning, nor of suppressing and burning Petitions, abusing and imprisoning petitioners, &c.

These things the souldiery beholding and observing, endeavored to restore their *Agents* to a competent power and ability, to make good the faith of the Army to the people, but then they found the hottest opposition from *Cromwell* and *Ireton* with his faction of Officers, as who ever cals but to mind the busines of *Ware,* when Col. *Eyer* was imprisoned, and M. *Arnold* a private souldier was shot to death for promoting and assisting the work of the souldiery in reference to the *solemn Engagement of the Army,* may know.

And then it may be remembred how insolent & furious *Cromwell* deported himself against the honest observers of *the faith of the Army,* it being then made death to observe the *Engagement,* or but speak for the *Agitators*: O let that day never be forgotten! let not the bloud of that innocent *person* be here had out of remembrance, till justice be had for the same; neither let our Engagement or the perfidious perjured subverters thereof be forgotten; for here the Engagement was utterly cast aside, and the *Adjutators* laid by, and after that no more *Agitators* would be permitted, but the sentence of death, imprisonment, and cashierments for all that endeavored the reviving thereof was denounced: here the right of the soldiery was clearly destroied, and the Gen. Officers became lords of the name of the Army, assuming the same to themselves, and fitting the impression thereof upon all their future actings, to the abuse and surprisall of the Army; although in deed and in truth no transacting since by *Cromwell, Ireton,* and their Officers, though in the name of the Gen. Councel of the Army, wil be accounted or imputed to the act of the Army, for it is no Gen. Councel, neither doth it represent the Army, neither hath it the Authority or Commission of the Army therin; for it is another Councel, differing from that of the *Engagement* of the Army, that was by *election*, this is *by force* and *obtrusion*, in that the soldiery were represented, in this only the Officers, that is to consist of those Gen. Officers concurring with the Engagement, two Com. Officers, and two soldiers chosen out of every Regiment, this is only a Councel of war, whose power doth extend to no transaction in the name of the Army, as Commoners, but only to matters of war, as souldiers : therefore their propositions and tamperings with the King, their march up to *London*, their violent secluding of so many members from Parl. their *triall* and *execution* of the *King*, of D. *Hamilton, Holland,* and stout *Capel,* their erection of the *high Court,* of the *Counsel of State,* and their *raigning in,* & *overruling the House,* their *stopping the Presses,* committing *violent outrages* and *cruelties* therupon, their *usurpation* of the *civil Authority,* &c. are not to be esteemed as actions of the Army, they are not to be set upon the score of the soldiery, for the soldiery hath no mouth in their Councels, neither have they therin to do.

Thus it may well be conceived, that their clothing themselves with the glorious Garments of that *Engagement,* with their manifold Declarations, Remonstrances, &c. was but in order to what time hath since made manifest, to heave out *Stapleton* and that faction, to grasp the sole dominion into their own hands: for by their fair speeches and fawning dissimulations, they courted the Souldiery and honest party of the Common-wealth into a strong delusion, even to believe their lyes, their enchantments, and sorceries: Never were such Saints, such curious Angels of light; *Pharaohs* Egyptian Sorcerers were short of these in their Art. And when by that means they had compassed their ends against *Hollis* and his, they were so far from insisting upon the premises of their former promises and vows, that they resolve upon an *Hocas Pocas* trick with the *King,* and so set upon the work (to make him a Pandor to their dominion and power, to make him a skreen betwixt them and the people) and they drive it to a bargain, *Cromwel* to be made Earl of *Essex,* and that (beside his *George* and blew Ribband) to be a *Knight* of the *Garter,* his own son to be Bed chamber-man to the Prince, and his Son in law *Ireton,* either Lord Deputy of *Ireland,* or at least Field Marshal General of *Ireland,* and his own Son (that commanded the Gen. Life Guard) said that the *King* had cast himself upon his father and brother *Ireton,* to make his terms for him, and restore him again : [2] And to that end, they frame expedients sutable to his *Prerogative Principles,* cunningly interweaving the same in their business called the *Proposals for the setling a just and lasting Peace* (as they called it) in the heads whereof were couched the several foundations of Regal Tyranny, *seating the whole power and authority of this Nation, fundamentally in the Kings will, making the same supreme, or a law paramount, to all the determinations of Parliament :* This is the unanimous voice of the 1, 2, and 3. particulars, under the first general Proposal, and the last is a seal to them all. But this expedient failing them, as to their exorbitant intents, they cast off those robes of *Royalty* with which they had rendred themselves acceptable with the *King's* adherents, and laid aside the *King* and them, finding the way of *an Agreement of the People* to be much affected and endeavoured after among the Souldiery, they also invest themselves with that *Robe,* to hide their deformity from the Army; and the better to allay all motions after the same, they confess and acknowledge the excellency and goodness of the premisses, they only find the same unseasonable; and this was drest out in such taking Saint-like language, as the religious people might best be surprised, not suspecting any venemous thing to be lurking under the leaf of their holy and sacred pretences: they call Fasts (a certain fore-runner of mischief with them) cry, and howl, and bedew their cheeks with the tears of hypocrsie and deceit, confess their iniquity and abomination in declining the cause of the people, and tampering with the King; and humbly, as in the presence of the all-seeing God, acknowledge the way of *an Agreement of the People,* to be the way to our Peace and Freedom; and even then, as soon as they had wiped their eys and their mouths, they proceed even to death, imprisonment or cashierment of all such in the Army as promoted or owned that Agreement; and to fan and cull all such Asserters of the Peoples Freedoms out of the Army, they proceed to disband 20. out of a Troup; by which the honest party of the Souldiery was very much weakned, and all the promoters of Freedom discouraged, and the people struck into desperation; which gave rise unto the second war amongst our selves, and invasion of the Scots: But the same by the great blessing of God being over, they finding the old affection of the Souldiers not yet quenched or much cooled, and great motions in the several Regiments after the Freedom of the Nation; they then

[2] This was delivered by Lieut. Col. Iohn Lilburn, and offered by him to be made good upon his life, at the Bar of House of Commons.

formalize again, and to keep the honest party in suspense, and to wait upon their motions, and to cease from their own; and the better to make way to the ambitious intents of those Grandees, they then as a cloke, take up the way of an Agreement again, to present themselves amiable unto us; and a great pudder they make in their Councel about an Agreement, and one they brought forth, but such an one as was most abhorred by such as most fought after the way of an Agreement; so inconsistant it was with the true foundations of equal Freedom and Right; but by this means they so far prevailed over the most constant and faithful friends to the People, as to beget an acquiescence in them for a season, till they in the mean time so far effected their business, as to the introduction of an absolute platform of Tyranie, long since hatched by *Ireton*; for it was he who first offered that expedient of Government by way of a Councel of State, which was soon after the Armies engagement neer New-market-heath, and which ever since he hath kept in the vail, but now the vail is taken away, and it is now presented to the view of all men; But no sooner was this Monster born into the world, but it devours up half of the Parliament of England, and now it is about adorning it self with all Regal magnificence, and majesty of Courtly attendance, &c. and like the 30. Tyrants of *Athens,* to head it self over the people: This is, and yet this is not our new intended King, there is a king to succeed, this is but his Vice-roy: O *Cromwel! whither art thou aspiring?* The word is already given out amongst their officers, *That this Nation must have one prime Magistrate or Ruler over them; and that the General hath power to make a law to bind all the Commons of England :* This was most daringly and desperately avowed at *White-hall*; and to this temper these Court-Officers are now a moulding, he that runs may read and fore-see the intent, a *New Regality !* And thus by their *Machiavilian* pretenses, and wicked practises, they are become masters and usurpers of the name of the Army, and of the name of the Parliament; under which Visors they have levell'd and destroyed all the Authority of this Nation: For the Parliament indeed and in truth is no Parliament, but a Representative Class of the Councel of War; and the Councel of War but the Representative of *Cromwel, Ireton,* and *Harrison*; and these are the all in all of this Nation, which under these guises and names of Parliament, Army, General Councel, High Court, and Councel of State, play all the strange pranks that are play'd.

Deer Countreymen and fellow-souldiers, you that by your adventerous hazards and bloud have purchased a precedency in your Native and just Rights; Consider and weigh these things in your hearts, for surely none are more deeply concerned than your selves, none are more highly infringed of their Rights than you; You are not so much as suffered (how oppress'd or abus'd your selves, how sensible of the miseries of the publike soever) to represent your desires or apprehensions to the Parliament; while you are souldiers, you (in their account) are no Free-men, neither have an equal right in the Common-wealth with other of your fellow-members therein. The General now tells us, *if we will petition, we must lay down our swords;* these were his own words unto us. It seems he hath forgot the contest of the Army (in which he concurred) with *Stapleton* and *Hollis* about their right of Petitioning as Souldiers; Why then (if this must be their received maxime) did he and the General Councel (as by usurpation they call it) present their petition, since we presented ours, and not lay down their swords and their high places, and petition as private Commoners? We are confident it would be an happy day for England, would they but practise that doctrine they preach unto others; But alas deer friends, it is but in this case with them as in all others, they condemned *Stapleton* and *Hollis,* because they were not the *Stapletons* and *Hollis's* themselves; they condemned privat correspondencies with the King, because they were not the corresponders themselves; they condemned the force offered to the Parliament by the tumult of Apprentices, &c. because they were not the forcers themselves; they condemned that monstrous declaration of the Parliament against the Souldiers petitioning; they condemned the imprisoning petitioners, and burning petitions, because they were not the Declarers, Imprisoners, and Burners themselves: As who, that doth but consider their waies, may not plainly discern.

But to trace the foot-steps of those Foxes yet a little further, we shall discover their dealings with us. When they heard that the Soldiers were about a petition in behalf of themselves and the people for whom they had engaged, they thereat were highly offended and enraged, and desperate motions upon it were made in their Conventicle (by themselves stiled the General Councel) some moved for an Act of Parliament, that they might have power to try, judge, condemn, and punish all such, whether of the Army or not of the Army, as should disturb them (as they now call it) by petition to the Parl. or otherwise; and upon the modest reply of one, who desired that the execution of civil affairs might be left to the Magistrate, Col. *Huson* answered, *we have had tryal enough of Civil Courts, we can hang* 20. *before they will hang one*; and in the Lobby at the Parl. dore, the said *Huson* breathing out bitter invectives against us Petitioners, who then were waiting at the dore for an answer to our petition, said thus openly, *O that any of them* (speaking of the Petitioners) *durst come into my Regiment, they should never go out; we shall never be quiet till some of them be cut off for examples, and then the rest will be quash'd; there are* 10. *about this Town that better deserve to be hanged, than those Lords that are at their Tryal before the high Court.* And now the Colonels, Lieut. Col. Maj. Capt. of this Gen. Councel, are now moulding up to that sweet temper, insomuch that about *March* 6. they concluded on the Act, it must now be death to petition, or for any Country-man to talk to us concerning ours and their Freedom : This enforceth us to put you in remembrance of their former words, for out of their own mouths they are judged.

In the Book of the Armics Declaration, *pag.* 17. we humbly represent in their and our behalfs, as followeth: 1. *That whereas it pleased the Honourable Houses of Parliament, having received information of a dangerous Petition in the Army, to declare and immediately to publish in print to the Kingdom, that that Petition did tend to put the Army in distemper and mutiny, to obstruct the relief of Ireland, and put conditions on the Parliament: And declaring the Petitioners if they shall continue in the promoting and advancing that Petition, shall be lookt upon, and proceeded against, as enemies to the State, and disturbers to the publick Peace.*

We cannot chuse, but with sadnesse of Spirit be deeply sensible that so humble and innocent Addresse could beget so strange an Interpretation.

Yet now *Stapleton* and *Hollis* being removed, are not they in the same steps? do not they call the Humble and Innocent Addresses of the Souldiers to the Parliament, Disturbance to their proceedings, and to the Publick Peace? And do not they seek for worse than a Declaration, an Act of Parliament, to put to death for Petitioning? And even as *Stapleton* and *Hollis* would have divided and broken the Army, under the pretence of relief for Ireland, do not these men now do the like? it was formerly opposed and condemned by them, it is now their own expedient.

In the particular charge against the 11. Members, *pag.* 83. *Article* 5. That the said M. *Hollis*, Sr *Philip Stapleton*, and M.

Glyn, have been and are obstructers and prejudices of several Petitioners to the Parliament, for redresse of publick grievances: And the said Mr *Hollis,* and Sr *Philip Stapleton,* in the moneth of *May,* last past, did abuse and affront divers Petitions, offering to draw their swords upon Major *Tuleday,* and others of the said Petitioners, causing *Nicholas Tew* to be imprisoned in Newgate, and to be detained a long time there, for no other cause, but for having a Petition about him, which was to be presented to the House: O how carefull were they then, of the freedom of the People to Petition!

In the eighth Article, *fol.* 85. *Hollis* is charged with procuring of the foresaid Declaration against the Souldiers petitioning, as a thing to the great dishonour of the Parliament, to the insufferable injury, the just provocations, discouragement, and discontent of the Army, &c.

O *Crumwell,* O *Ireton,* how hath a little time and successe changed the honest shape of so many Officers! who then would have thought the Councel would have moved for an act to put men to death for Petitioning? who would have thought to have seen Souldiers (by their Order) to ride with their faces towards their Horse tailes, to have their Swords broken over their Heads, and to be casheered, and that for Petitioning, and claiming their just right and title to the same? Such dealing as this was accounted in their Representation of *Iune* the 4. and 5. 1647. to be against the right both of a Souldier and a Subject. And in *pag.* 33. it thus saith, *And if our liberty of Petitioning for our due be denyed us, and be rendred such a crime (as by the said Order and Declaration.) we cannot but look for the same, or worse, hereafter, not only to our selves, but to all the free-born People of the Land in the like case.* And so this President (if it stand good) would extend in the consequence of it, to render all Souldiers under this Parliament the worst of slaves, and all Subjects little better. And though there hath been of late in other mens cases, too many dangerous presidents of suppressing Petitions, and punishing or censuring the Petitioners, &c.

Then they could say, (*pag.* 35.) *Let every honest English man lay his hand on his heart, weigh our case, and make it his own,* (as in consequence it is) *and then judge for us and himself.* But if we now lay our hands on our hearts, and weigh their present case, what may we say for them or our selves? we may forbear pronouncing the sentence they have said for themselves and us.

In the Declaration, *Iune* 14. 1647. *fol.* 44. *We desire, that the*

*right and freedom of the People, to represent to the Parliament by
way of Petition, their grievances may be cleared and vindicated.*

In the Remonstrance, *Iune* 23. 1647. *fol.* 58. They account
the suppressing of Petitioning in the Army, an infringement of
the Rights and Liberties, both of Souldiers and Subjects. And
(*fol.* 60. of the same Declaration,) *a putting the faithfull servants
of the Parliament and Kingdom out of the protection of the Law.*
Divers other passages of moment out of their own Declarations,
Remonstrances, &c. might be cited: but here is sufficient to condemne their violence against, and justifie the Souldiery in Petitioning.

Was there ever a generation of men so Apostate so false and
so perjur'd as these? did ever men pretend an higher degree of
Holinesse, Religion, and Zeal to God and their Country than
these? these preach, these fast, these pray, these have nothing
more frequent then the sentences of sacred Scripture, the Name
of God and of Christ in their mouthes: You shall scarce speak to
Crumwell about any thing, but he will lay his hand on his breast,
elevate his eyes, and call God to record, he will weep, howl and
repent, even while he doth smite you under the first rib. Captain
Ioyce and Captain *Vernam* can tell you sufficient stories to that
purpose.

Thus it is evident to the whole World, that the now present
interest of the Officers is directly contrary to the interest of the
Souldiery: there is no more difference betwixt them, than betwixt
Christ and Belial, light and darknesse: if you will uphold the interest of the one, the other must down; and as well you may let
them bore holes through your ears, and be their slaves for ever,
for your better distinction from free men: for what are you now?
your mouths are stopped, you may be abused and enslaved, but
you may not complain, you may not Petition for redresse; they are
your Lords, and you are their conquered vassals, and this is the
state you are in : If a Souldier commit but a seeming fault, especially if by their tentred far fetcht consequences they can make
it but reflect on their prerogative greatnesse : Oh to what an
height that crime as they call it, is advanced? what aggravations
and load is laid upon it? and if there be never an Article in their
out-landish Mercinary Articles of Warre, that will touch them; yet
they find one in their discretionary conclave, that will doe the
businesse, for there must be no standing against the Officers; they
must be impeached only by their Peers, the Souldier must not say
Black is their eye; if they say the Crow is white, so must the Soul-

dier; he must not lisp a sillable against their treacheries and abuses of the State, their false Musters, and cheating the Souldiery of their pay, though it be their constant and familiar practise: that Souldier that is so presumptuous as to dare to Article against an Officer, must be casheered: Quartermaster *Harby* was but the other day casheered, but for delivering in a Charge of Delinquency against Lieut. Col. *Ashfield,* for his perfideous confederacy with treacherous *Lilburn,* that betrayed *Tinmouth* Castle: and dayly honest men are casheered for complaining against their Officers: no interest must now stand in the Army, that is against the interest of the Officers, we must all bow to their Lordships, and lay down our necks under their feet, and count it our honour that they will but be pleased to tread upon us, but like worms we must not turn again, upon pain of death, or casheerment. This makes us call to mind the saying of *Ireton* to honest Major *Cobbett* of Snow hill, who for joyning with the Agents of the Army asked him, *if he were not deluded in his understanding in joyning with the giddy headed Souldiers:* and advised him *not to run against the interest of himselfe and the Officers.* And now we have plainly found what that interest was, it was long a forging, but is now brought forth: but like a Viper, we hope it will gnaw out their own bowels.

But now dear friends, that you may see that their Conclave of Officers at White Hall hath suckt into it the venome of all former corrupt Courts, and interests that were before them, we shall shew you how the Court of the High Commission, the Star chamber, the House of Lords, the King and his Privy Councel are all alive in that Court, called the General Councel of the Army.

First if you do but remember, the King to his death stood upon this principle, That he was accomptable to none but God; that he was above the Parliament, and above the People. And now to whom will these be accomptable? to none on Earth. And are they not above the Parliament? they have even a Negative voice thereover: Formerly the Commons could passe nothing without the concurrence of the Lords, now they dare passe nothing without the concurrence of the Conclave of Officers: we were before ruled by King, Lords, and Commons; now by a General, a Court Martial, and House of Commons: and we pray you what is the difference? the Lords were not Members both of the House of Lords, and of the House of Commons, but those are Members both in the House of Officers, (the Martial Lords,) and in the House of Commons. The old Kings person, and the old Lords, are but removed, and a new King and new Lords, with the Commons, are in one House; and so under a more absolute arbitrary Monarchy than before. We have not the change of a Kingdom to a Common wealth; we are onely under the old cheat, the transmutation of Names, but with the addition of New Tyrannies to the old: for the casting out of one unclean Spirit they have brought with them in his stead seven other unclean Spirits, more wicked than the former, and they have entered in, and dwell there; and the last state of this Common wealth, is worse than the first.

Now as for their High Commission and Star-chamber practises, if you will be pleased to view over an Epitomy of our several Examinations before them; you may have a perfect Embleme of those Courts before your eyes; and to that end (and not out of any vain-glorious folly,) we have subjoyned an Abstract of their Interrogatives, with our Answers; together with their Sentence they passed upon us. But first we desire you to take notice, that the matter which they made the occasion of advantage to proceed against us, was a Paper which we delivered to the General, a Copy whereof (lest you should not have seen it) we herewith present you: and then we shall proceed to our Examinations.

To his Excellency *Tho*. Lord *Fairfax*, and his Councel of Officers.

May it please your Excellencie, and your Councel of Officers,

WE have lately made our humble addresse unto the peoples Representors in Parliament, concerning some relief to our selves and the Commonwealth, by way of Petition, the meanest and lowest degree of an English mans Freedome that we know of, and yet the same (to our astonishment) hath much distasted and imbittered divers of our Superiour Officers (in this Councel convening) against us, as we perceive, and that even unto death.

We therefore being willing to avoid all occasion of offence and division, and to cleare our selves from all imputations thereof, that in Justice and Reason may be conceived against us, desire, that you would be pleased to consider, that we are English Souldiers, engaged for the Freedoms of *England*; and not outlandish mercenaries, to butcher the people for pay, to serve the pernitious ends of ambition and will in any person under Heaven. That we do not imagine our selves absolved from the solemn Engagement at *Newmarket* Heath, but to be still obliged before God and the whole world to pursue the just ends of the same; and you may remember your many promises and Declarations to the people upon that accompt, which like the blood of *Abel* cries for justice upon the perfidious infringers and perverters thereof in this Army. You may further remember, that it hath been a principle by you asserted and avowed, that our being Souldiers hath not deprived us of our Right as Commoners, and to Petition the people in Parliament, we do account in the number of our Birthrights; and you may remember that in the time of the domination of *Stapleton & Hollis,* you complained against their then endeavour to suppresse the liberty of the Souldiers to petition, as an insufferable infringement of the right of the Army and people; and we hope you did not then condemn it in them, to justifie it in your selves: when the power was theirs, it was then condemned; but now it is yours, how comes it to be justified? In the point of Petitioning, we expected your encouragement, and not to have manacles and fetters laid upon it: it is not the bare name or shadow thereof will satisfie us, while we are gull'd of the essence of it self; it is a perfect freedome therein we desire, not therein to be subjected under the Gradual Negative voices of a Captain, a Colonel, your Excllency, or this Councel, to passe the test from one Negative voice to another for its approvement, we account as the most vexatious Labyrinth of thraldom that in this point can be devised, worse then all the opposition and infringements of *Stapleton* and *Hollis;* we had rather that in plain terms you would deny us our right of petitioning, and pronounce and proclaim us absolute Slaves and Vassals to our Officers, then secretly to rob us of the right it self. God hath in some measure opened our eyes, that we can see and perceive; and we desire plain dealing, and not to be met half way with smooth Expedients, and Mediums facing both wayes, with specious and fair pretences, to overtake our sudden apprehensions, and unawares steal upon us, and so be defeated, as too often we have been, to the woe and misery of the people, and of us: but *The burnt child dreads the fire.*

Further we desire you to consider, That the strength, the honour and being of the Officer, yea and of this Councel (under God) doth consist in the Arme of the Souldier. Is it not the Souldier that endureth the heat and burden of the day, and performeth that work whereof the Officers beareth the glory and name? For what is, or what can the Officer do without the Souldier? If nothing, why are they not ashamed to deny us our right to petition?

We have long waited in silence, even while we could perceive any hopes of any reall redresse from them. But now finding the Military power in an absolute usurpation of the Civill Jurisdiction, in the place of the Magistrate executing that authority, by which the sword of the Magistrate, and the sword of war is incroached into the self same hands under one Military head, which we disclaim and abhorre, as not having any hand or assent therein at all. And we find a strange and unexpected constitution of a Councell of State, Such as neither we or our fore fathers were ever acquainted with, intrusted with little lesse then an unlimited power, & with the whole force both of Sea and Land, into which is combined the most pernitious interests of our rotten State, Lords, Lawyers, Star-Chamber Judges, and dissenters from the proceedings against the King, And which hath already swallowed up half our Parliament, and we fear to be an expedient to cut off our Parliaments, for ever; for if this Councel of State survive the Parliament, how shall we obtain a new Representative, if the Parliament sit but till a new one be ready to take their places, farwell Parliaments farwell Freedoms.

Further we find, the just and legall way of triall by twelve men of the neighbourhood in criminall cases, utterly subverted in this new constitution of an High Court, a President for ought we know, to frame all the Courts of *England* by, and to which our selves may be as well subjected as our enemies. And considering not one oppression is removed, not one vexation in the Law abated, or one punctillio of freedom restored, or any fair hopes at all appearing, but oppression heaped upon the back of oppression, double cruelty upon cruelty, we therefore from those many considerations, betook our selves as English men to make our address unto the Parliament, as the proper refuge and authority of the people for our and their addresse, in which by birth we challenge a right, as also by the price and purchase of our hazard and blood; and our Civill Rights we cannot yeeld up, we shall first rather yeeld up our lives.

And thus after the weak measure of our understandings, we judge we have given a rationall and full accompt of the occasion and reason of our Petitioning, and we hope satisfactory to your Excellency and this Councell, humbly praying that you will make a charitable and fair construction thereon.

And we further desire, that you will take speciall notice of the serious Apprehension of a part of the people in behalf of the Common wealth, presented to the House by Lievt. Col. *John Lilburn,* & divers other Citizens of *London,* and the Burrough of *Southwarke, Feb.* 26. now published in print. To the which with due thankfulnesse to those our faithful friends the promoters and presenters thereof, we do freely and cheerefully concur, to stand or fall in the just prosecution thereof, as the most absolute medium to our peace and freedom that hath been produced, and we hope it will produce an happy effect upon this Councell, to prevent the otherwise inavoidable dissolution and devision that will ensue upon us all, which to prevent, shall be the faithfull endeavours of.   Sir,

March 1.   *Your Excellencies most humble*
   1648.   *Servants and Soulders,*
                   Robert Ward.   Symon Grant.
                   Thomas Watson.   George Ielles.
                      William Sawyer.

The Examination and Anſwers of ROBERT WARD, *before the Court Martiall,* March 3. 1648.

1. **B**Eing call'd in before the Court, the President demanded of him whether he owned the Letter, or no: he answered, Yea; and did admire he should be committed to prison for delivering his judgment to them.

2. They asked him where the said Letter was written, and who was present at the writing thereof: He answered, he thought that Court had abominated the Spanish Inquisition, and Star-chamber practice, in examining him upon Interrogatories, contrary to their own Declarations; and he would rather lose his life, then betray his Libertie.

3. They told him, he had not wit sufficient to compose such a Letter: He answered, The Letter he did own; and as for worldly wisdom, he had not much; but he told the Court, he hoped he had so much honesty as would bear him out in this action; and desired them to remember what *Paul* spake, how that God did chuse the foolish things of the world to confound the mighty.

4. They said, That notwithstanding what he might think of himself touching honesty, they would not be afraid to proceed in

Judgment against him: To which he answered, they might do what they pleased, for he was in their hands, and they might take away his life if they would: but he assured they would bring innocent bloud upon their own heads. They answered, They did not much passe what he did say.

5. They did ask why they did print the Letter: To which hee answered, That he had been in prison, and it was impossible he or they should print in prison.

6. They asked how he proved the Civill and Military sword to be both in one hand. To which he answered, That some that sate in Councel with them, did likewise sit in the Parliament and Councell of State, contrary to what they had propounded to the People in their Agreement.

7. They asked what he had to say concerning the Councel of State. He answered, They did consist of corrupt persons; *viz.* Starchamber Judges, corrupt Lords, dissenters from the Proceedings against the late King, and of taking away the House of Lords; and trusted with little lesse then an unlimited power: now considering the persons, he told them, it seem'd to him *very dangerous.*

8. They asked him what he had to say concerning the subversion of our Liberties by the High Court of Justice. He answered: that it was a President (for ought he knew) to frame all the Courts in *England* by; considering that the lesser doth conform it self to the greater, and to which himself might be brought to tryall as well as others and so deprived of all liberty of exception against Triers.

9. They asked what he said concerning that clause, That no oppression was removed; the King and House of Lords being taken away, the chief cause of all oppression. To which he answered, That it was not the taking away of the King and House of Lords that made us free from oppression; for it was as good for him to suffer under the King, as under the keepers of the Liberties of *England*; both maintaining one and the same thing; *viz.* the corrupt administrations in the Law, treble dammage for Tythes, persecution for matter of Conscience, and oppression of the poor.

10. They asked what he thought of the serious apprehension of part of the People, in behalf of themselves and the Commonwealth, delivered to the Parliament by Lieutenant Col. *John Lilburn* and divers others: To which he being about to answer, they put him forth with confidence that he did own it.

After this they were all committed to prison again : and after three hours call'd again before the Court, and there Sentence read; at which time he told the Court, That they might as well take away his coat as his sword; it being his own proper goods, and never drew it against any but the Nations declared Enemies: and he did appeal from them, to a just God, before whom both they and he should one day appear to give an account of their actions : For the speaking of which, they told him, that by the Articles of War he did deserve death. He told them, it was more than he knew; and so was carried again to prison. And for this deportment, the Marshal General told him he had no more breeding then a Pig.

The Examination and Answers of Simon Grant.

THe President asked him whether he did own the Letter : He answered, he did. Then they asked him when he saw the Letter: He told them, before he came to the Generall. They demanded, how long before: Hee told them, two hours. They asked, when, and at what house, and where he did see it first? But apprehending they had not wherewithall to condemn him, but High-Commission like sought an advantage out of his mouth, he replyed, if they had any thing against him as matter of Charge, he desired that they would draw it up against him, and if they would give him time, he would answer it. Yes (said Colonel *Baxter*) and then he that wrote the Letter, would write the Answer. To which he replyed, It was his pleasure to say so. Then the Judge Advocate asked him, whether he did apprehend the Martiall Sword and the Magisteriall Sword were encroached into one another. He answered, he did apprehend it was so; because he did see daily, that many Souldiers did go about to draw and pull men out of their houses, as well as the Civill Magistrate, yea and more. Then he was asked whether he did own all the Letter : He answered, he did own it all. They told him, there were many lyes in it; and asked whether he did own them. But he replyed, that (as he conceived) there was none : he had set his hand to it, and would own it. Many more such like catchizing Interrogatories they put to him; but as frivolous as these.

The Examination and Answers of Tho. Watson.

THe President first demanded of him, whether he did own the Letter: He answered, he did own it. Then Col. *Huson* standing in the Court, told him, he had proclaimed open Wars against the Generall and the Councell. He answered, that Colonel *Huson* had past sentence upon him, it was in vain for him to say any thing. One of them replyed, that he knew not the practice of the Court. He answered, that they had no reason to accuse or condemn him for declaring his mind in reference to his Freedom, because they had declared in their own declarations, that in such things a man might write and speak his own mind freely. Nevertheless (he told them) if they had a Charge against him, and would produce it, he would answer it, if they would give him time; although they were not capable to judge him, because they declared he had abused the General and the Councel: and he had never heard, that they who were the Accusers, ought also to be the Judges.

Colonel *Baxter* asked him, Who wrote the Letter. He answered He came not to accuse himself or friends. Then he asked where it was written, and in whose house? He answered, In *London*. *Baxter* asked, why he gave orders to have it printed so quickly? He replied, How can you prove that? Then the Judge-Advocate told him, it would have been better for him if he had confest, he had found more mercy from the Court, for his obstinacie would gain him nothing. To whom he replied, They had a limited power, and could do nothing but what God permitted them, and they must once appear before a righteous Judge: but as for their Censure, he valued it not. So he was remanded back to prison.

The Examination and Answers of George Jelles.

THey demanded if he would own the Letter? He answered, he would, his hand was to it. They asked if he did write it? He answered, he did own it; and desired to know whether they would judge him in matters relating to the freedom of the Commonwealth by their Martial Law? They told him they would, being a Souldier. To which he replied, He was also Commoner of *England:* but if by their Martial Law he must be judged, he desired to know by what Article, in regard he had broken none? It was answered, upon the Article for Mutinie; and it was death. He replied, he had made no disturbance in the Army; and told them, that in the time of the predominance of *Stapleton* and *Hollis,* they then declared the Souldiery might petition the Parliament; but now the power was in their hands, the Souldiery had lost the Liberty thereof; and so desired God and the whole world might be Judge betwixt them. And upon his desiring of them to know whether they had seen the *Agreement* or no, they answered they had. He replied, it was therein concluded, that the Military sword & the Civil sword should not be encroached under one head. They answered, it was so, but that was left to the next Parliament to alter. But we wish they would tell us when that shall be; it is to be feared, it is never intended; for it is scarce imaginable they will ever venture the test of a new Representative, except they keep it under the sword, as they do this: let us have but a free successive Parliament, and wee'll run the hazard of it.

Thus he that considereth their catching questions, and but remembreth the *High-Commission* and *Star-Chamber* proceedings shall find no difference betwixt these Courts, but in name. Wherefore all English Souldiers or Commoners, that have the least spark of true love to themselves and their Countries freedom, are bound now or never, to unite them selves against those Apostates, those Jesuites and Traitors to the people : Those are the *Levellers* indeed; for what have they not levelled? There is no trust or confidence ever any more to be had in them: for they have broken their faith with all parties, by which they have advanced themselves to this height of dominion into which they are intruded; and now they reigne as Kings, and sit upon the Throne of their Predecessor, whom they removed, to take succession over the people.

And now we shall give you a Copy of their Sentence they passed upon us, the which *Baxter* being President (as they call it) pronounced as followeth.

Gentlemen; for so I think I may without offence call you, for as yet you are Souldiers; but truly you are not long to continue so : For you are guilty of high crimes, as your Letter here by you owned doth manifest, being scandalous to the Parliament, Counsel of State, High Court of Justice, and tending to breed mutinie in the Army; for which you have in an high measure deserved death; but through the great mercie of the Court that is waved, and truly they have waved the Sentence again and again, and now they are come as low as possibly they can: and it being late, I shall declare unto you your severall Sentences, which are as followeth.

You shall ride with your faces towards the Horse-tailes, before the heads of your severall Regiments, with your faults written upon your breasts, and your swords broken over your heads, and so be cashiered the Army as not worthy to ride therein; & a Proclamation to be made, that none shall receive you into any Troop, Company, or Garison. And this I would have you look upon as a great mercy of the Court.

Which sentence was accordingly executed upon us, in the Great Palace-yard at Westminster, *March* 6.

Thus you may see to what passe we are brought. What they have done to us, in the consequence thereof it doth extend equally to you all; for what they have done to us to day, you are liable to suffer to morrow. Thus you may see, they are Wolves in Sheeps clothing, Foxes in the habit of Saints; and their foosteps are in some measure traced and laid open unto you, from their beginning of engageing with the Army to their present Residence in *White-Hall* : So that from hence we may safely conclude with the saying of Col. *Disborrough* to Mr. *Bull* : that they did not intend to keep the Engagement, but provided the Acquiessing businesse at *Ware* on purpose to make void their engagement, we shall say no more at present, only add a coppy of a petition to the Parliament on which the Soldiers of the Army are proceeding.

To the Supreme Authority of the Nation,
The Commons affembled in Parliament:

The humble Petition of the Souldiery under the Conduct of THO. Lord FAIRFAX.

Sheweth,

THat we esteem the liberty of addresse by way of Petition to this Honourable House, a prime and most essentiall part of Freedom, and of right belonging to the meanest member of this Common-wealth.

That we humbly conceive our being Souldiers to be so far from depriving us of our share in this Freedom, as that it ought rather to be a confirmation thereof to us; we having with our utmost hazard of our lives been instrumentall in preserving the same.

That the power of the Officers doth onely extend to the Marshalling and disciplining of the Army, for the better management and execution of marshall Affairs, and that we submitting thereunto, do perform the utmost of obedience that can be required of us as Souldiers. All which notwithstanding, as we are in the capacity of Common-wealths men, we judge our selves as free as any other of the People, or as our Officers themselves, to represent by way of Petition, to this Honourable House, either our Grievances, Informations, or whaesoever else may tend either to the Right of our selves, or the benefit of the Common-wealth. And this is no more then what our Officers themselves have declared to be our Right, and without which we should be our selves the worst of slaves.

That the extraordinary actings of the Army, distinctly of themselves, in reference to the Common-wealth, are grounded upon our solemn Engagement at *Newmarket* and *Triploe* Heath, *June* 14. 1647.

That the Souldiery by that Engagement hath an equall Right and Propriety in and to the Transactions of the Army as Commoners.

That the Officers in matters of that concernment are not (without a free election and consent) the Representers of the Souldiers, as Commoners; but are onely their Conductors in Military matters.

That by vertue of our solemn Engagement, nothing done or to be done, though in the name of the Army, can be taken as the sense or the act of the Army, so as to be imputed to the Army, that is not agreed unto by a Councell to consist of those generall Officers who concur with the Engagement, with two Commission Officers, and two Souldiers to be chosen for each Regiment; or by the major part of such a Councell.

That if your Honors conceive it meet in your actings to concur with the actings of the Army, then it is necessary that with the sense of the Officers you also require the sense of the Souldiers, else not to account of it, or trust to it as the sense of the Army; and without this, we conceive, you cannot be safe, for it is small security, as to the act or faith of the Army, to receive the sense of the Officers, without the concurrence of the Souldiers in Councel, as aforesaid.

That being ejected and deprived of our Right and property in that Councell, we still conceive our selves at freedom to Petition this House; but yet in the late exercise thereof (amongst some of us) we have been very much abused and menaced; and Orders thereupon made by the Generall-Councell, to interrupt our free access to this honorable House, subjecting our petitions for approvement, to pass the Test from Officer to Officer, by which the sense and understanding of the Souldier is surprised and over-awed to the pleasure of the Officer, that he must neither hear, see, nor speak but by the eyes, ears and mouth of the Officer; so that the Souldiers right of petitioning is hereby taken from them; for to Petition in that case, can be at most but the bare sence of a few Officers; inconsiderable in comparison of the Souldiery, and so not the minde of the Army, for the Officers disjunct, make not the Army.

That to our great grief we are inforced to complain to this honorable House, that some of us, to wit, *Simon Grant, Robert Ward, Thomas Watson, William Sawyer* and *George Jelles* were sentenced by the Court Martiall, to ride with their faces towards their Horse tails; to have their Swords broken over their heads, and to be cashiered the Army, as unworthy therein to bear any Arms, counting it as a mercy of that Court, that their lives were spared; the which sentence was accordingly executed upon them in the great Palace-yard at Westminster, March the sixth: and all was but for petitioning this House, and delivering a paper of account of that action to the Generall-Councell, which is ready, if call'd for to be produced. The consideration whereof doth exceedingly agrieve us, to think that we should in vain undergo our former hardships, that in stead of addition to our Freedoms, we should in this opprobrious manner be rendred the worst of slaves, for we take it as done to our selves: and that to be deprived of our Rights both as Souldiers and English-men, as unworthy to petition or bear Arms, and that by such as are such glorious pretenders to Freedom, is a matter of amazement to us, considering the Crime (as they call it) was no other then above-mentioned.

Wherefore from these weighty Considerations we are enforced to apply our selves again unto this honourable House, and to desire,

First, That as heretofore and according to Right we may be as free to petition this Honorable House, as other our fellow-mem-

bers in the Commonwealth; and that we may with free and unin-
terrupted accesse approach with our Petitions (though by enforcement) without our Officers, as the Officers have done in declining
of us; and that for our clear satisfaction you would declare unto
us, that it is the undoubted freedome of the Souldiery to Petition
the Parliament, either singly of themselves, or joyntly with their
Officers, or with any other well-affected of the Nation whatsoever,
otherwise we cannot but look upon our selves as vassals and mercenaries, bound up by the pleasure and understandings of other
men.

2, That the power of the Officers and present Councel of
the Army may extend only to the Marshalling and Disciplinating
thereof; and that in matters which concern the Common-wealth,
we may not be concluded by these Debates, or any thing of that
nature taken as the Judgment of the whole Army, but of the
Subscribers only, unless we shall personally or deputatively give
our approbation and consent thereunto.

3. That you would require a revocation of their Order prohibiting us from Petitioning, but by our Officers.

4. That our forenamed fellow-Souldiers, by Order of this Honourable House, may be restored to their former places in their
respective Regiments.

5. That according to our solemn Engagement, we may not be
divided nor disbanded either in part or in whole, or any of us
engaged for Ireland, or any service whatsoever, untill full satisfaction and security be given us in relation to our Rights both as
Souldiers and Commoners, that we our selves, when in the condition of private men, and all other the free people of England, may
not be subject to the like oppression and tyrannie as hath been
put upon us.

6. That the desires of our former Petition which in most particulars hath been shadowed forth by a Petition of the Officers, as
also the serious Apprehensions of a part of the people, in behalf
of the Commonwealth, presented to this House Feb. 26 by Lieut.
Colonell Io. Lilburn, may be speedily taken into consideration,
and effectually accomplished, that so we may be more and more
encouraged to venture our lives in the protection and defence of
so good and just Authority.

And your Petitioners shall pray, &c.

FINIS.

Document 18

A MANIFESTATION

[William Walwyn]

Appeared April 14, 1649. Reprinted from a photostat of the original pamphlet in the McAlpin Collection of Union Theological Seminary.

A Manifestation is undoubtedly the work of William Walwyn. The whole pamphlet is couched in the conciliatory phrases typical of Walwyn, who according to his own testimony never lost confidence in his enemies' response to reason.[1] Walwyn had not signed *The second Part,* and Lilburne was surprised to see him under arrest on the morning of March 28. Apparently, for several months preceding his arrest, Walwyn had withdrawn from Leveller agitation;[2] but since the Leveller leaders presented a united front to the world, the grounds of difference with his comrades remain hidden in obscurity. One can only surmise that Walwyn thought it useless to continue agitation against an all-powerful military clique, whereas in Overton and Lilburne the iron will to resistance was still impenetrable, however slight the chances of success. Walwyn did not join with his comrades in condemnation of the Council of State on April 4. His sending forth of *A Manifestation* on April 14 is evidence of his desire to live at peace with his Independent antagonists, though deploring their errors, meanwhile defending Leveller principles as a moderate, sensible solution to the constitutional riddle. Walwyn is particularly anxious to prove to the world the unselfish, patriotic motives of the Leveller chiefs. The tone of the pamphlet is often defensive, suggesting that Walwyn was alarmed by the barrage of misconceptions that had been levelled at his party. He insists that

[1] *Walwyns Just Defence,* p. 12. Unlike Lilburne, Walwyn seldom uses quotations or authorities. *A Manifestation* is devoid of both devices. The pamphlet contains not a hint of Overton's biting satire. His enemies' accusation (*Walwins Wiles,* p. 5) that Walwyn was the author of *A Manifestation* is justified on every point of internal evidence.

[2] *The Picture of the Councel of State,* p. 2.

the Levellers have abhorred both anarchy and communism, they have sought to establish a rational and orderly government, taking into account the depravity of man, yet persisting in their aim of reducing the government "as near as might be to perfection." "Tis somewhat a strange consequence," writes Walwyn ruefully, "to infer that because we have laboured so earnestly for a good Government, therefore we would have none at all." [3] The Levellers have already declared, says Walwyn, their support of private property. Their concern, indeed, has been to bring the country "to such a passe that every man may with as much security as may be enjoy his propriety." [4]

Notwithstanding Walwyn's conciliatory accents, he strikes several bold notes in *A Manifestation*. In referring to the communism of the early Christians, he praises their "heavenly mindednesse," pointing out only that their sharing of property was voluntary, not compulsory. Refuting the charge that the Levellers are the king's agents, he insists that opposition to kingship had its "rise and originall from us," the Leveller party. The four leaders have seen so many men change from honesty to hypocrisy, from love of liberty to love of power, that they might even doubt themselves; but they have guarded against all such human frailty by the *Agreement* itself, which limits and defines the prerogatives of magistrates and governors. By no means have the Levellers lost hope of solution by the *Agreement*. They are indeed now engaged, writes Walwyn, in revising and amending it, to have it signed by the people and thus prepare the way for an orderly, democratic, constitutional revolution. In stating this intention, Walwyn writes with an assurance that it is impossible to believe he felt. The only thing wanting, he suggests, is the signatures of the "well-affected." In spite of Independent swords and the opposition of the Rump, the will of the people will prevail. It was this blindness, real or affected, to the realities of power, that distinguishes the Levellers from the army officers, particularly Cromwell. The chief ideological strength of the Levellers was also their critical weakness: Expert propagandists as they were, they were too rational and logical, appealing too confidently to the idealism of their contemporaries, scorning the predominating power of self-interest, jobs, livelihood, safety of friends and fami-

[3] *A Manifestation*, p. 391 of this volume.   [4] *Ibid.*, p. 391.

lies. To Lilburne and Overton, if not to Walwyn, prison had been almost a normal habitat, while their families suffered privation. They were last-ditch idealists, born centuries too soon, impatient, impulsive, unwilling or unable to gauge the barriers that barred the way to their utopian England.

A Manifeſtation

FROM

Lieutenant Col. *John Lilburn*, M^r· *William Walwyn*, M^r· *Thomas Prince*, and M^r· *Richard Overton*,

(Now Priſoners in the T o vv e r of *London*)
And others, commonly (though unjuſtly)

STYLED

LEVELLERS.

Intended for their

FVLL VINDICATION

FROM

The many aſperſions caſt upon them, to render them odious
to the World, and unſerviceable to the *Common-wealth*

And to ſatisfie and aſcertain all M E N

whereunto all their Motions and Endeavours tend, and what
is the ultimate Scope of their Engagement in the

PVBLICK AFFAIRES.

They alſo that render evill for good, are *Our* adverſaries:
becauſe *We* follow the thing that good is.

Printed in the year of our L o r d, 1649.

A
MANIFESTATION
FROM

Lieutenant Colonel *Iohn Lilburn*, Maſter *William Walwyne*, Maſter *Thomas Prince*, and Maſter *Richard Overton* (now priſoners in the Tower of *London*) and others, commonly (though unjustly) stiled *Levellers*.

S Ince no man is born for himself only, but obliged by the Laws of Nature (which reaches all) of Christianity (which ingages us as Christians) and of Publick Societie and Government, to employ our endeavours for the advancement of a communitive Happinesse, of equall concernment to others as our selves : here have we (according to that measure of understanding God hath dispensed unto us) laboured with much weaknesse indeed, but with integrity of heart, to produce out of the Common Calamities, such a proportion of Freedom and good to the Nation, as might somewhat compensate its many grievances and lasting sufferings : And although in doing thereof we have hitherto reaped only Reproach, and hatred for our good Will, and been faine to wrestle with the violent passions of Powers and Principalities; yet since it is nothing so much as our Blessed Master and his Followers suffered before us, and but what at first we reckoned upon, we cannot be thereby any whit dismayed in the performance of our duties, supported inwardly by the Innocency and evennesse of our Consciences.

'Tis a very great unhappinesse we well know, to be alwayes strugling and striving in the world, and does wholly keep us from the enjoyment of those contentments our several Conditions reach unto : So that if we should consult only with our selves, and regard only our own ease, Wee should never enterpose as we have done, in behalfe of the Common-wealth : But when so much has been done for recovery of our Liberties, and seeing God hath so blest that which has been done, as thereby to cleer the way, and to afford an opportunity which these 600 years has been desired, but could never be attained, of making this a *truly happy* and *wholly Free* Nation; We think our selves bound by the greatest obligations that may be, to prevent the neglect of this opportunity, and to hinder as much as lyes in us, that the bloud which has been shed be not spilt like water upon the ground, nor that after the abundant Calamities, which have overspread all quarters of the Land, the change be onely Notionall, Nominall, Circumstantiall, whilst the reall Burdens, Grievances, and Bondages, be continued, even when the Monarchy is changed into a Republike.

We are no more concern'd indeed then other men, and could bear the Yoke we believe as easily as others; but since a Common Duty lyes upon every man to be cautious and circumspect in behalfe of his Country, especially while the Government thereof is setling, other mens neglect is so far we thinke from being a just motive to us of the like sloath and inanimiadvertency, as that it rather requires of us an increase of care and circumspection which if it produces not so good a settlement as ought to be, yet certainly it will prevent its being so bad as otherwise it would be, if we should all only mind our particular callings and imployments.

So that although personally we may suffer, yet our solace is that the Common-wealth is therby some gainer, and we doubt not but that God in his due time wil so cleerly dispel the Clouds of Ignominy and Obloquy which now surround us by keeping our hearts upright and our spirits sincerely publike, that every good man will give us the right hand of fellowship, and be even sorry that they have been estranged, and so hardly opinionated against us : We question not but that in time the reason of such misprisions will appear to be in their eyes and not in our Actions, in the false Representation of things to them and improper glosses that are put upon every thing we do or say : In our own behalfs we have as yet said nothing, trusting that either shame and Christian duty would restraine men from making so bold with others good Name and Reputation, or that the sincerity of our actions would evince the falsehood of these scandals, and prevent the Peoples Beliefe of them; But we have found that with too much greedinesse they suck in Reports that tend to the discredit of others, and that our silence gives encouragement to bad Rumors of us; so that in all places they are spread, and industriously propagated as well amongst them that know us, as them that know us not, the first being fed with Jealousies that there is more in our designs then appeares, that there is something of danger in the bottom of our hearts, not yet discovered : that we are driven on by others, that we are even discontented and irresolved, that no body yet knowes what we would have, or where our desires will end; whilst they that know us not are made believe any strange conceit of us, that we would Levell all mens estates, that we would have no distinction of Orders and Dignities amongst men, that we are indeed for no government, but a Popular confusion; and then againe that we have bin Agents for the King, and now for the Queen; That we are Atheists, Antiscripturists, Jesuites and indeed any thing, that is hatefull and of evill repute amongst men.

All which we could without observance pass over, remembering what is promised to be the Portion of good men, were the damage only personall, but since the ends of such Rumors are purposely to make us uselesse and unserviceable to the Commonwealth, we are necessitated to open our breasts and shew the world our insides, for removing of those scandalls that lye upon us, and likewise for manifesting plainly and particularly what our desires are, and in what we will center and acquiess : all which we shall present to publike view and consideration, not pertinatiously or Magisterially, as concluding other mens judgements, but manifesting our own, for our further vindication, and for the procuring of a Bond and lasting establishment for the Commonwealth.

First, Then it will be requisite that we express our selves concerning Levelling, for which we suppose is commonly meant an equalling of mens estates, and taking away the proper right and Title that every man has to what is his own. This as we have formerly declared against, particularly in our petition of the 11 of Sept. so do we again professe that to attempt an inducing the same is most injurious, unlesse there did precede an universall assent thereunto from all and every one of the People. Nor doe we, under favour, judge it within the Power of a Representative it selfe, because although their power is supreame, yet it is but deputative and of trust; and consequently must be restrained expresly or tacitely, to some particular essential as well to the Peoples safety and freedom as to the present Government.

The Community amongst the primitive Christians, was *Voluntary, not Coactive*; they *brought* their goods and laid them at the Apostles feet, they were not enjoyned to bring them, it was the effect of their Charity and heavenly mindednesse, which the blessed Apostles begot in them, and not the Injunction of any Constitution, which as it was but for a short time done, and in but two or three places, that the Scripture makes mention of, so does the very doing of it there and the Apostles answer to him that detained a part, imply that it was not esteemed a duty, but reckoned a voluntary act occasioned by the abundant measure of faith that was in those Christians and Apostles.

We profess therefore that we never had it in our thoughts to Level mens estates, it being the utmost of our aime that the Common-wealth be reduced to such a passe that every man may with as much security as may be enjoy his propriety.

We know very well that in all Ages those men that engage themselves against Tyranny, unjust and Arbitrary proceedings in Magistrats, have suffered under such appellations, the People being purposely frighted from that wich is good by insinuations of imaginary evill.

But be it so, we must notwithstanding discharge our Duties, which being performed, the successe is in Gods hand to whose good pleasure we must leave the cleering of mens spirits, our only certainty being Tranquillity of mind, and peace of Conscience.

For distinction of Orders and Dignities, We think them so far needful, as they are animosities of vertue, or requisite for the maintenance of the Magistracy and Government, we thinke they were never intended for the nourishment of Ambition, or subjugation of the People but only to preserve the due respect and obedience in the People which is necessary for the better execution of the Laws.

That we are for Government and against Popular Confusion, we conceive all our actions declare, when rightly considered, our aim having bin all along to reduce it as near as might be to perfection, and certainly we know very well the pravity and corruption of mans heart is such that there could be no living without it; and that though Tyranny is so excessively bad, yet of the two extreames, Confusion is the worst: Tis somewhat a strange consequence to infer that because we have laboured so earnestly for a good Government, therefore we would have none at all; Because we would have the dead and exorbitant Branches pruned, and better sciens grafted, therefore we would pluck the Tree up by the roots.

Yet thus have we been misconceived, and misrepresented to the world, under which we must suffer, till God sees it fitting in his good time to cleer such harsh mistakes, by which many, even good men keep a distance from us.

For those weake suppositions of some of us being Agents for the King or Queen, we think it needful to say no more but this, That though we have not bin any way violent against the persons of them, or their Partie, as having aimed at the conversion of all, and the destruction of none, yet doe we verily beleeve that those Principles and Maxims of Government which are most fundamentally opposite to the Prerogative, and the Kings interest, take their first rise and originall from us, many whereof though at first starled at, and disown'd by those that professed the greatest opposition to him, have yet since been taken up by them and put in practise: and this we think is sufficient, though much more might be said to cleer us from any Agency for that Party.

It is likewise suggested that we are acted by others, who have other ends then appear to us; we answer. That that cannot be, since every thing has its rise amongst our selves, and since those things we bring to light cannot conduce to the ends of any but the publike weale of the Nation.

All our Desires, Petitions and Papers are directly opposite to all corrupt Interests; nor have any, credit with us, but persons well known, and of certain aboads, and such as have given sound and undeniable testimonies of the truth of their affection to their Country: Besides, the things we promote, are not good onely in appearance, but sensibly so: not moulded nor contrived by the subtill or politick Principles of the World, but plainly produced and nakedly sent, without any insinuating arts, relying wholly upon the apparent and universall beleefe they carry in themselves; and that is it which convinces and engages us in the promotion thereof. So that that suggestion has not indeed any foundation in itself, but is purposely framed, as we conceive, to make us afraid one of another, and to disable us in the promotion of those good things that tend to the freedom and happinesse of the Common-wealth.

For our being Jesuits, either in Order or Principles, as 'tis severally reported of us; Though the easiest Negative is hardly proved; yet we can say, That those on whom the first is principally fix'd, are married, and were never over Sea : and we think Marriage is never dispenc'd withall in that Order, and that none can be admitted into the Order but such as are personally present. 'Tis hard that we are put to expresse thus much; and haply we might better passe such reports over in silence; but that we beleeve the very mentioning of them publickly, will be an answer to them, and make such as forment them asham'd of such generally condemned wayes of discrediting and blasting the Reputation of other men. For the principles of Jesuits, we professe we know not what they are; but they are generally said to be full of craft and worldly policy; and therefore exceedingly different from that plainness and simplicity that is apparently visible in all our proceedings.

Whereas its said, we are Atheists and Antiscripturists, we professe that we beleeve there is one eternall and omnipotent God, the Author and Preserver of all things in the world. To whose will and directions, written first in our hearts, and afterwards in his blessed Word, we ought to square our actions and conversations. And though we are not so strict upon the formall and Ceremonial part of his Service, the method, manner, and personall injunction being not so clearly made out unto us, nor the necessary requisites which his Officers and Ministers ought to be furnished withall as yet appearing to some of us in any that pretend thereunto : yet for the manifestation of Gods love in Christ, it is cleerly assented unto by us; and the practicall and most reall part of Religion is as readily submitted unto by us, as being, in our apprehensions, the most eminent and the most excellent in the world, and as proceeding from no other but that God who is Goodnesse it self : and we humbly desire his Goodnesse daily more and more to conform our hearts to a willing and sincere obedience thereunto.

For our not being preferred to Offices and Places of profit and credit, which is urged to be the ground of our dissatisfaction, we say, That although we know no reason why we should not be equally capable of them with other men, nor why our publick Affection should be any barr or hinderance thereunto : Yet on the other side, we suppose we can truly say of our selves, that we have not been so earnest and solicitous after them as others : and that in the Catalogue of Sutors, very few that are reckoned of us, are to be found. We are very sorry that so general a change of Officers is proposed, which we judge of no small disparagement to our Cause; and do think it best, that in removals of that kinde, the ground should not be difference in opinion, either in Religious or Civil Matters, but corruption or breach of Trust; considering the misery which befalls whole Families upon such Changes; and that discontents are thereby increased : Whereas we hold it necessary that all wayes of composure and acquieting those storms which the preceding differences and distractions have begotten, be with utmost care and prudence endeavoured.

And whereas 'tis urged, That if we were in power, we would bear our selves as Tyrannically as others have done : We confess indeed, that the experimentall defections of so many men as have succeeded in Authority, and the exceeding difference we have hitherto found in the same men in a low, and in an exalted condition, makes us even mistrust our own hearts, and hardly beleeve our own Resolutions of the contrary. And therefore we have proposed such an Establishment, as supposing men to be too flexible and yeelding to worldly Temptations, they should not yet have a means or opportunity either to injure particulars, or prejudice the Publick, without extreme hazard, and apparent danger to themselves. Besides, to the objection we have further to say, That we aim not at power in our selves, our Principles and Desires being in no measure of self-concernment : nor do we relie for obtaining the same upon strength, or a forcible obstruction; but solely upon that inbred and perswasive power that is all good and just things, to make their own way in the hearts of men, and so to procure their own Establishments.

And that makes us at this time naked and defencelesse as we are, and amidst so many discouragements on all hands to persevere in our motions and desires of good to the Nation; although disowned therein at such a time when the doing thereof can be interpreted no other but a politick delivering us up to slaughter, by such as we took for Friends, our brethren of severall Churches; and for whom with truth of affection we have even in the most difficult times done many Services : all which, and whatsoever else can be done against us, we shall reckon but as badges of our sincerity, and be no whit discouraged thereby from the discharge of our duties.

For the dis-satisfactions that be upon many good mens spirits, for that they are not ascertained whereunto all our motions tend, and in what they will center,

Though, we conceive, they may have received some general satisfaction from what we have formerly at severall times propounded; yet since they were not disposed into such a form and condition as to become practicable; we have, with the best care and abilities God hath afforded us, cast the same into a Modell and Platform, which we shall speedily present unto the view and consideration of all, as the *Standard* and ultimate scope of our Designes, that so (in case of approvall) it may be subscribed and returned as agreed upon by the People. And thus far, we conceive, we may without offence or prejudice to Authority, proceed; and which we the rather do, because we know no better, and indeed no other way or means (but by such an Agreement) to remove (as much as may be) all disgusts and heart-burnings, and to settle the Common-wealth upon the fairest probabilities of a lasting Peace, and contentfull Establishment.

The Agreement of the People which was presented by his Excellency and the Officers of the Army to the Right Honourable the Commons in Parliament, although in many things short (according to our apprehensions) of what is necessary for the good of the Common-wealth, and satisfaction of the People; particularly, in that it containeth no provision for the certain removall of notorious and generally complained of grievances: And although it hath some things of much hazard to the Publick,——— yet, had it been put in execution, we should scarcely have interrupted the proceedings therof, since therein is contained many things of great and important concernment to the Common-wealth. But seeing the time proposed therein for reducing the same into practice, is now past, and that likewise the generality of the people have not, or do not approve of the same, for the reasons (as we suppose) fore-mentioned : We have thought fit to revise it, making onely such alterations therein as we conceive really necessary for the welfare, security and safety of the People, together with additional Provisions for the taking away of those Burdens and Grievances which may without reall prejudice to the Management of publick Affairs be removed.

And because it is essentiall to the nature of such an Agreement to take its rise from the People, we have therefore purposely declined the presentment thereof to the Parliament : and conceive it may speedily proceed to Subscription, and so to further practice, without any interruption to this Representative, untill the season prefix'd in the Agreement, for the assembling another : By whose immediate succession, without any intervall, the Affairs of the Common-wealth may suffer no stop or intermission.

Lastly, We conceive we are much mistaken in being judged impatient, and over-violent in our motions for the publick Good. To which we answer, That could we have had any assurance that what is desired should have otherwise, or by any have been done; and had not had some taste of the relinquishment of many good things that were promised, we should not have been so earnest and urgent for the doing thereof.

Though we know likewise it hath been very customary in such heretofore as never intended any freedom to the Nation, to except only against the season, and to protract the time so long, till they became sufficiently impowred to justifie the totall denyall and refusall thereof. However, the main reason of our proceeding as we do, is, because we prefer the way of a settlement by an Agreement of the People before any other whatsoever.

And thus the world may clearly see what we are, and what we aym at : We are altogether ignorant, and do from our hearts abominate all designes and contrivances of dangerous consequence which we are said (but God knows, untruly) to be labouring withall. Peace and Freedom is our Designe; by War we were never gainers, nor ever wish to be; and under bondage we have been hitherto sufferers. We desire however, that what is past may be forgotten, provided the Common wealth may have amends made it for the time to come. And this from our soul we desire.

Having no mens persons in hatred, and judging it needfull that all other respects whatsoever are to give way to the good of the Common-wealth, and this is the very truth and inside of our hearts.

From the Tower,
   April 14. 1649.

John Lilburne
William Walwyn
Thomas Prince
Richard Overton.

AN AGREEMENT OF THE FREE PEOPLE OF ENGLAND

Appeared May 1, 1649. Reprinted from a photostatic copy of the original pamphlet, Thomason Collection, E 552 (23).

The third *Agreement,* anticipated by Walwyn in *A Manifestation,* appeared with the name of the printer and the *imprimatur* of Gilbert Mabbott, licenser for the Independents. Certainly it was eagerly awaited by thousands to whom Lilburne and his fellows were now more than ever martyrs to the cause of Leveller principles. This eagerness of the Leveller following may account for the willingness of the printer to risk Independent repression and Mabbott to brave the ire of his employers.[1] The intensity of Leveller pressure for the new *Agreement* is indicated by two unacknowledged petitions for the leaders in one day, May 2.[2]

Written in the Tower, no doubt after long discussions among Lilburne, Walwyn, and Overton, the third *Agreement* represents their ripest reflections on the crucial constitutional dilemmas of the Puritan Revolution. Unlike the first *Agreement,* which was only a constitutional abstraction, and the second, which added to the abstraction a directive to Parliament for the redress of specific grievances, the third *Agreement,* composed of thirty articles, incorporates all the Leveller demands of their most important petitions. It therefore represents a fusion and synthesis of the cumulative experience of the radicals, not only in the solution of social dilemmas, but also in their mastery of propaganda methods. Petitions and the *Agreement* were now thoroughly interwoven. The constant mention of the *Agreement* in the pamphlets and newspapers of the day demonstrates the success of the Levellers in popularizing both the central abstractions of their democratic blueprint and the specific demands of their petitions.

With Independent strategy fresh in mind, the Levellers in

[1] *Old Parliamentary History,* XIX, 111. [2] *Ibid.,* XIX, 119.

their third *Agreement* show a profound distrust of authoritarian power and a greater confidence than ever in the judgment of the voting public. They stipulate that even the minister of each parish is to be elected by the people. Fearing long tenure in any political office, they for the first time in an *Agreement* explicitly require annual Parliaments and annual elections of all local officials, no Parliament member to succeed himself (Articles XXVII, VIII, and IV). The Rump is to dissolve the first Wednesday in August, its successor to meet the next day and sit regularly for four months (Articles V and VIII). Should the Rump fail to order the election of a new Parliament, then, say the Levellers confidently, the people will proceed to elect their representatives, their power being superior to that of any Parliament (Article VI). Parliament is forbidden to set up a Council of State; it may appoint a committee invested with only those specific powers that are consistent with the *Agreement* and published for the inspection of the citizens (Article VIII). Forbidden to act as a court of law, Parliament must not set up a court of justice or usurp the functions of the executive (Article XIIII). Nor must it appoint, or cause to be appointed, any army officers except the general and his staff; all others are to be elected by the citizens of the towns and counties in which the troops are raised (Article XXIX). Thus would the Levellers have destroyed the authoritarian efficiency of Cromwell's army and referred even military leadership to the judgment of the voting citizens. "Nothing," they conclude, "threateneth greater danger to the Common-wealth, then that the Military power should by any means come to be superior to the Civil Authority."

The third *Agreement* is notable for the significant addition of planks that hitherto the Levellers had either omitted or subordinated to the status of recommendations. For the first time excise and customs are expressly prohibited, any interference with foreign trade (Articles XVIII and XIX), and imprisonment for debt (Article XX). Furthermore the *Agreement* forbids capital punishment except for murder "or other the like hainous offences" such as a violent attempt to overthrow the constitution (Article XXI). No person "excepting such as maintain the Popes (or other forraign) Supremacy" may be disqualified for religious beliefs from holding public office. Thus the third *Agreement*, like its predecessors, the first two *Agreements* and the three great Leveller petitions, anticipated the patterns of democratic pressure that inaugurated the American republic and the English constitutional reforms of the nineteenth century. The Levellers undoubtedly lacked, however, a deep awareness of the incongruity of their proposals with the political education of the English people. Had their own republic been established,[3] it could hardly have been less abortive, or based less on force of arms, than that of the Independents. Acceptance of such radical measures waited upon processes of economic change and educational pressure that no revolution could have telescoped into a few decades.

[3] Though the abolition of kingship and Lords is assumed in the third *Agreement*, the Levellers do not incorporate a plain provision to this end. This is a curious omission, unexpected to a greater degree than in the first and second *Agreements* of 1647 and 1648. In *Englands New Chains* the Levellers had criticized the Independents for not providing against the restoration of king and Lords in the officers' *Agreement*. Yet this they had not done themselves in *Foundations of Freedom;* nor do they include it in their most mature and complete constitutional blueprint. The subsequent willingness of the Levellers to accept a kingship restricted by the *Agreement* does not fully explain the omission of two such crucial political issues.

AN
AGREEMENT
OF THE
Free People of England.

Tendered as a *Peace-Offering* to
this diftreffed *Nation*.

BY

Lieutenant Colonel *Iohn Lilburne*, Mafter *William Walwyn*,
Mafter *Thomas Prince*, and Mafter *Richard Overton*, Prif-
oners in the Tower of *London, May* the 1. 1649.

Matth. 5. verfe 9. *Bleffed are the Peace-makers for they fhall be
called the children of God.*

++

A Preparative to all sorts of people.

IF afflictions make men wise, and wisdom direct to happinesse,
then certainly this Nation is not far from such a degree
thereof, as may compare if not far exceed, any part of the
world: having for some yeares by-past, drunk deep of the Cup of
misery and sorrow. We blesse God our consciences are cleer from
adding affliction to affliction, having ever laboured from the beginning, of our publick distractions, to compose and reconcile
them: & should esteem it the Crown of all our temporal felicity
that yet we might be instrumentall in procuring the peace and
prosperity of this Common-wealth the land of our Nativity.

And therefore according to our promise in our late *Manifestation* of the 14 of *Aprill* 1649. (being perswaded of the neces-

sitie and justnesse thereof) as a *Peace-Offering* to the Free people of this Nation, we tender this ensuing Agreement, not knowing any more effectuall means to put a finall period to all our feares and troubles.

It is a way of settlement, though at first much startled at by some in high authority; yet according to the nature of truth, it hath made its own way into the understanding, and taken root in most mens hearts and affections, so that we have reall ground to hope (what ever shall become of us) that our earnest desires and indeavours for good to the people will not altogether be null and frustrate.

The life of all things is in the right use and application, which is not our worke only, but every mans conscience must look to it selfe, and not dreame out more seasons and opportunities. And this we trust will satisfie all ingenuous people that we are not such wilde, irrationall, dangerous Creatures as we have been aspersed to be ; This agreement being the ultimate end and full scope of all our desires and intentions concerning the Government of this Nation, and wherein we shall absolutely rest satisfied and acquiesce ; nor did we ever give just cause for any to beleeve worse of us by any thing either said or done by us, and which would not in the least be doubted, but that men consider not the interest of those that have so unchristian-like made bold with our good names ; but we must bear with men of such interests as are opposite to any part of this Agreement, when neither our Saviour nor his Apostles innocency could stop such mens mouthes whose interests their doctrines and practises did extirpate : And therefore if friends at least would but consider what interest men relate to, whilst they are telling or whispering their aspersions against us, they would find the reason and save us a great deale of labour in clearing our selves, it being a remarkable signe of an ill cause when aspersions supply the place of Arguments.

We blesse God that he hath given us time and hearts to bring it to this issue, what further he hath for us to do is yet only knowne to his wisedom, to whose will and pleasure we shall willingly submit ; we have if we look with the eyes of frailty, enemies like the sons of *Anak,* but if with the eyes of faith and confidence in a righteous God and a just cause, we see more with us then against us,

From our causelesse captivity in the   *Iohn Lilburn. William Walwyn.*
  Tower of *London, May* 1. 1649.   *Thomas Prince. Richard Overton.*

The Agreement it selfe thus followeth.

AFter the long and tedious prosecution of a most unnaturall cruell, homebred war, occasioned by divisions and distempers amongst our selves, and those distempers arising from the uncertaintie of our Government, and the exercise of an unlimited or Arbitrary power, by such as have been trusted with Supreme and subordinate Authority, wherby multitudes of grevances and intolerable oppressions have been brought upon us. And finding after eight yeares experience and expectation all indeavours hitherto used, or remedies hitherto applyed, to have encreased rather then diminished our distractions, and that if not speedily prevented our falling againe into factions and divisions, will not only deprive us of the benefit of all those wonderful Victories God hath vouchsafed against such as sought our bondage, but expose us first to poverty and misery, and then to be destroyed by forraigne enemies.

And being earnestly desirous to make a right use of that opportunity God hath given us to make this Nation Free and Happy, to reconcile our differences, and beget a perfect amitie and friendship once more amongst us, that we may stand clear in our consciences before Almighty God, as unbyassed by any corrupt Interest or particular advantages, and manifest to all the world that our indeavours have not proceeded from malice to the persons of any, or enmity against opinions ; but in reference to the peace and prosperity of the Common-wealth, and for prevention of like distractions, and removall of all grievances ; We the free People of *England*, to whom God hath given hearts, means and opportunity to effect the same, do with submission to his wisdom, in his name, and desiring the equity thereof may be to his praise and glory ; Agree to ascertain our Government, to abolish all arbitrary Power, and to set bounds and limits both to our Supreme, and all Subordinate Authority, and remove all known Grievances.

And accordingly do declare and publish to all the world,
that we are agreed as followeth,

I. THat the Supreme Authority of *England* and the Territories therewith incorporate, shall be and reside henceforward in a Representative of the people consisting of four hundred persons, but no more ; in the choice of whom (according to naturall right) all men of the age of one and twenty yeers and upwards (not being servants, or receiving alms, or having served the late King in Arms or voluntary Contributions) shall have their voices ; and be capable of being elected to that Supreme Trust those who served the King being disabled for ten years onely. All things concerning the distribution of the said four hundred Members proportionable to the respective parts of the Nation , the severall places for Election, the manner of giving and taking of Voyces, with all Circumstances of like nature, tending to the compleating and equall proceedings in Elections , as also their Salary, is referred to be setled by this present Parliament, in such sort as the next Representative may be in a certain capacity to meet with safety at the time herein expressed : and such circumstances to be made more perfect by future Representatives.

II. That two hundred of the four hundred Members, and not lesse, shall be taken and esteemed for a competent Representative ; and the major Voyces present shall be concluding to this Nation. The place of Session, and choice of a Speaker, with other circumstances of that nature, are referred to the care of this and future Representatives.

III. And to the end all publick Officers may be certainly accountable, and no Factions made to maintain corrupt Interests, no Officer of any salary Forces in Army or Garison, nor any Treasurer or Receiver of publick monies, shall (while such) be elected a Member for any Representative; and if any Lawyer shall at any time be chosen, he shall be uncapable of practice as a Lawyer, during the whole time of that Trust. And for the same reason, and that all persons may be capable of subjection as well as rule.

IIII. That no Member of the present Parliament shall be capable of being elected of the next Representative, nor any Member of any future Representative shall be capable of being chosen for the Representative immediately succeeding : but are free to be chosen, one Representative having intervened : Nor shall any Member of any Representative be made either Receiver, Treasurer, or other Officer during that imployment.

V. That for avoyding the many dangers and inconveniences apparantly arising from the long continuance of the same persons in Authority ; We Agree, that this present Parliament shall end the first Wednesday in *August* next 1649, and thenceforth be of no power or Authority : and in the mean time shall order and direct the Election of a new and equall Representative, according to the true intent of this our Agreement: and so as the next Representative may meet and sit in power and Authority as an effectuall Representative upon the day following ; namely, the first Thursday of the same *August,* 1 6 4 9.

VI. We agree, if the present Parliament shall omit to order such Election or Meetting of a new Representative ; or shall by any means be hindered from performance of that Trust :

That in such case, we shall for the next Representative proceed in electing thereof in those places, & according to that manner & number formerly accustomed in the choice of Knights and Burgesses ; observing onely the exceptions of such persons from being Electors or Elected, as are mentioned before in the first, third, and fourth Heads of this Agreement : It being most unreasonable that we should either be kept from new, frequent and successive Representatives, or that the supreme Authority should fall into the hands of such as have manifested disaffection to our common Freedom, and endeavoured the bondage of the Nation.

VII. And for preserving the supreme authority from falling into the hands of any whom the people have not, or shall not chuse,

We are resolved and agreed (God willing) that a *new Representative* shall be upon the first *Thursday* in *August* next aforesaid : the ordering and disposing of themselves, as to the choice of a speaker , and the like circumstances, is hereby left to their discretion : But are in the extent and exercise of Power, to follow the direction and rules of this agreement ; and are hereby authorised and required according to their best judgements, to set rules for future equall distribution, and election of Members as is herein intended and enjoyned to be done, by the present Parliament.

VIII. And for the preservation of the supreme Authority (in all times) entirely in the hands of such persons only as shal be chosen thereunto—we *agree and declare:* That the next & al future Representatives, shall continue in full power for the space of one whole year : and that the people shall of course, chuse a Parliament once every year, so as all the members thereof may be in a capacity to meet, and take place of the foregoing Representative : the first *Thursday* in every *August* for ever if God so please; Also (for the same reason) that the next or any future Representative being met, shall continue their Session day by day without intermission for four monthes at the least ; and after that shall be at Liberty to adjourn from two monthes to two months, as they shall see cause untill their yeer be expired, but shall sit no longer then a yeer upon pain of treason to every member

that shall exceed that time : and in times of adjurnment shall not
erect a Councel of State but refer the managing of affairs in the
intervals to a Committee of their own members giving such instructions, and publish them, as shall in no measure contradict
this agreement.

IX. And that none henceforth may be ignorant or doubtfull
concerning the power of the Supreme authority, and of the affairs,
about which the same is to be conversant and exercised : we
agree and declare, that the power of Representatives shall extend without the consent or concurrence of any other person or
persons,

1 To the conservation of Peace and commerce with forrain
Nations.

2 To the preservation of those safe guards, and securities of
our lives, limbes, liberties, properties, and estates, contained in
the Petition of Right, made and enacted in the third year of the
late King.

3 To the raising of moneys, and generally to all things as shall
be evidently conducing to those ends, or to the enlargement of
our freedom, redress of grievances, and prosperity of the Common-
wealth.

For security whereof, having by wofull experience found the
prevalence of corrupt interests powerfully inclining most men
once entrusted with authority, to pervert the same to their own
domination, and to the prejudice of our Peace and Liberties, we
therefore further agree and declare.

X. That we do not inpower or entrust our said representatives to continue in force, or to make any Lawes, Oaths, or Covenants, whereby to compell by penalties or otherwise any person
to any thing in or about matters of faith, Religion or Gods worship or to restrain any person from the profession of his faith,
or exercise of Religion according to his Conscience, nothing having caused more distractions, and heart burnings in all ages, then
persecution and molestation for matters of Conscience in and
about Religion :

XI We doe not impower them to impresse or constraint any
person to serve in war by Sea or Land every mans Conscience
being to be satisfied in the justness of that cause wherein he
hazards his own life, or may destroy an others.

And for the quieting of all differences, and abolishing of all
enmity and rancour, as much as is now possible for us to effect.

XII. We agree, That after the end of this present Parliament, no person shall be questioned for any thing said or done in reference to the late Warres, or publique differences ; otherwise then in pursuance of the determinations of the present Parliament, against such as have adhered to the King against the Liberties of the people : And saving that Accomptants for publick moneys received, shall remain accomptable for the same.

XIII. That all priviledges or exemptions of any persons from the Lawes, or from the ordinary course of Legall proceedings, by vertue of any Tenure, Grant, Charter, Patent, Degree, or Birth, or of any place of residence, or refuge, or priviledge of Parliament, shall be henceforth void and null ; and the like not to be made nor revived again.

XIIII. We doe not impower them to give judgment upon any ones person or estate, where no Law hath been before provided, nor to give power to any other Court or Jurisdiction so to do, Because where there is no Law, there is no transgression, for men or Magistrates to take Cognisance of; neither doe we impower them to intermeddle with the execution of any Law whatsoever.

XV. And that we may remove all long setled Grievances, and thereby as farre as we are able, take away all cause of complaints, and no longer depend upon the uncertain inclination of Parliaments to remove them, nor trouble our selves or them with Petitions after Petitions, as hath been accustomed, without fruit or benefit ; and knowing no cause why any should repine at our removall of them, except such as make advantage by their continuance, or are related to some corrupt Interests, which we are not to regard.

We agree and Declare,

XVI. That it shall not be in the power of any Representative, to punish, or cause to be punished, any person or persons for refusing to answer to questions against themselves in Criminall cases.

XVII. That it shall not be in their power, after the end of the next Representative, to continue or constitute any proceedings in Law that shall be longer then Six months in the final determination of any cause past all Appeal, nor to continue the Laws or proceedings therein in any other Language then English, nor to hinder any person or persons from pleading their own Causes, or of making use of whom they please to plead for them.

The reducing of these and other the like provisions of this nature in this Agreement provided, and which could not now in all particulars be perfected by us, is intended by us to be the proper works of faithful Representatives.

XVIII. That it shall not be in their power to continue or make any Laws to abridge or hinder any person or persons, from trading or merchandizing into any place beyond the Seas, where any of this Nation are free to Trade.

XIX. That it shall not be in their power to continue Excise or Customes upon any sort of Food, or any other Goods, Wares, or Commodities, longer then four months after the beginning of the next Representative, being both of them extreme burthensome and oppressive to Trade, and so expensive in the Receipt, as the moneys expended therein (if collected as Subsidies have been) would extend very far towards defraying the publick Charges ; and forasmuch as all Moneys to be raised are drawn from the People ; such burthensome and chargeable wayes, shall never more be revived, nor shall they raise Moneys by any other ways (after the aforesaid time) but only by an equal rate in the pound upon every reall and personall estate in the Nation.

XX. That it shall not be in their power to make or continue any Law, whereby mens reall or personall estates, or any part thereof, shall be exempted from payment of their debts; or to imprison any person for debt of any nature, it being both unchristian in it self, and no advantage to the Creditors, and both a reproach and prejudice to the Common-wealth.

XXI. That it shall not be in their power to make or continue any Law, for taking away any mans life, except for murther, or other the like hainous offences destructive to humane Society, or for endevouring by force to destroy this our Agreement, but shall use their uttermost endeavour to appoint punishments equall to offences : that so mens Lives, Limbs, Liberties, and estates, may not be liable to be taken away upon trivial or slight occasions as they have been; and shall have speciall care to preserve, all sorts of people from wickedness misery and beggery : nor shall the estate of any capitall offendor be confiscate but in cases of treason only ; and in all other capitall offences recompence shall be made to the parties damnified, as well out of the estate of the Malifactor, as by loss of life, according to the conscience of his jury.

XXII. That it shall not be in their power to continue or make any Law, to deprive any person, in case of Tryals for Life, Limb, Liberty, or Estate, from the benefit of witnesses, on his, or their behalf ; nor deprive any person of those priviledges, and liberties, contained in the P*etition of Right,* made in the third yeer of the late King *Charls.*

XXIII. That it shall not be in their power to continue the Grievance of Tithes, longer then to the end of the next Representative ; in which time, they shall provide to give reasonable satisfaction to all Impropriators : neither shall they force by penalties or otherwise, any person to pay towards the maintenance of any Ministers, who out of conscience cannot submit thereunto.

XXIV. That it shall not be in their power to impose Ministers upon any the respective Parishes, but shall give free liberty to the parishioners of every particular parish, to chuse such as themselves shall approve ; and upon such terms, and for such reward, as themselves shall be willing to contribute, or shall contract for. Provided, none be chusers but such as are capable of electing Representatives.

XXV. That it shal not be in their power, to continue or make a law, for any other way of Judgments, or Conviction of life, limb, liberty, or estate, but onely by twelve sworn men of the Neighborhood ; to be chosen in some free way by the people ; to be directed before the end of the next Representative, and not picked and imposed, as hitherto in many places they have been.

XXVI. They shall not disable any person from bearing any office in the Common-wealth, for any opinion or practice in Religion, excepting such as maintain the Popes (or other forraign) Supremacy.

XXVII. That it shal not be in their power to impose any publike officer upon any Counties, Hundreds, Cities, Towns, or Borroughs ; but the people capable by this Agreement to chuse Representatives, shall chuse all their publike Officers that are in any kinde to administer the Law for their respective places, for one whole yeer, and no longer, and so from yeer to yeer : and this as an especial means to avoyd Factions, and Parties.

And that no person may have just cause to complain, by reason of taking away the Excise and Customs, we agree,

XXVIII. That the next, and all future Representatives shall exactly keep the publike Faith, and give ful satisfaction, for all securities, debts, arrears or damages, (justly chargeable) out of the publike Treasury; and shall confirm and make good all just publike Purchases and Contracts that have been, or shall be made ; save that the next Representative may confirm or make null in part or in whole, all gifts of Lands, Moneys, Offices, or otherwise made by the present Parliament, to any Member of the House of

Commons, or to any of the Lords, or to any of the attendants of either of them.

And for as much as nothing threateneth greater danger to the Common-wealth, then that the Military power should by any means come to be superior to the Civil Authority.

XXIX. We declare and agree, That no Forces shal be raised, but by the Representatives, for the time being ; and in raising thereof, that they exactly observe these Rules, namely, That they allot to each particular County, City, Town, and Borrugh, the raising, furnishing, agreeing, and paying of a due proportion, according to the whole number to be levyed ; and shall to the Electors of Representatives in each respective place, give Free liberty, to nominate and appoint all Officers appertaining to Regiments, Troops, and Companies, and to remove them as they shall see cause, Reserving to the Representative, the nominating, and appointing onely of the General, and all General-Officers ; and the ordering, regulating, and commanding of them all, upon what service shall seem to them necessary for the Safety, Peace, and Freedom of the Common-wealth.

And in as much as we have found by sad experience, That generally men make little or nothing, to innovate in Government, to exceed their time and power in places of trust, to introduce an Arbitrary, and Tyrannical power, and to overturn all things into Anarchy and Confusion, where there are no penalties imposed for such destructive crimes and offences.

XXX. We therefore agree and declare, That it shall not be in the power of any Representative, in any wise, to render up, or give, or take away any part of this Agreement, nor level mens Estates, destroy Propriety, or make all things Common : And if any Representative shall endevor, as a Representative, to destroy this Agreement, every Member present in the House, not entering or immediately publishing his dissent, shall incur the pain due for High Treason, and be proceeded against accordingly ; and if any person or persons, shall by force endevor or contrive, the destruction thereof, each person so doing, shall likewise be dealt withal as in cases of Treason.

And if any person shal by force of Arms disturb Elections of Representatives, he shall incurr the penalty of a Riot ; and if any person not capable of being an Elector, or Elected, shal intrude themselves amongst those that are, or any persons shall behave themselves rudely and disorderly, such persons shal be liable to a

presentment by a grand Inquest and to an indictment upon misdemeanor ; and be fined and otherwise punish'd according to the
discretion and verdict of a Jury. And all Laws made, or that shall
be made contrary to any part of this Agreement, are hereby made
null and void.

Thus, as becometh a free People, thankfull unto God for this
blessed opportunity, and desirous to make use thereof to his glory,
in taking off every yoak, and removing every burthen, in delivering the captive, and setting the oppressed free ; we have in all the
particular Heads forementioned, done as we would be done unto,
and as we trust in God will abolish all occasion of offence and discord, and produce the lasting Peace and Prosperity of this Common wealth : and accordingly do in the sincerity of our hearts
and consciences, as in the presence of Almighty God, give cleer
testimony of our absolute agreement to all and every part hereof
by subscribing our hands thereunto. Dated the first day of *May*,
in the Yeer of our Lord 1 6 4 9.

John Lilburn.
William Walwyn.
Thomas Prince.
Richard Overton.

April 30. 1649.

Imprimatur.   Gilbert Mabbot.
FINIS.

London, Printed for *Gyles Calvert* at the black
ſpread-Eagle at the VVeſt end
of *PAULS*

Appendix 1

LILBURNE'S NARRATIVE

The story of Leveller collaboration with army and civilian Independents in framing the second *Agreement* Lilburne later told fully in *Legal Fundamental Liberties,* the first edition of which appeared June 8, 1649, and the second probably in late July.[1] No contemporary writer challenged the details of Lilburne's account, though an official declaration denied that the Levellers had published their *Agreement* first.[2] As the only source record of the collaboration and ultimate division on the principles of the second *Agreement,* Lilburne's story is invaluable. The following passages from his narrative are taken from the second edition of *Legal Fundamental Liberties:*

LEGAL FUNDAMENTAL LIBERTIES
pp. 33-42

And being come to *London,* my self, and some other of my friends, by two Messengers, *viz.* Mr. *Hunt* one of *Cromwels* (*) creatures, and another, sent a Message down to him to *Pomfret,* to be delivered to himself, and to debate it with him, and bring his express Answer back again speedily : the effect of which Message was,

That to our knowledg God had caused him to understand the principles of a just Government, under which the glory of God may shine forth by an equall distribution unto all men.

That the obtaining of this was the sole intended end of the wars : and that the war cannot be justified upon any other account, then the defence of the peoples right, unto that just Government, and their freedom under it.

---

[1] Lilburne says that the second edition was "occasioned by the late coming out of Mr. *William Prynnes* Book . . . *A Legal Vindication of the Liberties of* England." Prynne's book appeared July 16.

[2] *Legal Fundamental Liberties* (second edition), p. 41.

(*) *Who now hath three great and rich places upon his back, viz. Treasurer and Contracter for the sale of the Kings goods, and Contracter for the sale of his Lands.*

His Answer to which Message by Mr. *Hunt* was principally directed to the Independents ; some of whom appointed a meeting at the Nags-head Tavern by Blackwell Hall at Mrs. *Wilsons,* and invited Mr. *Wildman* and my self, &c. thither, whether we went accordingly, and where we met with Colonel *Tichburn,* Col. *John White,* Dr. *Parker,* Mr. *Taylor, John Price, and divers others* (where we had a large debate of things, and where the just ends of the War were as exactly laid open by Mr. *Wildman,* as ever I heard in my life.) But towards the conclusion, they plainly told us, The chief things first to be done by the Army, was first *To cut off the Kings Head,* &c. and force and throughly purge, if not dissolve the Parliament: All of which we were all against, and press'd to know the bottom of their center, and *in what they would absolutely rest for a future Settlement* ; and I plainly told them in these words, or to this effect.

Its true, *I look upon the King as an evil man in his actions, and divers of his party as bad, but the Army had couzened us the last year, and fallen from all their Promises and Declarations, and therefore could not rationally any more be trusted by us without good cautions, and security, : In which regard, although we should judge the King as arrant a Tyrant as they supposed him, or could imagine him to be, and the Parliament as bad as they could make them ; yet there being no other ballancing power in the Kingdom against the Army, but the King and Parliament, it was our interest to keep up one Tyrant to ballance another, till we certainly know what that Tyrant that pretended fairest would give us as our Freedoms ; that so we might have something to rest upon, and not suffer the Army (so much as in us lay) to devolve all the Government of the Kingdom into their wills and swords* (which were two things we nor no rationall man could like) *and leave no persons nor power to be a counter-ballance against them : And if we should do this, our slavery for future* (I told them) *might probably be greater then ever it was in the Kings time ; and so our last error would be greater then our first, and therefore I pressed very hard for an agreement amongst the People, first for a new Parliament, &c. utterly disclaiming the thoughts of the other till this was done. And this* (I told them) *was not onely my opinion, but I believe to be the unanimous opinion of all my friends with whom I most constantly conversed.*

At which the Gentlemen Independents were some of them most desperately cholerick : but my opinion being back'd with the Speeches of some others of my Friends, we came calmly to chuse out four and four of a side to debate and conclude of some Heads towards the accomplishment of an Agreement of the People : and (as I remember) their four were, Colonel *Titchburn,* Col. *White,* Dr. *Parker,* and *Jo. Price* ; and our four were Mr. *William Walwyn,* Lieut. Col. *Wetton,* Mr. *John Wildman,* and *my Self.* But *John Price* sent some of the company to tell us (after we were parted, and some of us drinking a cup of wine below) he would not make one, if Mr. *Walwyn* was one, for he had a prejudice against him. Unto which I replied, Mr. *Walwyn had more honesty and integrity in his little finger, then* John Price *had in all his body* ; and therefore no Meeting for me, seeing *John Price* was so base, unless Mr. *Walwyn* was one, though we had but two of a side : but the business being much debated and expostulated, Mr. *Walwyn,* and *John Price* both (for peace sake) were at present laid aside : and according to appointment (as I remember) all the other six met the fifteenth of *Novemb.* 1648. being Wednesday, at the fore-mentioned *Nags-head* ; and there, after some debate, unanimously agreed in these words, *viz. That in our conceptions, The onely way of Settlement is,*

1. *That some persons be chosen by the Army to represent the whole Body : And that the well-affected in every County (if it may be) chuse some persons to represent them : And those to meet at the Head-Quarters.*

2. *That those persons ought not to exercise any Legislative power, but onely to draw up the foundations of a just Government, and to propound them to the well-affected people in every County to be agreed to : Which Agreement ought to be above Law ; and therefore the bounds, limits, and extent of the peoples Legislative Deputies in Parliament, contained in the Agreement to be drawn up into a formall contract, to be mutually signed by the well-affected people and their said Deputies upon the dayes of their Election respectively.*

3. *To prevent present confusion, the Parliament (if it be possible) may not be by force immediatly dissolved ; but that the day of its dissolution be inserted in that Agreement, by vertue whereof it shall be dissolved.*

4. *That this way of Settlement, (if it may be) should be mentioned in the Armies first* Remonstrance.

5. *That the matter of the Petition of* September 11. 1648. *be the matter to be setled.*

Which Agreement of ours (as I remember) was immediatly sent away to the Head Quarters at St. *Albans* by Mr. *Hiland* of

Southwark, where (as it was afterwards told us) it was very well accepted and approved of by the great ones there ; whose high and mighty Declaration of the 16. *No.* 1648. (drawn by *Ireton* at Windsor, when he pretended to lay down his Commission) against the King coming to our view, we made divers objections against many passages in it, but especially at divers lashes that tacitely at the begining of it hinted at us: which we told some of their friends, could not be put in with a spirit of peace towards us, or intention of good to the Nation, in those good things we desired and propounded for it : But it was with many fair expressions salved up by them ; upon which we judged it requisite for some of us to go to Windsor, to speak with Mr. *Ireton* the Stear-man himself ; and accordingly (as I remember) Lieut. Colonel *Wetton,* Mr. *Petty,* Mr. *Wildman,* and *my self met there* ; and having drawn up our thoughts in writing, we communicated them to Col. *Tychburn,* Col. *White,* Mr. *Moyer,* and divers others of the Independent Party, who went with us to the Governors house, where we met with Mr. *Peters,* the grand Journey-or Hackney man of the Army ; And after we had acquainted him with our mindes, we delivered him a copy of our Paper, containing distinctly the Heads of what we desired, and intreated him to deliver them to Commissary *Ireton,* with whom we desired to discourse about them ; who sent us word, at such an hour he would come to our Inn at the Garter, to speak with us about them ; and accordingly he did, accompanied with a whole Train of Officers ; and a large and sharp discourse we had ; our principall difference lying at his desire in the too strict restraining *Liberty of Conscience,* and in keeping a power in the Parliament *to punish where no visible Law is transgressed* ; the unreasonableness of which was much spoken against by divers of the principall Officers with him, but especially by Col. *Harrison,* who was then extreme fair and gilded : And so little satisfaction had we at that meeting, from *Ireton* (*the Armie's Alpha and Omega*) that we despaired of any good from them, and were in a manner resolved to come away in haste to *London,* and acquaint our friends with our conceptions, and so improve our Interests *forcibly,* as much as we could, to oppose their intended designes. But Colonel *Harrison* coming to us again at ten a clock according to our desire, we had a private and large discourse with him, *and fully and effectually acquainted him with the most desperate mischievousnesse of their attempting to do these things, without giving some good security to the Nation for the future settlement of their Liberties and Freedoms, especially in frequent,*

free, and successive Representatives, according to their many
Promises, Oathes, Covenants and Declarations ; or else as soon as
they had performed their intentions to destroy the King, (which
we fully understood they were absolutely resolved to do, (yea, as
they told us, *though they did it by Martiall Law*) and also totally
to root up the Parliament, and invite so many Members to come
to them as would joyn with them, to manage businesses, till a new
and equall Representative could by an Agreement be setled ;
*which the chiefest of them protested before God, was the ulti-
mate and chiefest of their designes and desires.* I say, we pressed
hard for security, before they attempted these things in the least,
lest when they were done, we should be solely left to their *wills*
and swords ; by which, we told them, they might rule over us
arbitrarily, without declared Laws, as a conquered people, and so
deal with us as the poor slavish peasants in *France* are dealt with,
who enjoy nothing that they can call their own. And besides, we
plainly told him, we would not trust their bare words in generall
onely, *for they had broke their promise once already,* both with
us and the Kingdom ; and he that would break once, would make
no conscience of breaking twice, if it served for his ends, and
therefore they must come to some absolute particular compact
with us, or else, some of us told him, we would post away to *London,* and stir up our Interest against them, yea and spend our
bloods to oppose them. To which he replyed to this effect, It was
true in what we said ; *for he must ingenuously confess, they had
once broken with us and the Kingdom, and therefore acknowledged it was dangerous trusting them upon Generals again : But
saith he, we cannot stay so long from going to* London *with the
Army as to perfect an Agreement ; and without our speedy going,
we are unavoidable destroyed : For* (saith he) *we fully understand
that the Treaty betwixt the King and Parliament is almost concluded upon ; at the conclusion of which, we shall be commanded
by King and Parliament to disband, the which if we do, we are
unavoidably destroyed for what we have done already : and if we
do not disband, they will by Act of Parliament proclaim us Traytors, and declare us to be the onely hinderers of setling peace in
the Nation ; and then* (saith he) *we shall never be able to fight
with both the Interest of King and Parliament : so that you will
be destroyed as well as we : for we certainly understand that Major
Generall* Brown, &c. *are under hand preparing an Army against
us. And therefore I profess, I confess, I know not well what to say
to your Reasons, they are so strong ; but our Necessities are so*

*great, that we must speedily go, or perish ; and to go without giv-
ing you some content, is hazardable too.*

Well Sir, (said we) we have as much cause to distrust the Parliament men, as we have to distrust you ; for we know what and
how many large promises they have made to the Kingdom, *and
how little they have performed* ; and we also know what a *temp-
tation Honor, Power, and profit are even to those Spirits that were
pretty ingenuous and honest before* ; and when you have done
your work, and got, as you pretend, fourty or fifty of the honest
Members of the House to you ; alas, (said we) it will be a *mock-
Power* ; yet they may finde such sweetness and delight in their
pretended power, that they may fly to your swords for their protection, and bid us go shake our ears for our Agreement, and go
look it where we can catch it. And therefore we will trust generals no more to your fourty or fifty Members of Parliament, then
to you : for it's possible, if we leave the *Agreement* to their framing, they may frame us such a one as will do us no good, but
rather make us *slaves* by our own consents, if signed by us : and
therefore we pressed him that we might agree upon a *finall and
absolute Iudge* of the matter and method of the Agreement, that
so we might not spend moneths and years in dispute about it. And
therefore we would propound this unto him, That if their honest
friends in the Parliament, as they called them, would *chuse four*
from amongst themselves, and the Army *four from amongst themselves,* and the Independents *four from amongst themselves* ; we
that were nick-named *Levellers, would chuse four from among
our selves* ; and these *sixteen* should draw up the Agreement
finally, without any more appeal to any other ; and we for our
parts, so far as all our Interest in *England* extended, would be
willing to acquiesce in, and submit to the determinations of them
sixteen, or the major part of them : *And we would be willing the
Presbyterian party should be invited, and desired to chuse four
more to be of equal authority with the other sixteen. Provided,
They did it by the first day we should appoint to meet upon.*

Which Proposition he approved of extraordinary well, and
said, *It was as just, as rational, and as equitable, as possibly could
be* ; and said, *He doubted not but all Interests would center in it,
and be ingaged to acquaint them with it* ; and so we parted, very
glad that we were likely to come to some fixed agreement for the
future enjoyment of our dear-bought, and hard-purchased Freedoms.

And the next morning we went to the Gentlemen *Independ-*

ents, that lay the next door to us, who were almost ready to Horse for *London,* and we acquainted them with it, who liked it very well ; and with whom we fixed a night for several distinct meetings in *London,* to chuse our respective Trustees for this work, and also appointed a day to meet at *Windsor* again about it, and from them we went to Master *Cornelius Holland,* who then was the chief stickler for those they called honest men in the House of Commons ; and as I remember, we met Colonel *Harrison,* Master *Holland,* and Captain *Smith* a Member, and his Son in Law, in the street, and Master *Holland* seemed exceedingly to rejoyce at the Proposition, Colonel *Harrison* having told him of it before, which we repeated over again distinctly to him, that so in conclusion we might not be gulled through pretence of mistakes or misunderstandings, which we were continually afraid we should meet with ; so we went all together to Commissary General *Iretons* Chamber, to have his concurrence, which of all sides was taken for the concurrence of the whole Army, or at least for the powerful and governing part of it ; he being in a maner, both their eyes and ears. So when we came to his Chamber in the Castle, he was in Bed with his Wife, but sent us out word by Colonel *Harrison,* as he averred to us, That he did absolutely and heartily agree to the foresaid Proposition, which to avoid mistakes, was again repeated ; so we seemed joyful men of all sides, and appointed a day speedily to meet at *Windsor* about it, Master *Holland* again and again engaging for four Parliament men, and Colonel *Harrison* with Commissary *Ireton* for four of the Army, as we *Londoners* had done for each of our Tribe ; and so to Horse we went, and I overtook upon the Road, the whole gang of Independents, with whom I discoursed again and acquainted them all fully with the absoluteness of our Agreement, which they acquainted their friends with in *London,* who chose Colonel *Tichburn,* Colonel *John White,* Master *Daniel Taylor,* and Master *Price* the Scrivener ; And for our party, there was by unanimous consent of the Agents from our friends, in, and about *London,* at a very large meeting chosen Master *William Walwyn,* Master *Maximilian Petty,* Master *John Wildman,* and my self, and for the honest men of the Parliament as they were called, they had severall meetings at the Bell in Kings-street, and at Somerset house, where, as I was informed, they chose Col. *Hen. Martin,* Col. *Alexander Rigby,* Master *Thomas Chalenor,* and Master *Scot,* with one or two more, to supply the places of those of them that should be absent at any time about their occasions ; so when we came to

Windsor, the Army men had chosen Commissary Generall *Ireton,* Sir *William Constable,* and as I remember, Colonel *Tomlinson,* Colonel *Baxster,* Lieutenant Colonel *Kelsey,* and Captain *Packer,* some two of the which last four should alwayes make up the number ; so we had a meeting in their Councel-Chamber at the Castle, where we were all of all sides present, but only the Parliament men, for whom only Col. *Martin* appeared, and after a large discourse *about the foundations of our Agreement,* we departed to our Lodging, where Colonel *Martin* and we four, *nick-named* Levellers, lockt our selves up, and went in good earnest to the consideration of our *Agreement,* but much was not done in it there, because of their haste to London, to force and break up the Parliament (which Journey at all, was very much opposed by Mr *VValwyn,* and many reasons he gave against their march to London at all) the absolute dissolution of which, their friends in the House would no wayes admit of, although *Ireton, Harrison,* &c. commonly stiled it then a Parliament *that had forfeited its trust, a mock-parliament,* and that if they did not totally dissolve it, but purge it, it would be but a *mock-parliament, and a mock-power however ; for where have we, say they, either Law, Warrant, or Commission to purge it, or can any thing justifie us in the doing it, but the height of necessity to save the Kingdom from a new war, that they, with the conjunction with the King, will presently vote and declare for, and to procure a new and free Representative, and so successive and frequent free Representatives?* which this present Parliament will never suffer (*and without which the freedomes of the Nation are lost and gone,* and the doing of which can only justifie before God and man our present and former extraordinary actings with, and against legal Authority) and so all our fighting will be fruitlesse ; and this was their open and common discourse with more of the like nature ; and to those that objected against their totall dissolving or breaking the House (and the illegality of their intended and declared trying of the King, which also was opposed by us, till a new and unquestionable Representative was sitting) as I am able sufficiently, by plurality of witnesses to prove and justifie, yea when they were come to London, *Ireton,* &c. and some members of the House (in a Chamber near the long Gallery in White-hall) had a large conference, where, and to whom he stifly maintained the same to their faces, calling this *purged Parliament, a mock-power, and a mock-parliament,* which Members, I believe, if there were a necessity of it, I could produce to justifie it ; for I am sure one of them told me

the substance of all the discourse immediatly after it happened ;
So that if it be treason to call this a *pretended Parliament, a
mock-power, a mock-parliament,* yea, and to say in plain English,
*that it is no Parliament at all, then they themselves are the prime,
the chief and original traytors* ; and if this be true, as true it is ;
then there is neither legal Judges, nor Justices of Peace in England ; and if so ; *then all those that are executed at* Tiburn, &c.
*by their sentences of condemnation given against them, are meerly
murthered, and the Judges or Justices that condemned them are
liable in time to be hanged* (and that justly) *therefore,* for acting
without a just and legal commission, either from true Regall, or
true Parliamentary power ; see for this purpose the notable arguments in the 13,14. but especially 15 page of the second Edition of
my late Picture of the Councell of * State : But to return to our
acting to compleat the *Agreement,* all parties chosen of all sides
constantly met at White-hall after the Army came to Town, saving
the Parliament men failed, only Master *Martin* was most commonly there, and a long and tedious tug we had with Commissary
Generall *Ireton* only, yea sometimes whole nights together ; *Principally about Liberty of Conscience, and the Parliaments punishing where no law provides,* and very angry and *Lordly* in his debates many times he was ; but to some kinde of an expedient in the
first, for peace sake we condescended in to please him, *and so came
amongst the major part of the* 16 *Commissioners, according to our
original Agreement, to an absolute and final conclusion* ; and
thinking all had been done, as to any more debate upon it, and
that it should without any more ado be promoted for subscriptions, first at the Councel of War, and so in the Regiments, and
so all over the Nation ; *But alas poor fools, we were meerly
cheated and cozened* (it being the principall unhappinesse of some
of us (as to the flesh) to have our eyes wide open to see things,
long before most honest men come to have their eyes open ; and
this is that which turns to our *smart and reproach)* and that which
we Commissioners feared at the first (viz. That no tye, promises,
nor engagements were strong enough to hold the grand Juglers,
and Leaders of the Army) was now made clearly manifest, for
when it came to the Councel, there came the *General, Cromwel,*
and the whole gang of Creature-Colonels, and other officers, and
spent many dayes in taking it all in pieces, and there *Ireton* him-

(*) *See also the arguments for that purpose, in Mr.* Prinns *late forementioned
book, against the Tax of* 90. *thousand pound; Intituled a legal vindication of the
liberties of* England, *pag.* 3 4.9.10.44,45,46,47.

self shewed himself an *absolute King,* if not an *Emperor,* against whose will no man must dispute, and then shittlecock *Roe* their Scout, *Okey,* and Major *Barton* (where Sir *Hardress VValler* sate President) begun in their open Councel to quarrel with us, by giving some of us *base and unworthy language,* which procured them from me a sharp retortment of their own basenesse and unworthinesse into their *Teeth,* and a C H A L L E N G E from my self into the Field, besides seeing they were like to fight with us in the room, in their own Garrison, which when Sir *Hardress* in my ear reproved me for it, I justified it, and gave it him again, for suffering us to be so affronted : And within a little time after I took my leave of them, *for a pack of dissembling, jugling Knaves,* amongst whom in consultation ever thereafter I should scorn to come (as I told some of them) *for there was neither faith, truth, nor common honesty amongst them* : and so away I went to those that chose and trusted me, and gave publikely and effectually (at a set meeting appointed on purpose) to divers of them an exact account how they had dealt with us, *and cozened and deceived us* ; and so absolutely discharged my self for medling or making any more with so *perfidious a generation* of men as the great ones of the Army were, but especially the cunningest of Machiavilians, Commissary *Henry Ireton* : and having an exact copy of what the greatest part of the foresaid *sixteen* had agreed upon, I onely mended a clause in the first Reserve about Religion, to the sense of us all but *Ireton,* and put an Epistle to it, of the fifteenth of December 1648. and printed it of my own accord, and the next day it came abroad ; about which, Master *Price the Scrivener,* and my self had a good sharp bout at Colonel *Titchburn* his house, within two or three dayes after, *where I avowed the publishing of it,* and also putting my Epistle to it of my own head and accord. And after that I came no more amongst them, but with other of my friends, prepared a complaint against their dealing with us, and a kinde of Protest against their proceedings ; which with my own hand I presented to the Generals own hands at the Mews, the twenty eight of December 1648. being accompanied with Major *Robert Cobbet,* Mr. *Thomas Prince,* Mr. *George Middlemore,* Mr. *Robert Davies,* Mr. *Richard Overton,* Mr. *Edward Tench,* Mr. *Daniel Linton,* Mr. *William Bottom,* Mr. *John Harris,* Mr. *Thomas Dafferne,* Mr. *Tho. Goddard,* Mr. *Samuel Blaiklock,* Mr. *Andrew Dednam,* Mr. *John VValters,* and Mr. *Richard Pechel* ; and which was immediatly printed by *Ja.* and *Jo. Moxon,* for *VVill. Larnar,* at the sign of the *Black-moore* near

Bishops gate ; within two or three dayes of the delivery of which, I went towards my Journey to *Newcastle* ; and about five weeks after my arrivall in those parts, I heard that the Generall and his Councel had presented their *Agreement* to your House : which, when I read the title page of it, I found it to be upon the 20 of Jan. 1648. which is compleat 35 dayes after my publishing of that which is called ours.

And yet in the third and fourth pages of a Declaration of the proceedings of the General in reducing the late revolted Troops, *Appointed by his Excellency, and his Councel of war, to be printed and published,* May 22. 1649. and signed by their Order, *Richard Hatter* Secretary, and first printed at Oxford, and then re-printed at London, May 23. 1649. I finde these very words, viz.

The grounds and manner of the proceedings of these men that have so much pretended for the Liberty of the people, have been as followeth :

' There was a paper styled the *Agreement* of the people, framed
' by certain select persons, and debated at a general Councel of
' officers of the Army, to be tendred to the Parliament, & to be by
' them commended over to the people of the Nation : It being
' hoped, that such an Expedient, if assented unto, at least by the
' honest part of the people that had appeared for this comon
' cause, to which God hath so witnessed, it would have tended
' much to settlement (which you abhor and detest) and the com-
' posing of our differences ; at least have fixed honest men to such
' grounds of certainty as might have kept them firm and entire,
' in opposing the common enemy, and stand united to publike
' interest.

' The general Councel of the Army, and the other sorts of men,
' going then under the name of *Levellers (so baptized by your
' selves at Putney)* who (by their late actings have made good the
' same, which we then judged but an imputation) had (as now it
' appears) different ends and ayms, both in the matter & maner of
' their proceedings : That which was intended by those men, was
' to have somewhat tendred as a *test and coertion upon the people,*
' & all sorts of men and authorities in the Land : That which these,
' to wit, the Councel of the Army aymed at, was to make an hum-
' ble representation of such things as were then likely to give satis-
' faction, and unite, and might be remitted to M E N S J U D G -
' M E N T S , to be owned or disowned, as men were satisfied in
' their consciences, and as it should please God to let men S E E
R E A S O N for their so doing ; and that so it might not be only

'called an *Agreement,* but through the freedom of it, be one
'I N D E E D , and *Receive its stamp of approbation from the*
'*Parliament, to whom it was humbly represented.*

'*Hereupon those other men took* so much *dissatisfaction,* that
'they forthwith printed and spread abroad their paper, which was
'different from that of the Army ; using all possible means to
'make the same to passe : but with how little effect, is very well
'known. And finding by the Armies application to the *Parlia-*
'*ment,* that they were likely, according to their duty, *to stand by,*
'*and own them as the Supreme authority of the Nation,* they have
'by all means assayed to vilipend that Authority, presenting them
'to the people (in printed Libels, and otherwise) as worse (*) Ty-
'rants then any who were before them.

In which passage of the General and his Councel, I shall desire
to observe these things, *which plainly to me are in the words:*
and if they can make it appear that I mistake their words as they
are laid down, I shall cry them mercy.

First, *That they give a false and untrue Narrative* of the original occasion of that *Agreement,* to which by our importunate importunity they were necessitated, and drawn unto that little they
did in it as a *Bear* to the stake, as is truly by me before declared ;
and which, as the sequell shews, they undertook meerly to quiet
and please us *(like Children with rattles)* till they had done their
main work ; *(viz.* either in annihilating or purging the House to
make it fit for their purpose, and in destroying the King ; *unto*
both which they never had our consents in the least) that so they
might have no opposition from us, but that we might be *lull'd*
asleep in a fools paradise with thoughts of their honest intentions,
till all was over ; and then totally lay it aside, as they have done,
as being then able to do what they pleased whether we would or
no : for if they ever had intended an *Agreement, why do they let*
their own lie dormant in the pretended Parliament ever since they
presented it ? seeing it is obvious to every knowing *English* eye,
that from the day they presented it to this hour, they have had as
much power over their own Parliament now sitting, as *any School-*

(*) *And so they are, ye worse then the King,* comparatis comparandis, *for they*
have sworne, promised, and engaged to redeem the people from bondage, oppres-
sion and slavery, which the King never did; but rather was declared free and clear
from the penall part of the Law, at whose sacred feet, the Parliament in their
Petitions prostrated themselves, as a man that would do no wrong, nor be ac-
comptable for any, & yet they have chopt off his head for a tyrant, and when they
have done, walk superlatively in the worst of his steps, of treachery, murder,
rapine, and oppression.

master in England *ever had over his Boyes.* But to them it was presented (who scarce ought to meddle with it) on purpose, that there, without any more stir about it, it might be lodged for ever : *For alas, an Agreement of the People is not proper to come from the Parliament, because it comes from thence rather with a command then any thing else* ; so that its we, and not they that really and in good earnest say, it ought not so to do, *but to be voluntary and free.* Besides, that which is done by one Parliament, *as a Parliament,* may be undone by the next Parliament : but an *Agreement of the People begun and ended amongst the People, can never come justly within the Parliaments cognizance to destroy :* which the Generall and the chief of his Councel knew well enough ; and I dare safely say it upon my conscience, that an *Agreement of the People upon foundations of just freedom gon through with, is a thing the Generall and the chiefest of his Councell as much hates, as they do honesty, justice and righteousness,* (which they long since abandoned) against which in their own spirits they are absolutely resolved (I do verily believe) to spend their heart-blouds, and not to leave a man *breathing* in *English* air, if possibly they can, that throughly and resolutely prosecutes it ; a new and just *Parliament* being more dreadfull to them, then the *great day of Judgment* spoken so much of in the Scripture. And although they have beheaded the King, yet I am confidently perswaded their enmity is such at the *Peoples Liberties,* that they would sooner run the hazard of letting the *Prince* in to reign in his Fathers stead, *then further really a just Agreement,* or endure the sight of a new Parliament rightly constituted.

Secondly. Its plain to me out of their words, That they positively aver, that their *Agreement* was presented to the Parliament before ours was published in print ; which I must and do here tell both the Generall and his Councel, *is the arrantest lie and falshood under the cope of heaven :* for I have truly before declared, and will justifie it with my life, *that ours was printed above thirty days before theirs was presented :* yea, it was printed before theirs was half perfected. But it is no wonder, when men turn their *backs on God,* on a good *conscience,* on *righteousness* and common *honesty* amongst men, and make lies and falshoods, oppression and bloudy cruelty, *their sole confidence and refuge,* that then they say or swear any thing ; all which, if the Generall and his Councell had not done, they would have scorned and abhorred, in the face of the Sun, *to have affirmed and printed so many lies,* as in their foregoing words is literally (without wrestling) contained.

Thirdly, they positively hint, our dissatisfaction was taken at them for presenting theirs to the Parliament ; *which is also as false as the former :* for 1. Our dissatisfaction was above a moneth before declared in their open Councel by my self, &c. as Sir *Hardresse VValler* and divers others of them cannot but justifie. 2. Our dissatisfaction was long before taken, *upon the grounds by me before specified* : the manifestations of which dissatisfaction I presented to the Generals own hands the 28 of December 1648, accompanied and *subscribed with my own name, and fifteen more of my Comrades,* in behalf of our selves, and all our friends that sent us, which we also immediately caused to be printed. And their *Agreement,* as the Title of it declares, was not presented till the 20 of *Jan.* after.

Appendix 2

NOTES ON LEVELLER BIBLIOGRAPHY

The following notes, arranged in chronological order, are additions to my lists of Leveller pamphlets in *Milton in the Puritan Revolution*, pp. 469-83. I have gleaned new information from pamphlets sent me in photostat by the National Library of Wales (present custodians of the Thomason Collection) and by the Huntington Library of California, which has a large collection of Leveller pamphlets. Publication of Leveller bibliography, with suitable notes, is a project I expect to complete when passage to England is again possible.

JOHN LILBURNE

To all the brave, couragious, and valiant Apprentizes of the honourable City of London, but especially those that appertain to the worshipfull Company of Cloth Workers (of which company, if I live I hope to be a Free man). Reprinted at the end of *The Prisoners Plea for a Habeas Corpus,* dated by Lilburne "the 10. day of this 5. moneth of May, in the yeare of remembrances 1639." Lilburne mentions this pamphlet in *A Whip for the present House of Lords* (p. 26), saying that on the play day of the apprentices, he caused it "to be thrown in Moorfields amongst them." I have not seen the apprentice letter listed as a separated publication.

The Petition of Elizabeth Lilburne. September 23, 1646. Thomason 669 f. 10 (86). This petition, which was written by Lilburne to be presented by his wife, was later inserted in *Regall Tyrannie,* pp. 71-77.

The Oppressed Mans Oppressions declared. Jan. 30, 1647. Another edition of this pamphlet, set in larger type, is in the Seligman Collection of Columbia University.

The resolved mans Resolution. Appeared April 30, 1647. In *Rash Oaths* (p. 6) Lilburne mentions a second edition of this pamphlet, but I have been unable to locate it.

The Recantation Of . . . John Lilburne . . . 1647. Appeared May 13, 1647. In *Rash Oaths* (p. 56) Lilburne denounces this pamphlet as the work of his enemies.

A Copy of a Letter written to Coll. Henry Martin . . . . by Leiu. Col. Iohn Lilburn Iuly, 20, 1647. This letter appears at the end of *Jonahs Cry.* It was published as a broadside on July 20, Thomason 669 f. 11 (46).

The Ivst Mans Ivstification. Appeared June 6, 1647. A second edition of this pamphlet, which Lilburne often refers to as "my epistle to Justice Reeves", appeared August 27, 1647. It contains (pp. 24-28) a letter titled *To his much honoured friends the Councell of Adjutators,* dated August 27.

For every Individuall Member of the Honourable House of Commons. Thomason: November 13, 1647. Lilburne wrote afterwards that he delivered

425

this plea to the House on November 11. It is only four pages in length. Reprinted in *The peoples Prerogative,* pp. 77-81.

A new complaint of an old grievance, made by Lievt. Col. Iohn Lilburne, Prerogative prisoner in the Tower of London. Nove. 23, 1647. Thomason E. 416 (25). Dated by Lilburne at the end of November 23, 1647, 4 pp. Reprinted in *The peoples Prerogative,* pp. 62-66.

A broadside without title, labeled by Thomason "A Libell," opening with the following words: "All worthy Officers and Souldiers, who are yet mindful, That you Engaged not as a meer Mercenary Army." The writers urge the soldiers to "Chuse you out a Councel of Agitators once more." According to Thomason the sheet was distributed on April 25, 1649. E. 551 (21).

The Copie of a Letter, Written to the General from Lieut. Col. Iohn Lilburn, M. Richard Overton, April 27, 1649. A protest against the application of martial law to the case of Lockyer, Ash, Hockley, Osburn, Heyworth, and Goodwin, of Captain Savage's troop. 669 f. 14 (23).

A Salva Libertate. September 14, 1649. Erroneously dated 1648 in *Milton and the Puritan Revolution.*

RICHARD OVERTON

Though Overton was a prolific and versatile pamphleteer, his signed tracts are few. A whole series of satirical pamphlets in 1640-42, which I am now studying in photostat, sound much like Overton. Another series of "Sir John Presbyter" sallies of 1647 also needs investigation. I have already identified *The Nativity Of Sir John Presbyter* (July 2, 1645) as Overton's work. Tracts such as *The Last Will and Testamtnt Of Sir John Presbyter* (July 22, 1647), *The Lamentation of the ruling Lay-Elders* (August 14), *The Ghost of Sir John Presbyter* (August 11). *The Infamous History of Sir Simon Synod* (August 12), *Sir John Presbyter not Dead* (August 20), *The Tertian Ague* (August 17) need to be carefully examined.

A Perle in a dovnghill . . . John Lilbourne in Newgate. Thomason: June 23, 1646. In my opinion this was written by Overton, not by Walwyn. See p. 9 of this volume.

To the Parliament of England. The humble Petition of Mary Overton, prisoner in Bridewell. Thomason: March 24, 1647.

A New Found Strategem Framed In The Old Forge of Machivilisme, and put upon the Inhabitants of the County of Essex. Thomason: April 18, 1647. Overton's hand is clearly evident in this timely protest against disbanding.

To the Supreme Authority of England . . . The Petition of Richard Overton. Thomason: March 3, 1649.

The Hunting of the Foxes From New-Market . . . To White-Hall, By five small Beagles (late of the Armie). Thomason: March 21, 1649. 28 pp. By every test of internal evidence, Overton is the author of this tract.

Note on William Walwyn: *A Word in Season* appeared, according to Thomason, January 5, 1646. I have erroneously listed it as having appeared May 18, 1646. *Milton in the Puritan Revolution,* p. 482.

Appendix 3

NOTES ON TEXT CORRECTIONS

Except in the instances noted below, the text has been left unchanged in spelling and punctuation. When the errors or the original printer caused no difficulties in reading, we have allowed them usually to remain in the text. But in a number of instances the original errors impeded comprehension, hence the corrections. The changes are classified according to page and line (lines numbered from the top of the page).

Page	Line	Original Reading	Page	Line	Original Reading
114	16	the the people	217	43	shoul
116	6	beeause	218	1	thed substance
120	6	thei	218	2	Remonstrances;
124	25	opprssion	218	24	Freedom,e
125	33	[*doubtful*:]	225	20	Regiment,
		man, men	226	31	arising,
129	25	us any meanes	233	8–9	scndalize
141	9	o (for *of*)	232	14–15	concurrnece
147	7	surprzing	237	27	oeher
157	12	Exccllency	238	3	wae concluded
162	2	athorative [?]	238	27	of imbru ing
162	33	commmon	238	33	procceeded
165	33	*Suerty*	241	18	yonr dayes
171	14	J say	241	21	yonr selves
176	29	inurable members	249	28	*descent ar all*
		aere	252	22	sececond
178	5	thereuuto	265	9	*of m n*
178	13	Cheldren	266	40	Petition of *Right,*
180	9	wilbe	266	43	See *Rom.* 4, 15.
181	25	gobernation	268	24	Monopolics
185	6	evey	270	2	*one whele* year
185	16	peeservation	274	10	brins gnot
192	28	*Eaw.*	284	4	lesse thnt
193	24	thereone	284	37	*evpressions*
199	25	mained	287	25	doutbed
203	27	plead ᵖ	287	31	right or
210	23	desert or	288	19	epual
		deferr [*doubtful*]	288	28	dusines of
210	37	forth forth	288	40	State-Chamber
211	14, 15	the the	289	12	geneaally
212	13	peramount	290	8	as shoulp
213	15	3	290	22	for thei,
214	2	adantage	295	24	inconveniencies

427

Page	Line	Original Reading	Page	Line	Original Reading
298	3	or he present	347	4	7 That no
302	20	limbs, limbs	347	7	8 That the
319	13	change[?]	374	35	havzard
319	30	*Lualow*	375	6	faitful
328	6	*Ihon*	375	16	*Granul*[?]
341	2	eleven of of	377	1	might us
343	10	3 That	401	40	*Walliam*
343	30	4 That	405	4	thei King
343	39	5 For the	416	4	distruct
346	26	4 That	422	43	*pmurder*
346	31	5 That each	424	1	wresting
346	36	6 That in	424	10	Decomber

ERRATA

Page	Line	Correct Reading
12	21	*Naturall.*" 11
26	13	maintained." 2
30	6	The next day, May 30
67	22	more difficult
76	22	April, *The Armies Petition*
83	12	Phrased
93	10	*Freeedome* [*sic*]
102	23	*Agreement Of The*
108	5	preoccupied
131	8	*Agreement Of The*
142	24	*Agreement* 2 *Of The*
259	6	*Declaration Of some*
259	28–30	1 *A Declaration Of some Proceedings*, p. 17. In *The Triumph stain'd*, which had appeared February 10, Masterson had given the number as three thousand.

INDEX

This volume deserves a permanent place as a fundamental exhibit in the history of constitutional government and liberty in England, the United States, indeed the whole English-speaking world. . . . Mr. Wolfe has brought together rare pamphlets and tracts that are seldom available even in many of the largest libraries in England and America. . . . His work constitutes a well-rounded unity of thought and plan which forms an indispensable part of the whole record representing the struggle for constitutional government from Magna Carta to our own age.

As a contribution to critical scholarship, Mr. Wolfe's book serves many useful purposes. It makes easily available to inquirers everywhere numerous documents requisite to the study of a stormy and creative period in English history. No library that pretends to provide essential materials for English history can fail to have the volume on its shelves. No course of instruction in English history that rises above the most elementary level can fail to require an examination of the remonstrances, declarations, and appeals contained in this collection. . . .

Now that the history of ideas is beginning to receive in the United States some of the thoughtful attention it deserves, Mr. Wolfe's work possesses what may be called "current interest" in the strict sense of the words. In the materials he reprints and in the supplementary comments from his own pen are to be found early origins and formulations of ideas that have bulked large in the history of the Western world for more than two centuries. . . .

It is, therefore, to the history of civilization, as well as government and liberty, that Mr. Wolfe makes an enduring contribution.